# Man in the Middle: A Collection of Essays by a Red, White and Blue American

By: Eric L. Nachamie

While every precaution has been taken in the preparation of this book, the publisher assumes no responsibility for errors or omissions, or for damages resulting from the use of the information contained herein.

MAN IN THE MIDDLE: A COLLECTION OF ESSAYS BY A RED, WHITE AND BLUE AMERICAN

**First edition. April 1, 2024.**

Copyright © 2024 Eric Nachamie.

ISBN: 979-8224783793

Written by Eric Nachamie.

# Table of Contents


1. Introduction: Why I Have Written These Essays ............................................................ 1

2. We Must Stop Hate Against Asian Americans ............................................................ 7

3. Self-Driving Vehicle Systems: The Answer to Dangerous Roadways? ....................... 14

4. Crimes of Colonialism: Should Western Culture Be "Cancelled?" ........................... 20

5. Fair is Fair: An Honest Evaluation of Presidents Trump and Biden's Biggest Failures ............. 24

6. Initial Impressions Soon After the January 6th Insurrection (1/17/21) ................... 31

7. Violence in America - January 6th Insurrection Versus Inner City Violent Crime ...... 35

8. President Trump's Insurrection ................................................................................. 41

9. Violent Crime in America: Protecting the Citizenry ................................................ 46

10. The Tragedy of Tyre Nichols' Death at The Hands of Police ................................... 53

11. Have We Overcome Institutional Racism in The Workplace? ................................. 59

12. The World Is a Kinder and Safer Place When the United States Takes the Lead ...... 65

13. Hybrid Work's Role in Reducing Carbon Emissions and Improving Work-Life Balance ........ 73

14. President Biden Calling out "Semi-Fascism" Sect of the Republican Party ............. 77

15. The Cost of Healthcare for the American Family ..................................................... 82

16. Liz Cheney – A True American Patriot and Hero .................................................... 88

17. Too Many Greedy Charities and the Charities That I Endorse ................................ 94

18. Afghanistan: Biden's Big Blunder ........................................................................... 99

19. "Toxic Masculinity" On the Roadways .................................................................. 104

20. Confronting Urban Sprawl's Takeover of Rural Areas .......................................... 109

21. Flags Don't Belong on Cars ................................................................................... 116

22. Abortion Rights of Women Need Protection (with a Caveat) ............................... 119

23. Zero Population Growth - Now .................................................................. 125

24. Speed Cameras........................................................................................ 130

25. Young Woman under the Bridge........................................................... 135

26. The Southern Border............................................................................. 140

27. NFL Players Taking the Knee in Protest of American Racial Discrimination........................ 148

28. Early Thoughts on the COVID-19 Pandemic in 2020 ........................ 151

29. COVID-19 in the Fall of 2022 .............................................................. 153

30. New Year's Day 2020.............................................................................. 158

31. The Second Amendment......................................................................... 162

32. Reparations for Slavery .......................................................................... 168

33. CNN and Fox News – Levels of Bias ................................................... 174

34. Mike Pence for President - 2024........................................................... 180

35. One Nation – Only One Flag ................................................................ 184

36. The Reconnection (A Poem) ................................................................. 188

37. Reconnecting with Nature to Improve Our Quality of Life................. 190

38. Coexisting with Our Natural World:  Saving Our Planet and Saving Ourselves ..................... 193

39. The 1619 Project:  Leftist Propaganda or History Corrected .............. 196

40. My Personal Religious Beliefs................................................................. 202

41. Thoughts on Organized Religion ........................................................... 207

42. Which Lives Matter – Black, Blue or All?............................................. 211

43. Critical Race Theory (CRT):  How Should We Talk about Race in School?........................... 217

44. Dave Chappelle Is Wrong – Ye Should Be Called Out for Being Anti-Semitic ..................... 222

45. "Jews Will Not Replace Us" .................................................................. 228

46. Overcoming Negative Stereotyping of Southerners ............................... 233

47. Dangers While Driving: Too Fast, Too Close and Too Angry ................ 239

48. Long Live a Free Ukraine (written in late December of 2022) ............... 246

49. Quiet Quitting: The Self-Empowerment of the Employee ..................... 252

50. Final Thoughts: Let's Meet in the Middle .......................................... 258

Works Cited ........................................................................................ 271

# 1. Introduction: Why I Have Written These Essays

There is no lack of authors who write social and political commentary which is basically what I'm doing here. The obvious question then is why have I written this collection of essays? Do I possess some unique ideas or approaches that others have not discussed or expressed in an either more fluid manner, a more engaging style or from a more educated standpoint? I am sure that there are other writers who have more real-world experience when it comes to hard-core policymaking or societal improvement crusading. I do think it is important to provide a brief explanation as to why I have undertaken this effort of composing fifty essays.

The use of social media is now a primary way for public discourse to occur. It is an outlet for communication which millions of Americans regularly access. The ability for so many people to communicate with each other instantaneously is a recent technology that has become available to humanity. It is truly amazing. Billions of people around the globe now have access to express their opinions, whether these are well thought-out commentaries or impulsive responses. My concern is that those who are controversial and loud, as well as those on the edge of the political spectrums, receive significant attention on social media. Outrageous statements and proclamations, as is human nature, attract more viewers and readers (or followers) which lead to more advertising revenue for social media and online companies. So, I do give social media organizations, such as Facebook and Google, some credit for attempting to police false statements and hate speech, but the truth is that there is a financial disincentive to significantly rein in the social media environment as it currently exists. We find that in this environmental framework, those who are polite and address issues or political disagreements with a commonsense approach, do not get the level of attention as those who are loud and angry. No, the voices of reason and calm are all too often drowned out in the hyped-up world of social media.

Even the traditional media outlets from which Americans get their daily intake of news seem to be presenting news stories in a more biased format than in the past. I would say Fox News sets the bar extremely low as far as the network's performance in presenting news in an unbiased manner, per its constant right-wing rants. However, MSNBC is not far behind with its leftist slant, and even CNN often shows its more Democrat leanings. As I am writing this, I stop to pause to view a discussion on CNN about Governor Ron DeSantis of Florida flying Venezuelan migrants to Martha's Vineyard in Massachusetts. It becomes clear that the host and the Democrat strategist are on the same team against the sole Republican participant. American news media outlets, pandering too often to one side of the political spectrum, do not sufficiently support the dissemination of objective facts and civil debate.

I believe that the loud voices which seed distrust and turmoil on our political landscape do not represent most Americans who demonstrate in their daily lives that we are a fair-minded people. Yes, the truth is that Americans cannot agree on much these days - whether it is to wear masks during the pandemic, to believe in climate change, and on even what our children should or should not learn in school. I admit that we face intensive divisiveness in our nation on political issues, but there remains a basic ideal of fairness that most Americans share together. Our democratic society has instilled in us a sense of fairness that, in my opinion, will be what guides us to reaffirming a culture of interactions that is based on reason, compassion, and compromise.

I now return to the question as to why I set out to undertake this writing endeavor. I will describe below a bit about myself to answer this question more completely, but primarily I am of the opinion that to successfully oppose the multiple angry voices that are being expressed right now, that it will take many of us choosing to communicate, through various methods, the need to adopt civility as we engage in social and political discourse. A significantly larger number of citizens, than is currently the case, need to communicate a message of collaboration and cooperation to begin the process of addressing the bitter divisiveness in America. We can back off the ledge of more divisiveness, and even violence, in our American society if we have a groundswell of insistence on mutual respect in our open political debates. I am but one citizen, but my goal is to encourage many others to join in this civil discourse with an emphasis on "civil." We must collectively set an intention to treat others with dignity and respect in all communicative interactions.

As far as what I think I can bring to the table in this pursuit of achieving more civility and peaceful coexistence for all in our free society, I do have, I think, a unique perspective that adds value to the discussion. I am a North Carolinian with a New York, Jewish background. I live in a southern town of mostly devout Christians, and I have learned to respect my differences from others when it comes to religion. I am a Democrat who lives in a suburban (what used to be rural) mostly Republican, conservative town. However, I work in the nearby city/metropolitan area that seems so increasingly liberal in its policies, that the culture appears to me to be intolerant of anyone but those on the extreme left. I live where European whites are the majority, but in the city where I work (like other cities across the nation), there is a majority minority population, with African Americans and Hispanics in combination now outnumbering the number of white residents. As with other metropolitan areas in our nation, the city in which I am employed is composed of racial, religious, and political characteristics that are strikingly different from the nearby suburbs. It is not lost on me that I can drive a mere thirty to forty minutes and the population makeup can differ significantly from where I began my trip. Indeed, I admit that where I reside, and the location where I work are geographic factors that have shaped my outlook and politics. I work and live my life as both a member of majority and minority groups, depending on the situation and location.

Based on my identity and experiences, I have developed a great desire to communicate the message to others that protecting minority rights is just not our moral imperative as Americans, but protecting minority rights is the act of protecting the rights of all citizens. Let me explain. We live in an ever-increasingly diverse society. Each of us may experience even in the briefest of moments being the minority in the group. This recognition at the individual level can lead to a more compassionate world in which we all play a role in protecting individual liberties. What makes the United States such a unique and ethical society is that we have democratic rule by the majority, yet from our nation's inception, there has been a moral emphasis on respecting the rights of minorities.

My background and daily experiences have led me to have four core political approaches or beliefs that I endorse:

1. Often both sides of the political spectrum have valid points in their arguments that all sides must concede.
2. Compromising on issues and coming to the political middle ground is the best way to create a free society in which everyone feels that they have been heard. **We take the reasonable arguments of both sides of an issue and come to a decision in which no one gets everything that they want, but a decision in which most get something, and hopefully everyone comes to understand (if not fully accept) the valid viewpoints of others.**
3. As alluded to above, our Founding Fathers set up a unique governmental system in which we have the rule of the majority through free elections, but we also place a deep emphasis on individual freedoms. Our Constitution is the closest written document, in my opinion, to a perfect guide for creating a free and just society. However, without our nation's citizens throughout our history standing up to protect this free way of life, this most revered document would simply exist as a two-hundred-year-old printed intention of liberty – a theoretical dream of freedom that never actually blooms to fruition. **All Americans have a sacred responsibility to ensure the continued adherence to our Constitution and governmental systems created by our Founding Fathers.**
4. **The safety of all citizens (and families) is essential for the functioning of a free society.** This includes physical safety from outside threats (national security), as well as safety from local crime. I would say it also includes access to housing, health care, and safe transportation. Citizens and governmental representatives must work together to create a

safe environment for everyone. Safety is essential for our society to exist, and it is the foundational brick holding up our inalienable rights, as stated in our Declaration of Independence, to "...life, liberty and the pursuit of Happiness" (Kamps 36).

My middle-of-the-road, compromising approach to societal problem-solving is why I refer to myself so often as a "man in the middle. " We can move past blue and red state divisions to re-establish our Founding Fathers' ideal of a "United States of America." We have a history of uniting under our flag with its red, white, and blue colors. The pride that countless Americans have experienced when putting their hands over their hearts, pledging their allegiance to our red, white, and blue flag, comes from that almost sacred understanding that our nation at its core is just, good, and bound in liberty. Thus, my contention is that we should not think of America as separate red or blue states, but view them collectively as "red, white and blue" states. We can do this and silence any troublesome talk of civil war and prevent any future acts of insurrection. This is my explanation as to why I consider myself to be a "red, white and blue" American. The American ideal is one of looking toward the future with the most positive intentions. This can be seen in President Biden's continued message and recent statement ("Remarks by President Biden on Bidenomics") that, "America's best days are ahead of us, not behind us." This positive American vision has always crossed party lines as with President Reagan's common reference to "the shining city on a hill." We must all do our part to ensure this future of peace and prosperity for all Americans. It is this American idealism and pride when we look at our red, white, and blue flag with its promise of freedom for all, that we can collectively embrace.

One of my historical heroes is President Abraham Lincoln who led our nation through the bloody and costly U.S. Civil War. There are those who say that the United States has not been so divided as it is today since those dark days in the early 1860s. President Lincoln, from my perspective, not only worked closely with the United States military to ensure victory in the war but provided the guidance necessary to ensure that the national identity of our relatively young nation remained intact. Maintaining our collective, national vision was no small feat, I argue, during and soon after a time when our nation was being ravaged with internal war. President Lincoln's sincere communicative approach with the American people, in my opinion, solidified an American theme that our national love of freedom and democracy must always trump any intense political disagreement of the day.

Now, I do view my opinions as politically moderate – more liberal on social issues with a more conservative approach on economic and safety issues. However, some may consider a given opinion of mine as too far left or too far right to be on the middle of the political spectrum. I would encourage others to grade me as they wish. My primary goal is not to defend that all of my arguments or rationales always fall on the exact middle of the political spectrum, but to be part of a greater civil discourse that will lead to outcomes reached through compromise. Typically, decisions that come about through the democratic process of compromise are somewhere close to the middle ground based on the very nature of negotiation, but not always. When we live in a world of such polar opposite viewpoints, this process of give and take is the key to creating a more unified, peaceful society. Normalizing this process is the goal. We want to establish (or re-establish) a culture of compromise that leads to agreements that are not exactly down the political middle, but that all sides can live with so that we can all co-exist in relative peace.

In closing my introduction, I want to encourage others who have been afraid to speak out for fear of aggressive reaction from those who thrive in divisiveness, to step forward. I certainly must be honest in admitting that I have been in this group, often hesitating to speak out for fear of disapproval or rejection. It seems at first that it is easier to stay quiet rather than make waves, but then we experience that continual inner calling to stand up for what is right. At some point, we come to the realization that to achieve inner peace, we must speak up and take non-violent, but resolute action. As more of us voice the need for middle-of-the-road approaches, those on either side of the political spectrum will get aggressive. However, our collective of moderate voices can offset these uncivil communications and, sadly at times, calls for violence which are threats to our American way of life.

The very idea of our Freedom of Speech in our Constitution's Bill of Rights establishes the basic right to free political expression (Kamps 61, 66). Now, this does not mean that others do not have the right to strongly argue and debate in opposition to our opinions, but that the exchange of ideas should occur with some level of civility and certainly without any fear of violent reactions. We seem to have forgotten a key component of our democratic system, which is that after intense debate, we all come together as Americans committed to protecting every citizen's right to disagree with one another. This final step after the highly emotional verbal confrontations is what has been missing recently in our civil interactions.

One of my favorite movies is *The King's Speech*. It was such an inspirational, biographical account of someone who had to overcome an embarrassing speech impediment (stuttering) in order to have his voice heard by the world. The movie provides a general historical account of King George of Great Britain overcoming his challenge through perseverance and the right support, so he could communicate effectively to his people. King George's leadership, though ceremonial, was desperately needed at a time when the British people were facing the fascist threat of Hitler during World War II. One of my favorite lines from the movie was during a back-and-forth argument the king was having with his speech therapist and friend, Lionel Logue (*The King's Speech*). Mr. Logue virtually shouts to King George the question (paraphrasing), "Why should anyone listen to you?" The king responded emphatically (paraphrasing), "Because I have a voice," (*The King's Speech*).

Regardless of our "standing" in society based on economics, education, or social status, all of us should feel empowered to share our voices with the world. Through these essays, this is my way to express and share my voice.

# 2. We Must Stop Hate Against Asian Americans

———

### The COVID-19 Pandemic and the Rise of Hate Against Asian Americans

As a proud American of Jewish descent, I definitely feel a kinship with Asian Americans who have experienced verbal and disgusting, physical attacks against their community. These attacks increased significantly after the beginning of the COVID-19 pandemic with many blaming Asian Americans for the virus that began in a marketplace in Wuhan, China. First, there is plain ignorance by people, who can't quite grasp that it was solely the government of China that certainly was negligent in not doing more to warn the world about COVID. Individual citizens should not be blamed for this lack of governmental action. These Chinese governmental leaders should have worked directly with the WHO (World Health Organization) and should have taken immediate steps, such as closing down the borders of their nation, as soon as possible, once they realized the death and illness that COVID-19 caused. China is still a very repressive governmental regime that puts order, control and narrative over open communication or honesty.

It shouldn't be that much of a mental stretch for everyone to understand that the citizens of China and especially Chinese Americans, who are not Chinese citizens, are not to blame for the suffering caused by the COVID-19 pandemic. Particularly, blaming Chinese Americans many of whom are members of families who have been citizens of the United States for multiple generations is ridiculous. I do compare this behavior to Jews being attacked in America for disagreement over the Israeli-Palestinian conflict. The only difference for me is that I in no way compare the Israeli government, which is overall a democracy, to the totalitarian regime with state supported capitalism that is modern-day China. I do concede that Jews in America can be very pro-Israel, but to say that we are part of the Israeli government is not accurate. Certainly, treating Chinese Americans, whose families escaped from a repressive Chinese government, as representatives of that Chinese government is not logical. It is simply not the case. Many of us Jews living in America, as with Asian Americans, are from families who are multi-generational proud Americans. Jews who live in the United States are first and foremost Americans just as those of Asian descent are also citizens of the United States. The bias against certain groups who are just as American as any other group who has lived in the United States for generations is evident. How often are Americans of Russia or Western European ancestry verbally or physically attacked because of disagreements with the actions of these governments? It does not happen because white Americans are simply viewed as "true Americans," while too often bias comes into play with assigning racial minorities to their ancestral home.

A good example of this ingrained prejudice can be seen when President Trump during his administration commented that four minority Congresswomen should basically return to their home nations and fix those places. The former president described these nations as "corrupt," "broken" and "crime infested" (Cummings). Of course, except for one Congresswoman, these legislators were born in the United States. Alexandria Ocasio-Cortez, Ayanna Pressley, and Rashida Tlaib are all American-born citizens. Only Ilhan Omar was born in Somalia but has been a United States citizen since 2000. This sort of basic stereotyping is wrong and dangerous and in the case of Asian Americans, it has led to horrific acts of not only harassment, but violence. A note here that while I commend President Trump for some accomplishments (such as his focus on job creation and passing criminal justice reform), one key responsibility of the president that Mr. Trump miserably failed at, is to communicate to the citizenry that we are a nation of immigrants. It is so important for us as Americans to truly celebrate our great diversity and not use it as a tool for division and hate.

I must make an appropriate disclaimer in my statements of being sensitive as a Jew to mistreatment of Asian Americans. I am not an Orthodox or Conservative Jew, so I do not go through my daily life wearing a yarmulke. Unless someone asks, for the most part, I am viewed by the world as a Caucasian American of European descent. I may never fully comprehend what it feels like to be Asian or African American, but I do my best to realize that Americans from these groups have and do face mistreatment because there is no hiding one's race.

Now, regarding the COVID-19 pandemic, I gather in addition to simple-mindedness and ignorance of some, what we see here is more of an excuse to hate. People who are racists and bigots see any opportunity, such as the COVID-19 crisis and pounce on the excuse to hate others who are different. In this case Chinese Americans are the victims. Our leaders have been far too careless when it comes to publicly blaming China for this virus. Again, the Chinese government shoulders a great deal of blame, but comments by our former president, referring to the COVID-19 virus in slang derogatory terms (I will not repeat them here) is not acceptable. During the Pennsylvania Senate race, I even saw a statement from Dr. Oz blaming China for the COVID-19 pandemic (Chan). It is fair to call out the Chinese government, but our leaders must go further to explain that Chinese Americans are just that – Americans and are not in any way to blame for this horrible disease.

It should be noted that those blaming Asian Americans for COVID-19 with their warped logic don't recognize that Asian Americans have ancestry from a variety of Asian nations, not just China. Many Americans are of Japanese, Korean, Filipino and Vietnamese descent. Furthermore, a fact that I had to be corrected on (my apologies) is that Indian Americans are considered in the Asian category of nations as well, known as "South Asian Americans." I'm sure those wanting to blame the Chinese for COVID, would assume anyone with Asian ancestry to be open for verbal or even physical assault. These hatemongers aren't checking to see if the victim of their hate is Japanese or Filipino, they just want to hate. Our population needs more education on Asian American cultures and histories. I am not arguing for some type of extreme leftist diversity training that requires all white people to accept that they are "oppressors," but that some recognition that bias and hatred against Asian Americans does exist and needs to be effectively addressed and eradicated. We should emphasize messaging that incorporates the American "melting pot" ideal that citizens of the U.S. are of many races, ethnicities, and cultures. We need to accept all as true Americans. I want to stipulate that most Americans are accepting of others who are different from themselves. However, we need more of a public education emphasis on morality to quiet those voices calling for repulsive acts of violence to be committed against our fellow American citizens. I am in favor of getting tougher on criminals who engage in hate crimes, particularly those involving acts of physical violence.

We must all do our fair share to stop the violence against Asian Americans. It is simply and purely racism. It is appalling and disgusting that even in metropolitan areas that so often are havens of diversity, such as San Francisco and New York City, that Asian Americans have been gruesomely attacked. This violence is particularly disheartening when we are seeing senior citizens who are physically fragile being brutally beaten. It must stop. Along with educational campaigns in our schools and in our workplaces, community events that focus on Asian cultures could promote more tolerance. Any organized or even informal, social interactions between Asian Americans and other Americans could be helpful in replacing hate with compassion. I am not naïve enough to think that a few community events can turn every person who holds hate in her or his heart to become best friends with an Asian American, but some people will change, I contend. Also, the coming together of everyone who supports the Asian American community may dissuade those who seek to commit acts of hatred. As the saying goes, "there is strength in numbers."

### The United States Imprisoning Japanese Americans during World War II

I think a brief discussion of hatred against Asian Americans is not complete without providing some information on how Americans of Japanese descent were treated after the nation of Japan attacked Pearl Harbor, Hawaii on December 7th, 1941. Performing some generic research led me to discover that approximately 120,000 American men, women and children of Japanese ancestry were forced into concentration camps, known as "internment camps," during World War II by the United States government (Niiya). These Americans were forced from their homes and lives in the spring of 1942 due to an unjustified panic that they would spy for the Japanese government or assist Japan in coordinating an invasion of the West Coast of the United States. I must provide an overall apology to the Japanese American community, both for this past atrocity carried out by our government and to a somewhat lesser degree, the fact that I really was somewhat ignorant about the internment camps that Japanese Americans were placed in during World War II.

Reading about fellow Americans who were forced to leave their property and lives sometimes within just a few days is mortifying. The descriptions that Americans of Japanese descent have shared on their experiences on having to leave their homes with no more than what they could carry with them, communicate great feelings of anguish and desperation. As a huge Star Trek fan, I have been following George Takei's (who played Mr. Sulu on the original Star Trek television show) career for many years. His talent, humor and humanity have kept him in the spotlight throughout the decades. As a gay, Asian American, Mr. Takei is a role model for anyone navigating the difficult road that minorities often face when showing their true selves to the world. I recommend to anyone who wishes to get a first-hand account of what it was like for these families to be forced to leave their homes due to overwhelming racism to watch Mr. Takei's Ted Talk that is available on YouTube (Takei). Mr. Takei's great communication skills adeptly describes how as a small child, he, his parents, and siblings were forced to leave his California home and travel on a train of all things (reminiscent in my mind to how Jews were taken in mass to concentration camps in Eastern Europe) to their internment camps run by the United States government. A new federal agency, the War Relocation Authority, was tasked with relocating Japanese Americans to the interior of the nation, away from the West Coast to these camps. These internment camps provided very meager living conditions in barrack-style housing units that our fellow American citizens were forced to endure from 1942 until the end of the war in early 1946 ("Japanese American Incarceration").

George Takei's description of United States military personnel coming to his home and instructing the family that they had to leave their home is heartbreaking. His mother was in tears as she exited their home with his baby sister. They were taken by train to live in essentially a prisoner camp with barbed wire surrounding them with soldiers guarding the camp carrying guns. When the Japanese Americans were released after the war, they had nothing. Their property had been taken from them and they had to begin their lives again. Mr. Takei described how his family had to start over and they were penniless. His family lived on Skid Row in Los Angeles experiencing horrid living conditions because as with other Japanese Americans in this situation, they were not able to hold onto their homes and businesses while in federal custody. There are some stories of white Americans (I would say real Americans) who helped their Japanese neighbors by renting out their homes or helping with their businesses while the Japanese Americans were held in these camps, but most Japanese Americans lost everything and had to start over after the war.

The fact that so many Americans of Japanese descent succeeded after the war when discrimination against them was so prevalent, is a testament to their commitment to hard work and the American way of life. I come back now to the third decade in the twenty-first centuries when we are witnessing such violent acts against Asian Americans during the COVID-19 pandemic. I can't get out of my mind how Asian American senior citizens in places which traditionally have promoted acceptance and diversity, like the states of California and New York, have been attacked without warning. It is just barbaric. I call upon my fellow Americans and our leaders to come together in one voice of unity to proclaim that hatred and violence against Asian Americans will not be tolerated.

## Asian American Contributions to the World

I want to conclude this essay by discussing just a few of the many Asian Americans who have made tremendous contributions to our society and the world. First it is important to mention (as Mr. Takei did in his Ted Talk) the $442^{nd}$ Regiment of Japanese Americans in the U.S. Army who signed up to fight in World War II. As their fellow countrymen were being unjustly held in internment camps, these brave Americans were quickly becoming known for their heroic feats, including helping to liberate French cities from the Nazis (Takei).

The contributions of Asian Americans to science and technology are numerous and varied. I will mention three giants in science here, but I encourage readers to explore on their own the many Asian Americans who have made our world brighter due to their work.

First, Subrahmanyan Chandrasekhar was an Indian American astrophysicist who won the Noble Prize for Physics with William A. Fowler for his research on the composition and life cycle of stars. He joined the faculty at the University of Chicago in 1937 after attending university in India and at the University of Cambridge in England. Born in India, he became an American citizen in 1953. He trained as a physicist at Presidency College in Madras, India which is notable as his work involved a collaboration of both astronomy and physics. His work proved that white dwarf stars which are stars at the final stage of their active lives have an upper limit to how large they can get before exploding or turning into black holes. This finding is now known as the Chandrasekhar Limit. The Chandra X-Ray Observatory, named for this great scientist, was launched in orbit around the Earth in 1999. It can track x-ray emissions from very hot areas of the universe so that exploded stars, black holes, dark matter, and other astronomical environments can be imaged and studied. The satellite is operated by the Smithsonian Astrophysical Observatory in Cambridge, Massachusetts which collects data from Chandra and provides it to scientists for study. Please visit the website https://chandra.harvard.edu for more information on the Chandra X-Ray Observatory and the exciting, breakthrough information it is collecting on our universe. Additional information on Dr. Chandrasekhar can be found at multiple websites, including The Nobel Prize website www.nobelprize.org/prizes/physics/1983/chandrasekhar/facts/[1]. These websites for the Chanra X-Ray Observatory and The Nobel Prize provided me with extensive biographical facts that I detailed above about this Asian American scientist who gave so much to his field and the world.

A second great scientist that I wanted to highlight is Chien-Shiung Wu who was known as the "First Lady of Physics" ("Dr. Chien-Shiung Wu"). Dr. Wu was a physicist who was born in China in 1912 but came to the U.S. in 1936 where she obtained her PhD in Physics from the University of California at Berkley. She was a professor for many years at Columbia University in New York City. Dr. Wu worked on the Manhattan project that developed the atomic bomb. Also, her work led to improved Geiger counters to detect radioactivity levels. Dr. Wu was part of a team that won a Nobel Prize in 1957 for work on beta decay in which her experiment proved that identical nuclear particles do not always behave the same. The other two scientists on the team, who were men, were named as recipients of the award, but she was not publicly recognized ("Dr. Chien-Shiung Wu"). This lack of proper recognition displayed the widespread discrimination that women faced in the workplace during this time. Dr. Chien-Shiung Wu must be properly praised not only for her tremendous contributions to humanity's scientific knowledge, but for overcoming limitations that Asian Americans and women faced for most of the twentieth century. Indeed, Dr. Wu was truly an American pioneer in science and, I would say, a hero in civil rights. Please visit the website https://ahf.nuclearmuseum.org/ahf/profile/chien-shiung-wu/ for more information about Dr. Wu and her tremendous contributions to science. This website for the Atomic Heritage Foundation provided a significant portion of the biographical information on Dr. Wu's heroic rise in the science world that I discuss above.

Yes, there are many other Asian American and Native Hawaiian/Pacific Islander (AANHPI) individuals who have contributed so much to science. It is challenging to pick only three out of so many great Asian American scientific professionals to highlight but given our world's crisis in dealing with the COVID-19 pandemic, I did want to include Dr. Peter Tsai. Dr. Tsai is a Taiwanese American inventor who has a doctorate in material science (U.S. Embassy Tbilisi). He invented and patented the synthetic fabric used to make N95 mask filters (U.S. Embassy Tbilisi). Of course, the N95 mask became critical to protecting millions of people from contracting the COVID-19 virus. I just think it is fitting to mention Peter Tsai's contribution given the anti-Asian hate that surfaced with the COVID-19 pandemic. It should be noted that Dr. Tsai came out of retirement in 2020 to help with the pandemic by researching ways to sterilize the masks (U.S. Embassy Tbilisi). He undertook this effort to help protect medical professionals who were reusing masks due to limited

---

1. http://www.nobelprize.org/prizes/physics/1983/chandrasekhar/facts/

supplies. I would encourage anyone interested in getting a better insight into this great American to visit the web site https://www.taiwaneseamerica.org (search "N95" or "Kathy and Connie Tsai") and read the article, "Our Dad Invented the N95 Mask: Our Taiwanese American Story," written by his daughters Kathy and Connie Tsai.

## Closing

The list of Asian Americans contributing to our society is extensive and includes work in the realm of politics, sports, journalism, etc. One can look to Tiger Woods the golf legend as one of the world's greatest athletes whose diverse background includes Chinese, as well as Thai ancestry. Lisa Ling is a famous journalist and hosts *This is Life with Lisa Ling* on CNN. I am in awe of her unmatched ability to connect with those she is interviewing, as well as her tremendous talent in communicating the human story in each of her pieces to her audience. Finally, I do want to mention that our current United States Vice President, Kamala Harris is both the first woman and person of Asian descent (her parents were Indian and Jamaican) to hold this esteemed, high public office.

The list goes on and on of Asian Americans who have contributed so much to our nation and our world. I am personally thankful to Asian Americans who have shared so much of their traditional cultures with the rest of us. These cultural gifts include their diverse and sophisticated cuisines (more sushi please), their teachings on achieving inner peace (mindfulness meditation, Yoga and Tai chi come to mind) and their emphasis on achievement through simple hard work. What the COVID-19 pandemic showed us is that while we have made strides in creating a society that ensures Americans of all backgrounds and races are treated with equality and respect, we still have a long way to go. Asian Americans have demonstrated, time and time again, their dedication to the American way of life that consists of working hard, supporting our democratic values, and treating others with fairness. They are true Americans who set the example for others to emulate, whether they are newcomers to our nation or are citizens whose families have lived in the United States for multiple generations. All Americans need to stand in unity during this critical time when Asian Americans need us most to reject and defeat Asian hate.

# 3. Self-Driving Vehicle Systems: The Answer to Dangerous Roadways?

The other day I was driving to work, and I was stopped in traffic on a road that intersects with a major four-lane highway that proceeds into the city. At the time of morning that I typically travel on this road, there is traffic, but being stopped for so long on this road, I had assumed there must have been an accident. When I finally got closer to the traffic light at the intersection, I discovered there was an issue with the traffic lights. I quickly realized that for the traffic on my road, the light was flashing red for us to stop before entering the primary highway (typically drivers turn right to head into the City on the highway). The traffic flowing through on the highway had a flashing yellow light.

Obviously, this flashing light system is the default when there is a malfunction with the traffic light system, but on an intersection like this, it was just a horrendous series of accidents waiting to happen. Simply because of the volume of traffic traveling into the city with people going to work, it was extremely dangerous to pull into the intersection. None of the traffic on the main highway was slowing down at all through the yellow light. When it was my turn, I thought I had plenty of time with the tractor trailer approaching from a reasonable distance away, but when I pulled out, I realized I had to accelerate very quickly. The truck driver of course ignored the yellow light and did not slow down at all, and he continued to come toward me traveling in my lane at a speed well above the posted speed limit. This was extremely frustrating given he could have avoided rapidly approaching me by easily moving into the left-hand lane that was empty. I was able to speed up quickly enough, but not without quite a fright at 6:45 on a Tuesday morning.

It comes to mind whether this would be a situation in which an advanced, integrated system of vehicles communicating with each other per a type of internet (or intranet) system would work better. The vehicles and lights could all be connected into one integrated system. If the lights malfunctioned, the system would take over and process the vehicles in an orderly way through the intersection. Better yet, as some futurists envision, a transportation system could be developed in the far-off future in which all vehicles would be fully autonomous and linked through an advanced communications network. One of the many benefits of such a system is that the need for stop lights and traffic signals would be eliminated.

Everyone has their own personal opinions and experiences while driving, but I think it is quite evident that as society has opened back up after the peak of the pandemic, our roadways are more dangerous than they ever have been. People are impatient and short-tempered. Serious accidents have increased throughout the past few years. The National Highway Traffic Safety Administration provides an estimated figure of 42,915 fatalities in the United States for 2021 ("Early Estimates"). That is quite a large number of needless deaths. Unfortunately, we have traded safety for speed and convenience. As a society that cares about the health of our citizens, this trade-off must be reversed. Safety needs to come first and foremost, not convenience. Many argue that self-driving cars will save lives. Let us take a brief look at what options are being proposed.

### Technology Is the Key to Improving Vehicle Safety

I am a layperson when it comes to this technology, but my understanding is that the ability of a vehicle to drive independently of a human driver is measured in the industry on a scale from zero to five, with five being a level at which a vehicle can drive itself with no human interaction (Dow). Tesla is a leader in this pursuit. The company's technology as far as its self-driving ability truly is amazing, but even these cars are not level five self-driving. A quick review in early 2023 on YouTube can provide one with a real-world, point-of-view experience of driving a Tesla with the latest driver-assist technology. It really is a system where on an open road that is clearly marked, the computer system is able to maintain the vehicle with little assistance, however, the driver does in various circumstances have to take over and assist. It appeared that in a local road situation with many obstacles like buildings, other vehicles moving in a variety of directions and pedestrians, that the driver really needs to be more manually driving the vehicle rather than using the auto-driving function.

We are not there yet with self-driving cars being fully autonomous and some say this type of world is years away (Winton). Tesla seems to be the most optimistic in always proclaiming that in the near future we will truly achieve full vehicle autonomy, but others say the level of ability for an automated driving system to replace a human is in reality decades away.

There are a variety of ideas out there and the beginnings of some testing that show improvements can be made in the next decade or so. Tesla's tunnel plan involving self-driving cars take passengers in underground tunnels quickly from one area of a city to another is happening now in Las Vegas. They are planning a tunnel system that will take passengers to stops throughout the city. Currently, riders are able to avoid a forty-five-minute walk across the Convention Center area by instead taking a two-minute ride in the tunnel in a Tesla (Mihalascu). The vehicles do have drivers, so this is not a driverless system, but there are plans for such an autonomous system in the future. Perhaps this is the future of self-driving transportation in which passengers travel along a segregated self-driving environment without other vehicles driven by people. The goal is to have this system in Las Vegas throughout the city to provide stops at several locations.

One current transition challenge as we hopefully move away from mostly human driving to a large-scale self-driving system is the confusion that having both types of modes on the same roadways at the same time can cause. We are already seeing differences in how semi-autonomous vehicles perform compared to vehicles that are controlled solely by human drivers. Traveling distances between vehicles, braking behavior and even the speed of vehicles can be very different between the different driving modes. So, as with the Tesla tunnel format, an initial transition to all self-driving vehicles may involve setting up segregated areas of cities that would only allow self-driving cars. I realize a lot of people are opposed to having a transportation system in which humans are totally taken out of the loop. I do agree with this concern, somewhat, of giving up control, but if we can reduce traffic fatalities, accidents and reduce congestion, fully autonomous vehicle systems should be the future of vehicular transportation. The question is when will this technology be perfected? Yes, a truly autonomous, self-driving system may be years away, but I like the idea of setting up smaller geographic oases in which only self-driving cars are allowed. This approach would allow a gradual transition as more and more self-driving vehicle areas are set up throughout the nation.

When we think about the split-second decisions we make when driving, it is understandable that it would take an advanced artificial intelligent system for vehicles to safely travel on their own given the current traffic and roadway systems. The car pulling out right in front of us and the child chasing a ball into the street require immediate decision-making that computer systems are not capable of at this point. Per a YouTube video, a Tesla driver shows the viewers how he had to take over while traveling on a highway so his vehicle could accelerate fast enough given the tractor trailer coming up quickly behind him (of course he was honked at by the truck driver who insisted the Tesla driver speed up) (Brownlee 05:40-05:47). When one thinks about all the variety of issues that can arise while driving, such as navigating entering a busy intersection or how to travel safely on a rainy or snow-covered roadway, we realize how much mental energy is involved. The human mind is still the best judge on the road.

At this point, I do favor a system of integration and cooperation in which smart technology on every vehicle works with an active driver to greatly reduce vehicular accidents. We want both the vehicle driver-assist program to reduce human error, but we also need the human driver to take over in situations in which a driver-assist program is unable to safely navigate a given driving environment. One concern that may always be evident when we are talking about technology is the tremendous dangers involved if a vehicle's technology malfunctions. Particularly when we are talking about computer technology that increasingly is used in all facets of our life including vehicles, drivers must have the ability to take over when the vehicle computer or computer system has a glitch. If a self-driving vehicle begins traveling in an erratic manner, then the human driver must have the ability to immediately intercede and take over the driving function. In addition, with more technology and interconnectedness between computers, as we experience on the Internet, we know we will always have to be ready to defend against hackers' ill intentions to disrupt the system. The chance is always there that computer viruses can cause real world issues in such proposed vehicle driving systems. When our home desktop or laptop gets a virus, it can be a real headache, but nothing life threatening occurs. If a vehicle or interconnected vehicle system gets a virus through the computer system(s), then lives can be put in danger. Yes, in the foreseeable future, there are some technological and engineering issues, both on the vehicles and on the design of our roadways, that will have to be addressed to achieve a purely self-driving vehicle environment that is completely safe. Until that day, I favor a collaborative co-existence in which the vehicle driving system and the driver keep a check on each other to ensure safety for everyone on our roadways.

### Self-Driving Vehicle Wish List for the Near Future

What is my wish list for the near future? It is evident there are many challenges that I have no doubt will be mostly solved by minds, such as Elon Musk and other great scientists, engineers and car experts that will lead to a much safer driving experience with artificial intelligence technology. I would like to submit my wish list for what I want to see in the next five to ten years as being standard features on all new vehicles.

Yes, one of my hopes is that any current technological glitches are worked out so that they work well in a hybrid system (driver-assist technology with a human driver working together). We do see some warning systems included as features on some new vehicle models, such as the driver hearing a warning sound or feeling a vibration from the steering wheel if the vehicle is close to crashing into the vehicle in front of it, or if the vehicle is straying from its lane. I would like to see all cars with automated braking systems that will stop the car for the driver to avoid a crash. Drivers really do need this additional assistance and all travelers on the roads need this additional protection.

It would be a tremendous help in improving roadway safety if lane assist technology, that some vehicles already have, becomes standard on all new vehicles. Vehicles colliding with each other due to head-on collisions on two-lane roads make such technology indispensable. I'd like to see all vehicles come with lane assist technology to both prevent vehicles from straying into other lanes and to prevent crashes during lane changes due to blind spot situations. This help with blind spots really is needed. I have made it such a habit in my driving practice to check and then double check before changing lanes to ensure I'm not driving into another vehicle. As our roadways have become more congested, the issue of one vehicle changing lanes and the driver mistakenly not seeing a vehicle already in the lane is a real safety concern. Also, I've noticed while driving on multi-lane highways, that not only do I have to ensure that there is not a vehicle already in the lane that I am planning to move into, but I also realize that I have to scan very actively to ensure another vehicle from another lane is not attempting to move into the lane that I am about to merge into at the same time. This lane departure, prevention technology is also necessary for two-lane roads to prevent the tremendous danger of vehicles colliding head-on into one another. I have had multiple close calls, especially lately, in which the oncoming vehicles are simply traveling much too fast given the curve the driver is attempting to navigate. In these situations, drivers are too often demanding their vehicles perform in a manner that from a basic physics standpoint allows very little room for error. Their cars are traveling too fast given sharp road curves and the legitimate concern is the drivers will be unable to keep their vehicles in their lane, and thus will collide head-on with the vehicles coming towards them. Of course, in most cases the driver slows down at the last second or barely manages to maintain the vehicle in their lane, but increasingly this issue is a real concern with the current day environment of excessive speeding. We really do need more technological assistance to prevent accidents in these situations.

I also envision standard anti-tailgating technology in which a vehicle's driver assist system will simply ensure that the vehicle will not follow the vehicle in front of it at an unsafe distance (too closely). It seems that the safe following distance that can be set on some vehicles' cruise control systems can become an open area for other vehicles to merge into which, in effect, triggers the car's assist system to slow down and adjust the distance behind the new vehicle in front of it. Of course, a driver in a vehicle following the vehicle with the safe-following distance program, which probably is actively following too closely anyway, must continually react more. This is where it is clear to me that there must be some standardization of driver-assist programs among all vehicles on the road so that traveling can be more synchronized. The current environment in which we have vehicles with driver-assist programs sharing the road with exclusively manually driven cars does not work well together. If all cars are equipped with safe-following distance assistance, then proper spacing can be more easily achieved between vehicles. All cars having standard technology that results in all vehicles on the roadway reacting in the same way is needed.

Finally, I'd like to see a very effective and responsive, automatic speed adjustment system standard on all vehicles that adjusts vehicles' speeds due to environmental conditions. Such a driver assistance system would prevent vehicles from traveling too fast for current road conditions, whether vehicles are traveling on wet, icy, or snow-covered roads. I witness on a regular basis that a large number, if not the majority, of drivers attempt to drive at the same speed when it rains as they do on dry, sunny days when driving conditions are optimal. The hope is that technology can be developed to prevent accidents caused by vehicles traveling too fast for poor road conditions due to weather activity. The goal is safer traveling during inclement weather. Another aspect of this comprehensive safety system could possibly include technologically enhanced "smart" tires that could monitor the wetness (and slickness) of the road surface. This information could be shared and sensed by the vehicle's computer so that the vehicle speed would automatically be adjusted to improve safety. This type of system is desperately needed. It seems almost every time we have rainy or inclement weather, the accidents in my area just pile up. The reason is that drivers refuse to slow down. We need technology to help with this dangerous situation to correct for the fact that people too often refuse to slow down and drive safely. I contend that when drivers do not take responsibility, then we need to limit some of their independence on the roadways for the common good and safety of the populace.

## Closing

As our roads get more congested with more vehicles and people, it will be increasingly necessary to seek technological solutions to create a safer environment for all citizens traveling on our roadways. In the immediate future, planners, road engineers and car companies all need to work together to create a transportation system that significantly reduces car fatalities and accidents. In my opinion, with the current state of inattentive and aggressive driving that is increasingly the norm, we need to develop and implement new technologies as soon as possible to compensate for human failures. We need technologies that will result in lower vehicle speeds (I will talk more about speeding prevention later in this work), the elimination of dangerous tailgating, and safer vehicular travel during inclement weather situations. Our families and especially our children depend on us to ensure they always arrive safely at their destinations.

# 4. Crimes of Colonialism: Should Western Culture Be "Cancelled?"

---

## A Queen's Passing Triggers Criticism of Colonial Powers

As the world mourned the passing of Queen Elizabeth II on September 8, 2022, some politically active groups and individuals took the opportunity during this solemn event to protest crimes committed by colonial powers. These crimes included the murder and mistreatment of millions of native peoples around the globe. I have no personal allegiance to the British royal family and while those bringing up these past crimes were correct in their opinions, their timing was very inappropriate. I admit as an unsophisticated American, I don't quite understand the fascination and fandom that the British and many followers around the world express when it comes to "the Royals." However, having stated this, I do disagree with the growing trend of openly criticizing those who have recently passed, regardless of who they were, out of respect for family and friends of the deceased. The family and followers of Queen Elizabeth should have been allowed to mourn their queen in peace without judgement. Our open, Western culture certainly allows for open protest and the expression of opinions opposing the British royal family and the colonial culture the institution represents, but as a matter of appropriateness and civility, I would say this type of political speech should have been withheld until a more appropriate time. Would it have been too much to ask that the critics wait at least a month or so after the Queen had been laid to rest before coming out of the woodwork to rail against the monarchy? I do support the civil, societal norms of our Western culture which include the values of basic courtesy, compassion and respect for every family who is experiencing a loss. The British royal family, while a very public enterprise, still deserved to mourn peacefully. Now, having fully expressed my opinion on the timing of these critiques, I will now acknowledge their validity.

## Atrocities Committed Against Native Peoples by Colonial Powers

I definitely concur that atrocities, such as the slave trade and the virtual annihilation of native peoples in the Americas, do not paint traditional Western colonial powers in a favorable light when it comes to human rights in the past. The occupation of India by the British is another example of these relationships that were too much one-sided with cheap, indigenous labor being used to plunder the riches of the poorer nation. Currently, there is a call for the royal family to return a priceless jewel that Indians claim belongs to them (Guzman). The British through economic exploitation did, per many accounts, succeed in the transfer of trillions of dollars' worth of resources between the 1700s and the 1900s from India to Great Britain (Hickel).

It is no secret that Great Britain and colonial culture treated indigenous populations around the world savagely. Of course, Europeans referred to indigenous people around the world as "uncivilized," but time and time again we saw the "sophisticated" colonial aggressors as the ones who mistreated the people of India and First Nation peoples in the Americas, acting truly uncivilized and inhumane. India experienced severe famines under British rule with little assistance from the British government, while large exports of rice left India for Britain (Patel). The infamous Bengal famine between 1943 and 1944, saw three million Indians starve to death as Winston Churchill's wartime policy actions included transferring food from India to support the British and American war effort during World War II (Wilkinson, Bard).

Millions of indigenous people perished in the Americas as a result of European expansion. I was astounded and shocked to find out that out of sixty million people who lived in the Americas before the arrival of Columbus in 1492, only around six million were left around the year 1600 (Woodward). Violence against these groups and European diseases caused so many lives to be lost. In fact, researchers from the University College London found that this rapid decline of so many people led to a decrease in the Earth's temperature (Woodward). This tremendous decrease in population resulted in farmlands being re-forested, actually leading to a cooling of the planet's atmosphere by 0.15 degrees Celsius (Woodward). Of course, what is fairly being referred to as the American Genocide of Native Americans continued and culminated at the Wounded Knee Massacre in South Dakota (full disclosure: I am not an expert on the full history of the First Nation people in the U.S.). The U.S. Army in 1890 killed up to three hundred Lakota Indian men, women, and children (Blakemore). Native Americans were pretty much left to live on reservations set up by the U.S. government after that event. No, it was not until 1924 when Calvin Coolidge signed the Indian Citizenship Act (Shogan) that First Nation peoples were finally granted citizenship in a land that they had lived on for hundreds of years before Europeans arrived. When the Europeans came to the New World, they simply through use of force seized the land away from the original inhabitants. The impressive dedication of many Native Americans who signed up to fight for the United States during World War I helped in the effort to enact the Indian Citizenship Act ("Why We Serve").

## Western Culture Evolves into the Protector of Freedom

So how as a proud American and supporter of Western culture can I seemingly discount all these atrocities against indigenous peoples around the world that led to so much suffering, including the mistreatment of First Nation people and African Americans in the United States? It is the realization that while Western culture too often did not live up to its evolving ideals of basic human rights during colonial times, that in fact it was the West who eventually did implement these ethical ideals as real-world laws and practices. The atrocities of so-called "civilized" European society committed over centuries can never be forgiven, but what we can now say is that Western culture in the twenty-first century while, yes, imperfect, and sometimes hypocritical, is clearly the protector of liberties that continue to be extended to its diverse citizenry.

There is no doubt that we must be sensitive to those who were victims of the dark side of colonialism's past and seek as best as we can to find ways to make amends to the descendants of these populations. I do acknowledge this dark history of colonialism that we need to address and, yet I strongly disagree with the call by some that Western culture with its regrettable history should be completely rejected and shunned. The West from its grounding in Greek and Roman democratic government with an emphasis on individual liberty was adopted by the British. Great Britain did not live up to this democratic ideal in how the empire interacted with other nations and cultures, but it was this cornerstone ideal of liberty rising out of Western culture that can be seen in the American Declaration of Independence and Constitution of the United States. The U.S. and Western European nations fought despotism and fascism in World War I and World War II, thus establishing this alliance of nations as the primary protector of individual liberties in the world. Then, in the latter part of the twentieth century, we see this collective of nations overcome the tyranny of Soviet rule and welcome a plethora of Eastern European nations to join us as partners in freedom. This role of extending freedom to nations around the world, which in essence is extending individual liberty to increasing numbers of world citizens, should not be ignored by anyone who wishes to fairly evaluate Western culture.

The West, including the United States, continues to wrestle with prejudice and discrimination. Yet, when it comes to rights afforded to women and minorities, the West continues to make these strides. Yes, sometimes the extension of rights has been too slow of a process, but racial and religious minorities continue to seek refuge in the West, not Iran, Russia, or China. Now we are witnessing those in the LGTBQ (Lesbian, Gay, Transgender, Bisexual and Queer or Questioning) community standing up for their rights. The West is the leader again in establishing and protecting the rights of the members in this group who traditionally have faced severe discrimination and cruel treatment by society. There are still many nations where being gay or transgender is against the law and those that show their true selves are met with harsh punishments.

As of this writing in 2023, the West with its allies is the protector of freedom and democracy. We have a rogue Russian nation that has, without ethical justification, attacked the free nation of

Ukraine, causing the senseless death of thousands and displacement of millions. China seems to be intent on replacing the United States as the top "Superpower" with little regard for democratic rule and individual liberties, such as freedom of speech. Fundamentalist Muslim nations and societies continue to deny women their basic individual liberties. We see this in today's Iran and now Taliban-ruled Afghanistan. Women in such closed societies can face severe and even cruel punishments if they disobey the rules. Even straying from the Muslim dress code, requiring women to cover their bodies from head to toe can result in women experiencing severe physical punishment in some of these nations.

The West is not perfect, and the culture will continue to have to address its past, but I do ask those that reject all things Western in the campaign against former colonialism to review this altruistic function in preserving and protecting individual liberty that the West provides to our modern civilization. There is no nation or governmental system that has established and ensured the rights and liberties of the individual as fervently as the nations of Western democracy. The West has embraced and expanded the prevalence of national governments around the world based in democratic rule, while opposing governments based in tyranny or autocracy.

## Closing

I want to conclude by pointing out that one important attribute of Western culture is that it allows for dissent and protest. It even allows those who disagree with its existence to protest against it. Protesting against the government in other nations means long prison sentences and/or state-sponsored torture. Particularly in comparison to other repressive forms of government around the globe, those who completely wish to reject Western culture because of its origins in colonialism need to take a more balanced stance. We cannot ignore the historical oppression of colonialism, but we also must acknowledge the emphasis on individual liberties that these same nations did adopt as they evolved from their colonial pasts. The West is called upon now to continue its evolution as protector of individual liberties, while also doing much more to support indigenous peoples and their cultures that were so horrifically abused throughout history. We must also continue to make amends to the descendants of African victims of the transatlantic slave trade. Of course, we can never completely make amends for such catastrophic past crimes, but a truly just and free culture acknowledges its sins, attempts significant acts of atonement, and initiates legitimate efforts to ensure that the crimes and egregious behaviors are never repeated. In closing, it is not because of Western culture's past that I disagree with those calling for it to be "cancelled" or rejected, but because of what Western culture has evolved into as a true defender of democratic government and individual liberties, as we all can plainly witness in our twenty-first century world.

# 5. Fair is Fair: An Honest Evaluation of Presidents Trump and Biden's Biggest Failures

## President Trump and COVID-19

I felt, as many others have expressed, that President Trump missed a tremendous opportunity during the pandemic. Had he put the same level of effort into fighting COVID-19 as he did in attempting to downplay the virus for his political interests, he very possibly could have won another four years in office. President Trump could have been a champion of fighting back the pandemic and provided sound, resolute leadership. If Mr. Trump had rallied the nation as former president George W. Bush did, after the attack on our soil on September 11, 2001, he would have both better served the public in keeping deaths to a minimum during the COVID-19 pandemic, and he could have succeeded in the 2020 election. I think at the end of the day, the American people just felt they could not rehire President Trump after he didn't properly follow the guidance of the scientific experts nor really provide a consistent message on the pandemic. Trump also showed very little compassion to those suffering from COVID-19, as well as those who simply wanted to know how best to protect their loved ones. Joe Biden to his credit astutely seized upon the public's desire during a crisis for sound, rational leadership. This led to Mr. Biden's victory for the White House, in my opinion.

The Trump Administration led a very slow response to the pandemic as it was quickly spreading during the first three months of 2020. When deaths were quickly growing as a result of COVID-19 in the spring of 2020, the U.S. was already behind when it came to developing and distributing a reliable COVID-19 test on a wide scale to the public (Bronstein, Devine, and Griffin). In addition, we all remember the stories of medical professionals having to re-use their N95 masks because of a lack of basic protective equipment. It was March of 2020 before large orders for N95 masks and ventilators were ordered in bulk by the federal government (Wilkinson, Alissa). President Trump essentially portrayed the pandemic as a health event that would not seriously affect the United States to the extent that it was harming nations like China and those in the European Union. Mr. Trump was wrong.

Even if one has the opinion that there was no way to be more prepared in early 2020 for COVID in the United States, it was the next phase of the pandemic during the middle to latter months of 2020 that, in my opinion, really sealed Mr. Trump's guilt in being responsible for untold American deaths during the pandemic. Officially, the Centers for Disease Control (CDC) continued to emphasize the use of social distancing and the wearing of masks to limit the spread of COVID-19 during 2020 ("How to Protect"). Yet, Mr. Trump refused to wear a mask and the wearing of masks somehow morphed into a Republican versus Democrat issue. Devout Trump followers refused to wear masks, unfortunately leading to unnecessary deaths.

Now, in early 2023, the United States has seen over one million deaths due to COVID-19. I don't know how many of these we can blame on Mr. Trump, but I do credit his mocking of mask-wearing as a reason why thousands of Americans, many of his supporters, perished during the pandemic. I think it is important to point out the horror those dying from COVID-19 must have experienced. The inability to breathe easily and then needing to be put on a ventilator without knowing if one would ever wake up, is a thought that to this day leaves me feeling distraught for these poor souls. Those dying from COVID-19 in the early days of the pandemic could not even pass with their loved ones by their sides for fear of spreading the disease. During 2020 and 2021, we really were talking about a plague that left many citizens living in a constant state of fear. Simply to feel some sense of control, how many of us ran out and stocked up on too much bathroom tissue, creating a national shortage. I shamefully admit I was one of these people. So much more could have been done by the Trump Administration to alleviate all of the fear with proper planning, effective execution, and clear messaging.

I do want to pause to give credit to President Trump for his push to develop a vaccine for the COVID-19 virus in May of 2020 per his Operation Warp Speed. This monumental effort involved a cooperative collaboration between the U.S. Department of Health and Human Services, private sector pharmaceutical companies, and the U.S. Department of Defense ("Operation Warp Speed"). There is no doubt that the United States has been able to return to normal (given, a "new normal") much more quickly with the widespread distribution of the vaccines in early 2021. Mr. Trump had a great opportunity here to lead his nation. Science had quickly developed these truly miracle vaccines, yet President Trump still refused to voice strong support of the vaccine program. The former president could have addressed the rampant conspiracy theories that contended the vaccines were dangerous to the public. I want to note here that based on my personal factors, I was ecstatic to be one of those citizens who signed up as soon as I could to get that first dose in early March of 2021. It is important to note that more U.S. citizens died of COVID-19 in 2021 (415,000) in comparison to 2020 (351,000) due to many citizens not getting vaccinated and refusing to wear masks (Stobbe). As Mr. Trump was leaving office in January of 2021, he could have demonstrated his support for the vaccines by taking his inoculation in front of the cameras as President Biden would later do. Again, we have to give credit to the Trump Administration for Operation Warp

Speed, but the initial rollout of the vaccine per the federal government's distribution was reminiscent of the 2020 slow start to distribute masks and tests. The Trump Administration was committed to providing the vaccines to the states, but after that act, all implementation was left to each state to handle. The states needed more support in the implementation process. The Biden Administration does need to be commended for much better collaborating with the states to actually get vaccines into arms.

In conclusion, President Trump who at the time claimed that COVID would just "disappear" (Wolfe and Dale) did not live up to his responsibility as leader of our nation. He should have supported and echoed the message that our citizens should, for their safety, follow the sound medical advice from the CDC and other medical professionals on how best to protect against the spread of the virus. In addition, President Trump should have worked fervently in the early days of the pandemic to fast-track the manufacturing and distribution of proper medical equipment to the public. Mr. Trump was pushing to get our faltering economy back up and running again as unemployment ran rampant throughout the nation due to all the COVID shutdowns. What he refused to comprehend was that the economy was simply not going to improve until the COVID-19 pandemic had been contained. Indeed, even after testing positive for COVID-19 and having to check into Walter Reid Medical Center during early October of 2020, President Trump refused to adjust his messaging that masks should not be worn, and America needed to quickly open back up. Of course, President Trump, as leader of the free world, did and should have received the best available medical treatments. One outcome of Mr. Trump's bout with COVID-19 was that it demonstrated through the publicizing of the medications that he received, the issue with mass manufacturing and distribution. Mr. Trump received treatments in October of 2020 that were simply not widely available to everyday Americans. This was another missed opportunity. Mr. Trump, after recovering from the virus, could have dedicated the rest of his time in office disseminating to the public the medical experts' advice on how to prevent the spread of COVID-19. Finally, after losing the 2020 election, instead of spending his time falsely arguing that he was cheated out of victory and inciting an insurgency on January 6, 2021, he could have focused his energy on the rollout of the vaccine. Mr. Trump also could have volunteered his time as an ex-president to convince his followers to get vaccinated. It is sad to note that even as the Biden Administration focused on getting as many Americans vaccinated as possible in 2021, Trump followers in large numbers still refused to change their minds on masks and the vaccines. Too many died of COVID-19 because President Trump did not lead effectively on this issue.

### President Biden and Afghanistan

Now, however, if I am to be fair, President Biden does need to be taken to task for what truly was a dismal and embarrassing exit out of Afghanistan. I do not include myself in the majority of Americans who supported our withdrawal from the country. In order to discourage attacks, such as what occurred on September 11, 2001, from happening again on American soil, I did think it was in our national best interest to continue having a small, but effective force on the ground in Afghanistan. Also, I was of the opinion that once we established an expectation of rights and opportunities for women, that we had a moral obligation to ensure that those rights would continue to be protected. The withdrawal policy framework included a basic stance by the U.S. that we were in essence completely leaving the Afghan government and people to fight on their own against the Taliban. After working in collaboration for decades with the U.S. military, it would now be solely up to the people of Afghanistan to fight the Taliban if they wanted to keep their nation. President Biden acted as if the Afghan people weren't doing their part at all in the fight to keep their nation free. The Afghan military was fighting and dying (Knickmeyer) but due to a corrupt government, many were not getting paid (Copp). As the United States was preparing to leave, the Taliban began taking over large portions of the country. The U.S. was of the opinion that the Taliban could possibly take over the nation, but it would be months after that complete U.S. withdrawal (Turak, Ng and Macias). Again, I think by leaving some forces in Afghanistan, the Taliban resurgence could have been prevented. The line that should have never been crossed given the realities of 9/11 is that the Taliban should never have been allowed to rule Afghanistan or any nation. I reject the Biden Administration's argument that the Taliban have truly reformed their barbaric ways.

Focusing however on the actual exit of the United States military from Afghanistan, it is clear that this was a disaster. A seemingly unknown number of American citizens, as well as Afghan citizens who worked for the United States military were trapped in the country, fearing for their lives, and hiding from the Taliban. Then we had the IS-K (Islamic State of Khorasan Province) suicide bombing attack that killed thirteen American soldiers and some 170 Afghan citizens at the Kabul Airport during the withdrawal in August 2021 (Garamone). Many critics rationally argue that initial evacuations should have been fully completed before any troop withdrawals or Bagram Air Base was closed (Kheel). Also, all highly sensitive military aircraft, vehicles and weapons should have been properly collected and taken out of the country instead of leaving the items for the Taliban. Then, only after, people and U.S. property had been evacuated should the military exit have occurred. Indeed, I concur with the very rational argument that Bagram Air Base should not have been evacuated by U.S. military personnel until the evacuation of all U.S. civilians and those Afghans who had assisted in our operations had been complete.

An article on Politico.com written by Lara Seligman does an exceptional job of describing the decision-making process by U.S. military leaders as their pleas to President Biden to leave a small military contingent in-country was not going to be approved. The military changed the strategy then to pick up and leave as soon as possible to best protect against Taliban attacks (Seligman). This makes sense, as during this time of evacuation, U.S. forces would be more vulnerable to attack with fewer forces available to provide a proper defense or offense in response. The clear rationale of U.S. military leaders was that the longer the evacuation took, the more risk of attack the U.S. military faced. This article pointed out how some say the fast evacuation of Bagram Air Base on July 1st (2021) left the Afghan military feeling abandoned and disheartened (Seligman). Thus, the quick evacuation by U.S. forces, looks to have been a significant factor resulting in the Afghan military's almost immediate collapse. The Afghans certainly quickly gave up, allowing the Taliban to take over the nation in just days.

There are questions that do come to mind, as any reasonable person should conclude that this decision made by President Biden was a catastrophic mistake for the people of Afghanistan and for U.S. standing in the world. First, why did the president not take the recommendation of his military leaders that highly supported a policy of leaving a small contingency of U.S. troops in Afghanistan? The troops could have provided support to the Afghan military and keep a check on Taliban military aggression. Also, I question whether given the peace agreement signed on February 29, 2020, by the Taliban and the United States whether the Taliban's behavior justified the withdrawal of U.S. forces in the summer of 2021. The agreement outlined that there would be talks between the Taliban and the Afghan government on a permanent cease-fire, as well as a negotiation on a new governmental structure in which the Taliban would be integrated into as a member of the current government ("Agreement for Bringing Peace to Afghanistan"). It appears no real substantial movement was made on this front with the Taliban taking over large areas of land in the months immediately prior to the U.S. withdrawal. I do realize it may not have been feasible from a military standpoint to send troops back in after the Taliban took over essentially the entire nation as it quickly took over Kabul with the exit of the U.S. in days, but were there any discussions on doing something to address this new government entirely controlled by the Taliban? Finally, how would this bungled withdrawal be viewed around the world by our partners, as well as our rivals? Would the United States be seen now as weak and disorganized given how our exit from Afghanistan transpired. I do concede that our strong stand with Ukraine probably did repair some damage to the global, public image the United States suffered as a result of the fiasco in Afghanistan. The United States is clearly showing the world that Americans are fully backing the Ukrainian government with substantial funds and military hardware. However, I do wonder if Russia saw our withdrawal as a sign that Putin could invade Ukraine with little concern about any significant challenge from a

United States that appeared to be withdrawing from the world (after our exit from Afghanistan), instead of engaging with it. I won't go so far as to say that Russia would not have invaded Ukraine had we stayed in Afghanistan, but I do support an opinion that says our exit may have emboldened Mr. Putin's confidence in moving forward with his unjustified invasion.

There should be hearings by Congress and President Biden should have to account for this abysmal performance. The withdrawal from Afghanistan could have waited until after the end of the pandemic. This action by President Biden created another human catastrophe that just did not have to happen during this already time of great challenge. In my opinion, the decision to completely withdraw all troops from Afghanistan was poor and not in the long-term national security interest of the American people. The planning of the withdrawal demonstrated a great ineptitude for understanding the situation and indicates President Biden needs to be more thoroughly checked on his decision-making process.

I do think members of President Biden's team should be taken to task, but ultimately, I think President Biden had a "tunnel-vision" approach to Afghanistan, almost to the level that President Trump did in his efforts at downplaying the seriousness of the pandemic. Biden's agenda was to exit the war and romanticized the United States leaving Afghanistan after twenty years. He was intent on doing this as quickly as possible, regardless of the consequences of a fast, careless withdrawal.

I dedicate an entire essay in this work to President Biden's failure in Afghanistan which I encourage the reader to review, but I do think it is critically important to point out that leaving women and young girls to fend for themselves in retaining their rights to work, obtain an education and even dress as they choose under the ruthless, intolerant control of the Taliban is inexcusable. The United States made a commitment to support democratic processes in Afghanistan that allowed women to live as they choose - to either pursue a career or family (or both). President Biden turned his back on the 39.84 million citizens of Afghanistan (19.4 million of whom are female) ("Demographics of Afghanistan"). Many of these Afghan citizens simply wished to live as free people. It was not surprising that a large number of Afghans sought in desperation during the U.S. pullout to escape the soon to be hostile control of the Taliban. Some would say that the United States supported the Afghan government and this nation's economic development for twenty years from 2001 when the United States sought to fight those responsible for the attacks on September 11, 2001, up until Biden's pullout in 2021, and that was enough. My contention is that Afghanistan was a fragile democracy in progress in which voting was occurring. Also, the rights of women, as well as all citizens, were established, normalized, and protected during this twenty-year period. We had a moral responsibility to continue assisting in the development of democracy in this nation.

I also argue from simply a national security standpoint that the United States should have continued to keep a modest, military presence in Afghanistan, if for nothing else than to keep a check on Islamic terrorism in the region. It is understandable that the United States is now focusing primarily on the threats of China with its military expansionist policy and Russia with its invasion of Ukraine, but as the old saying goes, "We can walk and chew gum at the same time." The United States should prioritize its military focus on the threats from China and Russia, yet still be able to monitor the threats from radical, Islamic extremists in the Middle East. Continuing to station a modest military presence in Afghanistan accomplishes this. Indeed, we still have a small contingent of some 900 troops in Syria in early 2023 to, on the surface, prevent the resurgence of the Islamic State extremist group, but it appears there is also a foreign policy goal of limiting the influence of Iran in the region (Logan). Wouldn't leaving some troop levels in Afghanistan support this effort to prevent the spread of Islamist terrorism in the region and world, as well as to assist in keeping a check on Iran's military intentions?

## Conclusion

In closing, some have called for the impeachment of President Biden due to his abysmal performance in calling for the U.S. military to withdraw from Afghanistan. I do support and hope Congress opens a formal investigation. Perhaps now with the Republican Party controlling the U.S. House of Representatives an investigation will move forward. I concede that I am not a U.S. Constitutional attorney, but I do argue that a president can act in such a negligent manner that impeachment is appropriate. President Biden's behavior and actions are, I contend, very close to this line in his decision-making as Commander-in-Chief regarding this disaster in Afghanistan.

President Trump's botched COVID-19 pandemic response and President Biden's dismal decision-making regarding Afghanistan, simply render both ineligible, as well as unqualified, to be elected for second terms as President of the United States in my judgement. It is time for the nation to move on and elect a president in 2024 who uses sound reason and compassion in his (or her) decision-making process on a consistent basis.

# 6. Initial Impressions Soon After the January 6<sup>th</sup> Insurrection (1/17/21)

In my opinion, the insurgency at the United States Capitol on January 6, 2021, was the culmination of years of divisiveness instigated by President Donald Trump. His use of social media to express anger and hatred toward anyone disagreeing with him emboldened those fringe groups on the political right. Following his lead and aggressive demeanor on January 6th, after his vicious rant of falsehoods and his unsubstantiated claim that the election was stolen, some of his followers used violence to stop a constitutionally appropriate action, temporarily, by Congress. In most presidential election years, the confirmation by Congress of the Electoral College's vote outcome is pretty much an administrative step. This process of certifying the presidential election has essentially for generations been considered a formality by Congress. This infamous day, if anything, has taught us as Americans that the peaceful transfer of power must never be taken for granted.

Like so many Americans, I was appalled to see these instigators and, in my opinion, traitors overtaking the brave Capitol Police officers in a violent and barbaric fashion. When seeing the footage of these rioters breaking windows and pushing their way into the Capitol building, I felt like I was looking at something out of a banana republic or some apocalyptic fiction movie, the theme of which is the successful takeover of the United States by homegrown terrorists. It was shocking and heartbreaking to see the seat of our democratic republic being violently trampled by criminals and thugs. Our nation has been a beacon of freedom that for so long the world has looked to as the standard for all other societies and nation states to follow. It appeared on January 6, 2021, that our "City on a Hill," (a description that President Ronald Reagan used to describe our great Republic) was in serious peril. I feel in my heart that it was nothing less than Divine intervention, along with the actions of the brave and greatly outnumbered law enforcement officers that prevented the kidnapping and subsequent harm (including murder) of our Congressional leaders and the Vice President of the United States.

A few scenes come to mind that many of us witnessed on television or on the Internet. First, the breaking of the window at the Capitol, after which protestors climbed through and illegally entered into our nation's legislative home, was clearly a serious step outside the bounds of what some have referred to as just an animated protest. This was now a full-scale riot and insurrection against the people of the United States. I found this scene playing out extremely upsetting. My fellow

Americans were desecrating a site that all Americans should consider sacred ground. President Donald Trump failed in one of his core responsibilities as president – to "protect and defend" our Constitution, not to try to tear it apart just because he was a sore loser. Mr. Trump simply refused to accept the simple fact that he lost fair and square. This was an example of "mob mentality" if there ever was one. It is that transition from individuals using careful, independent judgement into a frenzied collective that allows mass hysteria and unchecked emotionalism to rule. The mob mentality of the insurrectionists led to violent acts against both property and people on January 6th.

The second event during this day of darkness for our nation that is imprinted on my memory, consisted of the repugnant behavior by the insurrectionists who were actually looking for members of Congress and Mike Pence in order to cause them bodily harm. Chants of "hang Mike Pence" were gruesome and savage. After all, Vice President Pence had been serving the nation in the Trump Administration for four years. Also, while I don't recall seeing the person on camera, I distinctly recall while the mob was rummaging through the Capitol a male voice calling out, "Nancy, where are you?" It was a very sinister, morbid voice that in its tone promised that if the mob found Nancy Pelosi, Speaker of the House, she would face serious and imminent physical harm. There are some who have already made excuses for the insurrectionists, claiming their intention was simply to protest for what they believed in on this infamous day. The intention of the mob was made clear from the chants and violent acts - to succeed in this insurrection against the United States government. In addition, some clearly had the desire to execute national leaders who were elected by our free democratic system, as created by our Founding Fathers.

A third theme I would say that caused me great concern, involved the expressions of hate by the insurrectionists. As an American who comes from a Jewish family, seeing the gentleman with the Auschwitz T-shirt was an offensive display of antisemitism and hate. Of course, just as upsetting to African Americans and what should be offensive to all those pledging allegiance to these United States, was the act by one insurrectionist walking through our Capitol waving a Confederate flag. Only the flag of the United States of America belongs in our house of American governance, standing as a symbol of freedom for all of our diverse citizens. A flag that represents an intention to leave our free Union in the name of upholding slavery should not be allowed inside the Capitol of the United States. A Confederate flag belongs in a museum, not in the hallowed halls of our U.S. Capitol. And yes, our national flag represents freedom and in that guarantee of freedom per the First Amendment of the Constitution we have freedom of speech. This guaranteed right to free speech does, in my opinion, extend to one's right to display the Confederate flag, but not on the grounds of the Capitol. The Confederate flag does not belong on such sacred ground and in such a sacred dwelling of individual liberty. The display of the Confederate flag in the Capitol was shameful and disrespectful of our national identity as one people living under one flag representing the ideal that all individuals have equal access to opportunity and enjoy political freedom. I found the horned "QAnon Shaman" and his unusual, Viking-like costume to be sending a clear message of Nordic purity and white supremacy. This individual, in his garb on full display during the group's curse-laden diatribes on the United States Senate floor, was totally inappropriate and lacking complete decorum for anyone who chooses to enter our national Capitol. I found it so strange and perplexing that the insurrectionists who had illegally and violently entered the Capitol paused reverently at one point to invoke a Christian prayer. I wonder if Jesus, a promoter of peace and non-violence, would support their behavior on this infamous day. The insurrectionists were clearly following the underlying theme of President Trump's "Make America Great Again" slogan. Indeed, whether Mr. Trump intended it that way or not, the coded message that many have adopted from this slogan is basically to "Make America White Again." There is clearly a desire by some (hate groups and others) to create a United States that is a white, Christian nation. In other words, the goal is to have a nation in which only white Christians live. Everyone else would need to leave or live as some type of second-class citizen or worse. The insurrectionists were fighting to take down the United States government and place Donald Trump at the head of a new government.

I do believe that anyone who committed illegal acts has to be punished to the full extent of the law, particularly those committing violent acts against individuals and property. It is worth noting I think that many of these rioters are expressing in their defense that they were told by the president to descend onto the Capitol and their actions were supported and endorsed by him. The United States House of Representatives did quickly and, in my opinion, appropriately impeach President Donald J. Trump for inciting a riot at the Capitol. It will be the courts that will potentially address the issue of whether the former president's speech and actions, or lack of action to more swiftly implore his followers to stop the insurrection were criminal behaviors. It is this citizen's hope that in the meantime, the U.S. Senate will convict Mr. Trump swiftly and ban him from holding public office in the future.

Late in the evening on January 6, 2021, and then into early January 7th, the U.S. Senate did certify the presidential election of 2020. Joe Biden was named President-Elect. Some Republican Senators had planned to object to the certification, but after the events of the day, the process overall went smoothly. Our institutions with the help at the last minute of Vice President Mike Pence and the Senate ensured that our government would continue. The lesson learned from this event is that we can have all the checks and balances that our wise Founding Fathers established for our way of government, but we all have a responsibility to hold our elected representatives accountable, so they carry out their duties in accordance with our democratic institutions. We must reject any political leader that selfishly seeks to violate our Constitution and simple norms of fairness to achieve or to retain power. Now, we can hopefully heal and one of the ways that we do this is by engaging our citizens in free elections and ensuring that people understand how our free system of elections is organized and executed. We also need to do a better job of teaching our children (and some adults apparently) about our Constitution, so our citizens adopt the legal and ethical foundation based in freedom that our Founding Fathers envisioned. American patriotism needs to be emphasized to instill a sense of duty and civic responsibility among all citizens. This sense of duty is necessary to ensure that our citizens whole-heartedly defend our constitutional republic so that our free society survives for all future generations. This event taught us that our freedom is truly fragile, and we must work every day to protect and defend it. The institutions set up by our Founding Fathers cannot by themselves protect and guarantee our freedom. The American people must work together as the most powerful oversight body of our government to "defend and protect" our Constitution.

# 7. Violence in America - January 6<sup>th</sup> Insurrection Versus Inner City Violent Crime

———

## Violence in Our Cities

One argument consistently made on right wing outlets, such as Fox News, is the contention that there's a double standard when it comes to criticisms and continued attention given to the insurrection that occurred on January 6, 2021, on the grounds of the United States Capitol. The argument is partially based around events during the first year of the pandemic in the summer of 2020 when there were protests in response to the George Floyd killing by a police officer. These protests that gripped the nation during that summer did on occasion, I do agree, lead to violent riots. It is fair to point out, however, that while there were violent incidents, overall, the protests were peaceful in support of the Black Lives Matter (BLM) movement (Chenoweth and Pressman). Fox News has been very vocal in expressing their message that while those on the left of the political spectrum decry the January 6<sup>th</sup> Insurrection, they do not condemn the violence of the 2020 BLM riots (Creitz). The other component of the Fox News message is that not only does the left not condemn the lawlessness of the BLM riots, but that the Democrats say nothing about the high level of violent crime that has increased across the nation in metropolitan areas (Creitz). As Fox News and Republicans often like to correctly point out, these are Democrat-led cities that are experiencing serious increases in crime (Montanaro).

I do concede that while again most protests during the BLM activities beginning in the summer of 2020 were peaceful, the violent eruptions were very concerning. I of course disagree with violence against individuals, but also the looting and crimes against property should not be tolerated. In addition, the practice of stopping traffic on major thoroughfares (and even minor streets) cannot be allowed. Public streets are intended for the free flow of vehicular traffic and by blocking a roadway, emergency vehicles cannot pass through to their destinations. I also dislike the idea of commercial vehicles, citizens and most importantly families being trapped in their vehicles, while angry protestors block roadways. This type of overly aggressive, illegal protesting can quickly lead to violent behavior. The images of rioters engaging in looting in major cities and blocking roads that Fox News and other media outlets shared with the public looked like a nation that was falling apart. I don't like the term "law and order" as it has been used to promote the use of aggressive police activities against minority and powerless communities (Cillizza, "The long, dark history"), but I certainly can see the point that law enforcement is needed to ensure that protesting is allowed, but that it is peaceful. Yes, Fox News has a point in calling out the riots of 2020 as unacceptable behavior and dangerous to public safety.

It is important to acknowledge here that in our free society protesting by its nature and per our First Amendment rights is supposed to be loud and verbally proactive. Also, protesting does need to occur in a public location in which the message of the protest can be heard by the public or by those who are the target of the protestors. So, I am not saying that protestors should be forced to express their constitutional right in an empty field away from the center city, but rules do need to be properly followed because the need to safeguard the public's physical safety takes precedent. We must find that balance in which the government creates an environment that allows protestors to communicate their messages through speeches, chants, marches, and demonstrations, but with limits to ensure the continued overall peace in every community in our nation is protected. It really is all about communication and coordination between law enforcement and the protestors. The reality is that the vast majority of protestors are concerned citizens themselves who want to make their communities better, not start riots that destroy communities.

According to the Centers for Disease Control and Prevention (CDC), 2020 was an extremely dangerous year in the United States with murders increasing by 30% compared to 2019 (Gramlich). Crime rates do vary from location to location across our large nation, but it does appear that in major cities violent crime had become a serious ongoing concern in 2020. Critics contend that Fox News sensationalizes some news items to reinforce the network's political outlook, but I do agree that we have a problem with safety for everyday citizens given the violent crime that we are witnessing. The environment has disintegrated in too many metropolitan areas in which the everyday citizen has to constantly be on guard and take extra precautions to avoid being the next victim. It is especially distressing to see video images of mothers with children and senior citizens becoming victims of crime, whether it is theft or assault. When we look at the inner-city killings in cities that are committed by young people attacking each other, I agree with Republicans that the cities have become dangerous places. Even a mid-sized city like Charlotte, North Carolina has endured a real catastrophe with young people murdering each other in the past few years. Hardly a day goes by now that a report on the news does not describe another murder in a high crime neighborhood involving teenagers.

Viewing this issue of violent crime on a national level, large U.S. cities including Chicago, New York and now, San Francisco are notorious in 2023 for their violent crime incidents. The recent news of high-profile national chain stores, such as Nordstrom, Whole Foods, Saks off 5$^{th}$ and Office Depot, leaving San Francisco due to the high rate of crime is deeply concerning. San Francisco for so long has been known as a national technology and banking hub (often rivaling Charlotte for the number two spot behind New York City as a banking center). Traditionally, the city has been considered an up-and-coming metropolitan area that was attractive to so many for being livable and safe. Rampant homelessness that has taken over near businesses and residential areas in the city, accompanied by a criminal justice system that apparently has not acted aggressively enough to arrest and imprison dangerous individuals, threaten the future of San Francisco. As someone in the political middle, I see the need to implement some more liberal policies, such as comprehensive drug treatment and mental health services for the homeless, while also implementing tough on crime policies from the political right to address the out-of-control crime. Local government, non-profits and the business community must act swiftly and effectively to transition this once great city back into a place where business and residents will want to return, instead of a place where many currently have decided to flee.

As we come out of the pandemic, a lot of industries still need new employees and law enforcement is no exception. We must support the brave and dangerous work that police perform every day. Yes, the mistreatment of African Americans by police is an issue that must be addressed effectively, but the calls by extreme liberals to "defund the police," don't acknowledge the reality that citizens do need the police to protect their communities from very dangerous criminals. We must hold corrupt and abusive police officers accountable for their misdeeds, but at the same time praise the vast majority of police officers who selflessly put their lives in potentially great danger every day as they work to protect the public. We want law enforcement to be a career choice that we praise as a society and in doing so, young people will want to become police officers. So, I concur with Fox News on their points that cities are experiencing very dangerous levels of crime and that we really need to support law enforcement and celebrate what they do. The message that needs to be sent to violent and serious criminals is that if you commit such heinous acts, you will go to jail for a long time.

This brings us to the bail reform movement. Fox News points to ultra-liberal cities that have enacted bail reform that they contend lets violent criminals out on low bail amounts (or no bail) with the ability to commit further violent crimes. Bail reform calls for more reasonable, lower bond amounts to be set for defendants accused of committing crimes with the idea that these individuals under our criminal justice system are presumed innocent until proven guilty. The intention is to allow these individuals to continue to work and support their families until a court hears their case. Supporters of bail reform point out that the current system discriminates against people based on their level of income with wealthy citizens being able to pay their bond, while low-income individuals must sit in jail for days, weeks or even months before their cases are tried. Unfortunately, it looks like a well-intentioned reform has gone too far when it comes to high-level, violent criminals. The bail reform movement is needed, in my opinion, although as many law enforcement agencies contend, too often now violent, dangerous defendants are let out of jail until their trials. This is the case even if they have past histories of violent behavior. The complaint is that defendants who have been accused of violent crimes, such as shootings, assaults and even murders are allowed to go free until their court cases. Law enforcement is now voicing this valid concern that they arrest violent criminals, only for them to be let out in a very short period of time, enabling them to commit another act of violence. Charlotte-Mecklenburg Police Chief Johnny Jennings during 2022 publicly came out against this practice of low bond setting for defendants accused of very violent crimes (Beckman & Ruffes). He discussed a case of a defendant who was let out after paying a low bond amount. The defendant was accused of shooting at police officers and into an occupied business. It is important to note that Chief Jennings did point out that some low-level crimes have had bonds set at an unfairly high amount (Beckman & Ruffes). I do see this valid point and while I support bail reform in general, it cannot go so far as to allow this type of revolving door for violent criminals, particularly those defendants who have previously had convictions of violent crimes.

## A Truly Violent Insurrection

So yes, crime in the cities is a major concern and I do agree somewhat that the rioting during BLM protests were not called out enough as being unacceptable by Democrats. Some on the far left even gave rioters and looters a pass, explaining it away as understandable given the history of hate in this nation. In my opinion, violence against a community is never justified regardless of the circumstances or reasoning. The January 6th insurrection in 2021 clearly appears to have been instigated by the former United States President to prevent a peaceful transfer of power. This collective action posed an unquestionably serious threat to simply the continued existence of our nation in its current, fundamental form of democratic government as intended by our Founding

Fathers. I discuss in further detail in this work my thoughts on the January 6th Insurrection, but I certainly contend that this threatening behavior against our Constitution and nation should have been a call to all Americans to reject the attack. Chants to hang the former vice president who was simply performing his constitutional duty to certify the presidential election were repugnant and medieval. This violent mob who literally took over the Capitol, seeking out congressional Democrats to assault or kidnap (the video footage showed at least one individual walking around the Capitol with zip ties to be used obviously to bound captives' hands), was clearly intent on destabilizing the normal operations of the United States government. The core basic foundation of a civil and safe society is to have a functioning national government. If we don't have a stable federal government, as we can witness throughout the world, a society can quickly disintegrate into lawlessness. President Trump does need to be held accountable for his instigation, but these were all grown adults who should have known better and were intent on attacking the normal functioning of the United States government. Fox News has done a tremendous disservice to its viewers by downplaying the seriousness of the events at the United States Capitol on January 6, 2021. The contention by Fox News is that the insurrection was just a harmless protesting event, and that the real threats to American society are the violent acts stemming from BLM protests and overall increase in violent crimes in the cities. This is a clever ploy to divert attention away from the seriousness of the insurrection and its participants' illegal and dangerous behavior. Clearly, this is unethical, narrative-making by Fox News which too often behaves as a cheerleader for Donald Trump, rather than an unbiased news organization.

However, I want to conclude by focusing on the issue of violence in America and acknowledge that Fox News has shared news events that are concerning and should be addressed. We need our national, state, and local governments to work with communities to better protect the safety and security of all citizens in these United States. The rights of protestors need to be protected, but the safety and free movement of the public in these communities ultimately must take precedent. Criminals who commit violent acts against law-abiding citizens and property need to be taken off the streets. Finally, as American citizens we do have the right to voice our opinions about politics and elections, however, anyone who attempts an insurrection against our United States government or commit acts of violence against law enforcement and property as occurred on January 6, 2021, needs to be dealt with harshly. I disagree with the attempt by Fox News' to downplay the level of violence committed and vitriol expressed by Trump supporters during the January 6th insurrection. Furthermore, I challenge the sentiment expressed by former President Trump and other Republicans who have referred to the insurrectionists as American "patriots." These individuals are traitors who need to be severely punished and deserve lengthy prison sentences, not treated as heroes.

## Closing

In conclusion, I want to point out that debating extensively on which set of violent acts (the insurrection on January 6th or violent crime in the cities) is more of a threat to our American way of life is, at the end of the day, not the best use of our mental resources. I contend that we need to address the rampant violent crime and lawlessness in our cities, while also working to stop the growing threat from right-wing, extremist groups and their supporters who wish to disrupt the constitutional, democratic processes of our federal government. Thus, we need to do address all sources of violence, regardless of their motivation. As a nation, we need to stop bickering and join together in unity to address both of these violent threats to our American way of life. A core, ethical underpinning of our American way of life is the concept that a society can only truly be free when all citizens live together in peace, safety, and mutual respect for individual differences. We must vow to work together as true American patriots to address all forms of violence which undermine our rule of law, democratic practices, and the inherent liberty of all of our citizens.

# 8. President Trump's Insurrection

—————

### President Trump's False Narrative That Led to Insurrection

There are those who still contend that the mass gathering on January 6, 2021, at the United States Capitol was simply an exercise by patriotic Americans who wanted to express their viewpoint that the 2020 presidential election was unfair. I will always defend every American's constitutional right to peacefully protest. Unfortunately, the event changed from a protest to an insurrection when participants began physically attacking law enforcement and barbarically forced their way into the U.S. Capitol, as members of Congress were performing their constitutional duty of certifying the presidential election.

The images that Americans saw on their televisions, tablets and phones were like something one would witness in a Third World nation during a military coup, not the peaceful transition of power in the world's beacon of freedom. American citizens were literally attacking the United States government, in essence staging an insurrection.

One of the key questions is to what degree President Trump is responsible for this protest event that so quickly transitioned into a violent insurrection. This attack brought harm to people and property in our nation's seat of democracy. The certification was indeed delayed until late that evening, so this was a very serious threat to our nation and way of life. I want to mention here that I am voicing my opinions based on what I have seen on the news, as well as what clear evidence was presented by the House Committee that was investigating the insurrection event. One can question the political motives of the Democrat-led House committee investigating the January 6th event, but this group of lawmakers clearly did a very extensive investigation, providing important information to the American people. I would refer the reader to the following Gov Info website to obtain detailed information on the findings of the committee:

www.govinfo.gov/collection/january-6th-committee-final-report?path=/GPO/
January%206th%20Committee%20Final%20Report%20and%20Supporting%20Materials%20Collection

My opinion is that while these supporters of the former president were all adults who, as they say, "should have known better" than to participate in a violent insurrection, President Trump does bear a significant amount of responsibility. Mr. Trump used his position as president of the free world to communicate a false narrative to his supporters, and anyone who would listen, that he was cheated out of re-election. After then President-elect Biden clearly and fairly defeated President Trump, the former president refused to concede the election to Joe Biden. Mr. Trump began his contentious campaign of claiming the election was "stolen." This false narrative and theme were consistently perpetuated by Mr. Trump and his closest allies.

I want to emphasize here that I wholeheartedly support every candidate's right to access all legal avenues if he, she, or they feel that election law was violated, thus preventing their victory. President Trump's legal team did in fact file several legal claims and I have no issue with these actions. The end results, however, were all the same – no court found that illegal activity occurred that unfairly prevented Mr. Trump from being reelected as president. Multiple courts of our nation's judiciary branch concluded that any accusations by President Trump that the election was "stolen" were simply unfounded.

### President Trump's "Stop the Steal" Rally

President Trump, after several weeks of refusing to support a calm, peaceful transition of power as is our democratic custom, only incited anger in his very strong base of supporters. Then, on January 6, 2021, Mr. Trump held an outdoor "Stop the Steal" rally at the White House. President Trump continued his false claim that the election was "stolen" and called on his supporters to march to the Capitol. The former president stated that he would march with them but did not. Mr. Trump later claimed that the Secret Service would not allow it (Benson). This does sound reasonable due to the challenges of protecting the president in such an open, vulnerable environment. It was during this speech that President Trump continued his claim that Mike Pence could stop the certification process as vice president. I defer of course to constitutional experts, but my understanding is Mr. Pence would have had no constitutional justification for taking any other action than to oversee the certification of the election. The election was in fact already decided by the people and through our Electoral College process. Donald Trump simply wanted Mike Pence to violate the U.S. Constitution and reject some electors, changing the outcome of the election.

During his speech, President Trump told his supporters something to the effect that if we don't fight for our country, we won't have a country left. As president of the United States, he called upon the people to act and fight against what truly was a non-existent threat to our democratic nation. This behavior is critical to ascertaining what level of responsibility that the former president had for the violence on January 6th. This is the president of the United States claiming that our presidential election was not legal and not fair. Our president was claiming the rightful winner of the presidential election was being prevented from taking office again. If Mr. Trump's argument that the presidential election was not decided by the people were in fact true (which it was not), then this would be a serious threat to our free system of government created by our nation's Founding Fathers.

Now, it is important to point out as some supporters of the former president have been saying, that the term, "Let's fight," cannot be strictly interpreted as a call to violent action. The word, "fight" can be and has been used as a figure of speech to encourage political, but peaceful and legal action to oppose policies that an individual or group wishes to rally against. It is important to look at the context of this situation in which Mr. Trump was claiming that our presidential election was taken illegally from the people. President Trump was in effect summoning his supporters to Washington D.C. on the day of the election certification to "stop the steal." Mr. Trump was lying to his supporters, triggering anger in them based on that lie that the election was "stolen." I think a rational person could conclude that a very large angry crowd who is convinced that the president of the United States was unfairly denied reelection, may very well engage in acts of violence to "stop the steal." This is exactly what occurred.

## Acts of Insurrection at the U.S. Capitol

Many of us watched live on television that upon reaching the U.S. Capitol grounds, protestors quickly became rioters who fought police officers and then upon entering the Capitol became, in my opinion, insurrectionists. We had Trump supporters breaking windows at the Capitol. We heard these individuals angrily chanting, "Hang Mike Pence." I recall hearing one of the Trump supporters calling out, "Oh Nancy," in a very disturbing, haunting voice. This individual no doubt had very sinister and violent intentions for the fate of Nancy Pelosi, Speaker of the United States House of Representatives. Fortunately, Speaker Pelosi was able to remain safe throughout the crisis. I find myself getting emotional at recalling that our members of the United States Congress on January 6, 2021, were forced to hide from a mob of insurrectionists when they were simply performing their constitutional roles in certifying our presidential election that President Trump had, without question, lost.

Republican congressional members pleaded over the phone with Mr. Trump to call off his supporters while they were hiding and fearing for their lives. President Trump took way too long to publicly address his supporters, finally asking them to go home after hours of rioting at the Capitol. Later, per a recorded video, we were to find out in a rare glimpse these days of bipartisanship, that Nancy Pelosi was in communication over the phone with Mike Pence. The Speaker expressed genuine concern for the physical safety of Vice President Mike Pence and his family (Cillizza, "Nancy Pelosi did"). Fortunately, due to the smart thinking of law enforcement and the Secret Service, members of Congress and Vice President Pence survived the ordeal safely. I recall viewing a video showing U.S. Capitol Police officer, Eugene Goodman, re-directing Senator Mitt Romney away from the path of angry Trump supporters. Officer Goodman has been correctly hailed as a hero for his selfless actions on the day of the insurrection to protect our legislative branch of government (LeBlanc). It is so important to understand the ethical, constitutional and, perhaps, legal crimes of President Trump when seeing this contrast. Capitol Police are attempting to defend our national, legislative building and its lawmakers, while President Trump apparently "gleefully" watches the chaos on television from the safety of the White House (Levin).

As of this point in time (I am writing this essay in late November 2022), hundreds of participants have been charged with their criminal involvement in the January 6, 2021, insurrection event at the U.S. Capitol (Popli and Zorthian). Depending on the severity of the criminal act, sentences handed out have varied from less severe punishments like probation, community service and the payment of fines, up to more severe punishments, including multi-year prison sentences for those committing serious violent acts. According to the U.S. Attorney's Office web site, Thomas Webster, a retired NYPD officer (and former Marine) attempted to attack a police officer with a flagpole ("Retired NYPD Officer"). Then, Webster tackled the officer and, in the process, choked the officer ("Retired NYPD Officer"). He was charged with five felonies and received a sentence of ten years in prison ("Retired NYPD Officer"). Yes, these criminals do deserve the punishments handed down by our system of laws.

I bring up Thomas Webster not just to highlight that the participants who committed violent attacks are simply criminals and anti-American actors regardless of their previous service to our nation, but to point out that it is obvious that President Trump did have an influence on these insurrectionists at the Capitol. No doubt, President Trump's rhetoric did work up some of his followers into a violent frenzy. Now, to be clear, I do think some participants used President Trump's rhetoric to give themselves a green light to cause mayhem on January 6, 2021. It is also without question, however, that President Trump in his lie about the election being stolen, did incite many to literally take up arms in an attempt to fight the United States government. President Trump in his false, inflammatory language endorsed mayhem at the Capitol on January 6, 2021, and mayhem is what occurred.

The other week President Trump announced he was making a run for re-election in 2024. Soon after on November 18, 2022, a statement was released on the Department of Justice website announcing that Attorney General Merrick B. Garland was appointing a Special Counsel to oversee two criminal investigations involving the former president ("Appointment of a Special Counsel"). These involved the classified documents found at Mr. Trump's Florida home and "...whether any person or entity unlawfully interfered with the transfer of power following the 2020 presidential

election or the certification of the Electoral College vote held on or about January 6, 2021"
("Appointment of a Special Counsel").

## Conclusion

In closing, I do respect the current, legal process calling for Special Counsel, Jack Smith, to conduct a thorough investigation of former President Trump's behavior. Given this, I don't think tremendous investigative resources are needed to conclude that former President Trump's actions were clear regarding the January 6, 2021, insurrection event. He did use his office of the president of the United States to carry out a false narrative campaign that the 2020 presidential election was "stolen." His behavior did influence thousands to come to Washington, D.C. on the day of the presidential election certification to "stop the steal." Mr. Trump did not live up to one of his core responsibilities as president which was to do everything in his power to ensure a smooth transition to the Biden administration after his election defeat. The former president had the responsibility to uphold the Constitution, as well as to set an example by displaying our shared American ideal of fair play. After all legal challenges had been exhausted, Donald Trump should have graciously conceded to Joe Biden. The desire of candidates to win an election is truly an essential component of a healthy, electoral process in a democratic system. The debating and arguing can get very heated, even verbally hostile at times, but it is never to rise to the level of violence. Elections are a war of words – that's it! Mr. Trump, time and time again, after losing the election had the opportunity to live up to his ethical and constitutional responsibility to facilitate the transition of power. The former president had a duty after losing the presidential election not to divide the nation, but to unite everyone behind President-Elect Joe Biden.

I leave any opinion on specific criminal charges to the Special Counsel, but one opinion I do emphatically share - President Donald J. Trump should never be allowed to run for re-election as president of the United States. The former president's disdain for our Constitution and democratic system, as well as his win-at-all-costs behavior is harmful to the health of our democratic Republic. I have no wish to see a former president serve jail time due to the insurrection or due to the other legal troubles that Mr. Trump is facing, but he should never be allowed to run for presidential office again based on his behavior leading up to and during the insurrection on January 6, 2021, at the United States Capitol.

# 9. Violent Crime in America: Protecting the Citizenry

I try to be fair in evaluating the merits of opposing political viewpoints. In order to accomplish this goal, I attempt to read and watch news from across the political spectrum. I admit that I am more partial to watching CNN, but I do watch Fox News on more than a regular occasion, I would say, to get that distinct viewpoint. While CNN was continually focused on the insurrection (correctly in my opinion) in the past year or so, Fox News had the general criticism that the events on January 6, 2021, were nowhere near the threat to the American way of life that violent crime is, particularly in the cities. Clearly, I concur that all violent acts and trends need to be addressed in our nation, but the attack on our government on January 6, 2021, was an immediate, direct threat that we as Americans needed to respond to and firmly reject. Given this opinion, however, as a citizen, I am concerned about what appears to be a very scary increase in lawlessness in our communities. There are a lot of different statistics on crime in America and violent crime rates can vary from location to location, however, while there are always those that disagree with any assertion, I do start my discussion based on the clear fact that overall violent crime has increased over the past few years in the United States, particularly in large cities (Bates).

Fox News focused on three areas of crime in its coverage over the past few years. The first area concerns the riots and looting coming out of the Black Lives Matter (BLM) protests beginning in the summer of 2020. The second area deals with bail reform that some have argued has led to an increase of violent criminals being put back out on the streets when they should be behind bars waiting on their trials. Then, the other area that Fox News has focused on involves incidents of illegal immigrants (I want to note that the tendency now is to describe these individuals as "undocumented" rather than illegal) committing violent crimes against American citizens. I want to take a look at each one of these crime categories and provide my opinions on the level that they pose as serious threats to the safety of the American people.

### Black Lives Matter Riots

First, I do want to address the riots that did come out of the BLM movement that Fox News appears to cite as a trigger for more acts of violence in America. It is a given that must be understood that the vast number of protestors supporting the BLM movement were peaceful loving Americans. Unfortunately, the problems involved small groups of individuals who did begin peacefully protesting as is their constitutional right, but then crossed the line into rioting, vandalizing property, and looting retail establishments. Some on the left seem to want to provide excuses for the violence and perhaps claim correctly that the impetus is from generations of frustration that is in their view understandably manifesting. While I can sympathize with the hurt and anger that African Americans rightfully feel because of past and current acts of racial injustice, I can no more condone the violence committed stemming from BLM protests than the violence committed by those criminal actors during the insurrection on January 6, 2021. We cannot as a civilized people allow violence and lawlessness in our streets, communities, or at the Capitol. My general opinion is that while there is still widespread support of the intentions of the BLM movement, the message of the movement has been significantly harmed by the visuals of violence and looting of stores in metropolitan areas. Some of these stores were not owned by large corporations, but by neighborhood, small businesses in these areas where violence overtook the peaceful BLM protests.

We must have peace and order for our society to function properly. Protests should be allowed in public areas so the message of the protestors can be communicated. A BLM march shouldn't be pushed to the edge of a city or town in an area that is out of the way where no one will be exposed to the message, but I do think that acts including blocking traffic on major thoroughfares, such as we witnessed during some BLM marches, does go too far. Public roadways need to be kept clear for moving traffic as a matter of public safety. Police, fire, and ambulances need to be able to access roadways that are clear so that they can get to any locations where help is needed.

I personally have never been in a traffic jam due to a protest stopping traffic, but I do recall having some concern and worry when hearing on the news that in the city where I work, there was such a protest action. Protesters in the center city entered a major thoroughfare and stopped all traffic. Citizens were protesting a police-involved shooting of an African American citizen that led to violence and looting in the center city. Again, I fully support the right to peacefully protest, but I also fully support law enforcement officers who work vigilantly to guide protestors away from major roadways to prevent protestors from stopping traffic. My rational fear is how quickly violence can erupt in this type of situation. I have imagined the difficulty of being trapped in one's vehicle on a roadway where angry protestors have stopped traffic. I have contemplated how I would handle such a challenge and have pondered how I should respond if a protest group, now an angry mob, began to approach my stopped vehicle. Would I try to back up my vehicle and turn around? If there was a vehicle right behind me, that might not be possible. Would I simply abandon my vehicle and try to leave the situation on foot? Leaving my vehicle may also be a dangerous move. Should I try to reason with the angry protestors and try to calm their escalating anger? This approach may not work. I think of the single mother in such a dangerous dilemma with small children in the backseat of the family vehicle. It is in planning for one's own survival and the protection of others that the thought of carrying a firearm becomes possibly a reasonable option. Yes, if citizens don't feel safe, they will look to other options, such as carrying firearms. The problem is that if we live in a civilized society, we shouldn't need everyone "packing heat." More guns mean more opportunities for their misuse. Therefore, it is a fine balance. I also don't want to discount the safety of the protestors who are in real bodily danger by attempting to stop potentially very fast-moving vehicles on a roadway or highway. We want to allow peaceful protesting, but it does need to be continually kept in check to prevent any escalation that could explode into violence against property and most importantly innocent citizens. This is where my harsher stance on violent crime is clear. As a civilized society, we cannot tolerate acts of violence even in the name of political speech.

I support the BLM movement and many other political efforts that focus on fighting inequality and promoting social justice in our nation and around the world. However, my support of any non-profit or political association requires a commitment by the entity to effect change through non-violent means. What transcended the Civil Rights movement of the 1960s that led to such strides in greater equality for African Americans was that it was founded in Dr. Martin Luther King Jr.'s insistence on a non-violent approach. When the nation and the world witnessed over their television sets the brutality that African American protestors faced from southern police officers, demand for change quickly intensified exponentially. My opinion is that protesting is by its very essence an in-your-face engaging activity, but once behavior crosses the line from words into actual acts of violence, regardless of the group's intentions, it is no longer an ethical endeavor that should be allowed to continue.

I disagree with Fox News on its poor support of the BLM movement, but I do agree that the riots coming out of some of these protests do need to be identified for what they are – violent, criminal acts against our citizens. Protesting in the name of equality is right and I praise the BLM movement for all the organization is doing in this regard. I hope the BLM organization continues to protest until true equality is achieved, but those who seek change through violence need to face the full consequences of the criminal justice system.

## Bail Reform

I agree with those on the political right (and some moderate Independents) who have a concern that our nation looks like it is descending into lawlessness with what seems to be violent criminals acting emboldened with no fear of police or the courts. Bail reform has been needed to prevent the accused from basically having to stay in jail or prison simply because they cannot afford to pay the bail until their court date. In our nation, we still follow the legal assumption that the accused are "innocent until proven guilty." The objection I have is that I think bail reform should primarily be extended to defendants that have allegedly committed non-violent crimes. We seem to have lost some common sense here. It should be evident that for public safety, particularly defendants with a clear history of committing violent crimes are individuals who should not be let out of jail before their trial dates. Fox News does a very convincing job of citing these cases when these previously convicted felons are let out who have extensive records of violent behavior who (guess what?) commit atrocious crimes while they are waiting for their court date. This can no longer happen.

I want to stress that I agree in principle with bail reform. We have created an indentured class in which citizens who have allegedly committed non-violent offenses are faced with months or even years behind bars because they cannot come up with the funds to pay bail. Many alleged offenders are not getting a court date in a timely manner because of backed-up, local court systems. Non-violent defendants should be free on little bail or no bail until their court dates. I'm even a little flexible on alleged first time offenders, who are accused of violent offenses, but have no criminal record. Individuals in this category of alleged offenders with a clean background should be allowed to continue working or required to find a job. I agree that there are some cases in which a citizen who has been accused for the first time of a violent crime may be required to be behind bars for immediate public safety concerns, but overall, I think these individuals should be out of jail working until they are proven guilty by a court of law. Additional tools can be used to track these individuals, such as the use of tracking, ankle bracelets. When they are not at work, they need to be required to be at their residences. The issue with so many alleged offenders being incarcerated, waiting on their trials, is that they are not earning incomes to care for their families, nor earning funds to be used to hire competent legal representation. This is not a negative viewpoint on hard-working, very capable public defense attorneys, just an acknowledgement that these public defenders have limited resources and huge caseloads.

Fox News has successfully pointed out the valid concern with bail reform when the network regularly shares stories of alleged offenders who, with significant histories of convictions for violent crimes, are let out to wait on their trial dates and subsequently commit more violent crimes. These offenders need to stay in jail until their trial dates. I agree that this is an area where bail reform has gone too far to the left and has lost any semblance of common sense. Alleged offenders who have long histories of violent crimes need to stay put, behind bars. This is the one way to ensure they don't continue to endanger the public.

I did want to note that an in-depth report, not produced by Fox News, but by CNN details the problem with low bail amounts coupled with non-profit organizations that pay the bail for defendants. A 240-pound homeless man violently attacked a senior citizen in a park and stole his camera during the spring of 2021, in Seattle, leaving the man with serious injuries (Kuznia and Abou-Ghazala). The senior citizen even returned to the park after the attack to ask the perpetrator for his camera back and was assaulted again (Kuznia and Abou-Ghazala). The judge in the case set the bail at only $5,000 which was paid by the Northwest Community Bail Fund (Kuznia and Abou-Ghazala). The report then detailed how this violent homeless individual in June of 2021 out on bail choked and stabbed a young man to death (Kuznia and Abou-Ghazala). Obviously, this dangerous individual should not have ever been allowed to roam free after his attack on the senior citizen, pending his trial.

## Violent Crimes Committed by Undocumented Immigrants

I am a firm supporter of legal and diverse immigration into the United States, as long as it is in harmony with our ability to handle the overall influx of people. There is an ongoing debate concerning undocumented immigrants in which many Republicans, such as President Trump, have cited the dangerous crimes being committed by these individuals. Fox News for some time now has described the arrival of thousands of immigrants coming to our southern border now monthly as an "invasion." This attitude seems to extend to both those attempting to cross illegally, as well as those attempting to enter through legal means. This divisive language demonstrates an anti-immigrant prejudice by the Fox News network. The reality is that the overwhelming majority of these migrants who are coming to our southern border are simply seeking safety or greater economic opportunities for themselves and their families. Many on the political left point out that statistics show that undocumented people in our nation commit crime at a lower rate than citizens of the U.S (Smith and Buchman). I do find myself, while I abhor the divisive rhetoric of Fox News, tending to agree that we have to improve our border security to prevent illegal entry and extensively review our entry processes for those seeking to enter legally. The safety of the legal citizens of the United States comes first and foremost when it comes to formulating acceptable, national immigration policy. In my opinion, the fact that the crime rate is lower for undocumented immigrants when compared to this rate for current legal citizens of the United States is not sufficient justification for downplaying the potential threats posed from these undocumented immigrants who are here illegally. We need to know who is in our nation.

I am in favor of some type of program that can allow for the earning of citizenship if undocumented immigrants come forward, but for those who do not notify officials that they are here, deportation must be an option. If just one violent crime, such as murder, is committed by an undocumented immigrant against a citizen of the United States, it is an unacceptable security failure. I do extend my opinion on the need to protect the safety of legal immigrants as well who are taking the legal steps to one day become U.S. citizens. The American people should not accept as the status quo that undocumented immigrants are here who have never been properly vetted by our federal government. We should reject the mass-panic rhetoric that Fox News endorses, but there should be some reasonable apprehension that our government does not know who has illegally entered the nation or if they have harmful intentions against the American people. Also, we are talking about millions of people – some 11 million per 2021 figures (Hook, Gelatt, and Soto), but we may not really know how many undocumented immigrants are now in the U.S. as of 2023. The concern here is both on a macro and micro level. The macro concern is that a terrorist group could enter our nation illegally with the intent on carrying out an attack, such as the detonation of a dirty bomb on U.S. soil or causing widespread damage to our nation's core infrastructure (for example, knocking out our power grid). A lot of death and suffering could be caused by such a terrorist group entering into our nation. Then, on a micro level, individuals who have not been properly vetted and have entered our nation illegally could pose dangerous threats to the safety of individual U.S. citizens. There is a legitimate concern about who is entering our southern border and for what reason.

I'm sure there are those on the political right who support a policy in which the United States allows very little or no immigration at the southern border. To them, closing the border means more than just security. It is an idea that we have let in our nation's fair share of immigrants from our southern neighbors, and we need to simply close off our nation to anyone else for a long time. This is not the policy that I endorse, but I do agree with Fox News that the southern border needs to be secure. Increasingly, I hear that the immigrants arriving are not only from Central and South American nations, but from nations all over the world. We may need to go to a different sort of application process for those who seek to immigrate to the United States, such as an application process that occurs in their home or neighboring countries. We do need a better set of procedures rather than allowing countless numbers of migrants who are now showing up at our border, regardless of if they are attempting to enter illegally or legally. When we are talking about thousands of people coming on a regular basis this puts tremendous strain on our resources for border security, legal processing and even providing immediate medical care to these new arrivals. I don't support a complete closed-door policy of not allowing any other immigrants in at our southern border, but as I discuss elsewhere in this work, we need to have a more organized process. We also need to look at ways that the United States can assist our neighbors in creating societies in which the desire or need to flee by so many can be greatly diminished. The answer is not realistic for the United States to take in everyone who wants to come here. That approach simply would not be sustainable given our resource availability and capacity. I fully support the American dream that involves the welcoming of immigrants who seek a better life in the United States, the cornerstone of global freedom. We still need to support this dream of so many around the world, but sadly with the large numbers of people traveling to our southern border, the immediate goal needs to be to secure our border and only allow entry to immigrants who have been properly vetted by the federal government. This may slow down the immigration process for those seeking to become new citizens of the United States, but we must put the safety and well-being of the current citizens of the United States first.

---

### Final Thoughts

IN CONCLUSION, I CONTINUE to contend that Fox News has failed miserably in acting as an ethical, unbiased news outlet by refusing to objectively cover the insurrection on January 6, 2021. This network has refused to properly admit how serious a threat this insurrection was and perhaps continues to be to our democratic system. Others may try again. Having made this objection against Fox News, I do have to be fair and concede that while the concerns about violent crime voiced on Fox News may be somewhat sensationalized at times, the network does discuss truly valid threats to the everyday lives of Americans. The federal, state, and local governments have the responsibility to act appropriately and effectively to protect the safety of American citizens. Fox News is correct in pointing out the failures of government in recent years to protect its citizens consistently and comprehensively.

When the news coverage shows looting and destruction of property as part of a BLM protest, it is valid for citizens to be concerned about safety. Any average citizen arrives at the reasonable conclusion that defendants who are accused of committing violent crimes and have histories of committing violence need to be held in jail until their trials. Numerous reports about defendants committing violent offenses while they are out of jail waiting for their trials because of bail reform are justifiably worrisome. Finally, many Americans are welcoming of immigrants and realize we have a moral responsibility to allow in people who are fleeing persecution. Having stated this, when we see our southern border getting overrun by so many people in such a disorganized manner, it is no wonder that we hear such horrendous stories on the news of American citizens being assaulted or murdered by undocumented immigrants.

One of the fundamental responsibilities of a democratic system of government is to ensure the safety and security of its people. Establishing a safe environment is the basic foundational block for a nation that from its inception has sought to protect each citizen's right to "...life, liberty and the pursuit of happiness" (Kamps 36). I contend that at times I am very critical of the approaches and content disseminated by Fox News, but to be honest, I must admit I agree with Fox News that we must get tougher on violent crime, not softer.

# 10. The Tragedy of Tyre Nichols' Death at The Hands of Police

It has been a few days since the Memphis Police Department released the video footage showing five police officers brutally beating twenty-nine-year-old Tyre Nichols. The beatings led to his death. The police pulled over Mr. Nichols for alleged reckless driving. Many of us have seen this footage from the January 7th, 2023, traffic stop that was widely distributed on Friday, January 27th by many media outlets.

First, I want to make it clear that my opinions on these interactions between Mr. Nichols and the Memphis police officers are based on video footage, information, and commentary that I viewed and reviewed primarily from CNN, beginning the weekend of January 27, 2023 (Caldwell). I do encourage the reader to review video and information about Tyre Nichols' horrific experience from the news source of one's choice. I found the video footage that was shown from vantage points of the officers' body cameras and an overhead city surveillance camera to be extremely grotesque examples of barbaric treatment of a fellow American. One of my frustrations is that the five police officers physically abusing Mr. Nichols were all African American. The George Floyd case was a clear example of the long-standing history of racist, white police officers mistreating and discriminating against African American citizens. Mr. Floyd was not being treated by the officer, who held his knee on Mr. Floyd's neck for several minutes, as a fellow citizen and human being. The higher frequency of African Americans being pulled over compared to whites behaving similarly, seems to be tied to police having a more consistent presence in minority areas (Gaebler, Cai and Goel). All too often, we see white police officers stopping minority drivers and in too many situations African American men have ended up being physically brutalized or killed.

My personal opinion has always been that we need more African American police officers to offset this imbalance of white officers who have mistreated the African American community on far too many occasions. It is clearly evident that racism against African Americans has too often been a component of traffic stops by the police. I don't want to make the mistake of extrapolating one event as a reason to change my opinion. I do think having more minority officers can help reduce the level of mistreatment of minorities by the police, but the obvious question is whether there is a cultural component in policing that encourages more aggressive behavior toward African Americans. I admit that when I first heard about this killing in Tennessee my mind immediately jumped to a stereotype of the officers. My assumption incorrectly was that a group of five white, "redneck" (probably weekend Klansmen-type) police officers were abusing this young African male citizen in horrific ways. This was an incorrect stereotype on my part, but how many news stories with video images have we viewed of white police officers violating the human and constitutional rights of minorities and African American citizens? It is evident that racism by white police officers is a serious problem for our society. Racism reduces the level of police protection and assistance that minorities deserve and desperately need. Also, when society views such immoral behavior by police officers, it begins to wear away at the public trust in the police. This public trust in our law enforcement is essential to ensuring the basic public safety in a civilized society is maintained. Safe communities require cooperative relationships between police organizations and the communities that they serve. Open communication between police and neighborhood residents is essential to effectively formulate and implement strategies to prevent crime, as well as quickly catch offenders when crimes occur. So, yes, I was just taken aback that five African American police officers turned out to be the culprits. How could this happen? Was this an isolated case of five bullies who happened to be African American or, again, are there cultural biases within law enforcement and other institutions that lead to such mistreatment of minorities?

Now, I am only expressing my interpretations based upon my personal viewing of the video footage provided by the Memphis Police Department of Mr. Nichols' traffic stop. After viewing the video showing the first interaction as Mr. Nichols' vehicle was pulled over, it was clear that these police officers were not professional and did anything and everything not to de-escalate the situation. These officers did not calmly approach the vehicle and ask Mr. Nichols to roll down his window to begin a civil discussion. They began screaming for him to get out of the vehicle. As commentators have expressed, Mr. Nichols actually appeared to be the only one attempting to calm the situation at this point, asking what he had done as these officers essentially tackled him.

Now, let me pause here please. Whether you call it "white privilege" or simply a biased culture in which whites in America have had advantages because they are in the majority, I don't believe as reckless (no pun intended since allegedly Mr. Nichols was being stopped for reckless driving) as these five rogue cops were, that they would have acted this way if they had stopped a middle-aged white male, such as myself. This is the issue. And yes, after watching the video, I do conclude that there could have been a different outcome if Mr. Nichols had laid fully onto his belly and swiftly offered his hands behind his back to be handcuffed. I do think it is fair to state that through the entire saga that played out on the streets of Memphis that night between police and Tyre Nichols, the struggle was continually centered around the police demanding that Mr. Nichols provide his hands to be handcuffed. I do want to provide a fair-minded evaluation, but I believe if Mr. Nichols were Mr. Nachamie being stopped, no one would have gotten beaten to the point of death and I may have gotten off with a warning or a minor traffic citation.

I am so sympathetic to the plight that African Americans find themselves in while driving. Yes, the phrase "driving while black" is a reality unfortunately in the "Land of the Free." African Americans are justified in feeling that they must drive perfectly to avoid being unfairly pulled over by police, and even if they do that, they still must fear police will think they are somehow "acting suspiciously" by being overly cautious. "Driving while black," is indeed too often the case in America. Mr. Nichols became frustrated and I'm sure tremendously fearful in the initial struggle with the police. He then ran. The videos are available from many sources on the Internet so I'm not going to provide a "play by play" of this upsetting footage, but I did want to note that it appeared the police officers became increasingly angered because Mr. Nichols ran away. As police used pepper spray against Mr. Nichols to obtain compliance, some of the spray got into at least one of the officer's eyes, which appeared to heighten the anger of the police. After chasing Mr. Nichols as he ran away, the struggle to get Mr. Nichols to present his hands to be handcuffed culminated in a horrific scene captured by an overhead street camera. The police were taking turns punching Mr. Nichols in the face and after Mr. Nichols fell to the ground, the treatment savagely continued with kicks to the head. I have a very limited knowledge of martial arts, but even to a layperson like me, it did seem that the police could have initiated other more controlled moves to capture the hands of Mr. Nichols to initiate the cuffing of his hands.

Mr. Nichols died from his injuries sustained while in police custody. Of course, these five officers have since been fired and are being charged with second degree murder.

## Short and Long-Term Solutions

We certainly must closely examine the culture of policing to determine how we can change such behavior too often displayed when the police interact with minorities. I do want to stress that I do feel the vast majority of police officers, white or black, are not racist and do their jobs to the best of their abilities in a fair-minded manner. However, as I've discussed above, we are having too many of these abusive situations when police pull over minorities. Better training obviously needs to happen that will adequately address any possible ingrained attitudes and beliefs that trigger inexcusably aggressive behavior by police when interacting with minorities, specifically African Americans. Now, in talking about deescalating the initial aggressive behavior by police during these interactions, we must concede that police are people who certainly can be influenced by their upbringing, as well as the culture of the organizations to which they belong, in this case their law enforcement employers. This interaction between the police and Mr. Nichols certainly can serve as a prime case study for social scientists to examine in order to evaluate the culture of policing. As a society, we need to answer the question as to whether there is an inherent bias against African Americans that exists even when the police officers are all themselves African American. One observation, and it is absolutely not an excuse for aggressive behavior, is the environmental reality that police are naturally more on guard when performing their duties in lower income areas which unfortunately can have a very high percentage of minority and African American residents. Low-income individuals who live in desperate living conditions with limited economic opportunities are more likely to look to criminal behavior to survive. Police have the unenviable position of being on the front lines of generational discrimination, bias and hatred that have left far too many African Americans living in these high crime areas with high levels of poverty and unemployment. Given this reality, we must provide tools for police to protect the law-abiding families and citizens who live in these high-crime areas in a way that doesn't result in these citizens feeling as if they are being targeted as criminals. We certainly should be able to develop police training programs that teach officers how to protect the public and themselves, while still interacting with the public and, yes, possible suspects in a polite, restrained, and tactful manner. The five officers who engaged in these barbaric crimes against Mr. Nichols obviously had a very poor skill set, as far as how to properly approach a citizen during a traffic stop, take a suspect into custody and probably, most importantly, how to keep their emotions in check. The poor behaviors displayed by these officers should be used in future training programs to demonstrate everything that police officers should not do in the carrying out of their duties.

We have to find ways to limit interactions with police and drivers unless completely necessary for the immediate public safety. I contend in cases of minor infractions, such as a taillight being out or an expired license tag, the police should not pull over the vehicle. The tag information of the vehicle should be recorded by the police and then administrative staff in the given police department should mail out a notice to the driver communicating that the issue has been observed and the driver has a certain amount of time to correct the problem, or a citation will be issued. The police are a quasi-military force which understandably must be ready to engage with dangerous, armed individuals. More training is needed, but if we can limit interactions which can quickly escalate during routine traffic stops, this will leave police to engage in more dangerous, immediate threats to public safety, such as an armed robbery or physical assaults. Now, I am not in favor of the completely hands-off approach being endorsed in some municipalities which has allowed massive shoplifting and theft because these acts are not classified as violent crimes. We have to have some reasonableness, but for minor traffic issues, we can make some changes to limit face-to-face interactions between armed police who have to fear they may be stopping armed drivers.

I want to point out that I do discuss in this work my support for a self-driving vehicle system or semi-autonomous driving system that will result in less casualties and fatalities on our roadways. I can envision a driving future in which interactions with police will be virtually eliminated because transportation systems will have the technology to prevent individual vehicle infractions before they occur. Can you envision a system that notifies the driver that a taillight is out or even drives the car autonomously with or without the driver to a service station so the taillight can be replaced? What about having the vehicle inspected annually in the same manner? If a vehicle is traveling erratically or the driver begins to speed excessively, rather than police having to pull over the aggressive driver, what if the vehicle automatically pulls over to the side of the road? The vehicle's onboard computer can provide vocal instructions to the driver to resume driving at a safe speed. This innovative transportation future would prevent drivers from becoming public safety threats through the use of technology and would eliminate the need for police officers to manually pull over individual vehicles. Again, less direct interactions between police officers and citizens will reduce the potential opportunities for these interactions to become violent.

Many changes need to be made and quickly to improve the behavior of police when interacting with all citizens. Improved training of police, along with a focus on building better relationships between police and citizens are critical action steps. These interactions with police that have led to the criminal deaths of African Americans are indications that we have a serious social emergency. African Americans have been the victims of social, economic, and governmental systems that have discriminated against them for generations. So, in my opinion, while we do need to stress the importance of police treating minorities with dignity, respect, and fairness, we must better address the underlying prejudice that pervades our society. We have to as a nation and world address discrimination and prejudice and continually fight to eradicate hate. How do we stop hate? How do we reduce discrimination? I don't have all the answers on this multi-generational, complex issue, but I do believe it begins with open communication and dialogue. We need to talk more in an open and free environment about race and diversity. This will involve those on the right admitting that past discrimination needs to be addressed, and for those on the left to acknowledge that making whites feel personally responsible for events that occurred before they were born is not justifiable.

Also, we simply need to do a better job of assisting African Americans in overcoming discriminatory practices that have limited their economic growth. Affordable housing, health care and childcare are critical for lower income families to succeed. In addition, along with financial support for higher learning, we need specific vocational training programs that can relatively quickly enable lower income citizens to qualify for good, high paying jobs. This is the United States of America. All neighborhoods in this nation should be at least middle-class. We can do this. Citizens in all neighborhoods should have the ability to live and thrive in safe communities, free of crime and poverty.

## Closing

We have lost another young man needlessly in America. Tyre Nichols was only twenty-nine years old. He was a father of a four-year-old son. As a father of a current college-aged son, I find myself getting overly emotional thinking of not having been able to be there as my son grew up and of him not having a father. It is a thought I don't want to dwell on for very long because of the emotional pain it manifests. I can only imagine the tremendous grief and inner torment the family of Tyre Nichols is experiencing after his untimely, completely avoidable passing. All children need to grow up knowing their parents. The connection between parents and their children is a sacred relationship that for so many tangible and intangible reasons we as a civilized society need to protect. Tyre should be alive and looking forward to achieving his American dream in a land that offers tremendous opportunities to its citizens. He worked for FedEx and enjoyed skateboarding and photography (Zdanowicz and Timm-Garcia). I'm sure he would have enjoyed sharing his hobbies with his son. We have a responsibility to Tyre's son to ensure that his father is simply not another statistic, but his loss will result in real change. We have the responsibility as a civilized people to make sure that every young person regardless of race is guaranteed an equal opportunity to pursue their own happiness. To date, we are falling far short of this truly achievable goal during the first quarter of the twenty-first century. We have a lot of work to do.

# 11. Have We Overcome Institutional Racism in The Workplace?

I think it is important to begin with explaining what I consider to be institutional racism. My definition may differ from how others define this term, but I think this is fine based on the intentions that I have set out to accomplish in this essay. **I define the term, "institutional racism" as both intentional and unintentional practices and aspects of an organization (or institution) that result in limiting opportunities for the advancement for people of color who do indeed qualify for such advancement**. There are different indications that demonstrate that institutional racism is inherent in any given organization. For example, even though there is a pool of qualified African American applicants for managerial positions, no African Americans are ever hired into these higher paid jobs, or they are always routed toward lower paid positions in the organization. This essay is not about goals or quotas for minorities, but I will say that another possible sign of institutional racism may be occurring when the percentage of African Americans in the general population of a geographic area is represented at a much lower percentage of a company's overall managerial staff. The African American population in the United States in 2021 was 12.1% of the overall population ("Black/African American Health"). This percentage differs from area to area, with metropolitan areas of the nation typically having a higher population of African Americans than this 12% figure. So, for example, if a given area has an African American population of 20% and a local company has a managerial staff which is only 2% African American, this could be an indication of institutional racism. In my definition, I do make the distinction that there has to be a pool of qualified minority candidates, without which an organization should not be chastised if there is a lower percentage of minorities in certain positions in comparison to their percentage of the overall population. Having said this, I do think for larger organizations who have the resources, there is a responsibility to mentor minority employees who are hired into entry level positions, as well as provide resources so that in the future, these employees will qualify for higher-paid or managerial positions. The philosophy that an organization is most successful when they invest in their employees is not new, but it is important to emphasize when we are talking about the upward mobility of African Americans in the workplace.

### Highly Successful African Americans in the U.S. Workplace

I work for a municipal government in the Southeast and the emphasis placed on diversity has led to a workforce with many more minority department heads than was the case even ten years ago.

We've had those who question whether such progress in our society means that the discrimination that minorities have endured for generations is over, and we can now declare programs to support upward mobility of minorities as no longer necessary. Others argue that these are just small steps in the right direction in fighting institutional racism, but the present work environment is far from a level playing field for minorities in the workplace. I do see quite a bit less white male executives at least in my work sphere and it is noteworthy that a majority of the department heads of the largest departments in my organization are African American. Progress has been made. One can always argue that in local government, African Americans, women, and other minorities now make up a high percentage of these executive positions compared to the private sector, and they probably would be correct. Governments in the United States generally do lead the way in promoting diversity, a practice that hopefully the private sector will follow. Even given this allowance, I would say that society is making strides in promoting African Americans to higher paid, executive positions.

Yes, we can look at government in the United States as leading the way to more diversity at top positions. The first person I would cite as representing progress in overcoming racism is former President Barack Obama. Mr. Obama was the first African American President of the United States. He was elected in 2008 and then four years later won reelection to serve a second term. Currently, our Vice President of the United States is Kamala Harris (of African and South Asian descent). These are very significant achievements given that the black population in the United States in 2021 was only 12.1% of the entire U.S. population ("Black/African American Health"). This means that African Americans are being elected by a diverse group of Americans. We also have Hakeem Jeffries who is the first African American leader of any party in Congress as he was elected on January 7th, 2023, as the minority leader of the Democrats in the House of Representatives. Mr. Jeffries will work with Kevin McCarthy who was elected Speaker of the House by the majority Republican Party. I was watching portions of the Alex Murdaugh murder trial the other day and caught myself being surprised that Judge Clifton Newman, who is presiding over the South Carolina court case, is African American. My surprise was not that Judge Newman is African American, but in my perhaps inherent bias against South Carolina, I assumed the state would not have any African American judges given its past racial strife. South Carolina has an extensive history of racial discrimination and injustice, stemming from the days of slavery in this former Confederate stronghold. I do apologize for my unfair stereotyping of the beautiful state of South Carolina in 2023. I'm sure my list of prominent African American leaders in government leaves many notable figures out, but the last dignitary I need to mention here is Ketanji Brown Jackson. Justice Jackson was sworn in during the summer of 2022 as the first African American woman Associate Justice of the U.S. Supreme Court.

I think it is important to recognize some of these highly successful African American professionals and leaders in science, industry, entertainment, and sports. Marvin Ellison is the CEO of Lowe's Home Improvement, a Fortune 500 company, and has a net worth of about $75 million as of 2021 (Haywood). Another giant in the business world, whose name I was not aware of before doing some research, is Robert F. Smith who is the founder of Vista Equity Partners, a private equity and venture capital firm (Taylor). Mr. Smith had an astronomical net worth of about $6.7 billion in 2022 (Taylor). I did want to also mention Janice Bryant Howroyd who grew up in North Carolina (Byng). Mrs. Howroyd is the founder of the ActOne Group, a personnel staffing company. This business endeavor led her to become the first African American woman to create and own a billion-dollar company (Byng).

Of course, there are some extremely successful African Americans in the entertainment industry. Oprah Winfrey, the talk show mogul, and pioneer is worth $3.5 billion in 2023 (Kumari). Rihanna and Beyoncé were worth $1.4 billion and $450 million, respectively as of the end of 2022 (Brown, Preezy). I'm a big fan of Rihanna but must admit as a devoted "Queen Bey" admirer, I was a little surprised at this difference. I'm sure, however, that Beyoncé will be just fine at this income level and, who knows, her latest album, *Renaissance*, which is a masterpiece, in my opinion, could possibly lead to an increase in her net worth. These entertainers and business leaders truly reach a certain popularity and income level when they are known by their first name, such as "Oprah, Rihanna and Beyoncé."

There are also some African Americans who are giants in the sports world (past and current) who are at least millionaires, and a few are billionaires. As of early 2023, Michael Jordan, former National Basketball Association (NBA) legend of Chicago Bulls fame is worth $2.2 billion with current NBA King Lebron James worth $1 billion (Kelly, Tim). There are other NBA past greats, such as Magic Johnson and Shaquille O'Neil, as well as more current stars like Dwyane Wade and Kevin Durant who are all worth hundreds of millions of dollars. We are used to seeing high dollar salaries for NBA stars, but there are other sports in which African Americans have succeeded financially. Tiger Woods, who many would say brought golf more into the mainstream as a spectator sport is worth $1 billion (Pereira). Floyd Mayweather Jr., the boxing champion, is worth $450 million (Christian). Patrick Mahomes, the quarterback, and Kansas City Chiefs two-time Super Bowl MVP as of 2023 is worth $70 million (Srinivasan).

Regardless of race, successful professionals in entertainment and sports, along with big business get a lot of attention. I think this is due to the intense media promotion that these individuals receive on a national, high-profile level. Wealthy business leaders, super star athletes and musical talents therefore may be more recognizable to the general public, but I did want to mention a few leaders from the scientific community who are African American. Dr. Mae Jemison, an engineer and medical doctor became the first black woman to go into space as a NASA astronaut on September 12, 1992 (Lindsey). I welcome anyone interested in science, particularly young people, to read up on Dr. Jemison's impressive and inspiring story.

I also wanted to mention one of the most well-known scientific figures in the United States who has contributed significantly to the world of Science. Per Biography.com, Dr. Neil deGrasse Tyson received his undergraduate degree in Physics from Harvard with a doctorate degree from Columbia University in Astrophysics ("Neil deGrasse Tyson"). In addition, per the American Museum of Natural History website, Dr. Tyson is the director of the Hayden Planetarium at the American Museum of Natural History in New York City, and his work has included research on star formation, as well as galaxy structure ("Neil deGrasse Tyson"). However, he is most known for communicating through interviews, television shows (such as *Star Talk* and *Nova*) and most notably his books, space science knowledge to the general public. If you have ever listened to one of his interviews or even have read one of his books, he breaks down somewhat complex scientific theories and concepts in a way that a non-scientific person can understand. Perhaps it is in Dr. Tyson's ability to communicate lessons in a method that uses both dramatic affect and, what I would describe as, an inspirational tone that so deeply captures the attention of his audiences. He makes learning about science interesting. As scientific knowledge advances, we increasingly depend on technology for everything from improvements in agriculture, the protection of the natural environment and even in the development of medications and surgical procedures to save lives. It is critical to our sustainability on many levels that scientists like Dr. Tyson reach out to the next generation and encourage them to continue this important work. In my opinion, Dr. Tyson is an American hero, and our nation and world are better because of his outreach efforts. I have a final word of praise for this scientific giant. In this era of misinformation and conspiracy theories, Dr. Tyson has in essence been a calming voice that has challenged society to adopt the use of fact-based, rational thinking to reach conclusions. He encourages this approach not only on scientific matters but on other issues that currently divide our society.

## The Continued Wealth Gap

I do come to an initial conclusion that when it comes to the achievements of African Americans in our society, that we do see many figures who have been highly successful and have contributed tremendously to the American culture. In addition, there are a lot of successful African Americans who have accumulated tremendous wealth. This cannot be overlooked. However, does this progress equate to the end of institutional racism? An outside observer may quip that we have President

Obama, Vice President Kamala Harris, Oprah, Michael Jordan, and Dr. Neil deGrasse Tyson, so certainly we have now overcome any remnants of a racist past.

My opinion is that we have a good start. Perhaps we have even turned an initial corner in the fight against institutional racism in the workplace, but we have more obstacles to remove. Yes, I think there are still issues to overcome regarding institutional racism. The reality still in America, and just a five-minute Google search will confirm this, is that African Americans are overrepresented in lower paid positions and still underrepresented in managerial and executive positions in the workplace (Connley). I think we have to be mindful that even though we have made headway on the hiring of African Americans into leadership positions, which may be seen by some as evidence that institutional racism has been resolved, we must realize that much more needs to be done. The reality is that the hiring of some African Americans into high-level or top positions does not mean that all forms of discrimination have ceased at all levels of an organization. It obviously can help with the culture, but the top executive leader is only one person. While a minority leader can set the stage for a new culture, it is quite a challenge for one person to quickly change a culture that may have deep roots of institutional racism throughout an entire organization.

The numbers do seem to be very clear in that as far as income and net worth, the average African American family is lagging significantly behind their white counterparts. For example, in 2021 per the U.S. Department of Health and Human Services based on U.S Census data, non-Hispanic whites had a median household income of $77,999 compared to non-Hispanic blacks with a median household income of $48,297 ("Black/African American Health"). This wide income disparity is logically reflected in the wide gap in net worth between white and black households. Whites with greater income have the financial ability to acquire more assets, such as savings, investments and equity per property owned. According to the website, usafacts.org, there was a staggering gap in average household net worth between whites and African Americans in the third quarter of 2022 (USAFacts Team). Whites had an average household net worth of $1,322,528 compared to African Americans with an average household net worth of $340,559 (USA[1]Facts Team). These figures display a tremendous disparity in which, on average, white households own about four times the amount of wealth of African American households. We indeed have more work to do in reducing this tremendous disparity in wealth between whites and African Americans in the United States.

## Conclusion

---

1. https://usafacts.org/articles/wealth-inequality-across-races-what-does-the-data-show/

The statistics support the argument that the hiring of top leaders of organizations who are African American is not a full indication that racism has been vanquished, but we can and should acknowledge that it is a very significant and supportive step in the right direction. It is also important to keep in mind that we need to still hold every leader accountable. The hiring of a minority director or head of a department does not mean that these leaders are flawless and cannot be constructively criticized. Also, in my opinion, the hiring of a woman or minority for the top spot in an organization does not automatically equate to an organization that will be any more progressive on employee issues, compared to organizations headed by their white male colleagues. I want to point out on a positive note that the tremendous success of professional athletes and entertainers does indicate that we have a marketplace that is more open to diversity than ever in our history. Every citizen is a unique individual and should be judged on her, his or their merits, but opening up opportunities to those who have traditionally been excluded is fair and right. We should continue to embrace and encourage diversity at all levels of our work organizations and in all sectors of our society. Also, I do agree with some form of goals to ensure that while race is not the primary reason a student is granted entry into a university or an employee is promoted into a position, we do want to create an environment that eliminates these dramatic disparities we continue to see overall between whites and African Americans.

My overall analysis is that while progress has been made in addressing institutional racism in the workplace given the success of some prominent African Americans, clearly much more has to be done to entirely eliminate inequities in opportunities for this group as a whole. I argue the continued challenge is addressing the past social constructs of institutional racism that have sadly left African Americans significantly behind their white counterparts when we examine levels of income and wealth. We must develop and implement more effective policies to eliminate this divide. African Americans need access to exceptional educational opportunities (beginning in the preschool years), affordable higher education and job training to prepare them for the jobs of the future. Finally, we must all work together to ensure that the doors of upward mobility in the workplace are wide open for qualified African Americans. Through a comprehensive effort we can eliminate the wealth gap and improve the lives of millions of Americans.

# 12. The World Is a Kinder and Safer Place When the United States Takes the Lead

We have Vladimir Putin in Russia attacking a free Ukraine, attempting to re-establish the old Soviet Union empire. China continues to expand its military presence in the South China Sea and seems intent on one day taking over the democratic island of Taiwan. Threats of terrorism from the Middle East have been somewhat kept in check thanks to the efforts of the U.S. military, but pockets of Islamic radicalism calling for the end of free societies continue to be a concern.

The U.S. is having its own issues, and many admit that this is a time period in which American society is highly polarized along political, economic, racial, religious, and geographic lines. We can't even agree on what our response should be to a pandemic or climate change. We must begin a process of cooperation and compromise in order to move past this time of extreme divisiveness in America. I think there is too much over-dramatization by some in the mainstream and social media outlets, who claim that our Founding Fathers' democratic experiment is at risk. I don't share this "the sky is falling" outlook, but I do think events like the right-wing January 6th Insurrection, as well as left-wing riots stemming from Black Lives Matter protests, do indicate there are threats and obstacles to us getting back to middle-ground reasonableness. Violence arising out of extreme political activism is a valid concern. I still have faith, however, in the reasonableness of the majority of the American people to come together in the middle of the political spectrum to solve our problems peacefully. I have no doubt that we will get back on track, but the question is how long this process will take.

The United States will survive, but my fear is that the longer it takes for us to deal with our demons, the more suffering there will be in the world. There is one firm belief that I hold for which no one will ever convince me otherwise – the world with the U.S. as its leader is a kinder and safer place for all. The United States is essentially ensuring that Ukraine still even exists, providing the nation with weapons to repel an initial Russian military surge that was intended to quickly defeat Ukraine in mere days. The war is now well into its second year. American influence keeps China's military and economic ambitions in check, as that nation seeks to replace the U.S. as the world leader. China is now a Capitalist nation but with a governmental system that has no interest in protecting the individual liberties of its people. The United States stands in the way of terrorists who wish to create a world where religious freedom and women's rights don't exist. It is a testament to the American system that with so much internal strife we can still provide such strong leadership and assistance for the good of the world.

We are still a tremendously powerful nation, but I must admit that I have great fondness for the last decade of the twentieth century. After the fall of the Soviet empire, Americans experienced the realization in the 1990s that no nation could compete on any level with the United States. Also, while there was political strife during this time, life in America seemed to be at least advancing in the direction of greater opportunity and the extension of rights for all citizens. It was a promising and hopeful time.

## The United States as the Sole Superpower in the Post-Soviet World

I am old enough to have been a young adult in the early 1990s when the United States was basically the sole superpower on the planet. The communist Soviet Empire had been defeated during the Cold War. The Soviet Union could not compete with the wealthy West and its economic system based on capitalism. Perhaps a simplistic way to explain the fall of the Soviet Union from a military perspective, is to say that the Soviets simply were no longer able to fund their military competition with the U.S., given that their economic system was collapsing. European nations in the former "Iron Curtain" were becoming democratic, capitalistic systems including Russia itself. The fall of the Berlin wall at the end of the 1980s seemed to mark in both a practical and symbolic sense that Soviet Communism was over. China was not yet the economic powerhouse that the United States would create and openly encourage, in the seemingly rational philosophy that by bringing competitive capitalism to the Asian Giant, China would naturally transition to and adopt a democratic form of government. The world seemed like a more stable and friendlier place where anything was possible. As the threat from Soviet Communism was fading, we could turn our attention on making the world in every corner more democratic and economically stable. Personally, I recall that this was a time of great expectations. America had reached its potential as world leader and we had little doubt that freedom would only expand around the globe, not recede from it. The world felt safe with a general vibe that achieving freedom for all world citizens was truly achievable. This was years before 9/11 when we realized that Islamic terrorism could indeed reach our shores, but in the early 1990s, this wasn't really a concern of the U.S. public. Yes, we did have the Gulf War when Iraq invaded Kuwait in 1990 to 1991, but there wasn't a sense in my opinion that the U.S. would really have any long-term conflict, at least not on a military level in the Middle East. The Gulf War was won due to exceptional military planning and execution by the U.S. with leaders such as Colin Powell, Chairman of the Joint Chiefs of Staff under President George H.W. Bush. I recall the almost comical images on the news of Iraqi soldiers quickly surrendering to the U.S. soldiers and in broken English expressed their love for President Bush. The United States was on top of the world and the chants of "USA is # 1" were commonplace. The sense was that the U.S. was the clear leader of the world, and the world was a better place with America in this position. Yes, we knew there would be skirmishes with small, rogue nations, but with our military might and the ability to move forces wherever needed without the concern of the Soviet Union (this was before the rise of China as a military power), we justifiably had great confidence that we could handle any global conflicts that may arise.

## Missed Opportunities and Misguided Strategies

One can now question in 2023 whether our policy on China for the past thirty years (or longer) was based on a sound strategy. The Chinese government in unique fashion adopted capitalism to some degree, but retained their totalitarian governmental system that limits individual rights and freedoms. At the time in the latter part of the twentieth century, the hope was that China would move closer to the U.S. and the West in governmental style. The achievement of both a democratic Russia and free China would ensure a freer and stable world.

The United States made some missteps in this effort at transitioning these communist nations to democracy. During the 1990s, after the fall of the Soviet Empire, we should have dismantled not just some, but the entire Soviet nuclear arsenal (and then could have destroyed many of our own nukes). In addition, the U.S. did too much celebrating and gloating over defeating the Soviets. We could have done so much more in the way of on the ground support and financial assistance to guide this nation that really did not have a lot of experience with democratic or capitalistic systems. A reasonable assessment decades later should conclude that our lack of support for Russia after the Cold War, led to the rise of a leader like Vladimir Putin who has led his nation into invading a free Ukraine and re-imposed a repressive regime, limiting the freedoms of the Russian People. Next time, and I do believe there will be a next time, we will need to provide more intricate support to Russia to ensure the Russian people achieve a true, successful transition to democracy.

Now, I don't place as much blame on U.S. policymakers regarding the China situation as I do with the Russian-failed transition to democracy. Perhaps transitioning so much of our manufacturing base to China, that has enabled this nation to become an economic powerhouse rivaling the U.S. (Kelly, William), was a bit too aggressive. I think it was a reasonable policy approach in the late twentieth century to believe that China as a capitalistic, competitive economic nation-state, would naturally sprout a free, democratic governmental system for the Chinese people. In retrospect, however, we should have moved more incrementally to ensure monetary wealth accumulated by the Chinese Communist Party would not be used to continue its behavior of limiting political rights of the Chinese people and expand its military presence. I recall going into Walmart in the late 1980s and early 1990s and apparel was actually advertised as "Made in America." The United States it clearly appears now went too far in moving such a substantial amount of manufacturing to China on a bet that didn't pan out as well for the U.S. We are currently in a situation as we head toward the end of the first quarter of the twenty-first century of facing a China that is basically economically bolstered with our assistance. China has, to our dismay, used its wealth accumulated through capitalism to build up the nation's military. The Chinese are now flexing their military muscle in their neck of the woods against nations like Taiwan, Japan, and South Korea, as well as moving their influence across the globe. Some would also say that making China our trading partner also cost the U.S. thousands of jobs that were shipped overseas. I am not an economist, but I do sympathize with the desire to bring back manufacturing jobs for American workers who have suffered tremendously during the globalization movement that moved the majority of our manufacturing overseas to nations like China.

## The United States Addressing Internal and External Conflicts

Yes, currently the United States is experiencing a lot of internal divisiveness, and we must find ways to unite behind our core beliefs of individual freedom, representative government and simply embracing fairness and kindness that Americans are known for around the globe. My solution, as part of the overall theme in my collection of essays, is that we need to compromise and meet in the middle on so many issues. I truly believe that by communicating effectively, we can reach reasonable solutions on the internal political issues that we are currently so divided on in our society. We need to emphasize our core beliefs of protecting individual freedom, while accepting rule by the majority. There is a balance that we can attain. My rationale is based on a core assumption that Americans overall are fair-minded people who support policies that support the greatest outcomes for the most people. This policymaking process entails allowing those on the extreme ends of the political and social spectrums the space to speak, but that rulemaking must occur through compromise at the middle. We can achieve this. Like the rest of the world, the U.S. went through a pandemic that highlighted some very unfair treatment of certain segments of our population. The working class and minorities who too often go through unavoidable exposure and the inability from an economic standpoint to access regular healthcare, were left especially vulnerable to COVID-19. We are experiencing, in my opinion, a normal element of a free society where groups clamor for change and reforms. These changes are occurring in the workplace and in society with citizens demanding better pay, benefits, and work-life balance to ensure simple equity of opportunity to live healthy, meaningful lives. We are re-examining how law enforcement can best protect the citizens, while also ensuring that minorities are not treated harshly and brutally as we saw with the murder of George Floyd. We will get through this time of division, but I do think it is important for us to realize that some harsh, divisive debate in a peaceful manner is part of living in a great democracy that values individual liberties and freedom of speech. We should not avoid highly charged debate, but we do need all sides to be willing to listen to others' viewpoints. The United States can adopt policies that are based on logical reasoning and compromise. We don't want to avoid passionate debates but engage fully in them. However, at the end of the day, we want to come together as one people, all who must pledge to support our democracy and freedom under one flag. This approach will ensure that we move toward a more peaceful coexistence with one another within our nation's borders.

I disagree with what seems to be a somewhat organized movement that arose more prominently in the years of the Obama Administration (I do concede I did vote for him twice without hesitation), that calls for the United States to play more of a minor role in the world. There seems to be a continuing, in my opinion, misguided political outlook that the United States based on its colonial, Western traditions is the cause of many of the world's problems through its overly interference of other nations' autonomy. This image portrays the U.S. of using its military and economic might, to enhance the status quo of American and European dominance while other nations suffer. I strongly agree that the U.S. has used its influence in the world at ill-advised times to achieve certain outcomes in its own interests. Given this admission, the United States based on its democratic and compassionate foundation, needs to prevail as leader of the world for the best chance at achieving a global reality in which every individual has a guarantee of freedom.

No doubt, the world is safer today because the United States has maintained its military superiority which clearly is needed with an aggressive Putin-led Russia and an increasingly bold-acting China. Fortunately for the world, the United States has begun to flex its muscles using our financial abilities to punish Russia with sanctions, as well as supply Ukraine with weapons that free Ukrainians are using to stave off the Russian assault. Putin and Russian leaders thought that they would have a cakewalk taking the nation of Ukraine and annexing the free nation back into their control as part of a new Iron Curtain in just mere days. Well over a year later, Ukraine is still holding its own because of the military assistance provided by the United States and NATO (North Atlantic Treaty Organization).

As far as China, the U.S. failed in its plan of transitioning the Red Giant into a democratic nation through capitalism. If China continues on its path of using its economic power to increase their military presence in an attempt to challenge the West, the United States will need to transition manufacturing away from China. The U.S. can look to other Asian nations and also bring back manufacturing to the United States. We no doubt should look to our neighbors to the South, such as Mexico and the nations of Central America, whose economies would benefit tremendously from U.S. investments in manufacturing. The COVID-19 Pandemic taught the United States that having so much of our manufacturing oversees can really lead to major supply chain issues pertaining to the availability of some basic supplies and even medications. Some have even asserted that depending too heavily on Chinese manufacturing is a national security issue. I agree that particularly in times of national or world emergencies, such as the pandemic, the U.S. needs easy access to a variety of goods and supplies, such as medicine, medical equipment, basic tools, etc. This is problematic if we are depending on the industrial manufacturing system in China for the majority of our nation's goods and supplies. As I alluded to above, as China continues to increase its aggressive behavior militarily, the U.S. needs to reassess if remaining such a significant trading partner with China is sensible. We have always desired to do business with the wonderful Chinese people, but if the economic wealth that the Chinese government attains from our business relationships is used to essentially develop their military to rival the U.S., this requires a major adjustment in economic policy. We don't want to fund the expansion of the Chinese military that could pose a serious risk to the national security of the United States. This behavior would not be logical. Yes, I would say it is now time to begin stepping back from relying on China for a significant portion of the manufacturing needs of the United States. This would hurt China, in my opinion, as without American consumers, the continued rise of the middle class in China could be at risk. This could also lead to the Chinese people becoming disenchanted with their Communist leadership and President Xi Jinping that perhaps could leave to democratic reforms.

I do not want to leave out the need of the United States to lead the fight against Islamic radicalism and extremism that is a threat to individual rights, women's rights, gay rights, and the freedom of religion for many in the Middle East and beyond. The United States needs to continue to play a peace-making role with Europe in the Middle East to create an environment which may not look exactly like Western democracy, but in which the practice of Islam does not equate to violence against those who believe differently. The United States can support Islamic nations that take on a more moderate, balanced approach to religious teachings through economic incentives that will reduce the tendency of the rise of fundamentalist, violent sects of Islam that too often use violence and brutality, including murder, to punish those who choose to express their individuality and self-determination. And yes, the United States needs to continue to work with Israel and the Palestinian people to achieve a permanent peace between the two sides. Nationhood must be achieved for the Palestinian people and Israel needs to be able to survive and thrive in a part of the world where too often their Islamic neighbors have called for the destruction of the nation of Israel. Israeli military and police have every right to protect the safety of the Jewish people but must ensure they do not adopt aggressive tactics toward Palestinian citizens.

It is clear to me that a world led by the United States in collaboration with our strong partners and allies throughout the globe can contain the spread of fascism, totalitarianism, religious intolerance, and extremism. There are numerous and powerful nations that oppose freedom for their people and the world. We can protect the rights of women, children, minorities, and all individuals by disseminating our democratic values to nations that desire our guidance. In addition, we can challenge through diplomatic and economic methods those nations whose governments are intent on keeping their populations in systems that provide little in the way of guaranteed rights and freedoms. The United States also should support free nations, like Ukraine and Taiwan, with military weapons and logistical support that are being attacked or threatened by their larger authoritarian and totalitarian neighbors of Russia and China.

## Closing

THE UNITED STATES IS experiencing an internal re-examination of our societal norms with views along the political spectrum being voiced by our citizens on a number of issues. How should we talk about race in school to our children? Up to what point in a pregnancy should abortion be legal, or should it never be legal? Should we enact more gun control laws to combat gun violence or does the need to protect the Second Amendment outweigh this concern? Do we need to do more to combat climate change or is this unnecessary since climate change is "not real?" Should we teach our children about human sexuality, including providing LGTBQ supportive information in school and, if so, at what age? We can address these disagreements by having open and honest discussion, not more division and tribalism. This is, after all, the United States and not a Third World nation of warring factions. We can do this, and I have no doubt the majority of Americans love their nation and want to work together for the benefit of all of its citizens. Our Founding Fathers provided us with a Constitution which implores every citizen to defend the rights of every other citizen to live freely and express their personal political opinions. The only way to protect a free society is to protect the free speech of all, regardless of how repugnant someone's views may be to us personally. We must keep this in mind that a free society requires us to be tolerant of the expression of a variety of opinions. This process can be highly confrontational. Currently, we all seem to be expressing ourselves vehemently and passionately which is great, but we are leaving out that critical element of a free society that requires us to listen (not just think about our response, but to really listen) to opposing opinions with open minds. We can all take that step away from irrational rigidity and accept that others who may oppose us with differing opinions can have very valid points that we should review.

Another key component that I think is critical in reaching compromise is that all sides need to acknowledge the truth of common facts or defer to expert professionals when evaluating how best to address an issue. This can be difficult when we all tend to naturally bring our biases to the discussion table, but it needs to be done. For example, what do the leading scientists say is happening with climate change? There will always be outlying positions, but if the majority of top scientists claim that climate change is real, then we must all agree to frame the debate based upon that common understanding. We have to begin from a rational standpoint that we will follow the facts and the expert opinions of those who know more than we do. At times that is not happening today in our divisive environment. We must make a commitment to review the facts first and do our best to leave our emotions or biases out of our personal evaluations. It is through open communication and dialogue that we can arrive at fair and reasonable solutions that bring us together as one people living in harmony with one another or, at least, acceptance of one another's differences. When the American people come together, as we have demonstrated time and time again, there is nothing that we as one people cannot achieve. This is due to our great diversity that brings so many ideas and thought processes together, that may initially clash, but when blended and organized, result in astounding outcomes.

Yes, while we are having a period of serious internal conflict, we face nations and extremist groups who threaten freedom throughout the world. We must realize that as great as the United States is, in terms of economic and military power, our nation cannot do it alone. We must join with our allies in Western Europe and Asia (including Japan and South Korea), among others, to defeat these threats to freedom and peace. This alliance of freedom led by the United States will defeat the threats now being posed to the world by Russia and China. The United States, however, must rise to the occasion to take on this leadership role. Americans are the glue that has held the world in relative peace and prosperity since World War II. Our help with Ukraine is a good sign that Americans are reasserting that the United States is the leader of the free world, as well as the moral foundation of our planet. Let's get our act together and retake our place in the world as the primary superpower. The United States needs to re-dedicate our commitment to working with our partners in liberty to oppose those who wish to extinguish freedom, instead of protecting and expanding it.

# 13. Hybrid Work's Role in Reducing Carbon Emissions and Improving Work-Life Balance

During the COVID-19 pandemic employers with primarily office employees allowed workers to transition to remote work in order to prevent the spread of the virus. Productivity in many instances went up as employees essentially were able to exchange at least some commute time for additional work time. In addition, by allowing employees some level of flexibility, they found a better work-life balance. This new arrangement led to happier, more productive employees. The new normal as we move past the height of the COVID-19 pandemic has been the adoption of a hybrid work schedule for many employees. The hybrid schedule involves employees working some days in the office with other days working remotely. My vote is for employees to have the choice to continue to work the majority of days remotely for the benefits I discuss below.

## Hybrid Work and Better Air Quality

A significant benefit that studies have predictably found is that remote working during the pandemic resulted in cleaner air. So, less vehicles on the road led to less carbon from vehicles being emitted into the air. One doesn't need to be a scientist to understand the obvious environmental benefits of remote working, but I did review a bit of the information available. One study by the University of Houston found that Washington D.C., Boston, and New York City each saw reductions in air pollutants by about twenty percent from March through May 2020, the height of the lockdown period, when compared to the previous spring months in 2019 (Strong). These findings are impressive, and we know that reductions in air pollution not only help with the reduction in carbon emissions which is causing climate change but help to reduce lung disease and other cardiovascular ailments. I recall listening to President Bill Clinton on a local radio show in the early 2000s, soon after he left office. He was being questioned by a somewhat conservative, local radio personality who did not believe that global warming was real. President Clinton had a great response. I'm paraphrasing after all these years, but basically, he explained that even if one doesn't believe that global warming is real, clearly, we want to live in a world that has clean air to breathe for ourselves and our families.

President Clinton's response just hit home with me as a simple rational explanation as to the entire environmental debate. One of the reasons why I consider myself a "Clinton Democrat" is that the former president has the ability to cut through the political semantics on an issue and provide a clear rational reason why a given policy is the best for all parties concerned. I think Americans today are seeking reasonable, common-sense solutions to problems and not overly complicated initiatives that too often don't work in the real world. President Clinton really was able to end the interview with this reasonable argument. It is rational that a society should be in total agreement that we want to protect the air, water, and land. We need clean air to live healthy lives. We need clean water to drink to survive. Our waterways and oceans need to be clean to support those ecosystems that support our planet, not to mention the fish and sea life that we eat. Finally, we need to protect the land where we grow our crops on from pesticides and other pollutants. Our land must also be free of pollutants that our cattle and other livestock graze on that we, of course, in turn depend on for human consumption. The reality is that we are all connected so anything we can do to keep our environment free of pollution must be done. I think we all should consciously focus on limiting driving trips to improve the environment. Eliminating commuting to work as much as possible can help in this environmentally friendly effort of reducing carbon emissions and improving our air quality.

We must make a commitment to improving our environment to alleviate climate change. We continually hear about electric cars and light rail mass transit which are intended to transition us away from gas powered single occupancy vehicles. I contend simply that we already have a big part of the answer – remote working. We have the technology to work and meet through highly advanced computers and social interactive networks. Humans are social animals. I agree that it is important to interact in a real-world face-to-face environment. However, the sustainability of our planet's ecosystems is in danger. Remote working works for our environment. Traditional office employees should have the option to continue to work at home and help our environment with occasional in-office events or meetings to bolster team cohesiveness.

### Hybrid Work and Work-Life Balance

I did want to discuss somewhat the work-life balance that many remote workers have reported to have achieved in contrast to the traditional office schedule. Workers who prefer remote work tout the benefits to both the employee and the employer. Overall, we did see many employees being more productive during the pandemic. Based on my personal experience, I think this was due to multiple reasons. Being able to sleep in an extra hour instead of getting up early for the morning commute helped me to feel better rested and ready to go when I did log on to my computer. Then, I think a lot of us actually worked longer in the afternoons during that hour or so when we would typically be driving home. I certainly began doing this. Also, a lot of unnecessary small talk and socializing is eliminated with employees working from home. Now, one of my concerns with the focus on productivity is that the humanity of employees can too easily be ignored, and

I do admit that for our mental well-being, all of us need that human interaction. Having said this, any argument proposing that employees need to return to the office five days a week to maximize performance is not credible given the overall, high level of employee productivity that was achieved during the lockdown, work from home period. Remote working does provide a very high level of productivity for the employer, on the whole, and for any case in which an employee is not performing up to par, the individual can always be required to come into the office more frequently. Again, overall, as studies have shown, for the vast majority of remote employees, off-site productivity is very impressive (Waltower).

Remote working has enabled employees to have more flexibility to improve their lifestyles, as well as meet the demands of both work and home. I can relate to parents who say it is much easier now even when they are at the office to slip out after four or five hours to pick up their child for an appointment. Then, they can get back online to finish their daily work tasks remotely. Gone are those days for parents when they felt as if they had to choose between keeping their jobs or picking up their sick child early from school. Remote work schedules are more civilized and certainly when organizations provide flexibility to their employees, workers will be more dedicated and loyal to their employers. Work location flexibility is a tremendous benefit for parents or any employee who is responsible for taking care of loved ones.

The other life-balance benefit of remote work that many have found is the ability to turn lunch hours into self-care hours. Some employees who used to sit in their breakrooms, at their desks or even in their cars eating their lunches, have now turned the lunch hour into a time of well-being or enjoyment. Some take a yoga class at the local YMCA or take thirty minutes to walk in the sunshine outside, followed by thirty minutes to eat. I used to be so tired when I got home from work and it would be a struggle to go for a run, especially during the shorter, cold days in the winter. Now, when I work from home, I run at lunchtime and when I finish my workday, I can relax. I am truly grateful for my remote workdays.

### Conclusion

Remote work has continued in 2022 and 2023 but in more of a hybrid fashion. I think companies have opted to continue to provide some flexibility to employees, but the general opinion of management is that some in-person interaction is beneficial to team-building and communication. I agree overall with this hybrid philosophy. Meetings can still be mostly virtual or over the phone. We are all used to this format now after three years. It works. I agree there is something to be said for informal, interactions between employees that promote goal achievement, and this can be achieved in a hybrid format with employees having opportunities to brain-storm on ideas together during the days that they are in the office.

When we are looking at reducing carbon emissions, the question is at what level of in-office work is necessary to ensure the effectiveness of the organization? This will differ from one organization to another, but the reality is that we are coming back into the office after a period when office workers were primarily off-site for in some cases two to three years. So, from a rational standpoint, it is difficult to make the argument that excessive multiple days in the office per week are necessary for the success of many work groups or organizations that perform the majority of their work via a computer screen.

My argument is that for any places of business that performed well during the pandemic when employees worked primarily off-site, organizations should adopt work schedules of no more than two days in the office each week. The benefits to the environment and to the work-life balance of employees are clear. We should come into the office when it is necessary for the critical functioning of an organization. Aside from that, flexibility for the employee needs to be the new standard. We can clean our air and achieve a better quality of life simply by skipping that drive back and forth from a brick-and-mortar building. I think we all have realized that with advanced computer technology, the future of greater flexibility for the office employee is now. Remote work proved during the pandemic that it could be just as productive as in-office work, if not more so (Maurer). Hybrid work schedules need to remain the new normal. Turning back the clock to a time of 40-hour work weeks or longer in the office does not benefit our environment, our work organizations, or our employees.

# 14. President Biden Calling out "Semi-Fascism" Sect of the Republican Party

### Confronting the Claim of a Stolen Election

At a Democratic Party event on Thursday, August 25, 2022, President Biden called out a sect of the Republican Party as having adopted a political platform rooted in "semi-fascism," and expressed how this sect is a threat to our democracy (Shabad, "Biden Blasts Maga"). He is being criticized by those on the right and particularly the personalities on Fox News who are insisting this is a slanderous statement against all Republicans. Fox News is also comparing this to former Secretary of State Hillary Clinton's assertion, per the 2016 presidential election, that Trump supporters were "deplorables." I can see a point in that case in which Secretary Clinton in that statement created an impression that she was calling all Republicans "deplorables." Mrs. Clinton's statement was problematic since anyone who supported the Republican candidate would be voting in essence for Mr. Trump and, thus, per her definition would be categorized as a "deplorable."

This situation with President Biden is different and he is correct. We can debate how the more conservative Supreme Court has affected freedom of religion and abortion rights for the individual or have other political disagreements which are part of a free political system, but in this case, I am talking about the rejection by some of a core ingredient in a free electoral system – the acceptance of the outcome of a free and fair election. President Biden is correctly calling out the false accusations and statements by these MAGA (Make America Great Again) Trump supporters who claim that our electoral system is unfair, and that former President Trump was cheated out of victory in the 2020 presidential election. If we don't have an electoral system that all political leaders adhere to and support, then our free system can begin to fall apart. Currently, we do have a segment of the Republican Party that to this day refuses to admit that President Biden was fairly elected without any illegal or unfair advantage afforded to him. Many Democrats were in shock when President Trump won his election in 2016 and even called for changes in the Electoral College process since Secretary Clinton won the popular vote. However, when it came time for the peaceful transition, President Obama welcomed then President-Elect Donald J. Trump to the White House. Now, we can recall that President Trump was a big supporter of the false claim that President Obama was not American born. Yet, we saw a gracious leader of our free democracy in Mr. Obama who played his crucial role in supporting a smooth transition from one U.S. President to another in a peaceful manner.

Trump and some of his followers did not live up to our American ideal of supporting a peaceful transition of government in early 2021. Trump himself through his social media use has continued to claim that the election was "stolen" and to this day will not concede that President Biden won fairly. I fully support any candidate's legal right to question an election through whatever legal options are available. However, Trump and his team could not provide any proof that he was cheated out of victory. President Trump instead of stoking anger among his supporters based on a false claim that led to an insurrection on January 6th, should have invited the former Vice President, President-Elect Joe Biden to the White House shortly after the election. Clearly, such an invitation extended by Mr. Trump would have been the honorable and right action that a sitting U.S. President should take to best protect our precious democracy. Again, candidates should be afforded every opportunity to dispute an outcome if there is any legitimate question as to the fairness of an election, but there must be that point at which the loser needs to graciously accept defeat. This acceptance of the outcome by all candidates is essential for the integrity of not only our democratic electoral system, but so that government can indeed move forward in a timely manner to serve the public. Our Republic was developed so that government leaders are not only elected by the people, but that they actually serve the people. Our nation's "claim to fame" when it comes to free elections, is that after everyone has had their say, the candidate with the most votes is acknowledged by all other candidates and their supporters as the winner. Then we move forward from the electoral phase into the governing phase in which, hopefully, policies can be formulated and implemented that support the American people. President Trump could have handled the election with class, and he would have been in a much better position to garner support for a comeback during the 2024 election.

Instead, to this day, President Trump, and many of his supporters (not main-stream Republicans like former Vice President Mike Pence who refused to succumb to Trump's pressure to obstruct the certification process of the 2020 presidential election) are leaning toward fascism. Refusing to admit defeat in an election in which your candidate lost is not supporting free elections, a fundamental component that our Founding Fathers included when they created our free government and society. Basically, this sect of Republican leaders and voters are simply refusing to acknowledge defeat in the face of clear facts. If everyone had this viewpoint, we would no longer have a democratic system of government. This is why I completely agree with President Biden. Not all Republicans, but these MAGA Republicans who desire for their candidate, who lost, to continue to retain power are leaning toward a fascist or totalitarian system that does not respect our free democratic, electoral heritage. These Republicans simply wished to retain power and disregard the votes of their fellow citizens who supported Joe Biden, the candidate who won the 2020 presidential election "fair and square."

### Solutions to Protect American Democracy & Final Thoughts

What we need is a new renaissance of ethics to support a healthy, free political and electoral system. I am focusing this discussion on the political process, but in today's society as divisive as we have become, we need to get back to the basics. This process will benefit society as a whole in many different facets of our lives, not just politics. I do want to emphasize that teaching our children about fairness in competition and being a gracious winner, as well as learning to lose with a positive acknowledgement to the winner are lessons that we all need to learn (and remember). Yes, we need to teach this basic lesson to our young children, but lately I think the issue has been with adults forgetting that winning at all costs is not ethical and does not promote a free society. Basically, President Trump and his supporters are acting like school-aged, sore losers who lost the kickball game in gym class, but continue to claim that they were cheated, when they were not. Indeed, we need to reinforce and teach the basic moral tenet of acting ethically and fairly to adults, as well as children.

A good step in communicating to the electorate that our voting system is fair to all candidates would be to initiate a campaign led by national and local elections officials. These election experts can educate the public on how their processes work to prevent cheating. It is also important to communicate to the public that candidates do have legal recourse if they feel an election process was unfair. I think it is helpful to share some refresher information to the public on how our elections, particularly presidential and Congressional races, are following the guidance of our Founding Fathers through the Constitution and their intention to create a free society in which everyone has a voice in electing our leaders. Our system was created out of the rejection of having a king who is not directly accountable to the people. Our Founding Fathers set out to create a government that was directly accountable to the public by way of elections.

Now, another component of this renaissance of ethics in politics would be to require the candidates (from local offices up to, yes, the presidential race) to take even a brief course on ethics when running for public office. The emphasis should be on teaching future leaders about our constitutional system and the need to support our free elections for the sake of the nation. Candidates need to understand that protecting our free electoral system is much more important than seeding distrust in the process for political gain. What we have seen, thankfully only a glimpse of with the insurrection on January 6, 2021, is that we need our political leaders and candidates, as well as our formal governmental institutions to support our democratic processes to absolutely ensure that our fair electoral system survives and thrives. Thankfully our formal institutions were able to withstand a threat to the free, presidential election, but if not for heroes of the day like Vice President Mike Pence, we could have had a real constitutional crisis. We need ethical candidates along with our formal institutions and practices to protect our free system and democratic way of life. All candidates should have to take a course, however brief, and sign a document attesting that if they lose the election and exhaust all legal avenues in the courts to oppose the outcome, that they then will agree to accept the final vote. This acknowledgement that they will accept defeat is essential and was a step that, let's face it, Donald Trump was never completely willing to do publicly.

Yet another initiative that is needed is for there to be a new "America First" campaign. This campaign could be called something different in its final form, but I quote the Trump Administration's catchy phrase in which the meaning was intended to express the need for American leadership to implement policies on the world scene that will benefit Americans rather than other nations, as has been the perception of some. A part of this agenda dealt with trade. President Trump (I would say accurately) complained that trade relations with China benefited the Chinese economy more than the American economy with the imbalance of manufacturing and jobs going abroad rather than staying in the United States. Yes, some American consumers did benefit from a plethora of cheaper Chinese-made products, but somewhat less expensive products on the store shelves is of little benefit to Americans who lost their manufacturing jobs due to the successful globalization effort to open up China's economy.

My use of this "America First" term has a different meaning. America First in my definition would be a campaign for political parties to re-commit their allegiance to the United States as one people and one government first, with one's political party affiliation and loyalty taking a back seat. We have become a nation in which a large number of citizens seem clearly to be putting their political party first instead of putting the focus of their support on our nation. This needs to change. Having a new emphasis on "country before party," as the saying goes can reduce the incredibly high level of divisiveness that now exists. We need to address this harmful tendency of political leaders to claim that members of the opposing political party are cheating, or our electoral process is in itself somehow unfair. America First means we get back to the basic ideals of what it means to be American by standing up for the liberties and rights of the individual. We also need to support and defend the formal processes that our Founding Fathers set up to create and protect a free society.

Finally, I would like to see in our schools that an in-depth Civics course becomes a requirement to graduate from high school. Along with this, a class in American government that includes a comprehensive curriculum covering our U.S. Colonial history with a focus on our constitutional system should be required for all students. I would also like to see an emphasis on ethics in our schools, both academically and through participatory interactions. Both teaching ethics in a classroom setting and teaching fairness through gym class or through other competitive activities (academic competitions come to mind), are necessary steps to educate our young people on how to interact with others to ensure a fair and kind society. It may sound clichéd but living by the "Golden Rule" of treating others as you would want to be treated, is really essential for a free and altruistic society to exist and thrive. What we have learned after January 6th is that we can have a Constitution and all the ingenious formal government institutions that our Founding Fathers created, but without the people to perform their part in supporting our democratic processes, our free system of government can surprisingly very quickly unravel, opening up the door for fascism or any other "ism" that revokes our individual liberties.

# 15. The Cost of Healthcare for the American Family

Paying for healthcare is a complicated issue. Do we need to move away from an employer-based system, adopt a single-payer "Medicare for All" system, or just add a public option to provide an additional affordable insurance choice? One idea is that an additional public insurance option could fill the gap for citizens who do not qualify for Medicaid but can't afford other insurance options. Do we need a supplemental insurance option for those whose current health insurance plans do not cover substantial parts of care needed? More Americans are having difficulty paying for their family's healthcare, so we need to take a look at all options on the table to create a better system to pay for the healthcare needs of American citizens.

## Medicare for All

At this point in time, I still support the current employer-based health insurance system but would like to see some reforms. I am a great admirer of Senator Bernie Sanders and agree with a lot of his opinions when it comes to how the American worker is treated. Salaries have not kept pace with the cost of living and the ability of employees to oppose mistreatment and abuse by employers seems to have gone backwards, not forwards as far as human rights advances. Senator Sanders, however, has not completely sold me on a Medicare for All option – yet (I refer those who wish to get more information on Senator Sanders platform to visit his website at https://berniesanders.com/issues/medicare-for-all/). My concern with such a system is that the Medicare for All approach may result in lower payments to hospitals and doctors to the point at which quality of care could be negatively impacted. When we hear about physician practices not accepting Medicare or Medicaid, the reason is because the payments are so much lower than what private insurance pays. Often, it seems that payments from private insurance actually supplant the lower payments received from the governmental insurance programs. If we go to a government-paid program for everyone, I question if this would result in a lower overall income for doctors, other medical staff, and hospitals. If funding is reduced, this could lead to lower levels of both service and overall medical care for patients. What we want to achieve is, yes, a reduction in cost for patients, but we also want to ensure we maintain our American, high-quality care. Let's face it, we need people to become medical professionals so salaries should be on the higher end of the spectrum for doctors, nurses and all the other technical staff that hospitals and medical practices need to function properly. We all witnessed during the COVID-19 pandemic how much our society depends on highly trained medical professionals who truly work miracles every day. These professionals should be paid salaries commensurate with the education, training and technical skill sets that they have acquired which enable them to provide such an exceptional, high level of care to the public. Therefore, I am cautious of any reform that would curtail our national medical system's ability to pay our medical professionals competitively high salary amounts. The goal is to reduce costs, but not to a point where there is inadequate funding for proper staff pay, advanced medical technology and patient-friendly medical facilities. I am concerned that Medicare for All may not be able to properly fund our medical system to maintain our current high level of care. Senator Sanders is correct in his desire to reduce costs for patients, but I'm not convinced yet that an all-public insurance system is the answer at this point.

### Steps to Reduce Healthcare Costs

The question of course is how we can reduce costs for patients, while still maintaining the level of care that we want for every American. Part of this cost-reduction process is to ensure that all citizens are able to afford regular health screenings, obtain their medications and be able to afford to live healthy lifestyles through employment opportunities that work for them. We know that through health screenings for various forms of cancer, heart disease and other ailments that when conditions are caught early, this can significantly increase the chances that patients can be healed. When early screenings are not performed, this leads to a lower chance that someone can be cured by medical care and, in addition, the cost will increase significantly when surgical procedures or other expensive treatments are required.

Also, when people can afford their medications, this is another way for them to be able to prevent ailments from getting worse or even from developing in the first place. When we think about diabetes or some type of hereditary deficiency condition, medications can prevent damage to the body from occurring. As with screenings, being able to take medications is a less invasive, lower risk and inexpensive option when compared to having to address medical ailments through surgical procedures when they more than likely fully manifest down the road.

I do agree with some personal responsibility proponents who say Americans have adopted unhealthy lifestyles that lead to serious, chronic illnesses and this is why the cost of healthcare is so high in our nation. They are correct in the fact that we all must do our part to exercise, eat a healthy diet, and find ways to reduce chronic stress in our lives. Of course, in order for one to live a healthy lifestyle, one basic requirement is to have gainful employment that supports healthy lifestyle choices. I concede this is a little bit of an aside, but we do have a societal issue of employees who are overworked and too often have to work multiple jobs to support their families. The everyday health of employees suffers due to a lack of downtime. We want Americans to be able to work 40-hour weeks most of the time so they can achieve a healthy work-life balance. All of us need time to detox daily and periodically take time off to keep stress in check. Especially for those who work full-time jobs and are also caregivers to family members, having leisure time off from work is essential to proper physical and mental wellbeing. Therefore, yes, taking personal responsibility for one's health must be emphasized, but this commitment must be combined with an employment system that supports and values the health of all employees. It is important to point out that our economic system must work for everyone so that all Americans can live healthy lifestyles.

### An Affordable Healthcare System for All

Let's examine further how we can best provide affordable, comprehensive health insurance coverage for all of our citizens. My current opinion is that Senator Sanders hasn't fully sold me on Medicare for All but if we continue on the current path, I may change my mind. I am at this point in favor of a public option, possibly an expansion of Medicaid for those with higher income levels who would not qualify for Medicaid in its current form. In addition, I would like to see a public or nonprofit option that could be used as supplemental insurance to cover expenses like co-pays and coinsurance that working-class Americans continue to struggle to pay. How many of us have insurance, but we put off screenings or non-emergency procedures because of the high out-of-pocket costs? There is a great need for affordable supplemental insurance.

One factor that would lead me to embrace Senator Sanders' Medicare for All plan more openly would be the continued unethical behavior by hospital systems savagely going after patients through lawsuits, property liens and turning them over to collection agencies for outstanding balances that many simply are unable to pay. The media has recently, in my opinion, begun to do a much better job of covering the numerous horrific situations for patients in which they face very aggressive collection practices by hospital systems throughout the nation (Levey). It's important to note that many of these hospitals are nonprofits and are required to provide a certain level of free care or financial assistance for those who are poor or indigent. There are cases in which patients with low incomes would actually qualify for financial assistance, but the aggressive hospital billing departments too often don't assist these patients, and instead, send these accounts straight to collection agencies (Levey). These individuals and families simply are unable to pay these often-astronomical charges. The incidents that many of us have read in the news or seen on television detail the catastrophic financial results on working class citizens due to these heavy-handed practices by hospitals to obtain full payment. People have had their exceptional credit, built over a lifetime, destroyed because of medical bills they can't afford to pay back. Some have lost their homes or property to hospitals who have sued them for non-payment. Talk about a case of "David versus Goliath." Hospital systems are very wealthy organizations that have vast resources to pay collection agencies and attorneys to go after everyday Americans. These practices need to be stopped through legislation as soon as possible. We need to find that right balance in which hospital systems earn enough to sustain and improve their services, while keeping costs reasonable for consumers without these aggressive collection tactics.

I believe we need a healthcare insurance system in which Americans can obtain affordable insurance that requires only small co-pays, deductibles, and co-insurance payments. The maximum out-of-pocket per year should be $1,000 for each covered family member. No more than that and below a certain income level it should only be $500 annually in out-of-pocket costs allowed. Yes, these may be arbitrary amounts that I am proposing and there would need to be more analysis conducted. I am basing these amounts on my personal experiences as someone who earns a middle-level salary (below six figures). It came as a shock to me personally that I could have insurance for myself and my family, yet the coinsurance and co-pay amounts could so very quickly increase to thousands of dollars. There were a few Emergency Room visits for a family member that resulted in additional out-of-pocket charges of over $2,000. Of course, what often happens is when one family member has an unexpected medical charge, then others in the family put off medical care, tests, or screenings. One of the problems with the current health insurance system is that even for individuals with health insurance coverage, the out-of-pocket expenses can still render access to complete care too expensive. It is important to point out that the issue of receiving affordable healthcare is magnified for those who can't afford health insurance and do not qualify for public programs like Medicaid in their states. Therefore, these uninsured populations sometimes only access proper medical care in an Emergency Room setting. As many experts point out, if the uninsured could access healthcare on a regular basis, we could eliminate some of the expensive surgeries and interventions that result when these individuals can only access care when medical issues develop into true medical emergencies. We need affordable healthcare for all citizens and for immigrants who are on a path to citizenship.

We also need to discuss the expense of medications that can be too cost-prohibitive for some to access. I concur that pharmaceutical companies should be paid adequately for the services and medications that they provide. The issue is that Americans pay significantly more for drugs than citizens in other nations (Hughes and Rapfogel). As I always say, I want the pharmaceutical companies to make millions of dollars in profit for the wondrous, miracle drugs that they develop, but not billions at the expense of Americans who can't pay for the treatments and the medications that they need in some cases just to literally survive. Yes, there has to be that market incentive for pharmaceutical companies to develop all these new life-saving drugs, but we must find a way to maintain this incentive, while also ensuring that every single patient who needs these drugs can afford to purchase them. Having a health insurance or prescription drug plan that covers the costs of drugs is important for patients, but I do think it is more important for drug companies to simply do more to reduce their very high prices. I want to note that when I discuss affordability for patients to be able to purchase medications, it is important to stress this means the ability to buy drugs in the amount recommended by the drug maker or a patient's physician. All too often, we hear of people in dire financial situations in which they cannot afford to purchase a drug in the proper dose or supply. They have to choose between paying their rent or purchasing the fully recommended supply of a medication that they need. It can be dangerous to the health of patients if they miss doses or must take smaller doses than prescribed because of the high cost of their medications. We want all citizens to have the ability to access the medications that they need in the appropriate supply and dosage without it causing undue financial stress on them.

## Conclusion

In closing, some say that medical care is a right and I don't disagree with them in theory, but we still have to find a way to fund it at a level which ensures that all citizens receive the highest quality medical care that our advanced American system has the ability to provide. I leave the reader with this opinion: If we as Americans cannot find a method to pay for healthcare that doesn't result in citizens having to choose between getting a medical test, buying their medication, or buying groceries for their families, then I would support some type of Medicare for All system, such as the one endorsed by Senator Bernie Sanders. I am certainly no health insurance expert, but it is obvious that something must be done to reduce costs for patients.

My vision for the optimal health insurance system would be one that has a spectrum of coverage options, including private insurance, Medicare, Medicaid, and a public option for those who don't qualify for Medicare or Medicaid. Also, as mentioned above, I would like to see supplemental insurance plans play a larger role in our health insurance system. Supplemental insurance is needed to cover co-pay, coinsurance and other out-of-pocket medical expenses that are not covered by patients' primary insurance plans. There are supplemental insurance plans available for critical care needs, long-term care, accidents and to cover other medical conditions. What I am envisioning here is something similar to the Medicare supplemental plans that provide gap coverage for medical services that basic Medicare does not cover. This type of affordable supplemental insurance would cover all supplemental costs for anyone not covered under Medicare or Medicaid. American families are having a tough time with high inflation and even an out-of-pocket hospital charge for an additional $1,000 to $2,000 can really be a financial burden for many. I see these supplemental insurance plans as a key in addressing the high out-of-pocket costs that citizens face today with insurance plans in their current forms. These supplemental plans could base premium rates on income level and could be offered through governmental or not-for-profit organizations. Hopefully, supplemental insurance could be funded through consumer premiums with possibly minor or moderate funding support from state and federal governments. Finally, supplemental insurance could be a tool that enables many Americans to access the preventative care and non-emergency care that they need without any significant out-of-pocket financial charges. There would of course be an overall financial benefit if more citizens sought preventative care and screenings, rather than risking undetected health conditions developing to the point that they must be treated with more invasive and costly procedures. Also, we want to ensure through regular medical insurance plans or through specific prescription drug plans that consumers only have to pay nominal out-of-pocket payments for the medications that they need. A key component to having a successful drug plan environment is for there to be negotiated pricing with the drug companies to ensure a fair balance between profit for the companies and affordability for patients.

The reality is that Americans at the end of the day just want quality healthcare at a price that they can afford for themselves and their families. As so many have pointed out when discussing this subject, Americans just want the system fixed. Let's get started.

# 16. Liz Cheney – A True American Patriot and Hero

After Liz Cheney lost her Wyoming seat in the U.S. House of Representatives Republican primary on Tuesday, August 16, 2022, her speech communicated a call to action to the people of Wyoming and the rest of the nation to join in the fight to protect our free electoral system. Former Representative Cheney has consistently shared a message that supporting the prior president's false claim that he was somehow cheated out of a second White House term is a serious threat to our American form of democracy. It is shocking and sad that many Republicans continue to claim this falsehood, even after the insurgent attack on our Capitol on January 6, 2021.

I agree that when we have an increasing number of elected leaders falsely claiming that elections are unfair or "rigged," it truly threatens the survival of our Founding Fathers' experiment in free elections. Representative Cheney was appropriate in her speech, citing the Civil War and the intention that was needed by President Lincoln and General Grant to ensure the union survived (Fung). While I don't subscribe to the opinion that others have expressed that we are close to an actual new civil war with fighting in the streets, it is not overly dramatic to conclude that we are at least in a critical juncture right now as our nation deals with extreme levels of political divisiveness. We need strong leadership to bring Americans together to reinforce our bond of freedom underneath our umbrella of a united union.

The answer to achieving an environment of common ground and civility for Americans who are so divided right now is for our elected leaders to follow Liz Cheney's example and reject "The Big Lie" propagated by President Trump and his inner circle. The "Big Lie" is of course the claim by former President Trump that he was cheated out of his second presidential election victory. Once our leaders say, "no more" and stand up for our Constitution with its free elections, instead of trying to subvert fair election outcomes to win, we will be back on the right track. Many will say our politicians will continue to follow the Trump train to reap the benefits at the expense of democracy. I think with Liz Cheney's leadership, at least some others will follow and choose to step forward and reject unfounded claims that our electoral system is broken. This is my hope at least.

### Where Liz Cheney Walks Others Are Beginning to Follow

Liz Cheney by rejecting to follow President Trump's antics has started a new beginning for our country. Yes, admittedly, we still have the majority of Republicans who seek reelection continue to try and appease the Trump base with claims that the 2020 presidential election was stolen.

Of course, significant numbers of these same Republicans acknowledge in private circles that they know the truth – former President Trump did lose the 2020 election to Joe Biden (Davis). However, even with Mr. Trump's new wave of support following his legal troubles and New York indictment (regarding the hush money payout to adult movie star Stormy Daniels using campaign funds), the fact that other leaders are now announcing their candidacies to become the Republican nominee for president in 2024 is a positive sign. These Republican leaders who plan to run against Donald Trump for president are still careful with their words, but the very fact that they are opposing his candidacy does say something about a general desire by the party to move away from the more reckless and divisive nature of "Trumpism." The candidates who have announced or are exploring the possibility of running include very high-profile Republicans. They include Nikki Haley, the former Governor of South Carolina, and United States ambassador to the United Nations under President Trump; Asa Hutchinson, the former Governor of Arkansas; Mike Pompeo who served as CIA Director and Secretary of State under the Trump Administration; Tim Scott, an African American, U.S. Senator representing South Carolina and Ron DeSantis, the current Governor of Florida. Also, on this list happens to be former Vice President Mike Pence who of course served in the Trump White House in this capacity. I thought it would be useful to this discussion to highlight these individuals because they are long-term Republicans who have held or do hold high political offices or positions in the nation. These are not little-known or fringe candidates that are contemplating running against the former president. It is true that they watch their words very carefully when it comes to how they speak about President Trump, but again the fact that they are publicly even considering running (Haley and Hutchinson have already thrown their hats in the ring as of the writing of this essay) against the former president, shows that Republican leaders are gently moving toward a post-Trump era for the party and nation. These potential candidates are not as open as Liz Cheney in their rejection of President Trump's harmful statements and actions that have contributed to such incivility in America currently, but I think it is a good sign of change for the better. Liz Cheney has laid the groundwork for others to follow in the process of rejecting Trump and his divisive manner and distractions, so we can properly address real issues affecting everyday Americans. We need a Republican party that does not carry out its business with false statements, controversies, and conspiracy theories, but a party that has legitimate and well-organized, formulated policies. I may not agree with all the Republican policies, but in the pre-Trump era, the Republican Party could always be counted on for being overall honorable, ethical, and fully dedicated to the ideal that our government should carry out its functions fully in alignment with our Constitution and system of government for the betterment of the American people.

**The Judicial System's Role in Providing Oversight on False Claims of a Stolen Election**

The hope is that more Republican leaders begin openly rejecting former President Trump's continued claim of being cheated out of victory during the 2020 presidential election. Liz Cheney has shown her tremendous leadership and patriotism in so openly opposing Trump's false claims. This demonstration of selflessness is clear, given that Representative Cheney took such a staunch stance against Trump given that she was seeking re-election in a pro-Trump Republican state.

It is important to point out that while Republican leaders have been overall slow to reject the dangers of "Trumpism," a third branch of government outside of the executive and legislative branches has stepped up to protect freedom. Americans who support our system of government should be thankful to our Founding Fathers who set up a system with checks and balances. The judicial branch of our government has effectively acted as a check on Trump's threat to America's presidential voting process. Our legal system (at both the federal and state levels) is now confronting and addressing these false statements regarding the 2020 presidential election by President Trump and his close supporters. We see that Dominion Voting Systems is now in 2023 involved in a $1.6 billion defamation lawsuit against Fox News whose on-air personalities have continuously and falsely claimed that rigged voting machines handed the 2020 presidential election to Joe Biden (Rubin). Fox News perpetuated the ridiculous claim that the election "was stolen" from former President Trump. In addition, the district attorney's office of Fulton County Georgia is investigating the Trump team (and Trump himself) regarding Donald Trump's efforts at influencing the outcome of the 2020 presidential election in Georgia (Kates). The reality in Georgia is that Joe Biden won by a slim, but clear majority. Trump's "perfect call" to Georgia's Secretary of State Brad Raffensperger asking for help with votes is now famous (or infamous) for demonstrating what any candidate running for any office should not do as part of the election process. When we add in the many insurrectionists being criminally charged and then receiving serious prison sentences, I think our judicial systems at both the state and federal levels are acting as they were intended to in providing appropriate levels of checks on the sinister intentions of the former president. Yes, our wise Founding Fathers included a robust and strong judicial branch as part of our system of government that has quite skillfully risen to this occasion of unconstitutional and potentially criminal acts by former President Trump. The former President of the United States attempted to retain his office by using methods that are simply clear violations of the fair and free electoral processes that are set out in our Constitution.

Representative Cheney has expressed her disapproval consistently on President Trump's antics and divisiveness, including specifically the former president's involvement in encouraging an insurrection. In addition, she provided significant support in the legal realm by serving as vice chair on the United States House select committee, created to investigate the insurrection at the

U.S. Capitol on January 6, 2021. Liz Cheney performed in this capacity on this committee as she was defending her seat in the Wyoming Republican primary election in a pro-Trump state. Clearly, she realized that with her anti-Trump stance, she had a slim chance of retaining her House Congressional seat. The work this committee performed of collecting hours of video testimony and innumerable documents provided very important information in communicating President Trump's misdeeds when it came to the insurrection on January 6, 2021. The televised hearings that the January 6th Committee held, provided some very compelling testimony that plainly communicated to the American people how reckless President Trump behaved on this day. I was both enthralled and educated from personally watching the televised hearings provided for the American public. The work Liz Cheney did on this committee led to a recommendation to the U.S. Justice Department that President Trump be criminally charged with obstruction and conspiracy regarding his behavior in attempting to stop or delay the electoral count on January 6, 2021.

The information gathered by the January 6th Committee detailed in length Mr. Trump's schemes at claiming that he was cheated out of a legitimate victory, as well as his efforts at encouraging Vice President Pence to take actions to block the legitimate, presidential electoral vote count. The recommendations also stated that President Trump should be charged criminally per his role in supporting and encouraging this insurrection against the United States that manifested in violence and anarchy at the U.S. Capitol on January 6th. Liz Cheney played a major role in ensuring that a comprehensive body of evidence was collected. This large amount of evidence is now being reviewed by Jack Smith, the Special Counsel appointed by the U.S. Justice Department, who is overseeing the criminal investigations regarding President Trump for both his actions on January 6, 2021 (Cohen, Perez, Murray and Grayer), as well as the former president's handling of confidential documents belonging to the U.S. government. I would encourage the reader to review the findings of this committee per the following website:

www.govinfo.gov/collection/january-6th-committee-final-report?path=/GPO/
January%206th%20Committee%20Final%20Report%20and%20Supporting%20Materials%20Collection

This was a case of the legislative branch acting as a quasi-judicial review body whose work is assisting the Justice Department in possibly charging the former president with serious crimes. Representative Cheney's insistence on putting the interests of the nation ahead of her own political career, as demonstrated by her work on this January 6th congressional committee, (investigating the insurrection at the U.S. Capitol on January 6, 2021), should be applauded by all Americans.

**Recognition for Adam Kinzinger**

I do want to include some recognition here for former Republican U.S. House of Representatives member Adam Kinzinger from Illinois. The Air Force veteran who served in Iraq and Afghanistan refused to follow along with Trump's false claim that the 2020 presidential election was stolen (DeBonis). Mr. Kinzinger regularly criticized President Trump for creating a more divisive environment in our nation through his insulting rhetoric against his opponents, as well as the former president's dissemination of false narratives, clearly created to achieve his political goals. Representative Kinzinger was one of a small number of Republicans including Representative Cheney who voted to impeach President Trump over his role in inciting the insurrection on January 6, 2021. Like Liz Cheney, Adam Kinzinger put his love of our democratic system and our Constitution ahead of political partisanship. He spoke out against Trump's behavior when the vast majority of Republicans would not and still won't. Kinzinger realized that by speaking out, it would be virtually impossible to be re-elected. He gave up any immediate political ambitions to do the right thing and oppose Trumpism in all its forms. As a veteran, Adam Kinzinger displayed his bravery by serving America in real war settings, but he also demonstrated great fortitude by standing up against the false claims by former President Trump. Mr. Kinzinger refused to go along with the fairy tale that the 2020 presidential election was stolen from Mr. Trump and, therefore, should also be recognized along with Liz Cheney as a true American hero.

## Conclusion

I want to point out in closing that my argument supporting the admonishment of those claiming that "The Big Lie" is true, in no way diminishes my full support of candidates' ethical and legal right to question an election process or outcome if there are legitimate claims or concerns. The United States is set up upon a system of fairness in elections. I wholeheartedly support any and all candidates, regardless of political affiliation, and the citizenry to express their right to question the outcome of elections if there are rational arguments to do so. However, in this situation the concern is that so many are incorrectly claiming that the election was stolen from President Trump, that it is leading unfairly to a lack of trust by portions of the population on the integrity of our electoral system. The former president and his team submitted many legal challenges that the courts found to be illegitimate. Indeed, just because President Trump and his supporters claim that he was cheated out of victory does not make it so. In this era of spin and false narrative-making, we must reject this false claim from a charismatic President Trump that his second presidential victory was somehow stolen from him. As a people, we must demand from our candidates and one another that when a candidate loses in a fair process, the candidate and his supporters accept the outcome. This is how a democratic Republic works. Leaders like Liz Cheney remind us that we do not live in a "banana republic" but in the United States of America and accepting defeat in a fair election is "as American as apple pie."

I do not agree with a lot of Liz Cheney's political stances, as I did not agree with her father, former Vice President Dick Cheney on some of his more Republican, conservative policies. Yet, I do not doubt this family's love of country and their dedication to the U.S. Constitution and our formal, as well as informal, systems of national government that are so deeply rooted in individual liberty and fair justice for all of our people. Some may say that I am going too far as a moderate Democrat in my support of a conservative Republican, but I would vote for Liz Cheney based on her understanding of the intentions of our Founding Fathers, as well as her desire to ensure the continuation of our national government, for any public office. When former President Trump and his followers attempt to claim victory in an election that he actually lost "fair and square," the constitutional Republic that our Founding Fathers created must be protected at all costs. This includes putting allegiance to the federal government of the United States over allegiance to any political party. My allegiance to Liz Cheney is firm as she spoke out to protect us from Trump's threat to freedom while others did not. Elizabeth "Liz" Cheney is an American hero who has worked tirelessly as a protector of our freedom. The United States needs her and people like her to serve in our national government. I look forward to seeing her back in the United States Congress or even in a future run for the White House.

# 17. Too Many Greedy Charities and the Charities That I Endorse

### Recurring Monthly Donation Requests

A few years back I was walking into a grocery store and a polite young lady was out front asking for donations to fund an animal rescue organization. Like a lot of Americans, I don't carry cash a lot because we all use debit cards, but that day I remember having a five-dollar bill. I attempted to hand the young lady the money, but her response was that they were only signing people up to give a certain amount each month. I explained I wasn't interested in that, but she could have the five dollars. To my surprise, she declined. Since then (and the name of the organization will remain nameless here) I have vowed not to give this organization funds. Any charity who wants a donation only if it is a certain amount and, in the manner, it requires (i.e. a monthly donation/payment) apparently doesn't need funds from me.

We have all seen the advertisements on television for save the endangered animal or for a disabled veterans' fund. There are so many truly great causes that do need financial support from the public. Some of these organizations do accept one-time donations, but the main focus increasingly is on providing a monthly donation. I just think this is asking too much of many potential contributors and, in my opinion, comes across as inappropriate. Many people want to donate. The amounts they give are determined by their level of passion for a given organization and, of course, their personal financial situations. Most Americans work very hard for their money. When an organization asks for a larger monthly payment (thinking of the $20 or higher range), it comes across as greedy and demanding. I also wonder if these fundraising organizations realize how much in potential contributions they are losing from people like me, who are not interested in a monthly payment which essentially turns into another monthly bill. Yes, another monthly bill to pay is what we all want and need, right?

The donation requests that seem to me to be more attractive to working class people, are the dollar donation requests or the round up to the next dollar programs that some retailers are sponsoring, that can be selected by the customer when paying at the check-out machines. I give a lot of credit and kudos to Walmart and CVS that have these round-up and dollar donation options. Some retailers like Family Dollar asked patrons if they wanted to donate a dollar and purchase a snack or drink for a first responder or hospital staff member during the COVID-19 pandemic.

I do want to stress that there are a large number of credible non-profit and charitable organizations that work miracles to find cures for diseases, protect the environment or even help people with the exorbitant expense of attending college. Many of us can and should give a dollar here or five dollars there on occasion to a good cause. If everyone who can donate just gives a small amount, it really can add up to millions of dollars to fund altruistic endeavors. My simple request to those organizations limiting donations to basically a monthly subscription service is that they rethink their strategy. Especially in these times of high inflation in which families are trying to make ends meet, adding basically another monthly bill on to the pile will increasingly lead potential donors to donate elsewhere.

We can create a donation environment that funds these great organizations without using high pressure sales tactics. Sure, have the monthly donation as an option for those interested and able to donate in that amount. However, we must return to the basic tenet of honest charitable organizations – "any donation big or small is gratefully accepted."

### Charities That I Endorse

I wanted to just briefly discuss some charities that I really feel do good work. These organizations that I am highlighting I endorse based on a variety of factors, such as my personal experience with them, their general reputation as performing quality work in a cost-effective way, and, of course, whether they seem to request funding in an honest, low-key manner. I want to stress that this is a subjective list and other sources, or consumer protection organizations may have invested more time in researching a large variety of nonprofits. My suggestion to the reader is simply to do your own research before donating any of your hard-earned money. A quick internet search of any of the organizations that I discuss will bring the reader quickly to the homepages providing information about the organizations and how to donate.

The top of my list is first the March of Dimes, a nonprofit organization which for decades has been dedicated to providing services to expectant mothers and newborn babies. The goal is to ensure that regardless of income or other disparity, such as race, mothers receive the services they need to support their health and the health of their newborns. The March of Dimes provides educational programs to mothers and families to help foster healthy pregnancies, as well as the funding of medical research to prevent birth defects and premature births. This nonprofit has always had the reputation in its eighty-five-year history of being honest with the vast majority of funding going to help mothers and babies, not to fund lavish salaries and other overhead components.

Secondly, I do have a very high opinion of St. Jude Children's Research Hospital. Typically, I frown on excessive advertising from charities and St. Jude is one of those charities that you see on television (I've even started seeing their ads on YouTube) on a regular basis, but they really provide exceptional services. The successful treatment of life-threatening diseases in children, such as cancer and immunodeficiency diseases among other conditions, is an endeavor that everyone should support. I think the commercials are great in that they show the children who have been helped by St. Jude. Also, the interviews of parents, who have very sick children, display the relief and gratefulness that these parents have, when St. Jude Children's Research Hospital saves their children's lives. If any charity is performing God's work, it is St. Jude Children's Research Hospital. Finally, all families who have dealt with the serious illness of close relatives, too often, have not only the stress of worrying about their loved ones, but also the financial worries. It is truly a testament to the caring environment of St. Jude that families never receive a bill from this hospital ("Is St. Jude really free?"). This is why I have given to St. Jude Children's Research Hospital and plan to give again to this honorable and ethical charity that is saving children's lives every day.

A third charity I have a high opinion of is the Red Cross. I have recently found out that many nations have a Red Cross nonprofit agency that is one of the first responders on the ground when natural and manmade disasters occur. We have the American Red Cross in the United States that responds to people in need, helps increase the blood supply for medical need, as well as provides safety classes to the public (CPR and lifeguard training come to mind). Currently, the Red Crescent organizations for Syria and Turkey are helping with the earthquake disaster that has killed thousands in those nations. One of the many aspects that I find admirable about the Red Cross organizations in different parts of the world is that they intentionally adjust to align with the cultures of the nations they serve. We have the Red Cross in the United States and the West to signify an association with the good deeds that Christians set out to do. Then, in the Muslim world the crescent replaces the cross to align with that culture and religion. Putting service ahead of religious association is an aspect of this organization alliance that is rare. When I say this, I am not condemning religious nonprofits like Franklin Graham's Samaritan's Purse. Religious organizations are often called by their faith to spread it to others. I do understand this, but the Red agencies perform a great service to communities by fitting in with their cultural and religious beliefs, which naturally facilitates getting help as fast as possible to those in need.

I have just a few more organizations that I'd like to mention. Operation Smile is an organization that treats children who suffer from cleft conditions. Children born with this condition have a gap in their upper lip and/or in the roof of their mouth. This condition can make breathing, eating, and speaking difficult for these children. Also, they are more likely to be picked on or bullied for their facial differences. This organization provides corrective surgeries to some thirty countries throughout the world. Operation Smile focuses on medical training so local physicians have the ability to make these miracles happen for their own communities. In many of these countries, families cannot afford the surgeries, so this organization provides the surgeries free of charge to families. The services provided not only include surgery, but dental treatment and speech therapy. In addition, Operation Smile provides mental and emotional support services for these children at every step of the process from preparing for surgery to the recovery process after the procedure.

The last organization I'd like to mention is any food bank, soup kitchen or homeless shelter located in one's own community. Americans are very generous people, and we send money all over the world, but sometimes as they say, "charity starts at home." The local Christian Ministries organization in my county is known for the "soup kitchen" that provides meals to homeless and those in need every day. This organization I learned also provides groceries, clothing, and financial assistance to support basic living needs (utilities and rent). We all have local food banks and shelters that we can donate to through either our financial support or through volunteering our time. We do need places like homeless shelters to house those who have nowhere else to go when they lose everything due to loss of employment, financial stress or even drug addiction. However, I think we need to do more to help people with their problems before they get to the point that they are living in their cars or in a tent on a vacant lot. As inflation has soared, families are in more need now than ever. You may have noticed that homelessness is no longer just an issue for the big city, but now is a crisis in the suburbs and small towns. This is a change. As a commuter, I'm used to seeing the panhandlers along the major roads in the city, but in the past few years, I now see homeless individuals surviving in tents in the downtown area of my small hometown. Food, shelter, and mental health support are desperately needed by many in our communities. There are some very high quality, front-line, non-profit organizations that are located in the cities and towns where we live that perform miracles every day. We should all seek out these charitable organizations and give what we can to help out our neighbors in need.

## Conclusion

In closing, I want to say that there is a lot of need in the world. I have named a few of my favorite charities and welcome the reader to do a quick internet search to obtain information on these organizations and the many other quality charities performing exceptional work for people in need. My opinion is that those who are financially able should give, but those who really are struggling to simply take care of their families and themselves, should not be pressured by aggressive fundraising to donate to a charity. My philosophy is that if many of us just gave a few dollars, here and there, to a variety of charities and organizations in need, the impact would be tremendous. I want to stress that before donating to any charity, one should do some in-depth research. We want to donate to those organizations that will do the most good with the money we contribute and stay away from organizations that spend too much on "administrative overhead." If an organization does not use our funds overwhelmingly and primarily on providing direct service to the needs of those for which the donations are made, then it does not deserve our money. Finally, I have discussed above my favorite charities, but I welcome everyone who can, to contribute to the areas that call to them. Charities and nonprofit organizations do great work to reduce suffering and bring peace of mind to so many. Collectively, we can support these quality organizations that make miracles a reality for multitudes of people every day.

# 18. Afghanistan: Biden's Big Blunder

I don't think even the staunchest Democrat supporter of President Biden can honestly defend his actions of completely pulling out troops from Afghanistan in August of 2021. This situation was stable with a relatively small contingent of troops in the country. Girls were going to school and women were working if they chose (with or without having to completely cover their faces). The Taliban was kept at bay and the citizens of Afghanistan, both men and women, particularly in urban areas, had the ability to live life in relative freedom.

We all remember the horrific images of crowds rushing American planes attempting to get out of the country. Video footage showed what looked like a person falling through the sky, after unsuccessfully holding on to the outside of an airplane. This image seemed to represent the panic of the Afghan people who were being left to live under the extreme, Islamic rule of the Taliban. The situation resulted in U.S. soldiers becoming easy targets for the Islamic State (ISIS-K), as our defenses were obviously weakened during the withdrawal. Thirteen troops perished in the attack in late August of 2021 by ISIS-K (ISIS-Khorasan) on the Kabul Airport.

The policy that was in place was working. The U.S. had a small, but effective military presence in Afghanistan. This did improve communication and collaboration between the two nations to address the threat more effectively from terrorist groups. An argument could be made that through face-to-face interactions, the birth and spread of new terrorist groups was prevented. The majority of Afghans saw the U.S. as peaceful and helpful. When the United States quickly left the country, the Taliban just as quickly reversed the extension of individual rights that the West had brought to Afghanistan. Citizens were no longer able to pursue their personal and professional passions and pursuits. They had to begin to follow the rigid, religious indoctrination of the Taliban.

The greatest injustice that has occurred when the Biden Administration pulled out our troops from Afghanistan is how it left women and girls with no future. Girls now are not allowed to go to school. Many women are not able to work for fear of retaliation from the Taliban. Now, women and girls must cover their faces and bodies with not even the basic freedom to express themselves in their dress. The organization, Human Rights Watch (HRW.org) describes that life in Afghanistan in 2022 was dire with 90% of citizens being classified as "food insecure," leaving millions malnourished or sometimes not having any food to eat for entire days (*Human Rights Watch World Report 2023* *17)*. The Taliban is severely brutal to anyone who even questions its leadership or policies with numerous cases of torture and killings. Many have been killed by beheading, a grotesque, inhumane and barbaric act that simply does not belong in any twenty-first century civilized nation.

Major segments of the Afghan media have been shut down and women journalists are not allowed to work, leaving them unable to contribute to their chosen career field. Any media outlets that criticize the Taliban are met with strict punishment, so essentially Afghanistan has no free press.

Gay and transgender relationships are met with a hard line, thus members of the LGTBQ community are at great risk for their safety if they openly live who they truly are or even engage in a relationship with others in the gay or transgender community.

The current situation for women and girls in Afghanistan is dire. Women who are heads of their households have been left basically in poverty because they are unable to work to support their families. The Taliban has decreed that women simply cannot work and there are restrictions on their movement (they are required to travel only with a male relative chaperone). In addition, if a woman does not wear an Islamic face covering in public, she can be severely punished. There are reports of women being flogged in simply cruel public displays (Bubalo), obviously intended by the Taliban to send a message that the rights women gained under a U.S. supported Afghan government have been permanently rescinded. No, women are no longer allowed to play a role in the government either through work or being elected to their parliament. I refer the reader to a comprehensive list compiled by the United States Institute of Peace detailing the severe limitations on girls and women in Afghanistan now that the Taliban government is in complete control of the nation, after the U.S. withdrawal in 2021 ("Tracking the Taliban's").

Media outlets in the United States and the West have done a good job of highlighting the state of girls' education in Taliban-ruled Afghanistan. What has been reported is basically that there is no education for girls under the Taliban. The news program, *60 Minutes* did an excellent piece on a girls school that basically escaped the Taliban as the United States military was withdrawing (Stahl). The school is named, SOLA, short for School of Leadership Afghanistan. The word "sola" in the Pashto language also means "peace" ("In the Pashto language"). A co-founder of the girls school, Shabana Basij-Rasikh was a child when the Taliban first took over in 1996. She received education only in secret. When the Taliban rule ended in 2001 as the United States became involved in the nation (per our response to 9/11), Shabana was then able to formally continue her education which eventually led her to travel to the United States to attend college (please visit sola-afghanistan.org). Shabana eventually would earn a degree in International Studies and Women and Gender Studies from Middlebury College in Vermont in 2011, as well as then earning a master's degree in public policy from Oxford University ("Our Founder").

The *60 Minutes* episode was both inspiring and heartbreaking. The teachers and students knew it could be a very long time before they would see their families again (Stahl). Shabana Basij-Rasikh, a true international hero, had dedicated her life to developing this school for girls in Afghanistan. I can only imagine what it was like for Shabana and her staff to have to destroy all the records of the girls who attended the school before their escape. They had to take this extreme act in order to protect the families of the girls who could face severe consequences, such as beatings or even death if the Taliban found out that these families had sent their daughters to school (Stahl). Leslie Stahl's interview of Shabana and her students skillfully communicated the heroic journey of some 250 Afghans associated with the SOLA organization who fled Afghanistan as the government was falling to the Taliban in August 2021. I challenge anyone who thinks that the U.S. withdrawal was a good idea to watch this episode of *60 Minutes*. Realizing the danger these young women and very young girls were having to endure simply to continue their education, demonstrates the complete lack of concern by the Biden Administration for those we left behind. SOLA was able to escape and is now continuing to educate Afghan girls in Rwanda. The school has found a home. My only wish now for the school is that if it ever becomes necessary, the United States will have a place waiting for these brave women and girls in the "Land of the Free," where girls can grow up to do whatever they want in a free society that cherishes and protects individual liberty.

Now, there has been a lot of debate about what our U.S. intelligence agency was saying would happen if the U.S. pulled out and if the pre-Taliban government would survive. The reports that I have reviewed indicate that no intelligence agency held a primary belief that the Afghanistan government would collapse in just days after the U.S. military left, but there were serious concerns of Afghanistan's ability to hold off a resurgent Taliban threat. Given this realistic threat that Afghanistan would turn back into an Islamic terrorist state, President Biden's decision to leave was unacceptable. Some military officials, including General Mark Milley, chairman of the Joint Chiefs of Staff, expressed that they recommended to President Biden that he leave a small contingent of 2,500 U.S. troops in Afghanistan (Shabad, "Contradicting Biden"). Perhaps this small number of military personnel could have acted as a buffer to keep the Taliban at bay. My opinion is that, if needed, additional forces could be called in to push back Taliban forces. Having that presence in the nation could have kept its people, and particularly women, free. Instead, Afghanistan has returned to a barbaric land where its citizens have no rights, no political power and increasingly, no food.

I cannot end this essay without mentioning the lives of 13 United States military service members and some 170 Afghans who were killed by an ISIS-K terrorist bomb at the Hamid Karzai International Airport on August 26, 2021. The U.S. military was simply a very easy target at the Kabul airport as thousands of Afghans were basically rushing to the Americans in an attempt to exit the nation as it was quickly falling to the Taliban. I recall witnessing the horrific carnage on the news that I had never even heard of the organization ISIS-K. Islamic State Khorasan (ISIS-K) is apparently an Afghan sect associated with ISIS that targeted U.S. forces (Mir). However, it is notable that this terrorist group also considers the Taliban an enemy (Mir). Yes, the withdrawal of U.S. forces and our attempt to evacuate Afghans, such as interpreters who supported U.S. military efforts, created a frantic environment in which ISIS-K saw a clear opportunity to kill and did so. We lost one Navy sailor, one Army soldier and 11 Marines of the United States military and of our American family. I don't want to, of course, overlook the numerous Afghans who lost their lives during this attack by ISIS-K just trying to escape the tyranny of the Taliban. Yes, indeed, this event capped off a disaster in which President Biden's decision-making abilities continue to be questioned, particularly when it comes to our foreign policy.

## Closing

The decision to completely exit Afghanistan was wrong on many accounts. President Biden's stated view of the war in Afghanistan was clearly that we should have sought retribution against al Qaeda and Osama bin Laden for the attack on the United States on September 11, 2001, and that was it ("Remarks by President Biden on Afghanistan"). He has expressed essentially that he did not believe the United States should have attempted to nation-build in Afghanistan ("Remarks by President Biden on Afghanistan"). The problem I have with this is that when he assumed his role as president, President Biden did not take into account that we had been in this nation for two decades. We at that point did have a moral responsibility to the people (women and girls in particular) to ensure that their free way of life would continue. Now, if this could only be achieved at great cost to the U.S. in lives lost, I could understand his decision, but the situation was stable.

Also, continuing to have a presence in the nation, allowed the United States to be able to combat terrorism more effectively, and keep the threat of Islamic terrorism in check. Part of this effort involved convincing the people of Afghanistan to choose freedom over religious oppression. Our presence was transitioning a nation to choose western ideals instead of close-minded intolerance. I want to mention again my recollection of viewing on the news the image of an Afghan clinging to the U.S. military airplane on the actual outside of the plane. We could all see the individual literally clinging to a hope of freedom before falling off the plane to their death. This image of such frantic desperation will always be imprinted on my mind as long as I live. As an American, I feel we as a people have failed the overwhelmingly good people of Afghanistan. Afghans, like the vast majority of all citizens in our world, simply wish to live in a free society. A small contingent of our forces could have continued to ensure this in a stable manner. I also argue that it is incorrect to think that the United States can withdraw from this part of the world and assume that the terrorist threat to us will not manifest again.

Finally, we don't know that Russia would not have invaded Ukraine if the United States had not withdrawn from Afghanistan. Reasonably, however, the United States leaving this nation after twenty years could have been interpreted as a signal to the world that the U.S. no longer wanted to involve itself militarily in foreign affairs. Leaving Afghanistan was an act of retreating, and as someone who voted for President Biden, my hope was that America would re-claim its role of leader of the free world after the Trump Administration's refusal to call out despots, such as Putin and North Korea's Kim Jong Un. My hope was that the Biden Administration would re-invigorate our foreign policy as a leader of the world. Leaving Afghanistan did not send the message that America was back and ready to engage with the world and support those who seek to live in freedom.

In summary, I agree with both Republicans and some Democrats who have called for special hearings on President Biden's decision to leave Afghanistan and/or on how the U.S. withdrawal from Afghanistan was executed. Whether from a military strategic standpoint to keep Islamic terrorists in check or from a human rights standpoint, particularly when it comes to women's rights, President Biden made a crucial and inexcusable error. Finally, the loss of thirteen military lives in this botched exit must not be overlooked. President Biden's decision was poor and did not properly consider the risks to our service members. They paid the price because of this decision to exit Afghanistan. The nation was stable with our limited involvement. I do think President Biden has had some significant successes, and I do support his overall policy in Ukraine. Unfortunately, President Biden's disastrous decision-making in Afghanistan should disqualify him from serving a second term as commander in chief of the United States.

# 19. "Toxic Masculinity" On the Roadways

The other day after dropping my teenage son off at the gym, I was driving home on a back road traveling at the speed limit when a motorcycle swiftly approached my back bumper. The two-lane road at that point has a double-line in the middle, indicating of course that passing is not allowed. The young male driver quickly disregarded that indication and appeared to be traveling closer to 65 miles per hour rather than the 45 miles per hour posted speed limit. Driving a vehicle at a speed faster than the posted speed limit leaves the driver with less time to react to a variety of roadway challenges, such as an object in the road or an unexpected sharp curve. Excessive speeding can lead to serious vehicular damage or bodily injury. Motorcyclists should desire to drive safely due to the fact that if they get into an accident, they have nothing around them to provide any protection. This reality for motorcyclists is in sharp contrast to those driving in enclosed vehicles which are made of metal that provide much more substantial protection. Yes, if a motorcycle collides with an SUV (Sports Utility Vehicle) or truck, the motorcyclist will suffer the brunt of that accident with significant bodily harm or even loss of life.

A few days later, I was on a road with a speed limit of 35 miles per hour. This was in my local municipality and the police had put up one of their electronic signs that display the driver's speed as he or she approaches the sign. I drove carefully to ensure that I was traveling at the speed limit and did my best to follow this speed as the road takes a steep downhill approach for about a quarter of a mile to the stoplight. A young, male driver in a muscle car impatiently drove very closely to my back bumper, tailgating me all the way down the hill. Apparently, the implied message of the speed limit tracking sign did not encourage him to slow down.

I don't like the term, "toxic masculinity," as I think we have enough stereotypical trigger words these days. There are so many positive aspects to being masculine, such as standing up for the fair treatment of all citizens, defending and protecting others who cannot protect themselves, as well as demonstrating moral leadership to others. And, yes, regardless of one's sexual orientation or gender identification, these are attributes of all moral people.

However, the facts are the facts and males, especially young males, are statistically dramatically more likely to engage in risky driving behavior, such as speeding and aggressive driving. This behavior leads to higher rates of accidents and fatalities for young men, as well as endangering everyone else who comes into contact with them on our roads and highways. Any general internet search of the National Traffic Highway Safety Administration or other reputable sites makes this fact clear. According to the Insurance Institute for Highway Safety and the Highway Loss Data Institute (IIHS-HLDI), statistics for 2021 revealed that teenagers were about three times more likely to be involved in fatal car crashes than those over age 20, and two-thirds of all teenagers who died in car crashes were males ("Fatality Facts 2021"). This is not to say that women never drive aggressively (especially those in the younger age groups). They do, however, based on statistics and from personal experience (purely subjective, I admit), I would counter that it is just not on the level of aggressive, risky behavior that young men display.

—————————————

### Some New Approaches to Increase Roadway Safety

IN MY PERFECT WORLD, how would I address this serious safety issue? First, I don't think anyone under the age of 25 (male, female or other) should be able to drive certain vehicles, such as very large pickup trucks, full-size SUVs, and high-powered sports cars. Particularly, I think these super-sized trucks should be off limits to younger drivers. These trucks have continually grown larger in size each year it seems. The amount of destruction to other vehicles and people that these vehicles can cause is tremendous. Also, different states and different municipalities have different stances on the use of speed cameras, but we do need a national program to place speed cameras on a massive scale throughout the country. We must send a united, national message to super speeders – if you drive at excessively high speeds, you will pay financially through citations or worse. I go into more detail on my opinions of speed cameras elsewhere in this work, but here I want to emphasize that we must put the safety of children and families first ahead of anyone's "need for speed." An increase in the enforcement of the laws by a variety of methods, such as speed cameras, red light cameras and just more traditional stops by police is needed. As I always contend, the danger to others traveling our roadways does not come from drivers traveling five miles over the speed limit, but from the excessive speeders who are traveling 15 to 20 miles per hour over the posted speed limit on our roads consistently.

We should agree that we all need to drive safely when we get behind the wheel, but I argue that when we are discussing larger vehicles and vehicles that are designed for high speeds traveling on our roadways, safe driving is critical to public safety. These vehicles, because of their size or ability to travel at very high speeds can cause serious accidents on the roadways because of these traits. In order to drive an 18-wheeler or a vehicle carrying a large number of people or a vehicle transporting dangerous chemicals, a lot of us are at least somewhat familiar with the requirement that a driver must obtain a Commercial Driver's License (CDL). Many who travel on our nation's highways can attest to the fact that just possessing a CDL does not in itself guarantee that the driver of one of these specialized, large vehicles will always drive safely. I'm sure many of us have witnessed impatient drivers of large 18-wheeled trucks traveling a bit too fast or following too closely to the vehicles traveling in front of them. Yes, these drivers are not perfect just because they possess CDLs, but I am still in favor of the additional training that this specialized license category represents. These drivers must obtain the required training in which they learn how to safely operate these much larger vehicles that enables them to pass the CDL driving test, implemented by the North Carolina Department of Motor Vehicles (CDL requirements can differ by state). We require drivers operating the largest trucks and vehicles on our public roadways to obtain CDLs because of the risks that these types of vehicles pose to passengers (think children on school buses) and to other motorists. It makes sense that additional training and certification is required of these driver operators.

I do see the need for additional driver and safety training as part of an overall policy to create a safer traveling environment for everyone on our roadways. This environment does include pedestrians and bicyclists who so often must cross and navigate streets occupied with heavy vehicle traffic. These eco-friendly travelers are especially vulnerable with no protection if they are hit by cars and trucks on the road. I do think it makes sense for owners of very large pickup trucks and full-size SUVs, as well as sports cars that have engines of a certain caliber to be required to take at least some type of short, specialized safety class in addition to the regular requirements for obtaining a standard driver's license. This class requirement would be noted on their regular driver's license and would have to be re-taken every few years as long as they operate these types of vehicles. Now, I'm sure vehicle manufacturing companies, as well as some citizens, may not like this additional requirement for drivers which could dissuade some car buyers from purchasing one of these vehicle types. Perhaps car companies could actually collaborate with state motor vehicle offices to certify their staff to provide this training to customers. The car companies could use this new emphasis on safety as part of their overall marketing strategy to communicate that they are concerned about everyone's safety on our roads, not just making a quick buck. I do think additional training could be a useful component of a greater movement that re-emphasizes the personal responsibility of all drivers to not only protect their passengers and themselves, but all others on the roadways.

I want to provide a bit more explanation as to why I feel drivers of larger pickup trucks and full-size SUVs, as well as sports cars with stronger engines should require more driver training. These are vehicles that young men want for their size and/or power. The problem comes in when aggressive male behavior leads to higher rates of vehicular accidents which the statistics clearly demonstrate. When these larger, super-sized vehicles collide with smaller vehicles, the passengers of the smaller vehicles are at significantly greater risk of injury and death. It is just simple physics that the larger, heavier vehicles, when colliding with the smaller, lighter vehicles will win the battle and will cause much more damage to the smaller vehicles (and the people inside the vehicles). I am amazed at the large size of some of these trucks. I have truly felt threatened for the safety of my passengers on many occasions when these tanks have tailgated me so closely that when I look in my rearview mirror all I can see are their front grills. Yes, we do need more requirements for those driving these large vehicles. As far as sports cars, these vehicles that have higher horsepower and are capable of traveling at very high speeds, in my opinion, should require additional certification to drive. These vehicles by their very nature encourage faster driving, which is not only indirectly messaged through their design, but somewhat directly messaged through very clever marketing. Cars capable of such higher speeds should only be driven by those who have taken additional driver safety training. When we combine this type of vehicle with an aggressive driver, then naturally the chance of an accident increases. We see time and time again that drivers of sports cars drive them very fast. These types of vehicles are designed to handle curves very well, but my concern has always been that an inexperienced driver can too often misjudge and demand that a vehicle performs in a certain way that physics dictates cannot happen. We need the drivers of these sports cars to drive at safe speeds and slow down when driving through curves and on all road environments.

## Closing

In conclusion, I want to stress that not all young males drive aggressively. I do wonder as the pricing for these super-sized SUVs, full-size trucks and sports cars continue to increase, whether younger drivers will be less able to purchase them, thus reducing the number of very young drivers traveling in such large and powerful machines. Yet, the statistics don't lie and many of us have experienced the aggressive and dangerous behavior of these drivers. We need better training for citizens who drive these types of vehicles and better enforcement of our laws to ensure safer roadways. Finally, I'm sure that there would be opposition to passing such unique legislation, but we must have a serious discussion if a teenager is ready to drive certain vehicles given their size or temptation to be driven very fast. I submit that a person needs to be older to drive these vehicles and young drivers should start off with sedans, small trucks, or mid-sized SUVs. We should emphasize the need for "starter vehicles" for very young drivers. In my opinion, it should be illegal for anyone under 25 years of age to drive very large pickup trucks, full-size SUVs, and higher-powered sports cars.

I did want to communicate that on a human level I do get it. The feeling of driving very large or very fast vehicles is exciting and fun. One feels powerful and cool behind the wheel of such impressive driving machines. Even I find myself in my sub-compact SUV a bit envious of those with the apparent means to purchase such impressive "rides." Yet, there is a lot of responsibility that should be required in order to drive these very large or very fast-moving vehicles. These trucks, SUVs and sports cars can cause a lot of damage and harm to other vehicles and people on the roads that share the same space. The purpose of having vehicles to use on our public roadways is not to look cool or to go fast, but to safely transport people from one destination to another. If these vehicles present too much temptation to drive aggressively or to speed excessively, we should question whether they should be allowed on our public roadways. I don't think anyone wants that outcome, but we do need to drive these vehicles carefully and responsibly to ensure the safety of everyone traveling on our roadways. All of us need to take the pledge, regardless of the vehicles that we own, to drive safely and courteously. Together, we can create a driving environment in which all of us reach our destinations safely and without incident every time that we get into our vehicles.

# 20. Confronting Urban Sprawl's Takeover of Rural Areas

I live in the Charlotte, North Carolina region which is an area with a significant growing population. Areas around my rural town where I have lived most of my life have succumbed to the transformation from smaller towns into suburban hubs. This transition occurred some years ago. The town I live in which is further north and west outside of Mecklenburg County (where Charlotte is located) has managed growth well for some time. We have had increases in the number of subdivisions, but mostly in the eastern areas closer to Mecklenburg County. I have observed in the past five years, however, a dramatic increase in the number of housing developments throughout my county. The Charlotte region has finally discovered us, and it seems almost daily that another lot that was vacant or wooded is now being cleared for more housing. The question is always how much population growth can be allowed without an area losing its more rural way of life and its original character.

## Costs and Benefits of Population Growth

A brief review of my local planning/zoning department's web site shows that requests for numerous large housing developments are being submitted for approval. Always, it is a balance – growth is preferred to stagnation and decline, but when dramatic growth occurs, a jurisdiction no longer has those attributes that attracted long-time residents and newcomers alike to the area. Growth can be very good for the economy in a given municipality or community. New businesses provide additional jobs and significant amounts of property tax revenue, particularly when these businesses construct expensive new facilities. Additional property taxes that can be used to increase the availability of public services, thus attracting new businesses which hopefully provide high paying positions to a community, can greatly enhance the quality of life for residents. An increase in residential growth which can follow or precede industrial growth (businesses do need people to work at their companies) has more of a mixed result as far as the financial benefits and costs for a local community. New residents who move to a community do add to the tax base in the way of property taxes, but these taxes must be used to pay for the construction of more roads, schools, hospitals, wastewater treatment plants and other core infrastructure, such as underground utility pipes and cable lines. As the population expands, more services, such as police, fire and sanitation will be needed. Local governments, in my opinion, in relishing over the potential increase in the tax base from more residents arriving, don't fully consider the scope and the expense involved in supporting the services and facilities that an increase in residents will require. Every place is different and there are benefits to growth, such as a more diverse population, more entertainment and dining offerings, as well as a wider variety of retail shopping opportunities. The question is to what extent changing the inherent nature of a community should be a determining factor when making these planning, zoning and land use decisions for a local municipality or county? As far as the cost of residential growth, the approval of new housing developments should only occur if the population growth can be accommodated by the corresponding increase in the tax base to support the increase in demand on existing services and infrastructure. I do think a municipality should propose a limit to population growth on an annual basis in order to both protect the character of a community and to ensure the growth can be fully paid for by available tax revenues.

We are seeing a transition in population in many states from rural to urban areas as people find better paying jobs and opportunities in thriving "sunbelt" or mid-west cities. North Carolina is no different than many states and we are seeing in the first quarter of the twenty-first century that population density is increasing in the outer rings of Charlotte, Raleigh, and other mid-sized cities. We are experiencing this urban sprawl particularly in southern and western states where land outside of metropolitan areas is cheap compared to land closer to the central business districts (Levitt and Eng). A certain level of transformation as suburban areas become more urban is expected, but in great frequency we are seeing rural areas in the outer geographical rings adjacent to these urban areas being transformed seemingly overnight.

Smaller jurisdictions which may not have the extensive land use laws and policies of larger municipalities have to play catch up to challenge very aggressive development. Clearly some areas are losing the fight to retain an inherent rural or small-town environment that previously characterized the area for perhaps hundreds of years. We should expect some of this growth, and growth does have its benefits as I've stated above. It certainly is more desirable for a town or rural area to have growth in population rather than having a loss in population. There are of course towns in our nation that once they started to lose population the trend continued leading to the "death" of the towns. The issue on the other end of the spectrum occurs when there is too much growth, particularly in a short span of time. A large growth pattern in population that is happening very rapidly can wreak havoc on a town's infrastructure and culture. We have to determine how we balance the tendency or even the desire for growth against the call to preserve the inherent environment and culture of those long-time residents of an area. This is challenging but what is clear is that towns that have doubled in size within a decade have experienced great upheaval and their original identities have been significantly altered. Large municipalities are much better able to handle significant increases in population, as urban planners in these locations design their cities for higher density living. Smaller towns and rural areas are by their very nature not as able to absorb great numbers of newcomers without tremendous strain on their infrastructures and financial resources.

## Personal Experience with Population Growth

My experience recently is probably typical of those who have resided in an area for years or decades and explosive population growth occurs. I had always seen some new housing units here and there, but in my county and hometown, it was very gradual growth that we experienced. The community where I live has traditionally experienced gradual growth in population due to the attractiveness of its small-town lifestyle and proximity to the major metropolitan area nearby. The population growth in the past five years in my area has differed from the traditional trend in its intensity. This new type of fast-paced growth I like to describe as a snowball that at first is small, and then as it travels down a steep, snow-covered hill becomes a very large snow boulder. This huge snowball takes on an inertia all its own and is hard to stop. Initially, I'd see some new construction here and there for single-family houses, with a few segments of condos in the center of town. Then, what seemed to be all of a sudden, I noticed several new single-family and multi-family residential developments being constructed. Furthermore, it was just not that more developments were going up that were noticeable, but that it seemed in several areas including where I live, any wooded areas along the roadways, however small, were being cleared for either small one or two-unit apartments or for single-family homes.

The transformation can be seen in our rural area's now clogged roadways that unfortunately have not been expanded to meet the increased population. I began to arrive home from work and found that I really couldn't go workout at the gym for a few hours until after "rush hour," unless I wanted to deal with extremely heavy traffic. I have noticed except for very early in the mornings or later in the evenings, that when I go shopping at the grocery store or Walmart there are always large throngs of people. This is a big change from my once sparsely populated, country hamlet. I have become good at dodging others coming around the aisles at the store to avoid my cart from crashing into other shopping carts. As a runner, I still enjoy getting out in the fresh air on our local Rail Trail, but there are times now that it becomes so crowded that having to navigate all the people as well as their pets becomes challenging and frustrating. Dog walkers love to get out with their pets, and I don't blame them, but as more people have used our trail, this has also brought more people who don't clean up after their pets. I used to run on the side of the paved trail when lots of people were out so there was plenty of room; particularly this was the case when parents were strolling with their children and pets. Unfortunately, I had to stop running on the side of the asphalt trail in the grass because of all the dog excrement that was accumulating due to irresponsible pet owners who were not cleaning up after their pets. We are experiencing the normal issues that come with a transition to a higher density residential environment, but to some degree this transition can be more challenging in rural areas. Even though growth is happening, it's as if people still retain the mindset in a former rural area that, "there are not that many people around, so my dog's poop along the trail won't be a problem for others." In addition, unlike urban areas, there aren't comprehensive transportation plans to build more roads or transit systems to accommodate more growth in former rural areas that are essentially now suburban in nature. There are no new major roadways where I live, and yet multiple residential developments have either been built or will be built in the near future. The schools are starting to get very full. One might argue that smaller areas that are growing in population will never reach the large population size of cities, so they can absorb the comparatively smaller total numbers of newcomers arriving when compared to these overall figures for cities. However, the important factor is the percentage increase in population that is occurring in an area that can determine the level of reasonable growth for a small town. The infrastructure in a rural area truly needs a complete overhaul to adequately address a high rate of population growth, particularly when it occurs in a short period of time.

## Reasonable Growth

The scenic, small, and quiet town where I reside just doesn't seem quite as quiet and small as it was even five years ago. It is still scenic with a small-town Main Street that gives off a Norman Rockwell vibe. Unfortunately, with so many trees being cut down and farmland being transitioned to residential and business uses, significant natural beauty has been lost. I want to be clear that some growth in a small town in the vicinity of a metropolitan area is understandable and, yes, desirable for the reasons stated above. I am in favor of reasonable growth in non-urban areas. Reasonable and sustainable growth planning, in my opinion, for rural towns would consist of allowing a 0.5% increase in population growth annually. This percentage may seem too conservative for some, but each locality can determine this percentage given their own environmental factors and circumstances. This amount seems reasonable to me as I review an example of say 10,000 residents in a fictitious town. Even at 1%, this would be 100 additional residents. Would one notice this increase of 100 people in their smaller municipality of 10,000 residents? I would say, yes, that a small increase in congestion would be noticed. In addition, if we saw this 1% every year of 100 or more new residents, it could soon pose a challenge to current infrastructure in a few years (again for this small-town population of 10,000). Given a 0.5% growth increase of 50 people, this may not be noticeable at all. Yes, there can be different factors affecting the rate of growth that a community can absorb without experiencing significant congestion. I am not a planning professional, but it seems that having stated limits on population growth may be a reasonable way for a locality to maintain a rural way of life. In my ideal situation, this percentage of 0.5% growth annually could increase, but only by some type of referendum in which the majority of residents vote to approve the increase in population. For example, perhaps a municipality has the opportunity to land a major technology company that would bring many much-needed jobs to an area. If the company were to relocate, it would result in an increase over the 0.5% annual allowed population growth rate. The citizens could vote and decide that the growth in population would not only be acceptable, but desired, given the increase in the standard of living for current and new residents who are relocating to work at the new company office or plant.

I'd just like to see current residents have more of a say in how their communities are allowed to change. A "Population Plan" could be part of a town's Zoning Ordinance. Zoning maps and designations by local Planning Departments do a great job of sectioning out what kinds of housing and business activities can take place in each geographical area. I am just not convinced, however, that these local ordinances effectively address potentially uncontrolled population growth (at least not in my area of North Carolina). Part of the approval of any new single-family subdivision or other residential housing designation (apartments, condos, or townhomes) should have to meet the requirements of any stated population plan to curb overdevelopment.

## The Need for Affordable Housing in Cities

I want to take some time to address the obvious reason for urban sprawl. Metropolitan areas have become increasingly expensive places in which to rent an apartment and to purchase a house or townhome. People who cannot afford to live in a safe neighborhood in the city will look toward the suburbs and further out on the fringes of the metropolitan region for affordable housing. The issue of affordable housing continues to affect many cities. Yes, some people like me do prefer to reside in the quiet suburbs, but there are those who would love to live the exciting and vibrant urban lifestyle, but simply can't afford it. We need to find ways to develop affordable housing options that are comfortable, adequate in space and that are safe for lower to moderate income citizens. An array of affordable housing is needed to meet the needs of people who are at different life stages. Recent college graduates, young families and senior citizens all have distinct needs and desires when it comes to housing. The development of more affordable housing is not an easy feat, but I do think more can be done to achieve this dream. Residential developments that are funded by both public and private non-profits can help to lower the price of housing for residents in urban areas. I would also like to see businesses and industries that are located in a city provide housing "bonuses" to their employees so they can live in a safe and comfortable home. I personally like the idea of a basic living income for those at a certain income level, provided by the local city or county government that could help families to afford housing in the city. Many families could use an extra $1,000.00 per month to help pay for rent or pay their monthly mortgage payment. The lack of affordable housing in metropolitan areas is a real dilemma in cities across America, but we simply have to continue to find ways to solve this problem.

## Closing

In closing, I want to point out that there are situations when localities do and should take in greater numbers of people, such as when citizens are fleeing natural disasters in their home states (Hurricane Katrina comes to mind), or refugees from Latin America, Afghanistan or Ukraine are fleeing potential persecution or great suffering in their home nations. I do believe that communities should open their doors during these times. Aside from these events, I contend that the desire of long-time citizens in a rural area to protect their way of life and environment should be respected. When an area experiences too much growth, the lifestyle and culture can change dramatically in a very short period of time.

I am a capitalist and I do believe in the benefits of a free market system. We truly do need real estate developers who build wonderful houses and businesses for our twenty-first century lifestyles, but the desire to build a very large number of residential units in an area must be balanced with the infrastructure available to absorb the new residents. The question as to whether the size of a new development will fit in with the current atmosphere of the community should be addressed by the developer before the project is approved by the local planning board. We also need to require these real estate developers to offset at least some of the additional infrastructure expenses through application fees or by providing affordable housing units to lower income individuals and families.

There are a lot of interests involved when it comes to determining an acceptable population growth rate for an area. We have the interests of the citizens who have lived in an area for generations, the desire of newcomers to live in a place that is attractive because of its lifestyle or geographic features and the business interests of real estate developers who, to be fair to them, are in the business of building housing in areas where people want to live. The balance must be found in allowing for sustainable growth, while protecting the attributes, such as a small town feel or rural lifestyle, that are attracting new people and businesses to a given area. In my opinion, managed growth is a sign of a healthy town or municipality since this is an approach that keeps a check on the problems of uncontrolled population growth, while also reaping the benefits of growth, such as more entertainment options and healthy interactions between diverse peoples. It is up to the citizens of each small town, mid-sized municipality, or major metropolitan area to determine what rate of growth is acceptable for them.

Finally, regardless of what level of growth a given community desires, we all have a responsibility to welcome newcomers to our hometowns and cities and treat them well. Those of us who live in desirable places where others want to come are already fortunate. We can reach that balance of preserving our way of life, while also sharing our good fortune with others.

# 21. Flags Don't Belong on Cars

As Americans, we take pride in our right to individual expression. We do this freely through how we dress, how we choose to wear our hair and even in the types of vehicles we drive. We are the land of the personalized license plate. Expressing ourselves as we choose is our birthright as citizens of the United States.

However, I think it is time to regulate the flying of flags on personal motor vehicles. Regardless of the message, whether sports related or political, these flags do not belong on vehicles traveling on our public roadways. First, they are at the least a distraction to others – we certainly don't need anything else to distract us with everyone on their cell phones. Secondly, these are additional items that if not secured to the vehicles can fly off, potentially causing serious vehicle damage and physical harm to other vehicles and travelers on the road. The more items that are allowed to be attached to the tailgates or to the exterior of vehicles, the more risk there is of an accident occurring just due to human error.

One afternoon driving home from work, I was behind a pickup truck that was hauling a large variety of objects. One of the objects was an old charcoal grill. Fortunately, I was driving safely and was not tailgating the truck because all of a sudden, the wind picked up the grill and it landed right in front of me on the highway. I was able to stop my vehicle safely and travel around the obstacle. Too often I witness vehicles traveling very fast with loads of items on their truck beds or on their roofs that don't appear to be adequately secured to the vehicles. Drivers seem to be getting worse in carrying out their responsibility of securing their loads to the exteriors of their vehicles. We don't need to add flags flying from vehicles to this mix. Yes, I increasingly witness vehicles with what appear to be very large flags flying behind them, attached to their tailgates. If the flag and/or flagpole or flag mount were to break away from the vehicle, it could cause immediate damage to other vehicles following from behind. This is especially the case with vehicles traveling at highway speeds. Even if just the flag (without the mount) were to break off from a vehicle, as large as some of these flags are, it could land on the windshield of another vehicle, causing a serious visual impairment to that vehicle's driver.

A third reason I am against allowing these flags to be flown from vehicles involves the flags with overtly political messages. I am thinking of the Confederate flags specifically, but political flags in general that may trigger conflict between motorists of different political ideologies don't need to be displayed from vehicles on public roadways. I was driving one afternoon, and a large pickup truck passed me. It had a large Confederate flag as well as a President Trump flag, both waving in the wind attached to the truck's tailgate. Now, I would have the same comment with an extreme left-wing group that promotes violence, but the Confederate flag in particular is a symbol that brings about strong opinions and emotions in people. When I saw this truck, I really had to remind myself that my immediate goal was to drive safely, not to look over and react in any way to what for me is a political statement that I find offensive. I discuss elsewhere in this work my opinions on the Confederate flag, but I say even for those who support a pickup truck traveling on the roadways with this flag, it is clearly a distraction mentally from the main task at hand of driving safely.

I want to make a distinction here in that while one may disagree with the political message a flag represents to the viewer, I am in no way saying that an individual cannot fly the flag of their choice on their private property. The distinction, however, is that I omit from this category privately-owned vehicles that travel on public roadways. I live in the South and while the practice is not as widespread as in the past, we still have individuals who promote the Confederate flag. Across the street from my son's high school, someone placed a very large Confederate flag on a flagpole in the yard. I cringe when I go by it and sometimes comment the owner needs to put up a flag of our nation instead, but I concur that in the United States, this landowner has the right to express himself on his own property. The messages that we send, however, on our public roadways do need to be more muted because of this natural tendency of such political symbols to evoke strong emotions. Our roadways seem to be more crowded than ever, and motorists appear to be more impatient and ruder coming out of the COVID-19 pandemic. We are also now a highly divisive society politically and we don't need to "add fuel to the fire," as the saying goes. This is especially the case while we are traveling together on the same roadway in vehicles that if they were to collide with one another, have the potential to cause great harm and even death. I have, therefore, concluded that flags that promote highly charged, political messages which citizens may disagree about, should not be allowed to be flown from cars from a public safety concern.

We do and should value our right in this nation to express our individuality and our cars in America say so much about us. Yes, if you want to purchase a pickup truck, a sports car, or a fuel-efficient hybrid, you are free to express your personality and values in our nation. Feel free to pay more for that personalized license plate or even place small bumper stickers on the rear of your vehicle if you truly want to express a political opinion. I do contend that a line is crossed when motorists fly these super-sized, controversial flags attached to their vehicles. These flags that send loud in-your-face statements to others sharing the public road go too far. They trigger strong emotional reactions, both positive and negative, from other motorists. These flags distract us from driving safely.

In conclusion, I would ask our state and federal leaders to address this issue and ban the practice of flying flags from all vehicles. Whether it is cell phone use or what appears to be the ever-increasing number of electronic visual displays within our vehicle "cockpits," we must reduce driver distractions. Again, there is the risk that yet another item being attached to a vehicle could always fly off due to human error and cause damage to other vehicles or bodily harm to other motorists. In addition, we need to leave the roadways just for vehicles transporting goods and people, not to have political discourse and/or debate. After all, our roadways already have enough rage on them; we don't need to add politics to the mix, particularly during this time of such divergent political viewpoints.

Public safety must come first, and this requires eliminating anything from our vehicles and roadways that detracts from every driver's responsibility to drive in an attentive and calm manner. We want all citizens to arrive at their destinations safely for all motor vehicle trips on which they embark. Enacting legislation that would prohibit the flying of flags from vehicles is an important component of a comprehensive, national safe driving policy.

# 22. Abortion Rights of Women Need Protection (with a Caveat)

Men generally are told to stay out of the abortion debate. Women argue that this is about their right to make decisions about their bodies. I do agree that women should have this exclusive decision-making autonomy during the first trimester of pregnancy. However, I do think that the life of the unborn child should be considered as the fetus develops past this first trimester. My viewpoint also includes the notion that while I defer to a woman's fundamental right to an early abortion, I seldom see any consideration for the wishes of the potential father throughout the pregnancy, which is unjust.

### *Dobbs v. Jackson*

Personally, I disagree with the Supreme Court's overturning of *Roe v. Wade* (1973) in the case of *Dobbs v. Jackson* (2022). I think it went too far in overturning a woman's constitutional right to an abortion and basically leaving the decision to each state to determine independently if the procedure should be legal at all ("Dobbs v. Jackson"). My viewpoint is that I do think that abortion should be legal nationwide, but strictly limited after the first trimester. This first trimester in a pregnancy seems to be a reasonable interval point that balances the right of women to access abortion with a very early pregnancy, against the rights of the unborn who increasingly attain development after this first trimester period. The exceptions that I would exclude from this guideline would be in the cases of rape, incest or pregnancies of very young teens who may not fully understand early on that they are pregnant.

The other circumstances in which the procedure should be allowed past the first trimester, that have become problem areas stemming from the *Dobbs* decision, include when a miscarriage has occurred or when a fetus, because of birth defects, will be unable to survive on its own outside of the womb. Hearing about these nightmares that women are experiencing is heart-wrenching. These are women who want to be mothers, but sadly when a miscarriage occurs or in situations in which fetuses would not survive outside the mother's body (due to significant abnormalities and defects), they need the abortion procedure to protect their physical, mental, and emotional health. Women from states like Ohio and Texas are facing this harsh new terrain both physically and emotionally when they have a miscarriage. My understanding is that the more time between when a miscarriage occurs and the necessary medical abortion procedure to remove any remaining fetal material (known as a D & C, dilation, and curettage) is performed, the higher the risk to the life of the woman. Even states with the most limited access to abortion, such as Oklahoma, do allow abortion when it comes to saving the life of the woman, but, unfortunately, too often now abortions have been delayed or denied because hospitals and doctors are afraid of being sued or face criminal charges in the wake of *Dobbs* (Felix, Sobel and Salganicoff). Women must now be in extremely dire health situations before they can obtain access to this proper medical care. It appears that they virtually do have to be on the brink of death before an abortion is approved in some states. This is unacceptable and cruel. In my opinion, once a medical doctor deems an abortion is medically necessary to protect the health of the mother, the procedure needs to move forward without anyone having to fear being sued or arrested.

## Men's Role in Family Planning

I ALSO WANT TO MENTION with the new, more restrictive abortion laws in many states, that we need to focus on the proper use of birth control methods and in particularly, I call out men to be more responsible. Women too often are left with the responsibility of handling birth control. In this post-*Roe* world, women who become pregnant are at risk, as mentioned above, of suffering complications for which they may not receive adequate or timely medical care in many states. In order to prevent unintended pregnancies, men should share more of this responsibility of family planning. If a man is already a father and does not intend to father more children, a procedure called a vasectomy is an option that prevents the biological ability to impregnate a woman. It is a reliable and permanent birth control solution that does not interfere with a man's ability to fully perform sexually. Men need to take initiative when it comes to birth control. Indeed, even if a man is not in a situation in which a vasectomy is a desired option, he has a responsibility to communicate and cooperate with his partner in the selection and use of highly effective birth control, or even multiple birth control options when engaging in intercourse. Sex is a very personal matter. I believe due to the concern of having an unwanted pregnancy and the chance of contracting a sexually transmitted disease (I think the current term is "STIs" – sexually transmitted infections), that intimacy should occur mostly in the confines of a long-term relationship. Sexual activity within either marriage or a long-term, committed relationship can support honest dialogue about how best a couple should approach subjects like birth control. Of course, individuals who are not married or are not in committed long-term relationships sometimes do choose to engage in sexual activity with others. I, personally, would be a hypocrite if I judged those harshly who engage in sexual relationships outside of these more formal relationship formats. The right to express one's sexuality with another consenting adult is part of living in a free society. My only recommendation for these individuals would be that when they engage in sexual behavior that they use effective safe sex and birth control products. Men need to take responsibility and before they engage in casual relationships, should on their own have multiple birth control products available for them and their partners. Given the post-*Roe* world, men need to properly support women in this uncertain time to prevent unwanted pregnancies by using effective birth control. Not only is abortion becoming less available in many states overall, but in cases in which women need abortion procedures for health reasons, as discussed above, the reluctance of medical facilities to provide timely service leaves women's health very much at risk. Men need to do their part to protect the health of the women in their lives.

### The Plight of Possibly More Abused Children

I differ from many on both of the extreme ends of the political spectrum as far as my viewpoint on abortion rights. Particularly in the first trimester, I do think abortion should be infrequent, but legal. I have become almost distraught at what seems to be regular occurrences communicated on the nightly news, describing horrific cases of abuse and murder of infants and toddlers by parents or other adults. Some incidents are cases of neglect which make one wonder how anyone can treat helpless children in such inhumane ways. When one hears about children in the United States who die of maltreatment or not receiving proper medical care, it is infuriating. Then, there are the cases of parents or other adults in the household physically abusing children and typically this abuse occurs over long periods. Tragically, in some cases the physical abuse ends in the death of a child. I don't support the death penalty in theory, but when it comes to the intentional neglect and abuse of children leading to their untimely and cruel deaths, I believe I could be convinced as to the merits of this punishment.

I bring up the issue of abuse of children because the question arises as to whether abortion should be an alternative for women and couples who truly don't want children. If a child is born and will suffer up to the point of murder, the ethical question arises if the option of an abortion soon after conception, when we are still talking more about the potentiality of sentient life, is actually more humane than the suffering that will occur for the child after birth. Again, I am speaking here about this option only in the first trimester and I realize those on the political right would say that the child still has a right to be born even into this circumstance. I concede they have a valid argument, but I'm not quite there with them. Yes, in theory the idea is that we would want the child to be born and for him or her (or they) to be taken away from parents and adults who are abusive, but clearly that doesn't always happen. Our foster care system struggled with demand when *Roe v. Wade* was the law of the land. Now, in a post-*Roe* world, the concern is with an expected rise of unwanted births, that cases of abuse and neglect could increase. Sadly, more children could be murdered by their abusers without a tremendous influx of resources from the public and private sectors to better serve these children through the creation of a comprehensive safety net.

The post-*Roe* world is one in which access to an abortion has been seriously and significantly limited in many states. This new environment requires society to increase funding for services to ensure that children who are unwanted will be placed in proper care. This will include proper screening of mothers and families who display behaviors and attitudes indicating that they may harm or neglect their children, as well as following up with at-risk children in their first years of life. Of course, this leads to the need for a foster care and adoption system that will require more adults to take on roles in our society as caretakers of these children. I do agree with those who criticize anti-abortion protestors and "right to life" proponents who correctly argue that those who are emphatically against abortion need to stand behind their political statements. If they are completely against a woman's right to choose (whether or not to have an abortion), then they need to volunteer their time and/or financial resources to supporting children in fragile home environments. More citizens need to step up to support these children in need. These individuals need to back up their political stances and become foster parents, contribute to children's nonprofits, or even volunteer their time to their local schools and community centers. The problem is there are those who fight so desperately for children to be born, but once they are born, these anti-abortion supporters are nowhere to be found. Non-profit agencies will have to collaborate alongside social services agencies to care for unwanted and abused children. Now, if we develop this comprehensive childcare, safety net, the anti-abortion advocates will have more of a reasonable argument when they try to convince women not to have an abortion, but to give their newborns up for adoption.

An issue that we are debating right now concerns parents' rights and their say on what their children are being taught and being exposed to in our schools. Parents should definitely have a significant say when it comes to what and how subjects are being taught in schools, as well as hold school systems accountable for mistreatment, such as severe bullying, that their children experience while at school. Schools, however, it should be noted, are overall very safe spaces that are in the business of educating and caring for our children. It gets overlooked how well and how often schools go above and beyond to educate, feed, and protect our young people. We know that the vast majority of parents would do anything to protect their children, but as we realized during the COVID-19 pandemic when schools were closed, teachers and guidance counselors do act as a check on any abuse that may be occurring in their students' homes. This is one reason why I am against home-schooling. Again, the vast majority of parents love their children more than anything in the world – as a parent, I can attest to this, but when children are enrolled in a community school, there is that extra layer of protection for them by being seen every day by adults other than their parents. Now, I don't know a lot about home schooling requirements, and I'm sure they differ by state, but even if there is an occasional home visit by a local school or social services agency, it isn't the same as a child being seen every day at school. My point here is that home is not always a safe place for children, and more people having unwanted children is a new reality that will demand more services from schools, social service agencies and even law enforcement to ensure that children are protected from abusive parents or other abusers in the home.

## Concluding Thoughts

There is no easy policy solution to this highly contentious issue for which so many have very passionate opinions on that will satisfy everyone along the political spectrum. This spectrum ranges from those who basically want all abortions to be essentially illegal, to those who want a woman's right to choose paramount well past the first trimester of pregnancy. The best we can do to balance the rights and interests of all when it comes to abortion, in my opinion, is to guarantee legal (and therefore safe) access to abortion for all women across the country, but primarily during the first trimester. I understand and concede that my stance is more limited for women than what was the U.S. Supreme Court's standard in the pre-*Dobbs* decision world. The previous standard held that women had the unchallenged right to an abortion up to the point of viability of the fetus (between 24 and 28 weeks of pregnancy) ("Roe v. Wade"). I support women's exclusive authority in the decision to have an abortion through the first trimester (12 weeks) of pregnancy. It just seems reasonable that after the first trimester, the right to life of the unborn child should increase and rather quickly be able to establish a standing in the situation. In addition, I do think fathers should also have a say as time progresses, particularly if a father of an unborn child makes a legal affirmation that he desires to take on all responsibilities (legal and practical) for parenting the unborn child. And, yes, I do acknowledge given the biological nature of pregnancy, that establishing a father's parental rights before the birth of a child is problematic, but I would say, not impossible.

My hope is also that individuals who engage in sexual activity do so responsibly, using reliable and effective birth control to prevent unwanted pregnancies. We also need science to develop more varied and effective birth control methods. Men now have a greater responsibility as a partner in the selection and use of birth control to protect the women in their lives from facing the increased uncertainties and dangers if they live in a state with very limited access to abortion, in comparison to the pre-*Dobbs* decision environment.

I do support abortion in cases past the first trimester in situations of rape or incest. In addition, in cases to protect the life of the woman, I also support the right to an abortion past my first trimester timeline. The medical determination as to whether a woman needs an abortion to protect her life needs to be left to a woman's personal physician and not the government.

To conclude, my overall policy stance is that abortion should remain as a woman's legal right, but except under certain circumstances (as discussed above), the caveat should be that this exclusive right is primarily valid during the first trimester of pregnancy. In order to ensure equal protection under the law, this should be the legal foundation throughout the nation under one U.S. Constitution. We should not have each state individually creating its own rules, such as has been the outcome of the *Dobbs* decision. The legal and ethical history of this nation makes clear that our constitutional rights are established and ultimately protected at the federal level, not on a state-by-state basis. Whether a woman has a right to an abortion and when during a pregnancy are core human rights questions that have implications for the mother, the unborn child and even the potential father. We need one legal standard that covers the entire nation. This is as it should be for Americans who look to our one United States Constitution with one Bill of Rights as the ultimate legal authority establishing and protecting our individual liberties.

# 23. Zero Population Growth - Now

The world population is now over eight billion people in early 2023. I want to emphasize that my stance on population growth in no way supports any sinister initiatives to reduce the world population. There are countless conspiracy theorists who love to conjecture that "the government" or the "Illuminati" are taking steps to greatly reduce the world's population. One of the latest and more dangerous conspiracy theories involves the insane idea that the COVID-19 vaccine is a way to sterilize the masses. Nor am I talking about a "China One" policy which limited each family to having only one child per couple. The plan was intended to curtail China's exponential population growth in the second half of the twentieth century. No, in the free world, we leave the decision of family planning up to each individual couple or family unit. I am not proposing any drastic measures to reduce our global population. It is important to point out that population estimates, including figures from the United Nations (un.org) estimate that the world's population will grow to 9.7 billion people by 2050 and then over 10 billion people by 2100 ("Our growing population"). These figures are staggering when we think about the high level of resources that humanity demands in order to shelter and feed the world's current population.

**Feeding the World**

What I do argue for is that on a national and international level we need to have a policy of zero population growth. According to the World Food Programme, 783 million people around the globe are hungry and 47 million are experiencing famine conditions ("10 Quick Facts"). The war in Ukraine, Global Warming, and high prices for food (due to global inflation) are some factors exacerbating the crisis. There are many honorable, international organizations, like the World Food Programme, that are staffed by altruistic people working to feed the hungry people of the world. My concern is if it is truly a global challenge today, aren't we setting ourselves up for an even more challenging obstacle to overcome if we add over 1.5 billion additional people to the planet's population by 2050. Yes, I think technology will be able to help as it does today. Technology and science have led to remarkable advances in farming and in the transportation of food products to feed many of the world's impoverished peoples. My essential argument is that we must be able to successfully feed the eight billion people who live on the planet in 2023 before we can assume that we will be able to feed 9.7 billion world citizens by 2050. Feeding the world's current population is increasingly challenging given factors, such as climate change and the intense demand on our planet's natural resources. Our changing climate is making farming more difficult due to more intense weather patterns. Also, we are now experiencing the depletion of seafood from our oceans and rivers because of overfishing. The saying, "Necessity is the mother of invention," (an English proverb that some reference back to Plato) does succinctly explain that where there is a desperate need, great minds come together to develop processes or technologies to meet that need (Martin). Modern farming has developed ways to efficiently produce our food to feed so many and, no doubt, science will continue to advance, but I have to ask if we shouldn't at least ensure that we have such technology available first before we add billions more in population to our already strained planet? For that matter, shouldn't we be asking ourselves if our planet can feasibly support a human population in excess of 10 billion?

I return to my argument that it is currently a challenge to feed our eight billion people. We have a lot of people to feed and the best way to ensure that we can feed them, as well as to ensure that our natural world and its wondrous ecosystems are healthy, is to voluntarily work to keep the current population from growing, and, hopefully, holding steady. Therefore, I support a zero-population growth policy for the world. The reader will have to forgive my dire tone, but I do consider overpopulation to be a critical environmental issue that humanity must address. We can and, I am sure, we will find ways to clean up our planet and protect our precious ecosystems, but adding more people who need resources for food, shelter, clothing etc. will not help with this endeavor. The need for more farmlands can lead to more deforestation, adding to the problem with global warming and climate change with less trees absorbing carbon dioxide. When one reads about overfishing in our oceans, it is obvious that this practice will lead to problems with food availability in the future, but also threatens the natural ecosystems that keep our waterways healthy. Industrial farming practices cause significant air, soil, and water pollution which, of course, degrade our available natural resources for future food production, as well as significantly harm the health of our planet (Hussain). As far as our farmland, I understand our industrial farming practices have put the health of our topsoil at risk – a very significant problem for the continued ability to grow the world's crops. Another problem with industrial farming methods has been the use of pesticides that too often end up as dangerous runoff, spilling freely and abundantly into our streams and waterways which harm the health of these precious aquatic ecosystems. Agriculture needs to continue its promising evolution toward more environmentally friendly practices. Organic farming protects and restores the topsoil in part by avoiding the use of industrial pesticides ("Healthy Soil"). There is also a movement toward plant-based diets, not just for our health, but because eating meat requires more natural resources, such as grazing land and water for livestock. Land is needed not just for animals to graze on but also to plant the crops to feed the animals. In areas, such as the Amazon, significant deforestation is occurring to provide land for grazing and to maintain cattle for the beef industry. Another significant environmental reason for reducing meat consumption is the methane that farm animals produce, leading to the production of greenhouse gases, thus more climate change ("Vegan Diets"). It is important to point out that when we clear land for animal food production and human habitation, this increase in proximity between humans and wild animals in their natural habitats can lead to the spread of diseases and illnesses, such as the COVID-19 virus. More pandemics can occur with deforestation.

Indeed, scientists and our food producers are working in an impressive fashion to develop more efficient and environmentally friendly methods to produce our food, but we are by no means at a point where we have solved the issue of feeding our eight billion citizens without continuing to endanger our planet's viability. We are taking a risk by leaving population unchecked and possibly incorrectly assuming that we will be able to advance food production methods in the future to feed millions more without massive environmental, global collapse. At this point, it is basic math. If our current food production system is putting a significant strain on the environment in order to feed our current population, adding millions more without intensive technological breakthroughs will continue to destroy the very ecosystems humanity depends on for survival. When we leave population growth unchecked, we are acting as irresponsible citizens of the world.

### Protecting the Earth's Ecosystems

We now live in a world in which we are too quickly using up our natural resources for the current population. A quick Google search provides the helpful and cautious explanation that if the world's current populations were to live an American middle-class lifestyle, we would need multiple Earths. Of course, we don't have four or five Earths. We only have one. The World Wildlife Fund (WWF) (www.worldwildlife.org[1]) is working to address what is being called a 6th Mass Extinction event occurring on Earth ("What is the sixth"). Due to the overuse of the planet's resources, we are witnessing a catastrophic rise in the number of species, including animals and plants, which are becoming extinct. The difference between this extinction event and previous mass extinctions (such as with the dinosaurs), is that this planetary crisis is due to human activity. According to the WWF, the extinction rate of our planet's species is 1,000 to 10,000 times higher than would naturally be occurring without the harm that humans are causing to our world ("What is the sixth").

The challenge is great just to meet the basic needs of the people in the world today, while at the same time protecting and also rehabilitating our natural ecosystems. We simply need to do more to protect our environment so that we can ensure that we have a sustainable, thriving planet for those living now and for all future generations who are yet to be born. We need to remember that without our planet's resources in the air, land, and water, not only will animal and plant species continue to

---

1. http://www.worldwildlife.org

decline, but in essence we are threatening the sustainability of the human race. The solution is to adopt a zero-population growth policy and take global steps to achieve this goal. Increased access to birth control is a key component of this process. Through a collaborative worldwide effort, low-cost and free birth control products need to be distributed globally, particularly to Third World nations in which access to healthcare treatment and resources can be very difficult to obtain by the general public. We do need to increase the standard of living in Third World nations. Yes, as people get wealthier, they desire more in the way of a modern lifestyle that demands more resources, however, they also have fewer children. We see this in Europe and the United States with the rise of modern women. First World women have the ability to decide if they want to focus on parenthood, their careers, or both (and on what timetable). When women have the autonomy to determine their own career and family pathways, this can naturally moderate and stabilize population growth. Women who are free to have careers as well as children, often decide to have children but balance this desire with career goals. This balancing of family and career can in itself lead to a limit on how many children women give birth to throughout their lives. The goal would be to achieve a higher standard of living for all people of the world, while coming up with ways to limit and manage resource use. It is my belief that we can manage our resources more efficiently to provide all world citizens with the basics of food, housing, and transportation, but this becomes increasingly unattainable if the population continues to grow at its currently projected high rate. Furthermore, I am not talking about a world in which it would be illegal for people to have multiple children, but the emphasis should be on population consistency. Two parents having two children is a reasonable new way of approaching the population crisis. We need to be open to a variety of innovative policy options to better manage this serious problem of keeping the human population from growing to such a size (and some say we have already reached this level), that we render our planet unable to support life as we know it.

## Closing

In conclusion, the first step in this process seems obviously elemental, but critical. The truth is humanity has yet to fully initiate this step of accepting that our current path of unchecked population growth is not sustainable. It is simply common sense that we must implement effective policies to address exponential population growth if humanity is to survive for any long-term basis. I am not a scientist, but at this rate of unchecked population growth, it seems clear that the survival of humanity (as we know it) past the twenty-first century is threatened due to the intense demands that we are making on our natural world. We owe it to future generations of the human species and, in my humble opinion, to the vast array of biodiversity on our planet, to adopt a global, zero population growth philosophy and policy immediately. Finally, as I briefly mentioned in my opening for this essay, I assure the reader that I do not support any hidden agenda that conspiracy theorists seem to enjoy conjecturing, including the notion that the world's governments are attempting to significantly reduce the global population. I do support a comprehensive and cooperative plan by the powers of the world to curb and discourage population growth. One possible benefit of such a policy, in my opinion, would be a future, moderate reduction in the total global population in which natural deaths would slightly outpace births. Yes, too much of a decline in births can pose a problem for the long-term survival of the human species, but a small decrease over a few generations would ease the strain and demand on the Earth's natural resources. I, therefore, leave the reader with a question. If the world's population contracted from eight billion to seven billion in the span of five or six generations through population planning (yes, a play on the term, "family planning"), would this be an optimal outcome to ensure the sustainability of Mother Earth and the human race?

# 24. Speed Cameras

The National Transportation Secretary for the Biden Administration, Pete Buttigieg, is endorsing speed cameras as part of a comprehensive plan to make our roadways safer (Ballasy). Mr. Buttigieg has received criticism for his focus on speed cameras as opponents claim it is just another way for local governments to establish a new type of revenue stream to support their endeavors (Verdon). I want to provide an explanation as to why I fully agree with Mr. Buttigieg's approach when it comes to speed cameras. Speeding has become a serious public health issue, in my opinion, and the use of speed cameras could really assist in creating a safer environment for the public. I begin with my personal experiences with speeding vehicles and my policy vision on how the use of speed cameras should be universally implemented.

**Speed Cameras Policy and Procedures**

When it comes to my opinion on the use of speed cameras, I say the more speed cameras, the better. I rarely have a day when I drive to work when someone isn't passing me who desires to drive fifteen, twenty or more miles per hour above the speed limit. I always shudder at the thought of these vehicles traveling at such high speeds along roads that are simply not designed for these super speeds. Increasingly, it seems that on the majority of trips during my commute to work, I experience at least one incident of a vehicle following me so closely that it is as if the vehicle is virtually connected to my tailgate. More often lately, my strategy is to pull over rather than coping with the stress of having someone right on top of me for three or four miles, when traffic is heavy and the driver tailgating me is unable to pass. I allow the aggressive drivers to go by and then I proceed on my route. These aggressive drivers are really pushing the limits of their vehicles' engineering by driving at very high speeds, while at the same time attempting to maintain their vehicles in their designated travel lanes. Frequently on two-lane roads, opposing vehicles travel so fast that I find myself reciting silent prayers. I hope desperately that these drivers will be able to maintain control of their vehicles in their designated lane and will not lose control, thus crashing head-on into my vehicle. Many motorists selfishly prioritize their desire to arrive at their destinations as quickly as possible over the safety and well-being of their fellow citizens on the roads. Another concern is how this clearly unsafe driving is a threat to all the children in the mornings who are traveling to their schools, whether on school buses or in their parents' personal vehicles. We need to take steps to stop irresponsible drivers from endangering our families and children on the roads. An individual's desire to speed or to not be late for work are not legitimate excuses to endanger others on our public thoroughfares.

It is time to stop the madness. We need a large network of speed cameras along our roadways. My recommendation is that the driver is allowed five (5) miles over the speed limit without a fine. If a driver travels at ten (10) miles per hour or more over the speed limit, however, a citation is generated and mailed to the registered owner of the vehicle that is recorded by the speed camera. I agree with the policy approach that some localities have adopted in which these camera citations would not count as points against someone's license. I am referring here to the points system that some states, including North Carolina, have in which a certain number of traffic violations count as points that are attached to someone's license. If a driver receives a certain number of violation tickets or serious citations that accumulate to a certain threshold number of points against their license, then their driver's license is suspended for a certain designated length of time. I concur with the rationale that for someone to receive a speeding citation that is counted as points against his or her license (which could eventually lead to them being unable to drive legally), a law enforcement officer needs to individually pull that citizen over while in the act of speeding. I am not an attorney and may not understand the full legal argument here, but as some have argued (correctly in my opinion) our legal system does and should require that someone accused of violating the law should be able to face their accuser. A speed camera is not an accuser, but a technological apparatus.

The general intent with using speed cameras to issue speeding citations is not to charge drivers criminally for speeding, but to impose monetary fines for excessive speeding. The goal is to charge drivers financial amounts that will discourage speeding. The penalty fee for a first speed infraction could be $100 for the driver. Then the penalty fee should increase by $50 for each additional infraction committed by a given driver during a calendar year period. My policy approach would emphasize the distribution of traditional and special grant funding from the federal government to be increased to states or cities that adopt the use of speed cameras, as well as establish speed limits that focus on safety first and not convenience. Initially, the citation income generated from the speed cameras could help pay for their purchase and installation. The ultimate goal of course is not to make more money for the state or local government from a continuous flow of citation income, but to affect a change in overall driver behavior which, if achieved, would result in significantly lower citation income from the cameras as time progressed.

### The Call to Increase Speed Limits

Some argue that current posted speed limits should increase because the problem is not specifically the high speeds at which some drivers are attempting to travel, but the different rates of speeds between vehicles, whether this be on a multi-lane highway or even on a two-lane road on which dangerous passing and tailgating occur. This argument contends that by increasing the speed limit, this keeps drivers from getting too close to one another. The rationale of increasing speed limits is that everyone is traveling at a speed that doesn't seem too slow for some but gives those who habitually drive at or very near the speed limit permission to speed up to a more reasonable speed, given the road conditions. There are certain situations in which I agree with this argument. I know of one road in my community where the speed limit is twenty-five miles per hour. This road has a very steep hill. Drivers must continually apply their brakes as they travel down the hill to prevent the pull of gravity from increasing the speed of their vehicles well above the speed limit. This doesn't make sense. However, I do have a safety concern when we change a speed limit from, for example, sixty-five miles per hour to seventy-five miles per hour. Different drivers have different personal practices, regardless of the speed limit, even if the posted speed limit allows vehicles to travel at very high speeds. For example, some routinely travel within five miles per hour over the speed limit as a rule to follow, but others have the "nine miles over" rule in which they intend to always travel nine miles over the posted speed limit. Many drivers are pushing the speeding ticket risk limits – they attempt to drive as fast as they can at speeds they assume the police would not consider fast enough over the speed limit to warrant a traffic stop. Thus, some are traveling five miles per hour over the speed limit while others are traveling nine miles per hour over the speed limit, with the accurate or inaccurate belief that they are safe from being pulled over by police. We all know that some drivers consider that as long as they are "going with the flow of traffic," they can travel well above the posted speed limit without ever receiving a speeding ticket. I would argue that if a driver does get stopped by law enforcement for traveling let's say twenty-five miles over the speed limit, that this "going with the flow" defense will not work, and it shouldn't.

I consistently witness on highways with speed limits of seventy miles per hour that there are drivers traveling near eighty miles per hour. I contend that traveling at nearly eighty miles per hour is simply too fast for vehicles to be traveling even on a straight, multi-lane highway. What occurs is that when speed limits are increased, we continue to have drivers traveling at different speeds. The only difference in the driving environment is that now everyone is driving faster. Now, I do agree that where suitable, higher speed limits with intensive speed monitoring by a variety of tools (including speed cameras and an enhanced presence of law enforcement officers on the roads) can achieve a balance of safety and convenience. Let us leave the speed limits where they are, and with the use of speed cameras widely and prominently placed along our roadways, habitual speeders will be faced with the choice to either slow down or pay financial penalties. My argument is that if a driver knows he or she will be issued a citation from a speed camera when traveling ten miles per hour over the speed limit, then we may see most drivers settling into that range of rarely going more than five miles per hour over the speed limit. Drivers who don't want to pay the speed camera fines will begin to drive within that cushion and will not want to get close to that ten miles per hour over the speed limit threshold.

I have one last comment about this movement to increase speed limits in an attempt to balance out speed variations. Particularly when the posted speed limits are already designated at higher speeds, it almost seems like the unstated goal is to settle upon posted speed limits at which drivers aren't bored while traveling. The reality is that the faster we drive, the less time we have to react to dangerous situations on the road. This is "Driver Education 101." When we combine higher speed limits with the same unsafe behaviors of tailgating and excessive speeding over the new speed limit, I reject the notion that the roads are safer. As I argued above, we continue to have the same speed variations as before but at just higher, more dangerous speeds. This is just physics. When vehicles collide at higher speeds, the higher velocities will generate more force. This increase in force raises the risk of injury and death for motorists involved in accidents at these higher speeds. I am in favor of reasonable speed limits that are appropriate for a given road environment and design. Some roadways are designed for highway speeds, so it makes sense for the posted speed limits to be higher on these types of roads than on other roadways. In comparison, narrower streets located in center cities that are more pedestrian-friendly should have much lower posted speed limits. These lower speed limits are necessary to protect the more vulnerable pedestrian population from being involved in an accident with a motor vehicle.

## More Technological Tools to Monitor Speeding

I don't claim to be an avid follower of televised court hearings, but I have been following the double murder trial of Alex Murdaugh since this South Carolina case is somewhat of a local event in my area. It was amazing to listen to the testimony of a technical expert who explained the reporting provided by GMC's OnStar system. The locations of where Mr. Murdaugh traveled on the night in question, as well as the speeds at which he was driving were all tracked by this system (Sharp). It is common knowledge that this system can even stop a vehicle that has been stolen. Of course, anyone who has had an app on their phone, such as WAZ, knows that our smart phones can track the speed we are traveling while we are being guided by the live directions of such an app. I'd like to see greater use of these technologies in addition to speed cameras. It would be such a tremendous tool for OnStar or a cell phone company to notify police when a given vehicle is traveling at a speed that is significantly exceeding the posted speed limit. I realize that there are those who will claim that this is "Big Brother" tracking our movements, but my opinion is that if a driver is traveling safely and reasonably, then there is no reason to track this information. It could only apply and initiate when unsafe traveling is occurring. Furthermore, I am no fan of excessive governmental intrusion into our lives, but the rest of us whose lives are being endangered by dangerous drivers have a right to be protected. Anyone who shows disregard for the safety of their fellow citizens, including families and children, needs to be effectively stopped from their behavior. Regardless of the formal legal definition of a crime, basically we are talking about behavior which is criminal in that excessive speeding is a real threat to the lives of other travelers sharing the road with a speeding vehicle.

## Closing

Currently, we are in a period in which people are very lackadaisical about observing speed limits and following other rules of the road. This is particularly the case as we hopefully are coming out of the COVID-19 pandemic. I certainly observe a lot more drivers ignoring stop signs and, on occasion, even red lights. We need to use additional technological tools because police can't be everywhere. Those drivers that are speeding should receive, at the minimum, citations that will hurt them in their wallets and pocketbooks. We need financial penalties in the form of citations to be issued to those who don't adjust their behavior. Finally, we must place more of an emphasis on public information and education to change bad driving habits like tailgating. I'd like to see more public service announcements on television and social media, as well as more signage along roadways that provide consistent messaging encouraging everyone to drive safely.

We have a responsibility to protect everyone from those who simply put their desire to get to their destination as fast as they can, above the safety of their fellow citizens. The use of speed cameras is just one tool, but I believe it can be an important tool that can successfully encourage motorists to drive safely for the benefit of everyone, including families and children, on our roadways. Financial penalties can be very persuasive in achieving behavioral change. It is time to take back the safety of our streets and create an environment in which speed cameras are an integrated component of our roadway landscape. I will continue to pledge my full support for Mr. Buttigieg's policy on speed cameras.

# 25. Young Woman under the Bridge

## My Run of Shame

It continues to haunt me. I was running on an early January evening along my town's Rail Trail. As the reader may be aware, Rail Trails are retired train corridors on which the train rails have been taken up and often paths are paved with asphalt. These paths are then used by walkers, bikers, runners, and others as places to exercise and enjoy nature. My intention was to get in a quick run before the real cold air set in - it was going to be a cold night with temperatures in the low 30s. If this had been the spring or summer, the trail would have been much busier with hours of daylight left and temperatures just starting to cool off from the daytime heat. At 6:00 p.m. on a January evening, it was already dark, and most people were smart enough to be settled comfortably inside for the long evening. Fortunately for me, as I ran along the trail on this early winter evening, the movement kept my body temperature just fine, even as temperatures were quickly starting to fall.

As I ran, I saw a young lady carrying what looked like was a box with a blanket over it. Many of us walkers and runners are in the friendly habit of waving or even just giving a nod to others as we travel the trail. I ran by and did a quick wave but no response. I thought nothing of it. Sometimes understandably women by themselves won't respond for obvious safety reasons.

We do have homeless people in our small, suburban county. I knew that, but I always thought it was a manageable issue. I have seen the men sleeping on the few benches we have in town. I was aware that we had a homeless shelter and basically a soup kitchen facility that feeds those in need daily at lunchtime. The truth is that I just never considered homelessness in my smaller town as the serious issue that it poses in larger cities. I realize now that while we are talking about smaller numbers of people in rural and suburban areas who are homeless when compared to these populations in major metropolitan areas, this issue is really starting to affect life in all areas of America.

I admit I have been guilty of stereotyping the homeless as mostly men who were experiencing mental health and substance abuse or other personal crises. Women, children, and families are unfortunately part of the homeless population, no thanks to the increasing cost of housing and other basic necessities. It is common knowledge that many working families are one or two paychecks away from being homeless, and in the current era of accelerated inflation, the issue is magnified.

The trail I run on is 1.5 miles in length and I typically run it in an out-and-back fashion to get a three-mile run in on any given day. I ran the course as I usually do on this cold evening. After running to the end of the trail, I came back up the trail that at one area passes under a bridge on the town's Main Street above. There are a few benches near this area, as well as a short concrete wall that connects perpendicularly to a ledge under the bridge that one could rest on, and people do. This ledge also provides some shelter from precipitation by the bridge above it. Homeless men sometimes rest under the bridge, even sleeping during the day on makeshift bedding. Also, teens and others who are not homeless sometimes congregate in this area. It was at this location that I saw the young lady again who earlier had been walking along with some personal items. She was now lying on her spread -out blanket with her head on a pillow, sobbing not so quietly.

I'm naturally a very reserved person, but as I went by I slowed down my run and asked her if she was okay. She did not raise her head. She actually covered her face with her arm, but she just gave me a "thumbs up" sign. It was a stupid question. Obviously, she was not "okay." I just told her that I hoped she had a better evening. Awkwardly I jogged away. That evening, I felt tremendous guilt as I do to this day that I didn't contact somebody to provide some type of support. I should have done more, even if it was to contact law enforcement requesting them to check on the young lady. I recall a sense of shame that night, as I settled into a warm house and warm bed with food in my stomach, that I did not act when I should have. I was eager to run the next day along the trail to see if she was still under the bridge.

Fortunately, no one was there when I ran by the next day. I hoped the young lady found a place to stay and did not have to spend the night in the cold. What we need are more services not just in the larger cities, but in every town and county in America (rural and suburban, as well as urban) to address both the immediate short-term and long-term needs in our communities to eliminate homelessness. Some cities are now housing homeless citizens in motels and hotels. I think this is a great option, particularly for homeless families or anyone in need. I envision a program in my area in which this young lady could walk along the Rail Trail and could access housing for even a night. Security phones, like we see on hospital and college campuses, should be available for citizens on the trail (or at other public areas, such as parks or post offices) to access, that dial directly to a public safety staff member. Calls can be made on these phones for not only a security issue, but also if the caller is having an immediate housing crisis. Both a police officer and a social worker could come out to assist. Area nonprofits and houses of worship could also assist in fundraising to pay for the homeless to stay at local motels. I am providing just a general idea of what could work without having expertise in this area. The key for towns with smaller populations, that traditionally may not have had to address the issue of homelessness, is for these localities to actively formulate policies to effectively help these citizens, not just ignore the issue, hoping that it just goes away on its own. Collaboration between social services agencies, mental health services, law enforcement, and non-profit organizations can lead to the development of creative solutions that will assist the homeless with obtaining short-term, immediate housing. In addition, substance abuse and mental health treatment, along with job training or additional educational opportunities are needed to help the homeless re-integrate into society and develop marketable skills that will enable them to achieve and maintain a secure life with permanent housing.

## We Need a Better Safety Net for Americans to Prevent Homelessness

I want to make it clear that I am firmly dedicated to our capitalistic economic system, but I do think we need to bolster and enhance our safety net system in the United States. It just seems to be common sense that it is much easier to support citizens financially during the period when they initially are facing economic hardships, than attempting to assist them when they have lost their homes. We need a system that will be there to provide financial support to protect citizens and prevent them from losing their homes, as well as enable them to continue to pay for their utilities and feed their families. We all live in a world economy that has upswings and downturns. During those economic downturns when people will lose their jobs, we need a more robust system in which unemployment is available for a time period that enables workers to obtain retraining in a new work skill that is in demand in our now very fast-paced economy. We also need a healthcare system that enables citizens to access quality, affordable preventative care so they can maintain their ability to work consistently until the age of retirement. In addition, our healthcare system must be reformed to ensure that citizens are shielded from very high medical bills stemming from the treatment of more serious medical conditions and ailments. All too often in today's predatory medical billing structure, citizens simply are unable to pay these exorbitant hospital bills and lose their homes after hospitals implement aggressive collections, as well as legal strategies to collect payments.

Furthermore, I do think that Andrew Yang's idea of a Universal Basic Income (UBI) that he endorsed during his 2020 presidential run, does have some merit. Mr. Yang's plan consists of paying every U.S. citizen over the age of 18, $1,000 per month ("The Freedom Dividend"). The idea of a basic monthly income for all Americans, that could be of particular benefit during difficult economic times, does need some further study. My only concern based on the stimulus checks that many of us received during the pandemic, is that any additional monies received from public sources should be sufficient to support families to make their lives a little easier while adults are employed, but not enable citizens the ability to stay out of work unnecessarily for months on end. We need to ensure such a UBI system does not discourage work or inhibit the development of a strong American workforce. In addition, a core benefit of a UBI program is that it could significantly help out Americans during harsh economic times when people are losing their jobs and may become unemployed or underemployed. I personally like the idea of an additional $1,000 per month for workers and perhaps a bit more for those with children or dependents. My opinion on the stimulus checks is that they really helped out a lot of families during the economic uncertainty of the COVID-19 pandemic when unemployment was very high, particularly in the service sectors. Personally, I used the funds I received for some home improvement projects that I had put off previously due to the expense. I finally got a garage door repaired that would screech loudly and I'm sure annoyed the neighbors for some time. In addition, I had a household emergency during which I had to replace a toilet that was 30 years old (the toilet replacement also included a high bill from a national plumbing company). It was just nice to have a little more support for myself and my family, but for others, the stimulus checks really helped with core basics like food, utilities, and clothing. So, yes, perhaps Andrew Yang's Universal Basic Income could help with the prevention of citizens falling into unfortunate circumstances in which they find themselves homeless. I am not an economist or an expert on Mr. Yang's plan (I could dedicate an entire essay reviewing and analyzing his innovative approach to UBI) , but his general theme is that as automation occurs, less full-time jobs may be available and needed, so we will require a plan in the future to provide income to many citizens. We will see how automation develops in the coming decades and perhaps there are better ways to support the incomes of citizens and families, but my primary point is that right now we need a more extensive and substantial, financial safety net for Americans. How we pay for this additional financial security is the question, but if other advanced nations are able to somehow provide enhanced social safety net systems for their citizens, then the United States can find a way as well.

### Closing: Helping the Homeless and Preventing Homelessness Today

As far as short-term solutions with the options that are readily available today to help people stay in their homes, there are many faith-based and non-profit organizations that help people pay for rent and utilities, as well as provide food. We need to fully support these organizations financially. Better collaboration between law enforcement, social services agencies, mental health organizations and even community colleges will be required to create comprehensive programs that help homeless individuals successfully move from living on the streets to finding placements with temporary housing along with job training. Programs are needed to assist individuals with acquiring the in-demand job skills to gain full-time, high paying employment. Training for the in-demand jobs of today and in the future is essential so these citizens can afford permanent housing. Our social services agencies do need to be out more in our communities so that they can identify homeless citizens and link them with emergency housing, mental health services or substance abuse treatment options. Also, when teenagers and young people find themselves living on the streets, social workers and law enforcement must collaborate to quickly locate these vulnerable youths and provide them with immediate, safe shelter until their living situations can be stabilized.

We just need to act more often and more effectively as a society to help out those in need. It is so easy to look away when we see the homeless on the sidewalk as we are sitting in our comfortable vehicles at the stoplight. How many of us judge these individuals as "lazy" or simply beyond anyone's help to make ourselves feel better. They are not our problem, right? Wrong. Each of us who is able to, must do better to help the homeless, even if it is a dollar or two donated to a homeless shelter. I am making a commitment today that I must do better to help out those in need. The next time I see a young woman sobbing under a bridge on a cold January evening, I will do better. This is my pledge. Let's work together to eradicate homelessness in the wealthiest nation to have ever existed on our planet. We can do this. As a people dedicated to compassion and morality, we are called to do this as Americans.

# 26. The Southern Border

## Lady Liberty

Like so many Americans, I have strong opinions on immigration. As a moderate and a pragmatist in 2022 and early 2023, I think it all comes down to balance. We still want to be a beacon of hope, but the reality is that we can only allow so many people into the United States annually in order to maintain our stability and sovereignty. We, of course, must ensure that our borders are secure to protect our citizens from those who wish to cause harm to America. Also, while many Americans want to help those in need, including those seeking to come here from nations to our south, we need to prevent excessive economic strains on our resources. According to the U.S. Census Bureau, we are already a nation of just under 335 million people as of the summer of 2023 ("QuickFacts"). We of course have many citizens with significant needs that we are ethically called upon to address. The United States does not have the seemingly endless land that it did in the 1890s as millions were arriving from Europe. During the end of the nineteenth and first half of the twentieth centuries, the United States had the space and resources to absorb many people and it was our responsibility to do so. Now, the reality is that we do have more limited resources with which to absorb very large numbers of immigrants, but I do think we still need to follow the spirit of Emma Lazarus' poem inscribed at the Statue of Liberty. Lazarus' poem, "The New Colossus" says so much in my opinion:

*Give me your tired, your poor, your huddled masses yearning to breathe free, the wretched refuse of your teeming shores. Send these, the homeless, tempest-tossed to me. I lift my lamp beside the golden door!*

It is 2023 and again I realize that we cannot let everyone in and we do have to have a nation with borders, but whoever you are, if Lazarus' words don't stir some patriotic emotion and realization that our greatness is not in our military and financial strengths, but in our generosity and compassion, then you miss the true meaning of what it is to be an American. Yes, our diversity is our strength and so often we see newcomers work extremely hard and outshine their second or third generation American counterparts. These first-generation Americans in great numbers become successful contributors to the American economic and social landscapes. Newcomers so often remind us of what the "American Dream" is all about – not about financial wealth, but about working hard and doing one's best to be an honorable citizen. Regardless of who you are or where you come from, Lazarus' words are a promise of fairness and opportunity for all. We are, as Francis

Scott Key states in his patriotic song, "The Star-Spangled Banner," "...the land of the free and the home of the brave." However, in my opinion, we are also and more importantly the land of those who uphold and protect what is right, fair, and kind. It is upon this ethical (American) foundation that I think our national immigration policy should be formulated and executed. It is a challenging dilemma with our current large population to determine how many more people we can accept and how often, but we do want to continue to be, as much as reasonably possible, a land where those who are in desperate need of freedom can come to seek refuge.

## A Reasonable and Fair Immigration Policy is Needed

Fox News on a consistent basis reports from the Mexican/U.S. Border. This politically right-leaning news network shows dramatic videos of waves of migrants attempting to cross the border illegally into the U.S. The contention from those on the right of the political spectrum is that the border is not secure, thus, the nation is at serious risk of literally being overrun by mobs of migrants. Fox News has described the situation at the southern border as "an invasion" (Fox News Staff). I do think this description is an over-exaggeration, but these large, unmanaged border crossings do potentially pose dangerous risks to our nation.

We need a middle ground – a compromise on the issue of immigration at the southern border. I do not agree with a total closing of the border as those on the far right would like, however, those on the far left seem to be firmly grounded in their unrealistic belief that the United States can absorb everyone who wants to come here. The U.S. Customs and Border Protection agents encountered 2.76 million people crossing our southern border in federal Fiscal Year 2022 (ending September 30, 2022) (Ainsley). This very large migratory movement is a national security risk. I have to agree moderately with those on the political right who say that we don't know who is coming into the nation. When we hear about how our border staff is being overwhelmed, no doubt, we have people in our nation who have recently crossed without proper screening or no screening at all. Therefore, I agree that we need tighter security at the border, but I do need to emphasize that the vast majority of those seeking to enter the United States are not terrorists - they are simply seeking a better life or escaping from political or other types of persecution. We must remember that simply just building a wall and closing the doors is not an option. We cannot let everyone into the United States who is attempting to migrate here (I wish we could), but we need to determine on an annual basis what is a manageable maximum number of migrants that we can allow into the U.S. We are confronting many serious issues in American society today, but we still have an ethical responsibility to help at least some of those who are desperately seeking refuge in a new home. As much as possible, let us share the great bounty and opportunities that are available in America.

So, while I find building a massive wall cost prohibitive, I do support more funding for border patrol agents. In addition, there should be strategically placed areas of physical barriers, supplanted with continual monitoring through the use of advanced technological tools to protect our southern border. The United States must admit those requesting asylum based on fear of persecution and allow them to be processed through the immigration courts. I do somewhat agree with the Biden Administration's new policy preventing those from seeking asylum from the U.S. if they have not first requested asylum from another nation that they traveled through on their way to the southern border ("What is President Biden's"). In addition, I contend asylum seekers should have to request this status only at one of our official ports of entry. If they enter at any other location, their request for asylum should not be heard and they should be promptly removed from the United States. Of course, we do need to ensure that we provide proper messaging, so migrants understand this rule. We should share this information through social media, as well as properly displaying signage along our border in a variety of languages, and particularly at those hot spots where migrants have a history of crossing the border illegally.

Also, I have my concerns about the Biden administration's new phone app, CBP (U.S. Customs and Border Protection) One, that I understand essentially must be used by asylum seekers in order to set up appointments, enabling applicants to formally seek asylum at U.S. ports of entry (Montoya-Galvez). Amnesty International has called the requirement to use CBP One as the only method to request asylum to the U.S. as a "...violation of international human rights law..." ("USA: Mandatory use of CBP"). I think the app is fine to offer as the primary option for asylum seekers and perhaps users of the app can receive some type of priority, however, at this point until we have a more comprehensive policy (as I discuss below) to assist those in the nations to our south who may wish to migrate to the U.S., we should still accept unscheduled asylum seekers at ports of entry who may be unable to access the app. Congressman Joaquin Castro in a letter signed by other House Democrats submitted to Homeland Security Secretary Alejandro Mayorkas complained about "...accessibility and equity..." with the CBP One app ("As Asylum-Seekers Report"). The app leaves out those without a certain level of technological knowledge, as well as those who have a language barrier ("As Asylum-Seekers Report"). I do see the app helping U.S. Customs and Border Protection staff since the information obtained from the app can be used to better manage large amounts of people seeking entry into the United States. Now, again, I do think that we have to be strict as far as only accepting those migrants for asylum consideration who do report to the ports of entry. The only situations in which migrants should be given leniency if they cross at locations that are not ports of entry, would include cases in which undocumented migrants are under immediate threat of bodily harm or when children are traveling alone. These circumstances must be taken into account. We must have an orderly, but humane asylum application process.

I agree that we need to strongly dissuade having such large numbers converge on our southern border. The United States should provide financial and other resources to nations, such as Mexico to help them absorb some of these migrants, as well as to improve the quality of life in the nations from which people are currently fleeing. I think having more of a presence on the ground in the nations from which people are leaving, would allow those seeking asylum status in the United States to do so from their home nation or in a nation where they currently are residing. This may seem a bit unconventional, but having some military bases in these nations could help out with the processing of asylum applicants, as well as possibly assisting these governments with transitioning to democratic systems. The truth is that we may need to get somewhat unconventional to ensure that our border is safe and to process asylum applications in a humane, but efficient manner. Our immigration approach also needs to discourage families, particularly with small children from trekking across very dangerous terrain with criminal smugglers who too often take advantage of those simply trying to get to the U.S.

Aside from seeking asylum due to the fear of persecution, a large number of migrants head to the United States undoubtedly to gain economic benefits. The United States does have a worker visa program, but I think we need a much more comprehensive program that links immigrants who are seeking work in the U.S. to businesses and industries in the U.S. which are short on workers. We should want to provide some opportunities to those seeking a better life economically. Again, unfortunately, we can't let everyone in who wants to come here and the desire to make more money is not a justifiable reason to seek asylum, but I'd like to see the development of a jobs program that links jobseekers in the nations to our south with specific positions needed by U.S. companies. Such a well-organized, national jobs program could essentially eliminate the desire of families to attempt this very dangerous journey for economic mobility. As I discussed above, I envision the establishment of U.S. military bases in these nations from which migrants are fleeing that among other services, could provide in-country facilities for U.S. companies to recruit employees in needed job areas. Such a program could coordinate transportation from these nations to the United States, which could possibly alleviate the congestion at the U.S. southern border. The reality is that many undocumented migrants enter the United States and do in fact find gainful employment. Let us create an above-board system that legally matches these migrants who desperately want to work, to the jobs that U.S. companies need filled. My contention is that we need two focused and distinct programs for those entering the U.S. from nations to our south – one clearly for asylum seekers and the other for workers seeking economic opportunities. There is no doubt that we can improve our current processes at the southern border, as well as our overall immigration policies.

Finally, if we don't want such high numbers of immigrants attempting to cross the border into the U.S., then the United States must do more to help our southern neighbors address their issues with abject poverty and organized crime. This means providing financial resources and in-person guidance to create democratic governmental systems, as well as business-friendly environments. The United States sends funds all over the world to help poor nations. I'm not saying that we should stop being generous to the world, but we should place a special focus on our southern neighbors in our own Western hemisphere. As we may be choosing to reduce our significant levels of commerce with China, perhaps we can pivot to increasing manufacturing in Latin American nations and improve the standard of living for our neighbors to the south. The great economic potential that so many have envisioned, involves extensive commerce between Canada, the United States, Mexico, and Central America. If we can democratize and bring up the standard of living through American capitalism in these Latin nations, people will want, no doubt, to remain in their nations of origin. We can do this.

### The Plight of Our Dreamers

An analysis of the immigration issue at our southern border is not complete without a discussion of the current state of the "Dreamers." These are young people who traveled with their families when they were young children to our nation and are undocumented. Many remember only being Americans. As a whole, the people of the United States have decided in a non-partisan way (which is very rare these days) that the Dreamers should have citizenship, or at least a pathway to citizenship and protection against deportation. I am pleased that in a bipartisan effort, Republican Senator Lindsey Graham (South Carolina) and Democrat Senator Dick Durbin (Illinois) have introduced a new bill in 2023 (Dream Act of 2023) to the Senate in order to provide conditional status to some 1.9 million young people ("Bipartisan Senators"). The bill would provide a path either through education, military service or through employment to gain full citizenship. Hopefully, after this issue has not been resolved for several years, we can at last agree to now help out these young people. These Dreamers can contribute to our society and achieve the "American Dream" of reaching their potential in our free economic and political system. Enacting such legislation would demonstrate that Americans are fair-minded people who refuse to cruelly send these young people to nations that they are not familiar with or even remember.

Most Americans agree with the Dream Act of 2023, but I do go further as far as my policy approach to all undocumented immigrants currently living in the United States. According to the Migration Policy Institute, about 11.2 million "unauthorized" immigrants lived in the United States in 2021 (Hook, Gelatt, and Soto). I assume that number has increased in the past few years, and we may not fully know the true number of undocumented immigrants now residing in the United

States. I would like to formalize a policy that allows these individuals to come from out of the shadows without fear and be provided with a reasonable pathway for them to continue to live here legally. Clearly, there needs to be some criteria, such as not having a violent criminal record, being employed, or attending school, as well as having lived in the United States for at least three years. A solid argument can be made that adults who have come here illegally should not be given the same opportunity as the Dreamers, but I do think for those who have been here for quite some time that we should provide not automatic citizenship, but a pathway for them to obtain this status. Let us start first at a place of consensus and as soon as possible take care of our Dreamers.

### Southern Border Policy Summary and Closing Thoughts

My overall policy philosophy on immigration begins with a basic premise that processing millions of migrants at the southern border as we experienced during 2022 is not feasible or sustainable. When the numbers of those attempting to cross the border become so large that our border security and immigration processing infrastructure is overwhelmed, the stability of our society is threatened. I also agree with conservatives that a secure border is essential to the national security of the United States and to the local security of Americans who could become victims of crime committed by immigrants who have entered into our nation illegally. I do concede that the vast majority of immigrants are peace-loving and simply seek a better life, but we also have to concede as a society, that one criminal act committed by one undocumented immigrant is a serious security failure. Our border security must be equipped with the tools to ensure that no one with criminal intentions can get into our nation. I have some confidence in our border agents in identifying which migrants should be allowed to apply for asylum and which should be immediately expelled, but with so many people, one wonders if some dangerous individuals are slipping through the cracks. We also have to ask with so many coming to our southern border, how many migrants who attempt to evade our border agents and security are successful? Again, I'm not in favor of a megalithic wall all along our southern border and my limited understanding is that the geography of the land would prevent the building of such a wall, but we must enhance our border security with some more physical impediments, as well as advanced technological tracking tools.

The primary responsibility of the United States is protecting those who are already here. A close secondary concern after border security, is the need to be humane to those seeking to immigrate to the United States. We also need to address the state of undocumented people in our nation. Yes, the Dreamers need to be quickly brought into the American family as citizens with the protections afforded all citizens of our great nation. The Dreamers account for about two million ("Bipartisan Senators") out of the projected 11 million undocumented immigrants who currently reside in the United States (as of 2021) (Hook, Gelatt, and Soto). I am in favor of providing a road to citizenship or at least a legal status classification for those deserving undocumented immigrants who live in the United States and who are currently contributing to the good of our society.

We need an immigration application process that is initiated in migrants' home nations or the nations in which they currently reside. A wide-spread and targeted communications campaign needs to focus on discouraging those who plan to make the dangerous trek to our border. This communications effort needs to emphasize that those who arrive at our border will quickly be returned to their home nations unless their asylum requests are clearly based on legitimate fears of persecution. A comprehensive jobs program matching immigrant workers to job skills needed by U.S. companies is another component to a successful immigration policy. Then, we need to develop an economic growth plan for these nations based on the Marshall Plan that we implemented in Japan and Germany after World War II. The Marshall Plan was tremendously successful in Japan and Germany. We can use this same framework to transition our southern neighbors into democratic and economically sustainable nation-states. I agree with President Biden that we want to assist in transforming these Latin American nations into havens of freedom that will support the dreams of their citizens. The goal is to eliminate the need and desire of current citizens in these nations to take a dangerous trip to leave their homes due to poverty, persecution, or crime.

I cannot and should not leave the subject about our southern border without stressing that we must have an immigration policy that is practical, but fair and compassionate. This means that those who are truly seeking asylum because of fear of persecution need to be heard and if their claims are legitimate, welcomed and protected. Each of us can put ourselves in their shoes and many of our recent ancestors who came to America were no different than these current migrants. They simply are seeking out the freedom that is America like so many before them. As someone with an Eastern European, Jewish background, I realize when my Russian and Polish great grandparents emigrated from their home nations to the United States in the late nineteenth century, the fact that the United States allowed them in is why in 2023 I enjoy such abundant freedom in the nation that I love. My grandparents were born in the United States and were able to seek their happiness here, while their counterparts in Europe dealt with Hitler and then the Soviet empire. We must not forget that many Americans in the twenty-first century are citizens of this nation because of a national policy that allowed immigrants to come to these shores. No, we cannot accept everyone into the United States who wishes to come here, but we are ethically called upon to accept as many as reasonably possible. We are Americans and that is what we do. Lady Liberty's message lives on and her light illuminates the way for those seeking freedom, opportunity, and justice. The torch She carries represents not just a message of freedom for America, but a hope of freedom for the world. May Her hope become reality one day soon with every citizen around the globe enjoying democracy and the guarantee of individual liberty with which to choose their own life's path.

# 27. NFL Players Taking the Knee in Protest of American Racial Discrimination

**(original essay summer of 2020)**

As the Black Lives Matter movement gains traction in the ethical endeavor to end racial discrimination in America, the issue of kneeling in protest during the beginning of sporting events as the "The Star-Spangled Banner" is played, has again risen to the forefront of public discourse. Some African American athletes have controversially taken a knee rather than stand during our national anthem to protest the history of racial discrimination in the United States. There are those citizens who very much support this method of protest to promote greater equality, while others consider it a great insult against a nation that has enabled many African American athletes to achieve tremendous professional and financial success.

I in no way assert that I can judge African Americans regarding the manner in which they protest. Only they can decide for themselves after the history of slavery, severe mistreatment, and discrimination how best they wish to combat continued prejudice. I consider the treatment of Colin Kaepernick, the former San Francisco 49ers quarterback, who essentially was run out of the NFL for his choice to protest by kneeling during the playing of the national anthem to be reprehensible. Also, I think those who claim that there is never a justifiable reason for citizens to protest against our federal government don't quite comprehend the meaning of freedom as it is guaranteed by our U.S. Constitution. We celebrate our liberties that we enjoy under our national flag that is praised by Francis Scott Key who wrote "The Star-Spangled Banner." Many experience a feeling of great patriotism and love for our free nation when hearing Francis Scott Key's lyrics in which he describes his firsthand experience of witnessing a victory by the United States during the War of 1812.

In my opinion, while African Americans absolutely have the right to protest racism as they see fit, I do not think the federal government should be the target and recipient of African Americans' justified anger and outrage. There obviously have been many socially inherent biases throughout our society at all levels of the private and public sectors, but the federal government of these United States (although stumbling at times) has continued to evolve in its role as protector of individual rights. This role of protector has included addressing the plight of African Americans in fighting racial discrimination.

There have been some very significant achievements that we can look to as shining examples of our federal government successfully extending rights to African Americans. We can begin with President Abraham Lincoln's Emancipation Proclamation to free the slaves (January 1, 1863). In addition, it should be recognized that the great ethical goal of the Civil War (1861-1865) was to end slavery in the United States. Our federal Union military was responsible for ending slavery by defeating the southern states which sought to secede from the Union and preserve the institution of slavery. Then we can look at victories for civil rights with the *1954 Brown versus Board of Education* ruling that found the "separate but equal" practice, pertaining to the policy of racially segregated schools in the United States, was unconstitutional. We can also examine the *Civil Rights Act of 1964* that essentially provided the legal foundation rendering racial discrimination illegal in the United States ("Legal Highlight"). It is noteworthy that while not specifically relevant to the rights of African Americans, our national government has enacted legislation that has extended rights to diverse segments of our citizenry, including women (suffrage), gay Americans (the legalization of same-sex marriage), the disabled (the Americans with Disabilities Act), etc. I argue that the federal government has been on the side of protecting, promoting, and extending individual liberties for all Americans, not acting as a barrier to them.

And, yes, I fully acknowledge that there has been unfair treatment of African Americans and other minorities by law enforcement, but I argue that the majority of these civil rights violations have occurred at the local level. As we've seen in the past, it has been the federal government that so often steps in to correct inappropriate behavior at the local and state levels. These corrective actions take a variety of forms including threatening to withhold federal funds if reforms are not made, enacting legislation to protect the rights of African Americans and prosecuting hate crimes when local governments fail to act. We are now seeing the effort at the federal level underway in which Congress and President Trump are cooperating to enact and implement new legislation and policies to reform unacceptable police practices.

Therefore, my suggestion is, yes, protest unfair, discriminatory systems that persist throughout our society, such as the biases in hiring practices, pay rates, banking (loans), law enforcement, healthcare, education, etc. My personal decision, and I do support the right of others to disagree with me, is that I will continue to stand during the singing of our national anthem and support our flag per this song's intention. The flag represents to me not a national government that is perfect or that has always gotten it right, but one that has continued to evolve in its role of protecting the rights of all Americans. As so many have said more eloquently than I, our flag represents a basic ethical tenet that every individual has the right to "...Life, Liberty and the pursuit of Happiness..." (Kamps 36) as set out in our Declaration of Independence.

I believe that this ideal of ensuring liberty for every citizen, that our nation was founded upon, provides the ethical foundation that will empower our society to finally overcome the racial bigotry and hatred that so many Americans are now fighting to end. It is this ideal that I have in mind when I stand with my hand upon my heart during the playing of our national anthem of the United States of America. Finally, as I stand in support of the freedom that "The Star-Spangled Banner" represents, I am also standing for this freedom that recognizes the right of others to kneel and protest our flag and national government. There may be no greater sign that one lives in a free and just society than the ability to protest against one's government without fear of punishment.

# 28. Early Thoughts on the COVID-19 Pandemic in 2020

**(originally written on July 30, 2020)**

Too many of us have forgotten our true American identity during this pandemic. We are the heroes of the world. The United States is the beacon of hope – the Statue of Liberty holding the torch guiding the way for those who seek protection from despots. We vanquished Nazis with our military might and took down the totalitarian regime of the Soviet Union in the Cold War face-off. Then, we stood together in solidarity after the horrors of 9/11 to confront terrorism.

However, today in Pandemic America in the summer of 2020, during what should be a time of great cooperation and compassion, we see squabbling about wearing masks and social distancing to prevent the spread of COVID-19. Somehow, the medical guidance to wear masks and perform social distancing has triggered a political argument. These actions are simply appropriate behaviors that all citizens need to participate in, which demonstrate civilized acts of decency and kindness to others. If everyone adopts the advice of medical experts to wear masks and practice social distancing as much as possible, then we will be able to open back up more segments of our society and get back to a more normal way of life. Like so many have pointed out, by each of us doing his or her part, this effort will enable us to turn the tide on the pandemic that is causing so much harm to so many. We can make great strides in getting back to a "new normal" by working together to stop the spread of COVID-19. This new normal of wearing masks and adopting social distancing will be with us for some time, but by using these tools, we will definitely be making progress in the right direction. We can get to that point in which less Americans are getting sick and dying, our medical facilities are not being overrun, and major sectors of our economy can begin to recover.

While Europe is opening up after they took strict measures, we look like selfish children going to political rallies and protesting at state capitals, proclaiming our right to get back to life as usual. There is an attitude of Me-ism that I and many other Americans, no doubt, find deplorable. I try not to read the numbers too much as they are simply overwhelming, but when I see that over 126,000 American citizens have passed due to the virus, it is simply unacceptable that people refuse to do their part. We must listen to the scientists and physicians. Yes, we all greatly desire to get back to life as usual and congregate again in public and retail spaces. The key to achieving greater freedom is accepting on a societal level that, at this point, we can only achieve this desired outcome by wearing masks in public and practicing social distancing from others who are not part of our immediate family.

So, let's all do better with masking and social distancing. We can do this – for our doctors and nurses who have worked so hard and deserve some rest. We can do this - to protect older Americans and others who are immunocompromised. We can do this - to protect the long-term health of our economy by reducing the spread of COVID-19 to more quickly be able to safely open up businesses and retail establishments. Part of supporting the health of all Americans involves ensuring that we have a healthy economy. All citizens fundamentally need gainful employment to provide shelter, food, clothing, and comprehensive medical care for their families. I am in no part calling for a return to the days of shutdowns, but we can only prevent new shutdowns by wearing masks and participating in social distancing. Then, we can move forward together as a healthy and economically stable nation.

We call upon our fellow citizens to live ethically by treating others with great compassion, particularly during times when society is facing a great challenge, such as during our current pandemic. Our religious and philosophical doctrines always teach us "The Golden Rule" – treat others as you would want to be treated. This ideal is the basic (while simplistic) meaning of what it is to be an American, in my opinion. We are called upon to treat others as we would want to be treated. We take care of others as we would want to be taken care of when we are in need. We must come together putting aside politics, pettiness, and ignorance to cooperate and show the world that we have not forgotten how heroes behave. We must remember that we are a nation not built on military might, nor built on economic power. We became the leader of the free world through demonstrating that anything can be achieved through cooperation, compassion, and vision. America, it's time you wake up and remember who you are. Let's reset and show this pandemic and the world what American heroes are capable of achieving when we work together as one people to confront a great challenge. The greater the commitment we make now to preventing the spread of this horrific disease, the sooner we will be to that joyous day when we can get rid of these annoying masks and welcome back all the smiling faces of the world.

# 29. COVID-19 in the Fall of 2022

### Time for a "New Normal"

I count myself as among those who have "COVID fatigue." I get it. I'm one of the few still wearing a mask in the grocery store and at work. I just had my fifth Moderna shot. I understand the fatigue. We are coming up on three years of this horrific pandemic. I haven't changed my full-pandemic behavior yet, but I hope by the spring of 2023 to start living my "new normal."

I have eased off my zealotry on at least mask wearing (although I still believe everyone needs to get the vaccinations). During the first and even the second years of the pandemic, I judgmentally looked down upon anyone standing behind me in the grocery store not wearing a mask. I recall driving by restaurants and thinking that the folks eating inside were just asking for COVID-19. Life, however, does need to get back to some sense of normalcy and to me that does not include wearing masks for the vast majority of the time. I do agree with the Centers for Disease Control and Prevention (CDC) which recommends that if you are in a high-risk health category, you should wear a mask for your protection in crowded indoor areas ("How to Protect"). Furthermore, if we can get more Americans vaccinated, then we have a better chance of reducing or preventing COVID-19 infection surges with people getting seriously ill ("How to Protect"). I also agree with the CDC that if you live in an area where COVID cases are quickly rising, that you should wear a mask during that high infection rate period ("How to Protect"). Except for these unique situations, I think we need to continue to focus on vaccinations, while easing off the emphasis on mask wearing.

Many restaurants suffered tremendously during the pandemic with too many having to close since they were forbidden from offering indoor dining. I think requiring children to wear hot, uncomfortable masks all day at school was a necessary evil during the height of the pandemic, but now we do need to eliminate that practice unless there is a community surge of COVID cases. Restaurants need to be open with indoor dining, so they can stay in business and their employees have jobs. Kids need to be kids and, yes, this means living life without covering up their smiling, inquisitive faces.

One area that we missed the mark on was how we handled children in school during the pandemic. As soon as vaccinations were available in early 2021 for teachers, students should have been back in class wearing masks. Particularly for younger children in the lower grades, they really needed that direct in-person interaction with their teachers to ensure core lessons were grasped. Students in high school could adjust more easily to the lecture-style teaching online, but there is a lot of work that now needs to be done so students in the lower grades can catch up to where they should be academically. We also learned the safety-net function that schools provide to students. Many students depend on schools during the year to obtain at least one substantial meal during the day. In addition, teachers and school employees act as a layer of protection for children since they see students every day. Teachers and school counselors are quite adept at noticing signs of abuse or neglect. Yes, the pandemic taught us that our public schools provide an array of core functions to ensure that the educational and basic needs of children are met. Finally, the pandemic highlighted the necessity of creating a system in which all children have access to computers and just as importantly, internet access to succeed academically.

### We Must Continue to Follow Medical Science to Prevent the Spread of COVID-19

I do agree with many who say it is time to move past COVID concerns dominating our daily lives, but the one insistence that I continue to stand by is that unless someone has a legitimate reason per their doctor (not based on what someone claims on a Joe Rogan podcast), everyone needs to get their vaccinations. I have to give President Trump tremendous credit for Operation Warp Speed that resulted in the development of these highly effective MRNA vaccines ("Operation Warp Speed"). Even though Mr. Trump's messaging on COVID was inexcusable, and for quite some time he refused to openly endorse everyone getting the vaccine, his vision was instrumental in fast-tracking the development of these vaccines. The MRNA vaccines, developed through collaboration between the federal government and our top pharmaceutical companies, are much more effective than what other nations, such as China and Russia, have produced. Former President Trump has recently become more openly supportive of everyone getting a COVID vaccine which is a positive step. We indeed need to trust the great medical minds of our era who are advising Americans to get fully vaccinated for protection against COVID-19. The medical experts correctly point out that the difference for many between experiencing mild cases of COVID-19 and landing in the intensive care unit (ICU) of a hospital, can depend on whether or not they have been vaccinated.

I have been fortunate in that ("knock on wood") I have not contracted COVID-19 as of the writing of this essay. There have been many who have caught COVID and some who have had the illness multiple times. I have followed all the guidance very closely, but I have heard of others who have done the same and have still contracted the virus. I suppose I do consider myself to be lucky, but I know I have increased my protection (and "luck") against contracting COVID-19 by wearing a mask consistently in public places and getting the full vaccination series. One prevalent projection for the future of COVID is that the virus will not be eliminated at this point because it is so widespread, but that in the future it will generally reflect the behavior of the current flu. I'm assuming that most of us will contract COVID at some point since the virus is now in mass-circulation, but with vaccines and with less severe strains, the hope is that these illnesses will be almost like any other minor to moderate cold or flu virus. Medical experts emphasize that we could be looking at getting an annual COVID-19 shot as we do with the flu, which seems reasonable.

Now, while saying that I completely sympathize with those who are fed up with the pandemic, I do believe as responsible citizens who desire to protect the health of our children and each other that we need to continue to take some precautions in the new COVID-19 era. We want to prevent any serious resurgence of the virus. The first action step to achieve this goal is for as many citizens as possible to get vaccinated. All of us who are adults remember having to get our vaccines when first enrolling in school as small children. Those of us who are parents are quite familiar with childhood vaccinations as a core method to protect community health. It has amazed me how this ant-vaccination sentiment just spiraled out of control when it came to COVID-19. The political right in the United States has a lot to account for as far as spreading propaganda against the vaccines. It has been so sad to hear about very ill people in our hospitals with COVID who refused to get vaccinated when they had the opportunity. The reaction of some of these patients has been deep regret that they didn't get their shots. Others are noted to have expressed anger with the false belief that the real threat was the vaccine, not the "imaginary" COVID pandemic.

I agree that we now should move away from wearing masks as a rule, but I do think it is appropriate that if and when we have other surges of COVID-19 cases, that we commit to our moral imperative of protecting others by again adopting the practice of wearing masks. I emphasize that resuming the wearing of masks by everyone (including healthy young people and fully vaccinated citizens who have had all of their booster shots) to prevent the spread of the virus, should only be required going forward during periods when COVID-19 cases are spiking. My message is that we need to leave our divisiveness in the past and work effectively together to keep the transmission of COVID-19 at bay. The hope, of course, is that spikes and surges of COVID cases will continue to become much less frequent as time passes, but if and when necessary, we all need to act responsibly to prevent community spread from getting out of hand.

## Returning to More of a Pre-COVID Life

My personal goal is by the spring of 2023 to shed the mask in most social situations and start living a new normal. I have even worn safety glasses at my work or in stores during the height of the pandemic, having read somewhere that while rare, the virus can enter our body through our eyes' tear ducts. I realize that I have been overly cautious to a fault, maybe even obsessive. It will be hard to shed the mask during the first few times I go maskless to a store or to work. I gather after so long of wearing a mask in public that it may feel almost unnatural. I'm sure any initial feelings of psychological discomfort from not wearing a mask will soon be overcome by the feeling of being free – to feel the air on my full face and to reveal to the world my entire expression.

The new normal for me is that I plan to stop wearing a mask. I will wear a mask for two reasons. First, during any period of high contagion of COVID when a surge of cases is occurring, I will wear a mask. Second, during the winter months when an indoor setting is crowded, I am planning to wear a mask. I typically receive the flu vaccine, but in each of the past three or four years, pre-COVID, I would always contract a pretty bad flu-like virus during the latter part of the winter. Fever, fatigue, and general cold-like symptoms are what I experienced during these illnesses. As so many others experienced, however, during the past two years, because I was wearing a mask in public, I did not contract any winter-time cold viruses. Therefore, my plan is that during cold weather periods, I will resume wearing a mask in crowded, indoor places. Other than in these situations, I don't plan to wear a mask. I think it is important to note that what we did learn, regardless of what some would say, is that masking does work (particularly in the case of N95 or KN95 style masks) to prevent the spread of illness.

## Closing

I don't think that President Biden's statement about the pandemic being over was the best choice of words (Williams), but we do need to establish a new normal in which we strike the right balance between protecting our physical health and protecting our mental health. We must continue to stress that everyone needs to get the miracle vaccines that are now widely available. It is also important to emphasize the need to resume wearing masks during any periods when COVID cases are surging in our local communities. We have now passed a very sad and horrific milestone in which over one million Americans have died from COVID-19. It is critical to recognize that we have a responsibility to act if and when necessary to prevent further community spread if the virus begins to surge again in its current strain or as a new virus variant. Having pointed out our responsibilities to prevent the spread of COVID-19, it is also important to remind ourselves that constant stress is not beneficial to our mental or physical health. As any mental health professional or resource would inform us, remaining on a "high alert" mental state for long periods of time is detrimental to our overall well-being. We need for our sanity after almost three long years to get back to a sense of normalcy.

I want to take a moment to point out the evolution that has occurred during these three years of the pandemic. We have gone from initially just social distancing to prevent the spread of COVID-19 to then masking with social distancing. Then, we transitioned to vaccines with some masking. My hope is that we are in a permanent new phase that stresses the vaccines, with masking only in certain situations. Our society should feel a sense of great achievement in the substantial progress that we have made in confronting COVID-19. The days of shutdowns for businesses, schools and social settings are over as we now have the resources to limit virus spread. Let us celebrate a new life without the constant daily, pandemic fear. It will not be the old normal, but yes, a "new normal." This means accepting that COVID-19 will continue to be a part of our lives, but we must move forward with the mindset that we can no longer allow this dreaded virus to control our lives.

# 30. New Year's Day 2020

New Year's Day is not my favorite holiday (that would be July 4th), but it is in my top 10. It's not religious so there's not that awkwardness in salutations. It's a secular holiday that everyone celebrates. This holiday is a perfect occasion for a "do over ". One can use the start of a new year as an incentive to make changes for the better. Yes, slimming down and improving physical fitness are popular New Year's goals for a lot of people in the Western world, but it's also a good time to dream about what you'd like to improve in your life (or in the lives of others) and then make plans accordingly. The beginning of 2020, of course, marks the start of a new decade – the 2020s. This is an optimal opportunity to do some long-term planning and think about personal goals we'd like to accomplish in the years ahead.

## Accepting Diversity

I suppose as someone who is civic-minded, I also ponder the question of what actions we can take locally and globally to make the world a better place as we begin the new year. I'd like to outline some goals that I think we as a society should adopt. First, I am in favor of a comprehensive initiative that encourages our society to be more respectful and accepting of diversity. All of us need to make much more of an effort at getting along with others who think differently, look differently, and live in different areas than we do. We could achieve great progress in creating a more peaceful society in the United States by showing more respect to and for one another. There's no doubt that people in New York City or California have a very different vision of the world than those in the Midwest or those in the Deep South. We should all come to the table with the mindset of leaving stereotypes at the door and be willing to listen openly to the opinions of others. Regardless of one's own political bent (or bias), open communication starts with respecting everyone's political values, whether those are rooted on the political left or stem from conservative, more traditional values found on the political right. In my opinion, as long as each of us approaches one another on matters of intense disagreement with an open and fair mind, we can make a lot of progress. I've always felt that when we interact on an individual-to-individual basis, we realize in many cases that people generally have more in common than differences. The truth is that the vast majority of us want peace, health and prosperity for our family, friends, and communities.

## Protecting Our Environment

Thinking from a global perspective, contemplating how best we can improve life for humanity, I'd like to see more of us listen to the established scientific community when it comes to how climate change is affecting our environment. Even if one doesn't believe in what the scientists are saying specifically about climate change, we can all agree that environmental laws protecting our air, water and land are imperative for the survival of critical ecosystems. Humanity should seek to protect our ecosystems which ensure the survival of all life on our planet, including our species. We have a responsibility to take care of our environment which in turn provides for our essential life needs (food, water, and air). I do find some fault with the political left on this issue. There seems to be a lack of recognition that many people throughout the world are just trying to go to work and take care of their families. Understandably, these working-class citizens of the world aren't going to respond very well to drastic reforms that will cause significant economic hardships. What we need is technological development that will enable large numbers of people to participate in improving the environment without major inconvenience or personal increased cost. An example is the transition in the next few years to more battery-powered vehicles. I have on more than one occasion been interested in purchasing a hybrid vehicle, but the cost was just too high to justify the purchase. I for one am excited about what appears to be more mass production of battery-powered vehicles which should lower the cost of these environmentally friendlier vehicles for everyone. Tesla has been the standard, but I'm reading about other companies, such as Ford, rolling out pickup trucks in 2021 that will run on battery packs. The goal is to ensure that citizens can maintain their standards of living, while at the same time reducing their carbon footprints. Through mass-production and competition between car manufacturers which should bring down prices, along with potential government tax credits, many more will be able to purchase these zero emission (at the tailpipe) vehicles. Indeed, if battery-powered vehicles can be sold at prices that are similar to internal combustion engine vehicles, then significant progress will be made. We want to work toward reducing the pollution in our air for our children and families in their home, school, and work environments. Electrified vehicles will help in this effort to clean the air. We need to continue to invest in cleaner energy options, such as wind, solar and hydro power that will provide the electricity for these new vehicles, as well as the power we depend on to run our modern lives. We should also reexamine the benefits that clean nuclear power could provide as a greener option in terms of limiting carbon emissions in comparison to traditional fossil fuels. A full transition away from fossil fuels won't occur overnight, but we must move in this direction with the understanding that it must be done in a way that is affordable for our citizens.

## Lowering the Costs of Healthcare and Higher Education

During this new decade, American society needs to formulate and implement policies that will lower the cost of health care and the cost of attending college for all citizens and students. Too many Americans have faced, are facing or will face financial strain because of healthcare or higher educational expenses. We need to come up with innovative approaches to lessen the financial impact of these ever-increasing expenses for higher education and health care. Can we look into tuition-free college for undergraduate students at public universities that is publicly funded with some assistance for living expenses through public and private grants? All public community colleges which provide training in career fields that are in demand, such as in the medical sector, public service, and technical trades (HVAC, electrician, etc. come to mind) should be free to students.

I'm not for "Medicare for All" (yet), but we must determine what policies we can implement to manage and mitigate these high health-care costs for citizens. I certainly don't think anyone should face financial ruin because of astronomical medical expenses. The heartbreaking stories of large, "non-profit" hospital systems seeking payments by hiring aggressive collection agencies and even suing their former patients, demonstrate that we need swift reforms. In addition to facing medical crises, too many citizens face tremendous psychological stress when they end up with medical bills that they simply will be unable to pay. Too many have lost their life savings and even their homes because of this predatory behavior. We need to collectively say that as a nation we will no longer tolerate this shameful behavior. I like the policy option that more moderates are looking at which proposes a total out-of-pocket spending limit of $1,000 for a covered member on an insurance plan. I think that if everyday people are paying high premiums for medical insurance coverage, which is so often the case, then $1,000 per year out of pocket should be the maximum amount per covered member that any family should be asked to spend on health care. This $1,000 limit would include all co-pay and co-insurance charges and that is it. Personally, I've had to become more educated on what my employer-based medical plan covers. I was incorrect to assume that my choice of a higher premium plan would insulate me from high co-insurance payments for myself and my family.

As many Americans are now demanding, we simply need a financial system that emphasizes supporting the upward mobility of working-class citizens who are struggling to support their families. This is the land of opportunity and I want there to be more millionaires not less, but the over-the-top profits that companies and stockholders are pocketing at the expense of the declining American middle-class must end. Our economy is based on a free-market system that encourages competition between businesses who seek to capture segments of markets for goods and services that they are selling in order to obtain significant profits. Maximizing profit is a core goal of business, but we do have to ensure that our capitalistic system (that I certainly believe in) does not allow businesses to accumulate exorbitant profits at the expense of adequate pay and benefits for employees. We must have a balance. Our economy is most successful for the most people when we provide an underlying support system for employees and their families. Job training, affordable health care and fairness in pay are all components of a policy that ensures America has a competitive workforce. I also must mention the altruistic theme of our economic and political systems which emphasize that we desire for our citizens to reach their potential in their careers and find deep joy in their personal lives. We are increasingly seeing the need to implement work-life balance strategies in society. I do have some criticisms of the European economic system that has more of a comprehensive safety net, socialistic approach when it comes to services provided to their citizens. The European model I argue is not financially sustainable over the long-term given the overdependence on governmental support for healthcare, early retirement, and other services. I do think, however, that the United States can learn some lessons from the European approach when looking at ways of reducing health-care costs for the individual, guaranteeing a fair amount of paid leave annually for workers and improving the standard of living for Americans overall. The United States is the richest nation in the world. We can simply do much better than the current status quo when it comes to adequately supporting the upward mobility of the working class and sustaining the standard of living for the middle class.

## Closing

As I close, I want to express my sincere New Year's wish that 2020 will be a transformational year during which our society will become kinder, more tolerant and accepting of all. A world in which everyone has access to healthy social interactions and abundant economic opportunities should be the norm, not the exception. We want a world in which the oceans are free of pollution and the air is clean for our children to breathe. Finally, we must act to protect all ecosystems so that they can support the diverse life found on our beautiful, blue planet now and for future generations. I wish my fellow Americans a very Happy New Year on this first day of 2020.

# 31. The Second Amendment

The gun debate is a subject on which both sides of the political spectrum need to gain some reasonableness in perspective. I do believe wholeheartedly in the Second Amendment and the right of citizens to protect their life, their families, and their property. As an American of Jewish descent, my reading up on the Holocaust indicates that the Nazis made it illegal for Jews to own guns (Halbrook). Basically, this gun control policy toward Jews made it no doubt easier for the Nazis to begin exterminating their "enemy." I also look to the end of the Civil War. It would have been quite the challenge to re-impose slavery upon millions of African Americans who took up arms and fought bravely for the Union. Along with providing protection at the individual level, gun ownership on a societal level does, I believe, keep some check on an ever-growing government that at any time can seek to impose limitations on individual rights and liberties.

### Balancing the Right to Own a Gun with the Need to Ensure Public Safety

I do believe, however, in some oversight on gun ownership since those using guns have the ability to cause tremendous harm and even death to others. When we witness horrific acts of violence, such as in the cases of young men firing automatic weapons upon both innocent shoppers in a grocery store in Buffalo, New York and children simply attending their last days in school before summer break in Uvalde, Texas, it is evident that we do need some reasonable limits on gun ownership. I do also agree that, yes, we do have some laws on the books to ensure violent or mentally unstable people cannot access guns, but sometimes they don't seem to be followed properly. Due to a clerical mistake, Dylann Roof who had an arrest record should not have passed the background test that enabled him to purchase a gun that he used to kill nine African Americans during a Bible study event at a church in Charleston, South Carolina on June 17, 2015 (Brown, Perez, and Lemon). Mr. Roof participated in religious activity with the members of the church for an hour before opening fire with a handgun.

Dylann Roof had to stop during his massacre to reload his weapon. Apparently, he desired an AR-15, but couldn't come up with the money for the more expensive weapon, as he explained during an interaction with police earlier in the year (Dahl). Certainly, more would have perished if Mr. Roof had enough funds for the semi-automatic weapon. These types of weapons can fire several rounds of bullets quickly without reloading. Weapons, such as the AR-15, have the ability to cause such devastating injury and death so quickly that they should be banned from purchase by the public, in my opinion. This type of powerful weapon should only be used by soldiers on the battlefield, not in a strictly civilian environment.

I do agree with laws that require waiting periods for people who want to purchase a gun. In addition, I support laws barring individuals with a history of domestic violence from purchasing firearms. These seem reasonable and prudent. If someone is in a violent mindset and attempts to purchase a firearm to "settle a score," the waiting period can provide a cooling off "time-out" during which tempers can calm. Also, victims of domestic violence have enough potential violence to avoid without their abuser having access to guns.

### A New Emphasis is needed on Gun Safety

Owning a firearm is a big responsibility and there should be initial training and continuing education required. A lot of proponents of safe gun ownership have pointed to Switzerland where men between eighteen and thirty-four are required to participate in military service. They are taught how to safely use guns. Switzerland has a homicide rate close to zero and 2001 was the last mass shooting event in the nation (Brueck). Increasingly, however, gun control has gotten stricter in this nation and the focus of having guns is for national security, not personal protection. Young teens are also taught how to properly handle firearms. Switzerland has a system which uses a civilian military to protect the nation. My understanding is that the National Rifle Association (NRA) had more of a focus on proper and safe use of firearms in its early days in the twentieth century in the United States. Today, the NRA is a rightwing lobbying group that basically argues that the Second Amendment prohibits the government from making any laws regarding limiting the ownership of guns by citizens of the U.S.

While I do support the Second Amendment protecting the rights of Americans to protect themselves and their families, as well as to participate in hunting activities, I do question at times if the gun culture focuses enough on safety. Gun ownership is more than a hobby or just an opportunity to play John Wick out on the target range (yes, I am a fan of this movie franchise). Gun owners must ensure that they are handling, maintaining, and storing their weapons in a safe manner at all times. I envision a national, comprehensive training program that is further tailored to each state's local gun laws that would be required for those who wish to own a gun. After the successful completion of the training, gun owners would receive a national gun owner's license, as well as a state license. I realize that there are those that contend the Second Amendment of our Constitution does not require that American citizens have to take a class or get a license to own a gun. I understand the concern here and a training program should simply encompass only what is reasonable for the safety of our communities and nation. Training requirements should in no way be used as a way to deny Americans of their constitutional right.

There are firearms safety experts and law enforcement officials who I'm sure have better ideas of what a comprehensive firearms training program for the citizenry should look like. My rationale is that any training should focus primarily on the core safety aspects of gun ownership. Training should include a substantial number of hours on a firing range during which time those applying for gun licenses are taught how to safely use and fire their weapons. Then, applicants need to be taught how to store their weapons properly. In addition, there needs to be extensive training and coaching on when it is appropriate, per local laws, to use the weapon or display the weapon in public, and when it is not. One serious concern is simply that gun owners have weapons that can be used to kill very quickly another individual or multiple people in a very short time. Prospective gun owners should be provided with substantial training in conflict management/resolution training, as well as anger management coaching. I am also in favor of annual or even every other year continuing education or training for those who carry guns. Many of us in our work life have "refresher training" courses that don't require the extensive time required that initial training or certification involves, but that highlight important key areas of knowledge to ensure that skills are maintained. I don't see a requirement for continuing education as an unreasonable burden placed on the rights of citizens – again, as long as the continuing education is reasonable as far as frequency and length of time involved.

## Closing

In conclusion, I do agree that the ability to own a gun is inherent in our U.S. Constitution's Bill of Rights under the Second Amendment as a core, fundamental right. However, this right must be balanced against the rights of others to live in peace, therefore, we do need to have some checks on those who choose to own guns. I am also firm in my conviction that gun owners must be trained properly in their use (as citizens are in Switzerland). Continuing education requirements that reinforce safe gun use procedures are essential, in my opinion, to maximize community safety. Unfortunately, I think a lack of training and proper screening has led to our nation experiencing regular mass shooting events. Also, guns are being stolen from irresponsible gun owners who do not properly secure their weapons. These stolen weapons too often end up being used to commit violent crimes in our cities and towns. Gun ownership can both be used to protect lives, as well as be used by those with ill intent to destroy lives. We must find ways to eliminate the latter, while promoting the former.

**Some Additional Comments on the Second Amendment per the Alex Murdaugh Trial**

I did want to include a minor addendum here at the beginning of March 2023 based on my viewing of the Alex Murdaugh double murder trial. I don't really follow a lot of these high profile, televised court cases, but this was somewhat of a relatively local case in my area as this trial was occurring in the "Lowcountry" of South Carolina. I did watch several trial sessions in February and March of 2023 via Court TV ("SC v. Murdaugh") and my discussion of the details of the case come primarily from these viewings.

The disgraced former attorney from a successful, wealthy family was charged and found guilty of murdering his young adult son, Paul Murdaugh, and his wife, Maggie Murdaugh. The crimes were committed on one of the family's estate properties. Mr. Alex Murdaugh was found guilty of these murders. The prosecutors argued successfully, per the swift verdict, that Mr. Murdaugh used two different guns to kill his wife and son. The apparent intention was to make it look like there were two different shooters. Of course, the defense attorneys are planning to appeal, but it looks like, based on Mr. Murdaugh changing his story about not being at the property around the time of the crime, the jury concluded he was trying to originally hide the truth. Aside from a successful appeal, this once high-profile attorney from a well-known legal family will now spend the rest of his life in prison. Indeed, before the trial, the picture of Alex Murdaugh's grandfather who was a circuit solicitor (now known as a district attorney) was removed at the order of the trial judge to prevent any influence on jurors. Mr. Murdaugh has had quite a fall from a position of great social and legal influence to now a convicted killer.

After watching a significant amount of testimony, it struck me how useful this case can be to any discussion of the Second Amendment. The testimony shared the gun culture of rural and southern America. I was a bit taken aback at the amount and variety of firearms that the Murdaughs always had around them, whether at their properties, in their vehicles or on their persons.

I don't have an issue with hunting as long as what is killed is eaten and not wasted. Personally, I find it upsetting to shoot an animal, but I am not a strict vegetarian (I am attempting to be more plant based but still do eat some meat). Obviously, I do realize where our meat comes from so I have no room to judge hunters. Also, at times I do understand when certain animal populations grow too large that hunting is necessary to keep animal populations in check to prevent starvation by the local species. The Murdaughs were avid hunters, so I have no issue with a certain number of firearms located at the rural property.

The issue that arises, however, is the prevalence and accessibility of guns when a family is experiencing a crisis. Here we have a lawyer who stole money from his clients in order to support his oxycodone painkiller addiction. The law was close to catching up to him. His son Paul had been charged with felonies in relation to a boating accident in which a young woman was killed and her family was suing the Murdaugh estate. The argument is that the lawsuit was going to uncover Alex's illegal financial activity and so to distract from that situation, he killed his son and wife. The defense continues to claim that this is a weak argument and that the real killers are still on the loose, but the conclusion of the jury is what I do defer to at this point, as to which explanation is most credible (the state's case versus the defense). So, we have a family in crisis and an abundance of firearms all readily available. One can understand the point of view of those gun control proponents who argue that if we strictly limit the availability of guns, crimes like this are much more difficult to carry out. I do think there should be some additional limitations on gun ownership for families going through crises.

One suggestion I have is that any individual who has been accused of a felony should have to immediately turn over their firearms to local law enforcement until his or her name is cleared. This would also include access to other firearms that would be easily accessible to the individual. In the case of Paul Murdaugh, my idea would be that his firearms (and apparently, he had quite a collection) would be taken away as well as the firearms of any immediate family members that he lived with at the time of his arrest. Again, I want to stress that a family in crisis should not have access to guns. Paul's legal troubles from being charged with crimes related to the death of a young woman, while a passenger on the Murdaugh family boat, clearly was a serious crisis. I contend that once Paul Murdaugh was charged with a felony, all of his guns and all the guns on the Murdaugh properties should have been seized. If the guns owned by the Murdaugh family had been seized due to Paul's legal issue, would he and his mother still have been killed apparently by Alex? We simply had a situation in which guns were abundant and readily available all over the properties.

Gun rights supporters may disagree with me on the above policy approach and argue that our legal doctrine of a defendant being presumed innocent until proven guilty would allow Paul Murdaugh to be able to retain his firearms until found guilty. I would disagree and would argue that if Paul Murdaugh were found innocent, this separation for a short period from his firearms would not be an overly burdensome intrusion on his rights. The need is to balance the rights of the individual against the need to protect the public.

I did want to share the above approach for those accused of felonious crimes when it comes to retaining or having access to firearms, but of course Paul was the actual victim in this situation. My stronger, I think, argument is that every gun owner should be required to take an annual drug test. When Judge Newman during the sentencing hearing was addressing Alex Murdaugh, it struck me as profound when Alex spoke to the court and stated that he would never hurt his family. The judge replied in essence that perhaps it wasn't the Alex he was seeing now in the courtroom, but the Alex who became someone else after taking several opiate painkillers. Alex Murdaugh had this addiction for several years. If he were required to take a drug test and if he had failed it (without a clear legal prescription for these medications), his guns would be removed per my approach.

Gun ownership is a fundamental right in our nation. I agree with that, but I'm sure the Founding Fathers would also agree that all rights have to be balanced against other rights. The ultimate right is the right to live in a nation in which each citizen's right to live peacefully without fear of bodily harm is protected through every means possible. We need training, continuing education, and drug testing to best ensure that those who own guns are doing so responsibly. Finally, I want to strongly emphasize that I do fully support the rights of Americans to safely use guns for hunting and for protecting their families. We are experiencing a crime epidemic, particularly in large cities. The police can't be everywhere, and I do have to be honest that at times I have seriously considered purchasing a firearm. It is our right as Americans to own guns, but we must do so in a responsible manner that focuses on the safe use of these weapons to prevent any unnecessary harm to ourselves or others.

# 32. Reparations for Slavery

## A Brief Argument in Favor of Reparations

When it comes to the question of whether reparations should be paid to African Americans stemming from slavery, my answer is yes. There is no doubt in my mind that the disparities between whites and African Americans are currently deeply rooted in the practice of slavery going back to the 1600s. It is clear from a commonsense standpoint that the institution of slavery set African Americans back tremendously in their future pursuits of the American dream.

Families were broken apart. Education was not allowed for slaves. Then, when slavery did end, racial discrimination continued. We witnessed throughout the late 19th Century and for the majority of the 20th Century, discriminatory practices resulting in very low pay for African Americans. Soon after the Civil War, there were many former slaves who were left to work on the same land they had as slaves for very little pay. Employers could mistreat and shortchange African Americans because the legal systems, particularly in the South, gave them very little standing against whites. Of course, when African Americans could get ahead economically, their new status was always at risk of being taken away through some newly devised legal or illegal method.

We are now aware of atrocities, such as the "Black Wall Street Massacre" in which a prosperous black community was destroyed by whites in Tulsa, Oklahoma in 1921. Homes and businesses were burned, approximately 100 to 300 lives were lost and approximately 10,000 African Americans were left homeless ("Tulsa Race Massacre"). This is one example of the establishment not even attempting to hide its racism. The wealth accumulated by successful African Americans was simply and savagely taken from them without any real consequences. Too often the criticism of African Americans has been that they just need to work harder and "pull themselves up by their bootstraps." The answer to this criticism is that throughout our history, racism and discrimination have prevented this group of Americans from advancing like their white counterparts. We have not provided an equal playing field for African Americans. The governmental and societal systems in our nation have traditionally demonstrated a reality in which innumerable hurdles have discouraged the black community from thriving. We must now take aggressive steps to address these past and some present injustices. I refer the reader to the Tulsa Historical Society and Museum website at www.tulsahistory.org/exhibit/1921-tulsa-race-massacre/[1] for more information on this horrific event.

---

1. http://www.tulsahistory.org/exhibit/1921-tulsa-race-massacre/

Now, I'm not entirely dedicated to a full governmental payout format. I think any reparation payments should be paid not only by the government, but also by any businesses or institutions which have a historical lineage of having prospered from slave labor. In addition, any large companies, such as the banks that have historically discriminated in lending or have been found to discriminate against African Americans through other practices, should be required to contribute to this national Reparation Fund. The largest American companies in the banking, real estate, manufacturing, and investment (Wall Street) industries should be asked to contribute to this effort as well. I see this as a public/private partnership.

I want to note that aside from First Nation peoples, African Americans are the primary recipients of inhumane treatment that was sanctioned by the government of the United States. The truth is that this mistreatment stemmed from a culture of prejudice ingrained in European culture long before the formation of our nation. I want to make it clear that while a lot of credible arguments can be made that other groups should receive large-scale reparations (and no doubt there are groups who have been discriminated against such as Asian Americans, Jewish Americans, Hispanic Americans, etc.), I contend that only the First Nation people and African-Americans are in a special category who should receive substantial financial compensation to properly and humbly acknowledge the distinct crimes against humanity that these two groups have experienced.

I do want to express my strong opinion that reparations should be paid to African Americans, but while I have a general idea of payout amounts (that I will detail below), I would ultimately defer to others with more expertise, as well as the African American community. It does seem cold and unfeeling to somehow assess a financial amount to fairly compensate for such past abuse and injustices. The amounts would be token payments and could never fully compensate for the unimaginable pain and suffering of the African American community. William Darity, an Economics and African American Studies professor at Duke University argues that reparations should be more than $11 trillion to close the wealth gap between whites and blacks in the United States ("What would reparations"). I think we want to have substantial payouts to African American families, but I don't support such monumental amounts that it causes tremendous financial strain on the government and the taxpayers. This is not to say that the true compensation cost of enslaved labor over centuries and generations (along with continued discriminatory practices against African Americans after the end of slavery) would not be in the trillions of dollars in today's funds, but I think we can achieve some core financial goals for the African American population without straining our nation's financial abilities to such a severe level. Indeed, if we want to look at both the financial value of work performed by slave labor and appropriate compensation for pain and suffering, the question is would we ever reach a fair amount that the United States as wealthy a nation as it is, could absorb.

## My Reparations Plan

My vision of a comprehensive reparations program consists of a three-pronged approach. The first is the establishment of a Reparations Fund that would involve the distribution of whatever amount is determined to be paid to every African American whose family has lived in the United States prior to and including the year 1964. My timeline is primarily focused on African Americans with family lineage in the United States before the 1964 Civil Rights Act, when the U.S. government essentially rendered racial discrimination illegal. I want to be clear that this is not to say that discrimination against African Americans has not continued to be a serious issue in our society during the latter part of the twentieth century and now in the first quarter of the twenty-first century, but the focus of my plan would be on the descendants of those families who suffered for possibly hundreds of years in slavery. Therefore, this would not include those relatively new citizens (or their descendants) who we have welcomed of African descent in the more recent past. I have seen different projections for the current African American population, but per the Pew Research Center (pewresearch.org), 47.2 million African Americans lived in the U.S. in 2021 (Lopez and Moslimani). Now, just for the ease of calculations I will use the figure of two million African Americans as having immigrated to the United States between 1965 and today. I do want to note, however, that based on the Pew Research Center, 3.8 million Black immigrants arrived in the U.S. between 1980 to 2019 (Tamir). Also of note is that my reparations plan would not include African Americans born in the U.S. who are descendants of these immigrants who arrived between 1965 and the current day. Therefore, my payout total approximation will be an overestimate compared to the actual, but again, I'm trying to simply provide a general snapshot of a reparations plan that can be easily calculated and understood.

Given this then general assumption of 45 million African American citizens who would qualify for reparations, if we paid each individual $10,000, we have an amount of $450 billion. I concede that this figure is a very large, tremendous amount and it is, but it is important to note that our federal government paid out $814 billion in stimulus funds during the pandemic ("Update: Three rounds of stimulus"). In addition, the payments would be paid immediately to adults 18 years or older, while children would receive the $10,000 payments when they reach adulthood, which would spread out payment distributions. My approach would not result in instantaneous millionaires, and some would understandably argue that the amounts should be more than $10,000 per person, but this amount is a symbol that could help individuals out somewhat and possibly help families significantly. My rationale here is that along with other facets of my plan, this is an effort to both apologize and assist the African American community with overall increasing their wealth. My plan, the Reparations Fund, would consist of a one-time payment or encumbrance (for those under 18 years of age) just for African Americans who currently are living in the United States at the time the plan is implemented, and not to future generations of African Americans who have not yet been born. We continue to witness harsh discriminatory practices against African Americans from the police, in the workplace and in everyday social settings, but the reality is that progress has continued to be made to defeat prejudice and hate against African Americans. As time progresses, discrimination will hopefully continue to dissipate with our society continuing to evolve into a more progressive and compassionate culture that rejects discrimination and bias.

A second initiative in this reparations effort would be to implement a grants program for African American first-time homeowners. This program would help with a down payment on a new home, but more significantly than some current first-time buyer programs. For example, up to a certain amount, African Americans could access grants to provide 20% of the purchase price for a down payment on the purchase of a home. This would immediately result in African Americans having equity in their homes and would reduce their monthly payments since they would not have to borrow the full-price amount of the home that typically would have to be all paid back through mortgage payments. This 20% down payment as many of us home buyers know also enables a mortgage holder to avoid paying for PMI (private mortgage insurance) that is set up to protect the lender in case a borrower defaults on the mortgage loan. A grant program could be supported by large banks, non-profit organizations, and the government. This type of financial support could really assist a lot of people to purchase moderately priced homes in middle-class neighborhoods. Now, this again wouldn't be a program in place for perpetuity and it would depend on how much could be devoted to the fund, but (and these figures are somewhat intimidating and hard to grasp) what about a national goal of $100 billion dedicated to down payment grants for African American families? Home ownership is a very effective way for families to increase their net values and overall wealth.

A third program that I would like to see implemented as part of a reparations program would include free tuition, housing and meals for African American students attending four-year public universities or free tuition with a living supplement for African Americans attending two-year community colleges. Too often, many students finish college only to face decades of student loan payments. This is of course a more serious problem for lower-income students and students of color. I don't want to put an amount on this goal, but just want to note that colleges and universities, both public and private, are exceptionally skilled at fundraising. Other non-profit fundraising could assist as well in funding these programs. Significant aid for the post-secondary education of African Americans would reduce the need for student loans significantly. The goal I think is that we prioritize the financial support for tuition and living expenses for full-time students in the African American community through endowments, grants, and public funding. My idea is that this program would begin as part of a reparations initiative for African Americans, but eventually extend to all students. We want our young people in this nation to obtain the education and training that they need to become productive citizens. This should not entail having to take on ridiculous amounts of college loan debt.

## Closing

In conclusion, as simply a layperson, I have laid out a few ideas that possibly could be implemented as part of a one-time reparations initiative for our nation to atone for the sin of slavery. We need to at least attempt to level the playing field on a financial basis. Society for hundreds of years did not provide the basic support needed for African Americans to attain and retain economic wealth. Reparations would be a reasonable way to begin to address the economic wealth gap between African Americans and whites due to slavery and the continued racism stemming from this institution in the United States. I want to emphasize that no program or amount of money can truly and fully make amends to African Americans whose ancestors were enslaved in the United States, but it is on us as an ethical people to take significant steps in this pursuit. Also, no plan will be completely fair to everyone it is intended to help, but if we are successful through a moderate payout plan, along with housing loans and funding for higher education for African Americans, we may just provide enough tools so that millions of our fellow Americans can rise up and out of the cycle of generational poverty. This is not about a "hand out" but about a "hand up" as the saying goes. What is more American that this approach of empowering our fellow citizens? We need to at least attempt to level the playing field. Society for hundreds of years did not provide the basic support needed for African Americans to attain and retain economic wealth. Reparations would be a reasonable way to achieve this. As far as the expense, yes, it will take a lot of financial support, but if we take a multi-year approach and obtain funding from many sources – government, non-profits, the large banks, and the many successful industries based in the United States, a comprehensive and effective reparations program can be established and successfully implemented with a reasonable burden placed on the taxpayers.

Finally, when we as a society discuss reparations for slavery, we understandably focus the debate in terms of how to financially repay African Americans for the economic wealth that was gained by others at their expense. However, in closing I want to stress that a very important part of the healing process for both African Americans and all Americans is acknowledging that while reparations may not be a perfect way to apologize, it is a method to formally proclaim that the unethical and inhumane system that was slavery was a crime against humanity. Perhaps then all Americans can move forward into the future, united as one people who are committed to protecting the individual rights and liberties of all citizens, regardless of their physical characteristics or traits.

# 33. CNN and Fox News – Levels of Bias

Up front, I admit that I am a registered Democrat so claiming that I have at least a moderate amount of bias is a reasonable assumption. I do think, however, that I can provide a relatively fair analysis of both CNN and Fox News. News networks are run by people who of course will have their own inherent biases. The question, in my opinion, is not whether there are inherent or noticeable political leanings displayed on each news network, with CNN leaning more to the left and Fox News to the right, but to what degree is this level of bias for each news organization? In addition, what steps do these networks take to ensure opposing viewpoints are offered to offset any intended or even unintended biases in reporting news or broadcasting opinion segments?

We have moved far away from a strictly facts-based presentation from yesteryear's 6 o'clock news format when a very small number of network channels provided the news. Now, we have a plethora of opinion-based programming, and this is to be expected in the world of cable news and the 24-hour news cycle. I would say to some degree that having a variety of media outlets providing different political opinions is a positive aspect for those of us who believe in the "marketplace of ideas" approach to free speech. We should desire an environment in which many opinions are allowed to be expressed and fairly evaluated on their merits. "Back in the day," Americans just had a few hours of evening news. Now, news channels of today have the resources to really present a great deal of both hard facts and commentary. I think one fair critique of CNN and Fox News is that they both need to do much better jobs of indicating when programs or segments are political-viewpoint oriented, in contrast to actual fact-based reporting of the news. I also contend that there are at least some moderate biases evident on both networks that can be seen in how a given news story is covered, or even whether a news story is covered at all. Let's take a look at a few important issues covered by these news networks.

### Fox News Is Correct - We Have a Crisis at Our Southern Border

I want to start with an example of an issue that I do agree with Fox News about – at least to some significant degree. While my "bleeding heart liberal" side feels immense empathy for our neighbors to the south, many of whom are desperately seeking a safer and better life, Fox News does aptly point out this security crisis. The constant flow of undocumented immigrants coming across the border without really knowing who they are is a national security concern. It should also be noted that it is just too dangerous for families and especially children to be making this journey to the United States from our neighboring nations in Latin America. We are unfortunately seeing more cases of very young children coming alone. The current movement of migrants leaves very desperate people in the uncaring hands of criminals who take their money to unsafely smuggle them into the United States. In addition, we are hearing more stories of girls and young women who are forced into sexual slavery by barbaric human traffickers. Furthermore, the practice of allowing migrants who are legally requesting asylum into the United States to be let free in our states and local communities, with a mere request that they show back up for their immigration hearings, really seems ridiculous. These migrants (unlike those who are illegally crossing our border) are admirably trying to follow the law by formally requesting asylum, but due to back-logged immigration courts, many people who we don't know a lot about are in our nation for months or even years awaiting trials. How closely are we monitoring these thousands of people? We of course want to welcome newcomers to our nation, but our national security requires us to perform an intensive screening and background check for every individual asking to come into our nation, even those who are following the law by claiming asylum at a port of entry. We must remember that protecting the current residents of our nation is the first and foremost responsibility of the federal government. The large influx of thousands of migrants each month is clearly unmanageable, whether they are attempting to cross illegally or declaring that they are asylum seekers through our legal process. I have my deep criticisms of Fox News personality Sean Hannity with his very politically right-leaning presentations, but I do concur with Mr. Hannity that other news outlets were late to the game in covering the border situation ("Sean Hannity: The mainstream"). There are simply too many entering our nation without appropriate screening, in my opinion. Asylum seekers need to be carefully screened and for cases that appear to be legitimate, these migrants should be placed on a list to have their cases heard before an immigration judge. However, it needs to be determined how many asylum applicants the United States can reasonably accommodate during a given time period (a month or quarter perhaps) who we will allow to enter into the U.S. to await their trials. After this reasonable limit of asylum seekers are allowed in to wait on their immigration trials, other applicants during this time period will need to remain in Mexico to await their trial dates. My approach here is somewhat of a twist based on President Trump's "Remain in Mexico" policy. I discuss further my policy thoughts on the southern border elsewhere in this work, but I am stressing here the need to be able to carefully screen, and then only absorb into the nation a number of migrants that will not overwhelm our immigration services, as well as local government services available within the interior of the nation.

My policy approach on the crises in Latin America includes an emphasis on the United States focusing on improving the lives of the people in the nations to our south, so they won't have this desperate need or desire to leave their home nations. We need to invest in their infrastructures, improve economic development inside these nations to strengthen their standard of living, and provide a better jobs program in the United States for industries that need migrant workers who can then access these jobs legally. We know that migrants are being hired to work in the U.S., but we want them to work here legally, not with an undocumented status. I clearly state that I am not in favor of a giant wall, but I am in favor of more measures to secure our border. Some additional physical barriers are needed, as well as additional staffing and technological aids (thinking drone technology, etc.) that will notify officials in real time of illegal entries across our border into the U.S.

Yes, our nation is one of immigrants, but if we allowed everyone to come into the United States who wanted to, our nation would quickly dissolve into chaos. Unlike other news outlets, Fox News does show what is actually going on at the border. What is clear is that our border security is beyond lacking, and the Biden Administration does need to be taken to task for the situation. CNN really has provided very little coverage on the border crisis. When CNN has provided coverage, the network has been late to the game and has not been critical enough of President Biden or Vice President Harris who was put in charge of the border. I want to point out here that I am a proud supporter of Vice President Kamala Harris who I consider to be immensely qualified to help lead our nation, but I have to concede that the chaos at the border speaks for itself. CNN's obvious left-leaning bias is evident in its subpar coverage of the chaotic situation at our southern border.

I do want to take a moment to lobby for the Dreamers. This group of young people arrived as small children with their parents who are undocumented, but essentially grew up in the United States. I do call for this group of undocumented immigrants who are in all reality fellow Americans, to be granted citizenship or at least a reasonable path to gain citizenship quickly.

Yes, I do agree with the theme presented by Fox News that we must have a secure border and limit border crossings. It doesn't mean we don't absorb new citizens into our nation from the nations to our south, but it does mean that we have to formulate and implement policies that ensure both the numbers of new immigrants don't overwhelm our systems, as well as ensure those being allowed in are not dangerous individuals. While I don't accuse CNN of supporting an open borders policy in practice, the network does come across as dismissing the obvious security issues with ever-increasing numbers of people crossing into our nation illegally.

## CNN Properly Covers Climate Change

One example of an issue for which I feel Fox News clearly presents an extreme, right-leaning ideology, is how the network views the issue of climate change. CNN does a very good job of presenting both news and documentaries about how climate change is causing real damage to our ecosystems, as well as connecting us to the natural world and all its wonders that in too many areas are disappearing. CNN's *Patagonia* series is excellent and I invite the reader to visit the website at www.cnncreativemarketing.com/project/patagonia/. Scientists are in general agreement that the planet is warming due to human activity (i.e. the over-release of carbon dioxide into our atmosphere causing global warming). Fox News simply rejects that global warming is causing significant harm to our critical ecosystems that are necessary to support all life on our planet. I agree that cutting off petroleum production too soon before fully developing other greener options will result in a very expensive and unreliable power grid. We have some work to do, but a planned green transition involving more wind, solar, hydro and (in my opinion) nuclear power options will be necessary to save as many animals and plants as possible from mass extinction due to our current climate change trajectory. We have to accept the fact that climate change if left unchecked will affect our ability to feed ever-increasing numbers of people. If plant and animal life suffer, feeding the human populations of the world (which continue to grow) will not be possible. Yet, Fox News vocalizes the same diatribe that we simply need to drill for more petroleum products. Their personalities contend that we can be energy independent on fossil fuels which is true, but there is never any discussion on the environmental impact of continuing to depend on fossil fuels to the extensive degree that we have been for our energy needs. According to Fox, there is no climate change and global warming doesn't exist (Tigue). This is very simplistic and dangerous political propaganda. If Fox News wants to be taken seriously as an objective news outlet and not a loudspeaker for the far right, the network's ownership, management, and on-screen personalities must come out openly in admitting that climate change is real and we all must work together to find cleaner energy sources to prevent further environmental catastrophes.

As a middle-aged citizen, I simply don't recall at any other point in my lifetime when the United States has experienced so many extreme weather events that are occurring constantly, one right after another. Forest fires occurring hundreds or even thousands of miles away negatively affecting the local air quality because they are so large, was unheard of just a few years ago. We have now experienced multiple times on the East Coast in the past few years, poor air quality because of fires as far away as Canada. It seems that hurricane season is getting longer each year with the warmer waters. Also, no longer are only coastal areas under threat from hurricanes and tropical storms, but areas located well into the interior of our nation now are at risk of severe tropical storm damage every season. Each summer now, high temperature records are continually being broken throughout the United States and across the globe. The facts can no longer be denied. The continued use of fossil fuels that are releasing tremendously large quantities of greenhouse gases into our atmosphere is causing global warming. We are no longer just hearing what the scientists are saying with the luxury of viewing them as just theoretical opinions. The science is being demonstrated by the extreme weather events that we are experiencing. Climate change is real and is a threat to delicate ecosystems. More forest fires due to hotter and drier environments, stemming from global warming

(Powell), mean poorer air quality that threatens the health of all life in the areas affected, as well as extensive damage to habitats (both natural and man-made). The increased temperatures in our oceans are forcing some aquatic life to find cooler waters toward the global poles in order to survive or face possible extinction (University of Glasgow). Higher temperatures can lead to more drought-like conditions, affecting farmers' ability to grow the large quantities of food needed to feed the world's population (Chandler). Indeed, farmers have a tall order in providing food to our approximately eight billion citizens of the world, and with climate change they are additionally challenged. When it comes to the realities of climate change, Fox News has done a disservice to the public in its coverage and attitude on the subject. CNN has not only done an adequate job, but should be recognized for providing consistent, comprehensive coverage of this global threat to life on our planet.

## Final Thoughts

In conclusion, both CNN and Fox News at times display specific biases along the political spectrum. I am not seeking a news environment that is simply providing around the clock facts with no opinions allowed. It is important to point out that any stories or reports presented on the news need to be verified (i.e. "fact-checked"). Also, opposing opinions need to be presented in an equal and fair manner. Both networks can do more to support the expression of a variety of opinions on our issues of the day. Yes, I think Fox News is somewhat more biased, but at times CNN shows left-leaning approaches to a fault.

One initial step that I think will help is ceasing the obvious practice of both networks tending to have one-sided conversations. Fox News will have multiple right-leaning, Republican correspondents and guests with typically a single left-leaning Democrat on a given discussion panel. At the same time, I do notice that CNN too often has four or five correspondents and guests on a panel who are clearly Democrats. CNN will only have one Republican commentator in the group. It all too often appears during these segments that the Democrats on CNN verbally "pile on" and at least mildly intimidate the Republican. When one witnesses a clearly Democrat-leaning show host cutting the Republican off or aggressively questioning the right-leaning guests, as opposed to providing "softball" questions to the Democrats, the ethics of the news network needs to be seriously questioned. The group of "inclusive" Democrats shows their disdain for anyone who thinks differently from them. Discussion segments on both networks should include an equal number of participants along the political spectrum as much as possible. This is a good first step. Another practice I support would be for these networks to clearly communicate to their audiences when a news show is a traditional news reporting program, as opposed to an opinion-based theme show in which the host is at times acting as a cheerleader for their political bent or candidates. For example, the *Hannity* and *The Ingraham Angle* shows on Fox News are political-opinion oriented and clearly have no intention of providing equal time for viewpoints that are in opposition to those of the Trump MAGA ("Make America Great Again") base. A story published by *The Hill* pointed out that even Rupert Murdoch, the owner of the Fox corporation, expressed that Sean Hannity and Laura Ingraham crossed the line in supporting former President Trump's false claims about the 2020 election (Mastrangelo). These shows are clearly biased in favor of one political viewpoint. I am not saying that these shows should change their formats, just that they should acknowledge they are not objective news shows, but strictly political opinion based.

A lot more needs to be done to reduce the friction between groups in our nation today. Part of improving our relationships with those whom we politically oppose is not just talking more to each other, but actually listening to each other. Another concern is that when we have differing viewpoints as to what the facts actually are to begin with on a given issue, communication is almost impossible. Our Constitution emphasizes the need for a free press. Our Founding Fathers understood that a free press is essential to a free society, as it carries out its crucial role of questioning our government in its actions and holding it accountable to the people who place their trust in the government. I would also add that a truthful and fair press is vital to the sustainability of a free society. The press has this sacred responsibility to be factual in its presentation of news stories and to provide access so that all opinions on an issue can be heard. This approach ensures that citizens are completely educated on a given issue and can best act as a check on their elected leaders' behavior. When the press disseminates accurate information, the public is empowered to hold their elected representatives ultimately responsible for their actions, as it was intended by the creators of our democratic republic.

In closing, I am calling on CNN and Fox News to take their journalistic responsibilities seriously in the sacred manner as outlined by our U.S. Constitution. The management and on-air personalities of both networks need to remember that their primary role is to present the news in an unbiased fashion and provide a forum for all legitimate political opinions to be heard. Finally, while I am not calling for the banning of political opinion shows in which one political viewpoint is dominant, there does need to be an effort by these news networks to curb a programming environment which essentially acts overwhelmingly as a cheerleader for one political party or one political agenda over another. CNN and Fox News have a responsibility to clearly communicate to viewers when they are presenting programming that is strictly political opinion based versus fact-based reporting.

# 34. Mike Pence for President - 2024

Former Vice President Mike Pence must be acknowledged and praised for his decision to uphold the U.S. Constitution and carry out his responsibilities as President of the Senate to ensure that the presidential election of 2020 was certified on January 6, 2021. Of course, the result of this certification process was the election of President Joe Biden. Mr. Pence faced severe and intense pressure from President Donald Trump and other Republicans who were basically demanding that he manipulate the rules to re-elect Trump. The refusal by the vice president to submit to President Trump's illegal and inappropriate demand is a testament to Mike Pence's dedication to our constitutional system and American way of life.

It was absolutely fine, in my opinion, for President Trump and his legal team to review and investigate any concerns or allegations of voter fraud per the 2020 presidential election. However, once those allegations were found to have no merit, the continual recitation of "The Big Lie" that Trump pushed, falsely stating that he was cheated out of victory, should have ceased immediately. Too many Republicans supported the lie which erupted into an attempted coup of our constitutional republic on January 6th.

There should not be any confusion on former Vice President Pence's legitimate, constitutional role in certifying the 2020 presidential election. Our U.S. Constitution makes it clear that the vice president has an important, but ceremonial function in his or her role during the counting of votes by the Electoral College during the certification of presidential elections. Article II, Section 1 Clause 3 of the U.S. Constitution is very clear in this, stating, "The President of the Senate shall, in the Presence of the Senate and House of Representatives, open all the Certificates, and the Votes shall then be counted. The Person having the greatest Number of Votes shall be the President..." (Kamps 54). It should be noted that the U.S. Constitution states very clearly in Article I, Section 3, Clause 4 that the United States Vice President is the President of the Senate (Kamps 51). The vice president's role in the certification of a presidential election is outlined clearly and in a very straightforward manner in our sacred Constitution.

The setting here that is important to recall is that former President Trump after losing the 2020 election carried out a rather aggressive public relations campaign claiming that he unfairly lost the election. Mr. Trump filed lawsuits in multiple states that he lost, such as Arizona and Georgia, basically claiming that he was cheated out of victory. All of his legal claims were rejected. The former president at the advice of conservative attorney John Eastman, supported a very creative and unconstitutional strategy, claiming that then Vice President Pence could in effect deem certain electoral votes of selected states illegitimate, and reject them. The obviously deceptive plan involved pro-Trump supporters unilaterally selecting new electors in states that Trump had lost, paving the way for then Vice President Pence to approve the vote of these, in reality, illegitimate electors (Cheney). This argument incorrectly claims that the vice president, the President of the Senate, has the authority to independently appoint the next president during this certification process by ignoring the true electoral votes by the states.

Several legal scholars have weighed in on the issue and regardless of political affiliation, it is clear that the consensus is that the U.S. Constitution does not give the vice president any power to change election results by the Electoral College (Fichera). Per testimony during the Select Committee to Investigate the January 6th Attack on the United States Capitol hearings, we get a very good sense of how close we were to a complete constitutional crisis and, in my opinion, the rise of a completely rogue executive leader, Donald Trump, running our nation outside of our democratic system of government. Greg Jacob, the vice president's counsel, explained during his testimony to the Congressional committee how Vice President Pence saw his role in the presidential election certification process ("Watch: Greg Jacob"). According to Mr. Jacob, Vice President Pence in December 2020 was of the opinion that the Founding Fathers had no desire to grant any one person, particularly a person running for office, the ability to affect the outcome of the electoral process ("Watch: Greg Jacob"). Mike Pence understood his duty to the United States Constitution per the election of the next president. His role was to preside over the process to count the votes submitted by each state's electors and that was the extent of his power endorsed by our United States Constitution.

We witnessed the difference between Mike Pence and Donald Trump on January 6, 2021. Donald Trump was intent, and let's be completely honest here, to do whatever he needed to in order to retain the presidency. Winning at all costs was Mr. Trump's intention, even if that meant not following our U.S. Constitution and rejecting democratic practices that our nation has followed since its inception. Trump's false claims that the election "was stolen" created a false narrative that he continued to endorse. Then, along with this narrative, Trump and his close associates endorsed another false claim that Vice President Pence could name him as the winner of the 2020 presidential election. When we combine these narratives that were intended to incite anger among his supporters with his call for a march on the Capitol on January 6, 2021, we all saw the outcome of former President Trump's deceit. The result was an insurrection at the U.S. Capitol that is now remembered as an infamous event. As Trump's supporters stormed the Capitol and fought an outmanned number of U.S. Capitol Police, the chants of "hang Mike Pence," were heard. It was due to the heroic actions of these police officers and, in my belief system, Divine intervention that prevented the murder of the vice president and members of Congress on this dark day in American history.

I think it is important to note that recent video has surfaced from January 6th showing that former Speaker (of the House of Representatives) Nancy Pelosi and former Vice President Mike Pence were communicating by phone as the horrific events were unfolding on this day. The collaboration by both American leaders is a great example of how both sides of the aisle can work together to problem-solve. Both leaders were in hiding with Speaker Pelosi showing great concern for Vice President Mike Pence and his family's safety during the insurrection (Cillizza, "Nancy Pelosi did"). These leaders were calm but emphatic with the military powers that the Capitol needed to be cleared as soon as possible for not only their safety, but so the certification of the 2020 presidential election could be completed. After the insurrection was calmed, then Vice President Mike Pence resumed the certification process late in the evening on January 6, 2021. I had never considered Mike Pence to be a great speaker, an effective speaker certainly, but not one of those speakers who brings people to their feet. On this night, Mr. Pence gave a short two-minute speech that I have reviewed multiple times and I found it to be exactly what the nation needed to hear. He condemned the violence and emphatically emphasized the need to uphold our nation's constitutional practices, including the certification process to elect the president. I found it inspirational, and it established a reset that our nation is a democratic republic with a Constitution that must be followed. His last line I will never forget. The former vice president simply said, "Let's get back to work" ("Watch: 'Let's get back to work,' Pence").

I vow to support political leaders with a clear, unyielding commitment to protect and support our free electoral system. As a moderate Democrat, my political viewpoints vary greatly from the former vice president's, but I am committed to putting country before party. When we view and examine former Vice President Mike Pence's actions on January 6, 2021, versus the attempt by Donald Trump to win at all costs and even refuse to take quick action to quell an insurrection, we should realize that Mike Pence is an American hero. All Americans should follow former Vice President Mike Pence's lead in defending our system of rule by the people through free elections, while rejecting leaders who seek to manipulate the system in order to obtain or retain power for their own personal ambitions. Based on former Vice President Mike Pence's actions on January 6, 2021, I feel that I am ethically obligated as an American to pledge my support to Mike Pence for President of the United States if he decides to run in 2024. I am a registered Democrat, but if

Mr. Pence is chosen as the Republican nominee, I will cross party lines to cast my vote for him as President of the United States. I ask others who share my love of country to do the same.

# 35. One Nation – Only One Flag

### The U.S. Civil War: The South Embraces the Confederate Flag

I have lived many years in the South, but I've never adopted an acceptance of flying the Confederate flag as a matter of regional pride. As someone with a New York, northern background, I admit I don't have the connection to the Civil War South that native-born southerners may have. I've had some very interesting discussions with very educated, well-intentioned people who claim the Civil War was the "war of northern aggression" and the South was fighting for "states' rights." I've tried to look at the situation from their perspective. I can understand in a wartime situation the terror that local citizens in the South, who may not have even owned slaves, may have experienced with Union soldiers coming to their land. I'd like to think that Union soldiers were always polite to the civilian population in the South, but of course we know of property being seized, as well as food taken from the women and children left behind by men fighting for the Confederacy. Many of us have read in our history books about Union General William T. Sherman's march through Georgia from Atlanta to Savannah that resulted in significant destruction of property (History.com Editors). Sherman's forces seized food, livestock, and items of value from the homes of southerners (History.com Editors). Known as "Sherman's March," this military campaign was not a peaceful endeavor, but was intended to essentially destroy the desire of southerners to continue to fight the Civil War (History.com Editors). Then, after the war during Reconstruction, the South really experienced very harsh economic times having to transition from a strictly slave-based, agricultural economy to catch up with the industrial-based North. It is no doubt that the nation could have done more to support a faster transition for the Southern states into the broader national economy.

Having pointed out these valid mistreatments against southern citizens, the fact, however, remains that the North did fight on the right side of history. The South's states' rights argument was motivated by the desire to continue the barbaric practice of slavery. The North fought to preserve the Union and end slavery as a legal institution in the United States. Rights of citizens protected by the federal government will always outweigh any theoretical, scholarly argument supporting states' rights that in reality limit the rights of the citizenry, or in this case, was intended to deny any rights to a segment of the population. I am a bit critical of today's movement to judge behavior of individuals hundreds of years ago based on current standards of fairness, equity, and emphasis on individual liberties for all citizens. Yet, the United States made the commitment in the early

1860s to free the slaves, while the Confederacy fought to maintain this inhumane institution. The elimination of slavery and the assurance that the Union would survive to become the world's golden light of freedom, were ethical outcomes which support the argument that the North was clearly on the right side of history.

Many Confederate flag supporters argue that flying the Confederate flag is based on "heritage not hate" as stated on many a bumper sticker in the South (Coski) (and in other parts of the nation no doubt). As stated above, I can understand the underlying resentment of the North and there is an independent spirit of the traditional South that must be admired. I concur with the point that protecting free expression and a southern, independent way of life against an overbearing "Big Brother" federal government is a valid concern. One has to realize, however, the context of what the Confederate flag has stood for throughout history.

### An Argument Calling for All Americans to Embrace the National Flag of the United States

After the Civil War and up until current times, hate groups, such as the Ku Klux Klan, have adopted the Confederate flag and have displayed it during their cruel, racist activities. The flag has been on display during acts of violence against African Americans. As hate groups have displayed the flag during marches and other assemblies, it has continued to grow not as a symbol of heritage, but as a symbol of hate and intolerance toward African Americans, Jews, and other minority groups. A symbol communicating such intense hatred for other Americans and groups should be rejected by society. The Confederate flag certainly has no overarching message of peace and unity in a land of ever evolving acceptance of diversity. Our national culture values freedom of the individual. We celebrate each other's unique traits, such as race, religion, creed, sex and gender identity or preference.

Even if there are some who truly fly the Confederate flag as a symbol of pride in their southern heritage, they should at least understand why others find it offensive. These individuals need to acknowledge that the flag represents slavery and hatred for African Americans. Also, the Confederate flag represents an attempt to secede from a nation that so many, before and since the Civil War, have sought refuge in because of our nation's guarantee of individual rights and liberties. There is a lack of realization by many who fly the Confederate flag that it stands in opposition to the flag of the United States and what it represents. I argue that you can fly the Confederate flag or fly the flag of the United States of America, but not both. It is not like flying a state flag and a United States flag that are partner governments under our democratic system. I contend that proud southerners (and they should be proud) need to find a new symbol to represent their love of their land. We can have a win-win outcome here with southerners being able to display their regional pride in a way that doesn't disrespect the flag of the United States or trigger trauma for African Americans.

I feel such a strong need as a patriotic American to communicate that we have a flag that should be the primary symbol of our heritage. Our shared American heritage is represented by a red, white, and blue flag that stands for inclusion and "justice for all." We should all take pride in our regional area and state in which we reside. When we have pride in our local area, this leads to a collaborative environment in which citizens want to maintain their quality of life or, if need be, improve upon factors that reduce that quality. Any local pride and love of where we live is fundamentally supported by the fact that our states and regions are components of a nation that ensures each of us has basic individual freedoms. In addition, we have quite an impressive economic system managed at a national level, but in a sense is executed by every state in the nation. We can all take pride both as residents of our states and of our nation that we are part of the wealthiest economy in the world – an economy that enables so many to achieve lives of abundance and fulfillment. As Americans, we are all so blessed to live in a nation that so many want to call home. We are experiencing a difficult time in the United States right now with so much intense division. Maybe part of the solution is for us to recognize the many political and economic benefits available to us as citizens of the United States. Our nation has now long been the leader of the free world. The United States has been the policeman of the world as no other nation or group of nations has the resources or intention to stand up for justice, fairness, and kindness. We are fortunate to have so many natural resources available to us to ensure a high quality of life. Basic rights for minorities and women have taken too long to be guaranteed, but we must acknowledge that our fundamental system of government has allowed freedoms to continue to be expanded to all. We must all join together and affirm our heritage of freedom that our national flag represents.

## Closing Thoughts

Yes, I conclude with my contention that southerners should be proud of their region. Some of the kindest, caring people come from the Southern United States. The independent nature of southerners is admirable and their distrust of a large, federal government whose power needs to be checked is understandable and perhaps praiseworthy. The federal government should certainly continually be checked by the people to ensure the government is representing the people's best interests. However, southerners should not be proud of the Confederate flag. This is a symbol that represents an attempt to secede from our nation, keep African Americans in bondage and to this day is used as a symbol of hate against minorities.

I do believe in political speech and expression even if it is of a hateful nature. Citizens in our nation do have the right to fly any flag that they wish as an act of free speech. I do differ from others who understandably would call the flying of the Confederate flag hate speech that should be banned. I want to provide some clarification here on my opinion. I agree that if the flag is used as an in-your-face action to intentionally intimidate specific individuals or groups, such as if a white supremacist group goes out of its way to confront African American citizens, I would consider that unprotected hate speech. I do fundamentally support freedom of speech, even when I find that speech to be repugnant. This is why I contend that the mere displaying of the Confederate flag as a general political statement should be protected speech under our First Amendment. I concede that it may not be so easy to distinguish between protected free speech and hate speech. I certainly have my concerns as an American with Jewish heritage on both the displaying of the Confederate flag and the Nazi swastika which are both symbols of hate and exclusion. However, I do think having true freedom of speech means allowing even disgusting speech a place within certain constructs. My goal is not to force my opinion on others, but I am imploring these citizens who freely display the Confederate flag to consider putting it aside and replacing it with the red, white, and blue flag that represents the light of freedom and hope for humanity. Change can only truly happen if individuals come to realizations on their own, such as freely deciding to stop displaying a flag that brings such distress to many citizens. My opinion is that all Americans should overwhelmingly wish to express their patriotism by displaying our national flag - not because it represents our significant world influence or military power, but because it represents a "melting pot" of people from around the world who have come together for "the great experiment" of democracy. As a very patriotic American, I argue that the world is a much colder, darker place without the United States of America..

It is simplistic to think that just flying the flag of the United States can overcome our differences. I also realize that not everyone shares my love of country. Admittedly, our nation is not perfect and has engaged in actions that we should not be proud of, such as the displacement of First Nation peoples. We do need to confront our past and current failures, but I contend that we are our best selves when we focus on our core American values of individual freedom, equal opportunity, and safety for all citizens. We are then best able to reset how we interact with one another. Let us remind ourselves that in the United States we solve our differences with compromise, compassion, and collaboration - not by beginning a new civil war. I implore all Americans, regardless of where you reside in this great land of ours, and regardless of what race you are or religion that you follow, to remember that we are all Americans. We are a people of one free nation who should all pledge our allegiance to only one national flag – the flag of the United States of America.

# 36. The Reconnection (A Poem)

I make a decision to connect with Mother Nature right here, right now - to step away from the computer, tablet, and smart phone, if just for a bit. It is time to be outside with nature, not observing it through a window.

Feeling the wind enliven my skin, I begin to remember that elemental connection humanity has with nature. I feel free again, like my friend the wind.

Walking and feeling the grass under my feet, my spirit rises with each step. I reconnect to that part of myself that somehow is fulfilled by just being here, living with the grass. Simply being in the moment with the green blades of life reawakens my spirit. I admire the true beauty of the lush lawn and breathe in its scents of chives and dampness.

I walk over to my friend, a tree, who I have ignored too often. Greeting her, I touch her rough bark, silently thanking the tree for the shade and beauty that she provides. I watch the tree's branches and leaves swaying with the wind, almost as if waving a "hello, where have you been?"

The Sun provides light that is rejuvenating. I enjoy bathing my arms and face in the Sun's warmth and energy. I thank the Sun for the warmth it provides and for sharing its light so life can exist here on Earth.

I see a small stream and venture over to it, listening to the water running as it has done for countless days. Sticking my hand in the water, I feel the softness and the strength that is this miraculous substance. I conclude that I want to be like water - so flexible and yielding, yet it can wear down mountaintops with its gentle, continuous movement that disguises tremendous power. Yes, I want to be able to flow with the challenges of life, but through consistent effort, overcome these challenges to achieve my goals.

I realize soon that I must return to the "real world" of doing this and that, to achieve whatever is the popular notion of "success." Everything in balance I decide. The technology that we have is amazing, but have we separated ourselves too much from our natural home? Have we lost an essential part of being human by spending so much of our existence in front of our screens in our climate-controlled dwellings? I sense a feeling of great energy in my reconnection with my new friends. I take a moment more to ponder the peace of walking on the grass, talking silently to the tree, bathing in the warm sunlight and feeling the stream's rush through my fingers.

Walking back home, I feel a sense of energy, strength, and peace from this reconnection to the natural world. Thoughts of watching the screens come to the forefront of my mind, but this time I pause. I close my eyes and listen to the wind. I make a promise to myself and my new friends that I will soon return, but now with the realization that I am not truly whole unless I'm in connection with the source of life which is our natural world.

An intense feeling of gratitude comes into focus - gratitude for the Creator's universe and for our Mother Earth to which all living beings are dependent upon for existence. I commit to do my part to protect Mother Earth in kind for the life and peace she provides to me and all of life. Call it a transformation, a spiritual awakening or just a new outlook on what is truly important in life. I call it, a Reconnection.

# 37. Reconnecting with Nature to Improve Our Quality of Life

I am no poet, but in my work above, "The Reconnection," I hope I am expressing to the reader how many of us in our twenty-first century lives have separated ourselves from nature and how reconnecting to the natural world benefits our overall well-being. A large part of this separation is due to the technology we use in everyday life. I certainly am in the camp that greatly enjoys being on my smartphone or watching television. Sometimes in my household it gets almost comical with my teenage son on his smartphone and laptop, while I am on my smartphone "surfing the Web." Of course, the television is on in the background as if anyone is really paying attention to that screen. We are incredibly spoiled with all of this technology right at our fingertips. I admit I love it. In addition, so many of us are on screens for work, whether at an on-site facility or now with a post-pandemic schedule, working remotely at home. The computers and all of this technology have made our lives more enriched. The concern, however, is that if we become so physically separated from the natural world in our daily lives, we won't reap the psychological and physical benefits of being immersed in it.

Many poets and artists romanticize life connected to the natural world through prose or paintings, etc. The calming effect of gazing upon a painting of a tree or seeing a picture of a favorite nature scene is something all of us have experienced. Robert Frost's poem, "Stopping by Woods on a Snowy Evening," comes to mind as an excellent example of this calming connection humanity can experience in nature. I believe this poem is so famous because it so well communicates the tranquility one can experience of being in the woods while snow gently and quietly falls, transforming the world into a winter oasis. It becomes almost a spiritual endeavor.

Simply spending time in nature on a regular basis has many benefits. The American Psychological Association (APA) points out that there is a link between spending time in nature and lower stress, a more positive outlook, a reduction in the risk of mental disorders and even better cognitive function and processing (Weir). It is also impressive that according to the APA, spending time in nature promotes one's happiness and can help to improve the mental state of someone who is experiencing serious, mental anguish or suffering (Weir).

Of course, we don't need any experts to explain the many benefits that we can experience by spending time in nature. We can discover these for ourselves. I am no Robert Frost. My poem is based on a combination of real experiences in nature and my imagined ideal natural setting that I merged together. My goal in writing this poem was to provide a vision that communicates the great sense of peace one can enjoy just by spending quality time in nature. We live in a world of always going and doing. Simply being in the natural environment grounds us. When we experience being in the natural world from where all living things have evolved, it truly is an exercise in renewal and resetting of one's mind, body, and spirit. How many of us use our smart phones to play natural sounds of the rain, blowing snow or simply of waves splashing on the shore of a beach? These sounds do bring on a sense of calm. I contend that when we realize we can experience these environments in the real world with not only the sounds, but the view, the sense of the terrain under our feet, the level of moisture in the air, the air circulating around our bodies, as well as any scents, we realize that being in nature is a necessity for our overall mental and physical well-being. No technology can substitute for the real thing.

It is important to add that along with all the benefits of connecting with nature that I've already discussed, the physical benefits to our health of being active in nature must not be overlooked. I contend as a life-long runner that exercising outside may help to keep one committed for the long-term to a healthy, active lifestyle. Running or walking along a scenic trail is much more enjoyable than doing the same activity inside the gym on a treadmill. Walking along the beach or taking a day-hike in the mountains are great ways to maintain a healthy weight and improve cardiovascular health, all while enjoying the great beauty of the natural environment. Of course, if one doesn't live near the beach or the mountains, just taking regular walks or bike rides in one's neighborhood or in a nearby park are accessible and enjoyable activities that will improve physical health.

Finally, exercising outside is a great way to foster community cohesiveness. Whether one is taking a walk with a few friends or joining a group that meets regularly, exercising outside as a social endeavor brings communities together. New friendships emerge and neighborhoods can be transformed into more inclusive settings when we all get off the screens, get outside and get to know one another in person.

We live in a technologically advanced society. I certainly am not campaigning to get rid of our technology. No one is taking away my iPhone (if I were texting I would insert a smiley face emoji here with my overused "LOL"), but too much screen time with no outdoor activity can be detrimental to our health and well-being. Our physical, mental and, I would contend, spiritual health can be greatly improved and enhanced by committing to spending more time outside. We should also commit to spending time outdoors not only on an individual basis, but we should do this as a social activity that will connect family, friends, and communities together. I assert that if more of us socialize together outdoors, the result will be a kinder and more peaceful world, not to mention more of us would be dedicated to protecting the environment. Humanity thrives when we live a connected life to our beautiful world, not when we separate ourselves from it. In closing, while this essay is not primarily intended as a call to protect our natural environments from deforestation and human development, I want to point out that in order for people to enjoy the outdoors, we need to protect our national, state, and local parks. These natural, minimally disturbed areas and green spaces need to remain and expand in size for the enjoyment of current citizens and for all future generations.

# 38. Coexisting with Our Natural World: Saving Our Planet and Saving Ourselves

I've discussed the many benefits of spending time in nature on a personal scale. I'd like to take some time to discuss the current state of our natural environment in a global context. One could write a book just about the imminent threat that our environment is now under because of mankind's reckless treatment and abuse of the natural world. My concern is that by separating ourselves from the natural world to such a significant degree, gradual, incremental-moving environmental catastrophes, such as global warming and pollution, may not receive the attention that they deserve until it is too late. As custodians of the Earth for future generations, we need to realize that protecting the environment locally, nationally and on a global scale is essential to humanity's survival. Thus, we need to re-establish a relationship with the natural world in which we can live our modern lives, but simultaneously co-exist with and support our life-sustaining planet. When we protect the environmental health of the planet, we will reap an abundant and wide spectrum of benefits for ourselves and for all life on Earth.

Ecosystems are dying and we must realize that not only does this affect a wide variety of plant and animal life, but without a vibrant natural world, we are endangering the future of mankind. We do need to listen to what the experts, the scientists, are saying. The planet is warming (popularly known as "global warming") due to climate change, and we must take heed to do all we can to stop this. Climate change in the form of global warming is mainly caused, of course, by the burning of fossil fuels. We know that we can't eliminate the use of these fuels overnight, but we must do all we can to improve and increase the use of renewable sources of energy (solar, wind, geothermal, and hydropower). Even the use of nuclear power plants which are now cleaner and safer than ever, should be included at least as an energy alternative to study. The reduction in carbon emissions by transitioning to electric cars, replacing vehicles that run on fossil fuels is one policy that is gaining momentum. Also, local food production to reduce the large-scale transportation of food products over long distances is another idea that could help. Technological advances have contributed to a more polluted world that depends on fossil fuels. Bright scientists are now working on new "green" technologies that can be used to clean the environment on a macro scale by moving away from fossil-fuel dependence. Indeed, carbon capture technology that actually removes carbon dioxide directly out of the air could be a game changer. As reported on the news show, *60 Minutes*, a Swiss company, Climeworks, has built the first facility that captures carbon dioxide in Iceland ("Carbon Capture").

The reality is that we are already experiencing environmental disasters that pose threats to the world's food supply. Due to hotter, drier weather, there is less farmable land. The now warmer oceans with higher temperatures and less oxygen have resulted in a less hospitable climate that is putting a strain on many species of sea life. Areas of once abundant fish that were used as seemingly boundless fishing locations for our food supply are no longer available. I was shocked and dismayed to find out that in just a few years, the Alaskan crab supply went from being in abundant supply to a situation in 2022 in which the fishing season had to be called off, due to a catastrophic dwindling supply of this seafood option (Ramirez). The question will be how long it will take to bring back this population that was just a few years ago thriving in the Bering Sea. It is shameful that, yet another life form is threatened because of global warming caused by human activity. The crab fishing industry that so many depend on for their livelihoods has been devastated and there is less of a delicious food item that many seafood lovers seek.

The United Nations International Children's Emergency Fund (commonly known as UNICEF), the organization that works to improve the lives of children living in poverty throughout the world, is following how climate change is affecting the availability of safe drinking water for children and families (please visit www.unicef.org). Higher temperatures mean some areas of fresh water are drying up (Reuters). Of course, this can create very serious crises in locations that desperately need more, not less, safe drinking water options. Also, as temperatures rise, glacier ice melts and sea levels rise, causing freshwater areas to have higher saline content ("Water and the global"). This result of climate change threatens the ability of many areas to continue to function as safe, freshwater sources. Finally, UNICEF and other organizations explain that as temperatures rise, unhealthy pathogens also increase in freshwater areas, potentially making them unsafe to be used for human consumption ("Water and the global").

I can go on and on about how human activity is harming our planet due to our excessive dependence on fossil fuels, our unsustainable use of the world's natural resources, and humanity's irresponsible release of pollutants into our natural environment. One needs only to look at the large amounts of runoff from agricultural animal manure and from pesticides used on crops which spill into our waterways, causing severe damage to ecosystems ("Industrial Agricultural"), as proof of the seriousness of the issue. Our agricultural system worldwide needs an overhaul to make it much more environmentally friendly. If human behavior does not change, the planet's ability to continue to sustain life will be limited. My hope is that the majority of us will realize this. We must act to protect our planet's environment before it is too late. I like to think of myself as an altruistic person who desires to protect all the varieties of species of plants and animals who call our diverse planet home. There is something intrinsically humane and moral about protecting all life forms and preventing the extinction of any animal or plant species. Ensuring that life continues to thrive on our blue globe floating out in infinite space, one could say, is our core moral imperative. I support the effort of many environmental heroes in their pursuit at leaving our planet in a better environmental state than we found it. The moral imperative is to ensure that future generations can enjoy the tremendous resources that the natural world provides to humanity. We can achieve this goal if we work to protect our environment now and move forward on a macro, societal level.

## Closing

In conclusion, I concede it is not realistic to think that everyone will join in an active environmental crusade to save the planet. What is realistic, in my opinion, is that by continuing widespread communication efforts, the vast majority of the planet's citizens will be convinced that in order to live our lives in peace and prosperity, we must come together on this issue and take creative actions to establish a sustainable, environmentally friendly way of life. We need to take actions individually, such as eating less red meat, the production of which involves large amounts of greenhouse gas emissions, and eating more plant-based sustenance on a more frequent basis. Opting for walking or bike riding rather than using an internal combustion engine (ICE) vehicle for short errands, is another good idea to reduce our "carbon footprints" and help out the environment. Technological advances must be a significant component in reducing our emissions and we must implement these technologies in practical ways. I've always wondered why all residential structures don't now have solar panels to complement traditional power sources. For that matter, since our metal vehicles are such great conductors of heat (we have all felt how hot our vehicle roofs get in the summer in the direct sunlight), I've pondered for some time why we haven't developed vehicles that have some type of solar-power component, such as the installation of solar panels on vehicle roofs. Society can and does need to find ways to live a modern life, while at the same time protecting the environment. All of us on an individual basis need to act by making greener choices in our lives. However, we also need to develop new green technologies that can complement these individual choices in order to effectively reverse the damage to our environment caused by human activity. The plain truth is that if we want to live in a healthy, abundant world that supports mankind in every way with food, water, and shelter, we must save our planet, in order to save ourselves.

# 39. The 1619 Project: Leftist Propaganda or History Corrected

The 1619 Project created and sponsored by *The New York Times Magazine* includes essays and poems from writers, such as the justifiably acclaimed author Nikole Hannah-Jones, who is the lead author of this literary collection. Nikole Hannah-Jones expertly and effectively communicates to the reader the horrific and barbaric treatment of African Americans in the now United States for centuries, as well as points out the many contributions that African Americans have made to our society (Hannah-Jones). The intent of *The 1619 Project* is to adjust the mainstream historical account of United States history, by placing the role of the enslavement of African Americans in our nation's past as a primary factor that determined how our society has developed and evolved.

## 400 Years of Struggle

The underlying theme of this work asserts that our history as a nation truly began in August 1619 with the arrival of the first African slaves in Virginia and not with the Declaration of Independence signed in 1776 or any other notable event in American history. The literary works for this program were first of course published in *The New York Times Magazine* in 2019. This initial assemblage of essays and poems has since expanded to include public forum lectures, the distribution of academic materials for schools and a book produced from a collaborative effort between Nikole Hannah-Jones and *The New York Times Magazine*. *The 1619 Project* explains much more thoroughly and compassionately than traditional sources, in my opinion, the struggles that African Americans have had to endure in the history of our nation. African Americans were denied any core basic human rights during slavery, were prevented from accessing any formal education for generations and had any wealth they could acquire too often taken from them through legal, but racist systems. There is no doubt that this distinct racial group has faced far too many obstacles in American society. The personal accounts shared through the essays and poems in *The 1619 Project* accurately and effectively communicate these atrocious mistreatments committed against African Americans throughout the past four centuries.

I do think the timeline of releasing these works four hundred years after the 1619 date is quite appropriate. This timeline theme communicates effectively that we are not talking about decades, but multiple centuries during which African Americans consistently suffered physical and emotional abuse. This abuse occurred both before and during the formal creation of the United

States. I think a core realization that one can take away from this "Project" is that we are talking about four hundred years of enslavement, apartheid and continued racial bias that African Americans have had to endure as a people. The length of time in which African Americans have been exploited, neglected, and savagely abused cannot be emphasized enough as we collectively examine this 400-year period. When we look at current comparisons of African Americans to other groups in America, we consistently see African Americans lagging behind in health outcomes and socio-economic successes. In addition to economic and social disadvantages that African Americans have historically experienced, it should be evident that life in America has had a serious detrimental impact on the mental health of African Americans. When those along the political spectrum debate whether additional public policies should be implemented to improve the lives of African Americans, *The 1619 Project* should be studied for its comprehensive information on the plight of African Americans during the past 400 years. The reality is that African Americans have had to overcome centuries during which the tools of success that so many Americans have had access to from the nation's inception, were not extended to them. This truth must not be lost on those who have often ignorantly proclaimed that African Americans simply need to "pull themselves up by their bootstraps."

## The Long History of Institutional Racism

*The 1619 Project* does an exceptional job of communicating how institutional racism continues to negatively affect the lives of African Americans. Our nation's history of slavery, apartheid in the segregationist South and simply terrorist acts by citizen-formed hate groups, such as the Ku Klux Klan, laid the foundation for continued inequities. I think *The 1619 Project* has been very successful in displaying how past injustices have led to such wide disparities for modern African Americans when compared to other Americans in areas of employment, housing, education and even in medical care. The work details how long-standing practices have led to these real-world disparities. Linda Villarosa provides an insightful look at the history of racial discrimination when it comes to the provision of adequate medical care for African Americans in her essay in *The 1619 Project*. A false argument with no objective credibility was perpetuated which claimed that Africans had significant physical differences from other humans, including the false claim that they can tolerate higher levels of pain compared to other races (Villarosa). A biased and simply incorrect rationale was used to justify physical overwork, brutal whippings and other inhumane physical punishments inflicted on slaves (Villarosa). These mistreatments became ingrained, normal occurrences in this economic and social system that protected the institution of slavery. Claims that African Americans were sub-human were, what I would refer to in modern times, part of a comprehensive public relations campaign by the South to protect the practice of slavery and downplay the institution's dehumanizing effects. This false, pain tolerance narrative continues to result in occurrences in which African Americans do not receive adequate amounts of medications to properly manage their pain due to legitimate medical conditions (Villarosa). The denial of proper levels of medication provided to African Americans that continues today is cruel, given that modern medicine can alleviate severe pain of those suffering from serious medical ailments often quite easily.

It is a tragic truth in the 21$^{st}$ century that continued racism too often means African Americans receive substandard treatment in medical settings in comparison to their white counterparts (Villarosa). Thus, African Americans on the whole experience a lower quality of life and shorter life expectancies.

I am not a historian, so I don't want to argue to the exact degree that African Americans have played in building our nation into the great economic and democratic power that it is today, but it is evident that African Americans have played a significant role in establishing the United States as the unmatched leader of the free world. Whether it is through their great work to build the architecture and physical structures of our nation or their development of a variety of musical genres in our popular American culture, African Americans need to be honored for the great contributions that they have made to our nation and Western society. No doubt, African Americans have been involved at every step of the way in shaping the United States into becoming the great world power that it is today. One can quickly perform a "Google" search and view the significant inventions and contributions of African Americans in the medical, science, entertainment, and other professional fields. We have a moral responsibility to continue to share the great accomplishments of African Americans and set the historical record straight. This needs to be an ongoing effort, not just a subject briefly discussed during Black History Month.

## Our Nation's Date of Birth

Now, I do have somewhat of an issue with placing the year of 1619 on the same level of prominence in our nation's history with the date of July 4, 1776, as *The 1619 Project* argues, particularly when discussing the authentic date of our nation's birth. I do see the immense value in establishing August 1619 as a point in our history that we as Americans should understand as having great historical significance. It was during this year when slavery and all the crimes committed against African Americans essentially began. Where I differ somewhat from *The 1619 Project* is that I do consider the year 1776, when the Declaration of Independence was signed, to be the year when our nation began its formal life as a consolidated nation-state, or the birth of the United States as we know it. The signing of the Declaration of Independence was the beginning of our national vision with a political ideology dedicated to the freedom and liberties of the individual. I do fairly and appropriately need to point out that Thomas Jefferson who so eloquently penned our Declaration of Independence, which established our American ideals of freedom and equality, was himself a slave owner. Our nation's historical relationship with race is indeed both troubling and complex. It is true that we have made great strides in extending rights and opportunities to African Americans, but as *The 1619 Project* very effectively communicates, this progress has been excruciatingly slow when we view the history of African Americans over this period of 400 years. Yet, I still contend that it was the great intention of freedom established in 1776 that marks our beginning as a future protector of individual liberties. Yes, we know that the Declaration of Independence and the United States Constitution did not immediately free the slaves, nor ensure equal rights for women. I do argue, however, that the intentions set forth in these documents did enshrine in words, the value that we as Americans place on individual liberties, basic human rights and equality that did lead to the amendments to the Constitution guaranteeing rights to African Americans, women, and others. One only has to look at the language of the 13th, 14th, 15th, and 19th Amendments to the United States Constitution that ensured the end to slavery, equal protection for all under the law, the right to vote for African Americans and the right to vote for women, for proof of the fruition of these initial constitutional intentions. 1776 was the year that our nation was placed on a righteous evolutionary path that continues to extend rights and freedoms to citizens of all backgrounds, races, genders, and religions.

We certainly must acknowledge that many of our Founding Fathers owned slaves and should not be glorified because of their use of slavery to build their personal wealth. I certainly think this fact needs to be clearly acknowledged, but this new movement to reject all aspects of our Founding Fathers because of slavery is to some degree holding them to the moral and ethical standards of the 21st century. I am not contending that they should be absolved of the crimes of owning slaves, but I think historical context and societal norms of the time need to be understood, even if we do not accept these norms today, which correctly, of course, we should not when it comes to the inhumane institution of slavery. My viewpoint is that we should not completely reject our Founding Fathers. This is particularly the case when we recognize their enlightened outlook which led to the creation and perpetuation of our free society. Therefore, I contend that while these men did own slaves, it was their work to establish a framework of individual rights that created the social and legal environments which later led to the end of this great crime against humanity - the enslavement of African Americans.

### Summary Analysis of *The 1619 Project*

I want to point out that in this brief essay I do not attempt to provide an in-depth review of all aspects of *The 1619 Project*. I am providing a general overview and expressing my opinion on whether this collection of works should be considered historically factual, thus, supporting an adjustment of how we as Americans should view our history, or if this program should be viewed as closer to an opinion-based tool that while limited in its historical claims, can still be used to communicate the horrendous experiences of African Americans throughout our history. Where I fall along the opinion spectrum is that I do think this should be viewed as a series of works that can be used to educate Americans on slavery and help explain how institutional racism has unjustly kept African Americans from accessing the vast opportunities that others have enjoyed in the United States. One theme of *The 1619 Project* that I do have some issue with, is the attempt to reformat our American identity from the traditional vision of the United States as being a nation based in freedom of the individual. This traditional vision includes the acknowledgement that we have had a past in which the barbaric institution of slavery was a great sin of our nation for which we should hold great regret for and continue to make amends for by working to eliminate all forms of racism. The adjusted national identity promoted by *The 1619 Project* consists of the assertion that America's birth and development were primarily based, founded upon, and connected to the institution of slavery. I am in no way attempting to downplay the significantly negative outcomes for modern-day African Americans resulting from the institution of slavery or reduce the responsibility that we as Americans must take on in doing all we can to make amends for this great crime against humanity. Yes, we admittedly have a long way to go in achieving a fair society based on race even in the

first quarter of the 21$^{st}$ century, but our nation's true developmental path has led it away from the enslavement of a people to the swearing in of Barrack Obama in 2009 as the nation's first African American president. This is progress that only a great nation founded upon the ideals of equality and individual liberty can achieve. Indeed, I believe America's true presence in the world has been as a leader in extending and protecting individual liberties for all. The United States is respected as the great protector of rights. This is our true identity and is why people from all over the world of all races, religions and ethnicities seek to come to our shores.

I do think *The 1619 Project* is a remarkable work and does have its place in schools and other environments as a great modality to communicate how the extensive history of slavery and discrimination has so negatively affected the quality of life for generations of African Americans. These literary works and programs also provide substantial justification for the need to formulate and implement policies to improve lives in the African American community. One of the great triumphs of *The 1619 Project* is its ability to facilitate American society in honestly and directly confronting the great American atrocities of slavery and racial discrimination.

A primary concern, however, that I do have, which is reflected in the approach of *The 1619 Project*, is this popular initiative in the current era on mostly the far-left side of the political spectrum, of rejecting all aspects of Western culture. Certainly, European Colonialism has a great deal to account for, as far as mistreatment and crimes against indigenous peoples around the world, including people from Africa, India, and the Americas. The British Empire alone is responsible for the brutal treatment and murder of millions. This history should not be ignored, but the evolution of Western culture into what has become the entity that has championed individual freedoms and morality also needs to be recognized. Western culture is responsible for the modern world's economic, social, and political institutions that have lifted millions out of poverty and have solidified the basic ethical tenet of protecting human rights. Admittedly, progress has been very slow through the centuries, but it must be acknowledged that it is from modern Western, cultural ethics that the free world now rejects the mistreatment and discrimination of minorities and women. I contend in closing that it is our modern Western culture that created an environment in which a program, such as *The 1619 Project,* has been able to be freely developed and openly discussed.

In closing, I encourage all Americans to read the array of essays and view online the discussions on the African American experience as presented in *The 1619 Project.* My hope is that *The 1619 Project* is highly successful in not only communicating the great injustices that African Americans have faced in our nation for centuries, but that it begins a collaborative movement to address past inequities, enabling African Americans to acquire the same levels of wealth and quality of life as any other group in our nation. When our society implements comprehensive initiatives to effectively address past abuses suffered by African Americans, as well as confront ongoing racial discrimination, only then will we be fulfilling the promise of freedom for all citizens of the United States. Finally, by focusing on our history of slavery and racial prejudice over a 400-year span of time, *The 1619 Project* must be acknowledged as a transformational, ground-breaking initiative that provides the justification for our society to recommit to a shared, ethical goal of genuinely achieving racial equality in the United States. Then, we can truly move forward as one unified nation of free people.

# 40. My Personal Religious Beliefs

## My Religious Background

I think it is important as I talk about my opinions on religion, that I provide some information on my religious background and personal beliefs. We all have different viewpoints based on our religious upbringings, our specific sets of experiences and our evolved attitudes toward religion in general. Yes, it does seem appropriate for me to share some personal history which could explain how I have arrived at where I am currently as far as my religious faith journey.

I am influenced by Judaism as this is my family's religion. Both of my parents were brought up in Jewish households. My mother came from a reformed Jewish family which is less strict at following the traditional Jewish rules like keeping Kosher. My father's family did follow more of a conservative Jewish life and they kept Kosher. I recall in my paternal grandfather's household there was the practice of not eating meat and milk items together. Many Kosher households even have separate utensils and dishes for partaking in meat and milk food products. This even goes so far as to having separate dishwashers for utensils and dishes used for meat and milk items to ensure there is never any intermingling between the different food categories. My childhood household in New York was definitely on the reform end of the Jewish spectrum. On occasion we went to Friday night services at the local synagogue as I recall, but my mother was not a fan of organized religion and while we definitely considered ourselves Jewish, we always had a Christmas tree each year. I'm sure this was to the disapproval of all our Jewish relatives.

I always provide an apology to devout Christians when I say that Christmas can be celebrated as a secular holiday as my family did. I truly mean no disrespect to those of this peaceful faith of Jesus. My mother was a history major and focused on British history in college. When she was living she could name off the lineage of the British monarchy going back centuries and describe in detail the lives of many in the royal family. She knew the history of how Christmas trees were originally Pagan in nature and had its roots in ancient times during the short, dark days in December, long before the beginning of Christianity. We had the understanding that the history of the Christmas tree was generally linked to the winter solstice and other celebrations of nature associated with Paganism. The goal by early Christian leaders to link this late December time of celebration for Pagans to the new holiday of Christmas was intended (very successfully I might add) to convert large populations more easily to the new Christian religion. I recall one Christmas in the late 1970s in New York that while we had a live Christmas tree in our living room, my sister and I had a small tree in the hallway near our bedrooms that was a white artificial tree. Interestingly after all these decades later, I now have a full-size white frosted (as if with snow) artificial tree that I get out every year from my backroom closet. This secular practice of Christmas with the tree and Santa Claus probably did make the transition easier when my parents moved my twin sister and I from New York City with a major Jewish population to North Carolina with a comparatively much smaller Jewish population in 1980. There were times when we felt different because we didn't attend church which was a very big part of life in the South, but when Christmas came around we shared in those traditions of the Christmas tree and opening of gifts on Christmas. Yes, we still celebrated Hanukkah, the Jewish festival of lights in December, but my family followed the practice of opening presents on Christmas. There are those devout Christians who do argue that the holiday that celebrates the birth of their savior has been commercialized and secularized. I certainly understand their concern, but, from my standpoint, the fact that everyone can join in the fun of Santa Claus, putting up Christmas lights and opening presents on Christmas morning, allows everyone to be included, regardless of their families' religious affiliations. In addition, many businesses would have a very hard time keeping afloat if it weren't for this annual holiday of shopping and giving. Everyone, however, should respect that this holiday from a religious sense is very sacred to devout Christians who celebrate the birth of their savior, Jesus Christ, on Christmas.

## My Current Religious and Spiritual Beliefs

The above information provides some background on my religious upbringing. I was Jewish but we didn't attend temple on a regular basis and loosely followed the traditions. We did not celebrate Christmas as a religious holiday, but more of a secular, cultural holiday. One may ask what my current beliefs consist of today as a middle-aged citizen. I would say I do consider myself a person of faith who does believe there is a God who consciously created the universe or universes. Judaism is what I would say I follow as my primary religious doctrine, but I do admit that while it is now becoming more religiously diverse, having lived in the homogenous South for the vast majority of my life, Christian doctrine is part of the social fabric here and has had an influence on me. My basic religious outlook is I don't proclaim to know which religion is right, but that I like to think that the general doctrine of being Godly through treating others well and doing good deeds for the world is what is ultimately important on a cosmic level. This is why I do think the religions of Buddhism and perhaps Hindu have had some influence as well on this outlook. I do believe somewhat in Karma even on a practical level that what you put out into the world, you receive back.

As far as the Christian influence on my life, I do try to follow Jesus' message of peace and forgiveness (although I do sometimes come short on the forgiveness part – I am working on it). I have even noticed myself invoking the name of Jesus at times in prayer, however, I don't place Jesus ultimately on the same level as to what I believe is one Supreme God. I do go along with the understanding that Islam, Christianity, and Judaism are all connected by the same God. Living in the "Bible Belt" South, I came to understand that a lot of Christians think of Jesus as God with the terms "Jesus" and "God" being interchangeable. Some may argue with me on this point, but this is how I see their practice and prayer process. Now I do want to state here that there is no doubt religious intolerance in rural America. I have had a mixed bag of experiences in the South with some asking about the Jews role in killing Jesus, while other Christians focus on the fact that Jesus was Jewish (and Jews are "God's chosen people"). What I want to focus on though and communicate is that while there are pockets of religious intolerance in the South and, no doubt, elsewhere in our nation, for the most part, I think rural southern Christians are honorable and moral people who are just trying to live in accordance with their faith. I admire the tremendous amount of good work that Christian groups perform in their communities and for people around the world. I call an overall Christian conservative town home and it is a peaceful place in which one can live in tranquility with others. This I feel is important to point out, as I do feel that Christians in the United States can be unfairly stereotyped as intolerant, ignorant people who don't support individual rights and liberties. The truth is that the United States has been since its inception, a nation with a majority Christian population that has evolved into the global protector of individual rights and liberties for people of all faiths, ethnicities, and races. It does need to be understood that this can only happen when those in the majority (in this case Christians) not only establish individual rights for themselves, but also protect the rights of those in minority groups. This is no small altruistic, moral accomplishment and the United States has set the example for the world of how to have rule by the majority with respect for individual rights.

I personally do believe, as I have stated, in the existence of God or the Creator. My perspective is that I like to think of myself as a person of faith who prays to God and seeks guidance, assistance, and peace. What I don't do is try to impose my belief system on others as the only true way to worship God. I fully accept that my beliefs could be wrong. This is a key concern that I have when people of faith treat their faith as scientific fact. Now, there can be reasoned interpretations as to why one should follow a certain religious doctrine or path, but we as humans in the twenty-first century need to acknowledge that one's faith is not fact-based. We cannot scientifically prove the existence of God, therefore, it is, yes, a belief based on faith. I find faith to be a powerful human attribute that requires someone to believe in a supreme being (or beings) just based on faith. This is the beauty and grace of the Divine in that our belief in God must come from faith and not science. Whether God exists is simply a question that cannot be answered by fact-based science. This does not mean God does not exist, only that in our world, it cannot be proven. Given this clear fact that one could be wrong in their faith-based beliefs as to what God actually is or is not, it continually perplexes me how different religious groups can turn to violence against others who may believe differently. I had a dear friend who I would have very serious political and social discussions with who recently passed. My friend shared his opinion with me several years ago that he felt it was almost a sin to try to stop someone from following the faith system that she or he felt was best for him or her. This has always stayed with me and has become a spiritual tenet upon which I live. Part of my core spiritual belief system is that I respect each individual's right to believe as he or she chooses. I believe in a God who is rational and fair. This leads to a rational line of thinking that a fair-minded deity would not punish someone for not following the exact "true" doctrine. I simply just don't believe in a God who is going to punish me and would have me burning alive in a hell-like environment for millions of years for believing in the "wrong" religion.

## Freedom of Religion

I believe in a God who wishes His children to have freedom of choice and wants us to make decisions based on how we can best live altruistic lives that bring benefits and blessings to others. Regardless of the way we choose to worship God, this is the only way that we can grow as followers of Him (or please pick the pronoun that works for you) is my perspective. We must freely choose to live morally and justly. Actions, not just beliefs, do matter. If we consider that any God would be one of kindness and love, then performing acts of kindness in the world is a measuring stick of how close we are to God's will. Again, these are only my personal religious beliefs. I do follow the Western model of thought so eloquently penned in our American Declaration of Independence that states, "...that all men are created equal, that they are endowed by their Creator with certain unalienable Rights, that among these are Life, Liberty and the Pursuit of Happiness" (Kamps 36). I would say that our Founding Fathers, in our Declaration of Independence and the First Amendment of the Constitution in our Bill of Rights (Kamps 66), would agree that there may be no more important right of a person than the ability to choose one's religion. I would argue that an individual's relationship with God is a sacred and private endeavor that all people of faith should seek to protect. This is why I support our secular form of government. The problem with theocracies is that only those in the majority religion are free while everyone else has to worship in hiding for fear of punishment or even death. The same crimes occur in governments that prohibit anyone from following a religion. A secular government, such as the one that our American Founding Fathers created, in which the government not only refuses to endorse any one religion, but intentionally does not involve itself in religion, is the only form of government that can ensure that all people have their basic right to religious freedom completely protected.

## Closing

As I have aged, I do find myself thinking about the ultimate question: Whether there is life after death? The desire in all of us to continue simply to exist is just a part of being a sentient, intelligent being. I do hope that our spirits live on and that there is some afterlife where we see our loved ones who have died again. Having expressed this point, I think there can be that tendency to excessively focus on the afterlife at the expense of living to the best of our abilities fully in the present world. One could make a convincing argument that the world would be a much better place if instead of constantly arguing about the right doctrine to follow to get into heaven, we focused on making the world that we are currently living in, a better place for all. Maybe this is the idea behind the part of the Lord's Prayer that refers to "...on earth as it is in heaven." ("The Lord's Prayer"). I'd like to think this biblical phrase is a call for us to do our part as servants of God to make our world a kind, loving and welcoming home for all of the world's citizens.

# 41. Thoughts on Organized Religion

### Religion's History of Hate

A lot of killing has been done in the name of religion. We had the Crusades in the Middle Ages between Muslims and Christians. Followers of Christianity were killed for their beliefs during the early days of the faith. The history of Romans throwing Christians "to the lions" in their barbaric arena fighting is well-known. Christians persecuted Jews throughout history for not accepting Jesus as their Messiah and held Jews responsible for the murder of Jesus. Then, of course, the history of Hindus and Muslims in India fighting and killing one another, extending into the modern era, is yet another example of religious bigotry and hatred. Northern Ireland experienced "The Troubles" from the late 1960s until the late 1990s. The Troubles involved very violent fighting between Protestants loyal to British rule and the Catholic minority who sought to end widespread discrimination which they experienced. We also have the Palestinian/Israeli conflict which currently appears to be under control, but there are always pop-up conflicts in which military personnel and civilians are killed. The world realizes that brewing just underneath the surface of this conflict is the constant threat of full-scale war. I realize that the Israeli/Palestinian conundrum is more than just a disagreement over religion and there are geo-political implications, but this tension in the Middle East does pit the Arab Muslim world against the Jewish nation of Israel supported by the United States and the Christian West. The violent and intolerant sides of religion continue to cause immense suffering and misery now well into the twenty-first century.

A significant criticism that I have of some religious groups is their tendency to adopt a mindset that becomes entirely intolerant of others' faiths and belief systems. We mostly see this in the conservative and more ultra-orthodox sects of religious groups whether Christian, Muslim, Jewish etc. To be honest, I have always admired those who are so devoted to their faiths that they follow the rituals and adhere to the doctrines diligently without question. After all, having complete faith in a religion and Supreme Being is a core attribute of an individual who truly is a follower of his or her chosen religious tradition. This unwavering faith is an admirable trait – one that I have struggled to adopt along my own spiritual and religious path. The problem begins when religious groups and individuals try to impose their beliefs on others and judge others, proclaiming their way is the only way to worship or live as people of God. I think this "only my way is correct" mentality that has led to countless lives being savagely extinguished throughout the ages, is tremendously dangerous.

Today we continue to have bloodshed in the name of religion. I'm primarily referring to the Middle East, but religious intolerance continues to plague many locations throughout the globe.

What I'd like to see among the world's religions is for all people of faith to join and adhere to the basic altruistic guidance and rules so common in many of the great religious texts. The core messages calling for fair and kind treatment of others, taking care of the poor, and simply doing our best to make the world a better place, should be the focal points of religions' guidance to followers in a diverse society of many faiths. Open and peaceful religious debate is healthy and promotes an environment in which seekers of faith can find the religious paths which call to them. However, too often religious zealots engage in hostile debate and interactions, which involve condemning one another's faiths for being "wrong." Their fellow citizens would be much better served if they instead chose to focus on the performance of good works for others.

The violent and intolerant aspects of religion must be addressed. Women are brutally punished (or worse) in Iran if they violate the strict dress requirements imposed upon them by the militant Islamist regime. We have also witnessed in the United States intolerance and violent attacks against gay and transgender people by evangelical Christians. Religious institutions should primarily dedicate their time and resources to spreading the message of love over hate. In addition, the tendency of religious groups to resort to violence and mistreatment of those who don't believe as they do, requires societies to be organized by secular governments. Secular governments, such as those in the United States and Western Europe, have played a vital role in ensuring equality and freedom for citizens of these nations to practice their own religious or non-religious beliefs in peace.

## Religion's Role in Acts of Kindness and Compassion

While not all religions openly work to convert others to their faiths, it is a given that religions have particular belief systems on a supreme being or supreme beings that they are sharing with the world from a well-intended, even altruistic mindset. All religions claim that they are the true path to God and/or the higher spiritual realms, so they wish to share this "truth" as they see it with others. One important question that people seek out religion to answer is, of course, what happens when we die? Religious groups wish to help others or "save their souls" by providing what they consider to be the correct way to worship God in order to be accepted into His kingdom after death. I have no problem with religious groups sharing what they legitimately feel are doctrines that will foster eternal peace for others in a loving and caring manner.

Most religious belief systems emphasize that by performing good deeds, having a strong faith, and committing to the practice of regular religious rituals, that followers will increase the likelihood that they will be accepted into Heaven (or whatever is the specific religion's understanding of the most comfortable existence in the afterlife). Many religious traditions do communicate the need to perform charitable works for the poor. Through acts of kindness and compassion, religious groups have and do have a tremendously positive impact on the world. This should be recognized as an area for which religious institutions should be taking the lead in the twenty-first century. The Catholic Church does tremendous work around the globe as far as providing medical care, food, education, and other much needed services, particularly in the Third World where the need is so great. There are also many Muslim organizations that work to feed the poor, such as Islamic Relief Worldwide. These religious charities do promote their faiths and there is a polite attempt at proselytizing, but sharing a message about one's religion while providing help to those in need is acceptable, in my opinion. This method is certainly more civilized than being tortured or murdered for not adopting the religion of the group in power or being "burned at the stake." Some would say help should be provided to others not to win a prize of getting into heaven, but just for the sake of being a good human being. I certainly see this argument and may agree, but I do give credit that overall, when religious groups help others, they are acting out of the love that their faiths are promoting.

I do understand religious followers' outlook that by sharing what they consider to be the legitimate doctrines of God that they are performing a tremendous act of kindness. The rationale from this standpoint is that by spreading the true teachings of God, followers of faith wholeheartedly believe that they are guiding others on the path to a safe and joyful eternity after death. I do greatly respect their genuine intentions to "save souls." However, I contend that we must also focus on our current life and all religious groups should dedicate themselves to alleviating suffering in our present world that we all share. It makes sense that a basic directive of a kind, loving God would be that we help out those in great need and regularly support one another. Feeding the poor, healing the sick and creating a world of kindness and peace are acts that at their basic foundation are from God's love or for those who are non-believers, from a place of living up to humanity's moral obligation. Religious groups and charities should be commended for their work to help the poor in meeting their worldly needs, in addition to offering the benevolent spiritual guidance and religious teachings of their faiths.

An area of good works that we don't speak about as often is the role that religious groups and leaders have played in the Civil Rights movement. The Reverend Dr. Martin Luther King Jr. through his Christian ministry in the 1960s was instrumental in the crusade against racial discrimination that African Americans endured in the Southern United States. Christian, Jewish, and other groups joined together to campaign against discrimination during this American Civil Rights movement. I could and probably should devote an entire essay to the tremendous progress our nation made in the way of civil rights that occurred because of the groundwork laid down by this great American hero. Dr. Martin Luther King Jr. demonstrated the power of non-violent protest that was based on his Christian faith emphasizing the promotion of peace. When citizens across the United States witnessed a religious leader show such devotion to remaining non-violent in the face of very bloody physical attacks that those protesting for equality had to endure, the nation rose up and proclaimed in unison, "No More."

## Conclusion

In closing, when I talk about organized religion I view it as a mixed bag. I think the zealotry of intolerant religious followers is a true threat to individual freedom and free societies. The vitriolic rhetoric coming from a variety of groups claiming that only their way is the true way to God, threatens the peaceful coexistence of all peoples. Again, I truly admire people of great faith, but I have to question their logic when they put so much value on their way of worshipping God to the vehement rejection of all other belief systems. The basic tenet of any belief system in a supreme being (or supreme beings), from my perspective, is that a true God is ultimately kind, compassionate and loving. In my opinion, a kind and compassionate God is not one who is going to punish His children for millions of years into eternity simply for following an incorrect path. To me, the intentions by an individual to live a life of caring for others and seeking out God's wisdom, that may be illuminated in perhaps many potential forms, should be the factors determining the level of one's Godliness. If religious groups take on the primary task of serving those in need, in addition to rejecting violence and hatred against those who believe differently from them, then I submit that we have the proper components of religion's ethical responsibilities to society and the world in the twenty-first century.

# 42. Which Lives Matter – Black, Blue or All?

―――

### The Black Lives Matter Movement is Born

The Black Lives Matter (BLM) movement formerly began in response to the killing of seventeen-year-old Trayvon Martin in Florida in 2012 (Morrison). The young man was targeted by a citizen participating in a local Community Watch program. George Zimmerman claimed that he killed Trayvon Martin in self-defense after he reported to police that the youth, who was wearing a hoodie, looked '...suspicious...' (CNN Editorial Research). Of course, many questioned why after making the report to the police, George Zimmerman didn't keep his distance from Trayvon Martin and let the police intervene if need be, instead of approaching the teen, an action which led to the deadly altercation. This case highlighted the problem of racial profiling in America. Trayvon Martin seemed to only truly be guilty of being a young black male wearing a hoodie.

The BLM civil rights initiative focuses on the statistics that continue to show that African Americans have higher rates of being killed during interactions with the police when compared to other races (Bunn). The BLM web site (https://blacklivesmatter.com) very clearly states that the organization's primary mission is combating violence against African Americans. The Trayvon Martin case in which his killer was found not guilty also initiated a new focus on a criminal justice system that critics claim too often gives the benefit of the doubt to police and others who kill African Americans.

In my opinion, the BLM movement truly became widely adopted and supported by white Americans after the grim video surfaced of George Floyd's death. Mr. Floyd was killed as a result of a police officer laying his knee on Mr. Floyd's neck for over nine minutes (on May 25, 2020) in Minneapolis, Minnesota (Levenson, Eric). This killing was caught on video for all the world to see. This event was the tipping point triggering mass frustration and anger over acts of violence by police, as well as societal discrimination being committed against African Americans. Protests spilled out into the streets in cities across the nation during the summer of 2020. People of all races and backgrounds came together to fight against hate.

I was personally inspired by the diversity and sheer numbers of citizens across the nation who congregated in public spaces during the early days of the COVID-19 pandemic to protest police brutality and discrimination against African Americans. The other intense emotion that I experienced was compassion for the expressions of frustration, anger, fear and simply fatigue from African Americans communicating what daily life is still unfortunately like for people of color in America. Many in the African American community expressed this sheer exhaustion from feeling as if they have to navigate their lives along a very fine line to avoid harassment from police, businesses where they shop, and their fellow American citizens. The common theme of "driving while black" was continually highlighted with African Americans communicating their accounts of being unfairly targeted by police, leading to unjustified traffic stops simply because of their race. The issue of economic opportunity, while not as immediate of an issue as violence against African Americans, was a core concern during the protests as well. Many expressed frustration with the tremendous challenge in the African American community of accessing cost-prohibitive education or training necessary to land higher paying jobs. The socio-economic divide between white and black citizens in America is striking with the average black family (per the 2019 Survey of Consumer Finances) having a household amount of wealth that is fifteen percent of that of the average white family (Bhutta, Chang, Dettling, Hsu and Hewitt).

## The Wealth Gap

In addition to the George Floyd killing, the wealth gap between African Americans and other groups during the COVID-19 pandemic was another significant factor that led to a summer in 2020 of African Americans and their supporters holding mass protests across the country. The wealth gap, as I discuss elsewhere in this work, became strikingly evident during the pandemic when middle class whites could work safely and remotely from home on their computers. This was in contrast to many African Americans who worked lower paying service sector jobs and had no choice but to go to work in person to support their families. Too often African Americans had to accept working in environments in which they had a higher risk of being exposed to the COVID-19 virus just so that they could financially survive. This was in early 2020, months before vaccinations were available. Many African Americans employed in the service sector, such as those working in grocery stores, public service and healthcare did contract the COVID-19 virus. Unfortunately, there were African American citizens who lost their lives after contracting the COVID-19 virus due to exposure in unsafe working environments.

Along with the higher risk of contracting COVID-19 due to their working conditions, the lack of access to healthcare and wellness options for African Americans was highlighted as well during the pandemic. African Americans because of economic disparities on average do not have access to general quality healthcare, adequate healthy food options, or the time or resources to engage in health-supporting exercise activities. This "Health Gap" between whites and African Americans does have clear ties to economic disparities. Many low-income individuals who often have to work multiple jobs just to "make ends meet" simply don't have leisure time available for respite, vacations or even for spending time with their families. The inability to take time off from work can result in employees experiencing chronic stress, fatigue, and burnout – all conditions that negatively affect the health of our citizens. Indeed, the prospect of a traditional American family vacation for those making lower wages is now virtually non-existent. A lack of paid sick time means that all too often those who can't afford a reduced paycheck must work sick. The "Great Resignation" during the pandemic for many Americans highlighted the mental and physical toll that overwork is taking on the quality of our lives, especially for those on the lower end of the economic spectrum which disproportionately includes African Americans. These obstacles to a healthy lifestyle were on full display during the pandemic. The calls for higher pay, more paid leave options, and access to high quality, affordable healthcare were part of this focus by the BLM movement to increase the health and wellbeing of those in the African American community.

Therefore, while I would say that the BLM organization is mainly focused on violence and discrimination committed against African Americans by the police or racist individuals and groups, the economic disadvantages that African Americans experience is a significant issue that is justifiably being highlighted by the BLM Movement.

## Opposition to the BLM Movement

THERE IS SOME OPPOSITION to the BLM movement, such as by those who endorse the "Blue Lives Matter" and "All Lives Matter" viewpoints. The Blue Lives Matter movement is somewhat of an opposing response to the BLM movement, as the individuals supporting this standpoint take the position that police overall are being unfairly characterized by BLM advocates. The Blue Lives Matter supporters argue that police work is by its very nature dangerous and essential, without which the safety of society cannot be protected and maintained. We do need to find some middle ground here between protecting the rights of police officers to defend themselves (and the community) from physical harm and protecting African Americans from suffering physical abuse due to the use of excessive force by overly aggressive police officers. I think most would agree that the vast majority of police officers are honorable and ethical public servants who try to be fair-minded when dealing with the public, including African American citizens. A history of institutional racism which has caused severe socio-economic inequities, has meant that a higher percentage of African Americans live in poor areas. Areas of economic blight and stagnation, of course, tend to have more crime. These areas, therefore, are more likely to experience increased interactions between police and African American citizens. The Blue Live Matters advocates support strict legislation that calls for harsh punishments for those who commit violence against police officers. The BLM proponents call for stricter legislation to hold police officers to account when they commit acts of excessive force. The case of George Floyd, of course, comes to mind as a prime example when a police officer outrageously overstepped any reasonable line of justifiable force given the threat to the officer. As the officer held his knee on Mr. Floyd's neck for nine minutes, it was obvious that Mr. Floyd was not a physical threat that required such brutality to protect the officer, or the public, from being harmed physically. My conclusion here is that we can achieve safety for everyone. We can give police the latitude to take actions to protect the public and themselves when justified, while doing much more to hold corrupt, racist, and overly aggressive police officers accountable. We can find that reasonable middle ground.

Then there is the All Lives Matter movement. I'd say this is not exactly a movement, but more of a reaction from those who found that the BLM movement was unfair by focusing only on the lives of black citizens. I would say that of course all lives do matter. Anyone, however, concluding that the BLM movement is one of exclusion which places the value of black lives over others does not comprehend a primary intention of the BLM movement. A major theme of the BLM movement is that black lives have been treated by society as "less than" for hundreds of years. This devaluing of people of color has led to institutional acts of racism that include violence from society, as well as from law enforcement. The BLM message here is that violent acts committed against African Americans would never be accepted by society if these same heinous acts were being committed against other groups. The goal of the BLM movement is for society to treat African Americans equally on the same level that any other group would be treated in our nation. African Americans are not seeking special or favored treatment, only equal treatment. This seems quite fair given our nation's history regarding racism. I do want to acknowledge here that violent crime committed by African Americans particularly in large cities is a valid concern and does need to be addressed. My belief is that a historical lack of opportunities has led to the development of high poverty areas in which large populations of African Americans turn to crime and violence to survive. Regardless of the core reason for high crime in African American communities, the police, and the general public (many of whom of course are African American) are exposed to this high violent threat. So, yes, in this context all lives matter as far as all citizens need to be protected from violent criminals regardless of the criminals' race. However, I don't think the BLM movement is advocating that African Americans should be able to commit violent crimes in our cities without fear of arrest and incarceration. Violent criminals of any race need to be taken off the streets for the protection of the public. The legitimate focus of the BLM movement involves the valid cases of police using excessive force in too many situations when they confront African Americans for apparent, non-violent infractions. There are some who claim the All Lives Matter doctrine is racist for not acknowledging the issue of historical violence and murder of black citizens without any accountability. I don't consider the All Lives Matter movement to be racist at its core and I absolutely agree that all lives matter, but I do think this group's approach is short-sighted and insensitive to the African American experience, which includes such a long history of physical, mental and emotional abuse suffered at the hands of a majority white American society.

## Conclusion

In answering the question posed in the title of this essay, my emphatic response is that each and every individual human life matters, regardless of race, occupation, ethnicity, religion, sexual orientation, gender, etc. As a society we must learn to live together as a civilized, advanced people who reject all forms of unprovoked aggression and violence. I only support the use of force when needed to protect the wellbeing of ourselves or others. Racism and the perpetuation of hate against groups of people must be addressed and eradicated for humanity to reach its true higher potential in maximizing the quality of life for all of our planet's citizens. Primarily, I agree with the argument that we must have a special focus on the lives of African Americans to ensure that they have the same quality and longevity of life as any other group. This includes addressing police brutality and violence committed by other citizens against African Americans, as well as working to correct the socio-economic inequalities that negatively affect the life outcomes for African Americans.

As far as the police, we must hold them to the highest of standards, requiring them to humanely treat African Americans in all facets of their jobs. Police need better training so they are properly equipped to interact with citizens who may be of different races from themselves. One policy that I support is Neighborhood Policing which calls for police to get out of their vehicles and become more involved in the neighborhoods in which they serve. Having more interpersonal interactions on a regular or daily basis can improve relations between the police and the African American community. In addition, including social workers who can act as buffers in deescalating tense situations between the police and citizens may also provide another useful reform. Furthermore, recruiting African Americans from their local communities to pursue careers in law enforcement could reduce the tension by addressing the "us versus them" mentality that has developed in the African American community when it comes to their interactions with police officers. This is particularly the case in areas where police officers have a reputation of acting overly aggressive in predominantly minority neighborhoods. I disagree with the policy proposal of "Defunding the Police." Our cities and towns do need law enforcement to ensure public safety is maintained, but this policy initiative (while overall misguided) has highlighted a great frustration in which police officers are viewed as too often initially identifying African Americans as criminals, until they are verified as law-abiding citizens (instead of the other way around). My contention is that by encouraging local citizens to become police officers who serve the neighborhoods in which they grew up, this approach could foster an environment in which citizens feel like the police are there to protect them and not to unfairly target them as potential criminals. I support this approach of people from the neighborhood protecting the neighborhood as one way to reduce this "us versus them" dynamic. Along with these policing reforms, we do need to recognize how dangerous a job it is to be a police officer. I conclude that we need to recognize the important mission of the BLM movement, but that does not need to compete with public support for the majority of police officers who are doing their best to protect all citizens. We should support both the BLM movement and those who wear blue uniforms who overwhelmingly take their pledge with the utmost commitment to "protect and serve."

Finally, I do agree that, yes, all lives matter, but the BLM movement argument stating, "All lives matter, when black lives matter," says it all. We need to have a special focus on the state of black lives due to the historical and continued existence of institutional racism. I recall viewing a television interview with one of my favorite actors, Samuel L. Jackson. He very well explained that the point of the BLM movement (and I'm paraphrasing here) is not that other lives don't matter, but that black lives matter too (Jackson). I truly believe that we are a great nation, but in order to live up to our best selves as Americans we must all work to ensure that black lives do matter and must be supported and protected. Blue lives matter and all lives matter, without question, but our racist history calls upon us all as citizens of our great nation to also stand up to hate by proclaiming in unison that "Black Lives Matter."

# 43. Critical Race Theory (CRT): How Should We Talk about Race in School?

## What is Critical Race Theory (CRT)?

Critical Race Theory or CRT for short has become a controversial subject in recent years. The controversy involves the question as to whether CRT is an appropriate approach to use when we talk to our children about race. Many a school board meeting around the nation have had visits from upset parents regarding the teaching of CRT as a component of their children's educational experience. After reviewing to some degree what the exact definition of CRT actually is, I must admit I'm still not an expert on the subject. My understanding is that CRT was created as the next step past the civil rights movements of the 1960s and 1970s, as a method to both teach about racism and implore citizens to act in ending racial bias in the United States. The concept involves the idea that institutional bias exists in many facets of American life and must be dismantled as the next significant step in ending racism. It does seem to require of whites an acknowledgement that the current legal, social, economic, and educational systems benefit them at the expense of African Americans. This acknowledgement calls upon whites to accept that they have a moral responsibility to take action to improve the lives of blacks who have suffered tremendously during slavery, segregation and now in our current era of continued institutional racism. CRT makes the reasonable argument, in my opinion, that ingrained or institutional racism is the primary reason for the socio-economic disadvantages that African Americans overall continue to experience in the United States compared to whites (Fortin).

## An Analysis of Diversity Training and CRT

The controversy has become quite heated as some parents are opposed to this format of teaching about racism to young children in our schools. The use of terms like "oppressors" and "victims," labels that can be internalized by individual students as a result of CRT lessons, have triggered complaints from parents. This controversy seems to have gained steam during the pandemic with children learning remotely and parents observing directly what their children are being taught in school. Some white parents argue that children should not be made to feel guilty about their race or feel the need to apologize for it. Even some African American parents have not supported the idea of teaching their children that they are "victims." I may differ in my opinions from Republican Senator Marsha Blackburn of Tennessee on a number of issues as a moderate Democrat, but I must agree that she has a legitimate argument when it comes to CRT. The CRT approach of teaching all too often does seem to lead students to internalizing these unhelpful group descriptions of "oppressors" or "victims" (Blackburn). Regardless of the intention of CRT teaching which I do not disagree with - to effectively address institutional racism in our nation, the approach is not a good fit for our young children.

I recall that some years ago I participated in a work-related, diversity training activity in which all the participants stood in a circle formation in the middle of the room. As different group categories were announced, such as "male", "female", "Christian", "non-Christian", "white", "black", etc., the members of the announced group would step in the middle of the circle. Then, we did a group assignment in which different groups were named and the class had to select who the advantaged group was and who the disadvantaged group was. An example of this advantaged versus disadvantaged group exercise involved the participants comparing two groups, such as white and non-white or heterosexual versus gay (at this time it was not prevalent to identify transgender and non-binary groups). The training participants were to specify which group was the advantaged (or dominant) group and which group was the disadvantaged or minority group. The intention of these exercises appeared to be to encourage participants to view society as having dominant groups that have enjoyed influence and opportunity, while the minority groups and women have been disadvantaged. Men have definitely enjoyed advantages that women have not had access to throughout the generations, and the vast extent of discrimination against African Americans by the majority white society is unquestionable. I do agree that identifying overall inequalities between groups can aid in discussing institutional bias and how to overcome it.

One aspect of the circle exercise approach in my diversity training, however, that I was not a big fan of, was the emphasis on sharing one's individual group identity. I felt rather uncomfortable when "non-Christian" was announced, and I was the only one who stepped in the circle. We can teach about diversity without this practice of very openly and vocally labeling individuals according to the groups that they belong to or to which they self-identify. Also, this type of diversity training format is limited in that it does not look at individuals and their specific viewpoints, intentions, or uniqueness outside of group dynamics. I felt these exercises were lacking in that they overemphasized one's primary group identity versus individual traits or other group identities of an individual. These other factors can make it more difficult to make a clear determination that an individual has specifically been the victim of institutional bias based on race. For example, I realize as a white male that I have some privileges, but once I get into the arena of religion, as a Jewish person, I can relate to others who lack the comfort of being in a majority group. No, I don't contend that I have ever experienced what it is like to have a physical, racial attribute, such as being African or Asian American, which leaves one as an easy target for hate. My point is that I find increasingly that diversity training (and now the CRT approach) seems to oversimplify group identity in a world in which individuals increasingly belong to multiple groups or have multi-racial identities. We can say that racial bias still exists, but in our multi-racial society we should not rush to judgement in claiming that specific individuals are the victims of discrimination without thorough investigation.

Now, I do admit that diversity training has the intention of addressing unfair treatment at the group level, so it is somewhat understandable why group differences are the focus. I do think diversity training, however, has a responsibility to do a better job of noting that while institutional racism certainly has played a significant role in majority groups enjoying advantages in society (which must be addressed), this is not a justification to dismiss that the decisions and actions taken by individuals are also factors when it comes to outcomes for individuals. I do question whether some diversity training programs become too aggressive at claiming that lower achievements by individuals in minority groups are almost always exclusively due to institutional biases against them. We must acknowledge that more progress needs to be made to ensure equal opportunity, while also emphasizing that some outcome differences may be simply due to individuals' inherent talents, as well as their decisions and actions.

I do support diversity training in school and in the workplace, but we have to reexamine how we discuss race, particularly with school–aged children. Yes, reviewing the teaching approach when it comes to diversity is especially important for children in elementary school. I am fully supportive of an educational system that discusses slavery and continued racism in our society. Teaching the historical context which explains why African Americans are behind other groups in areas, such as wealth and income, is important so that all citizens can work together to create a society that provides sufficient economic opportunities to everyone. The problem I find with the CRT approach is that it leads children, even if indirectly, through a classification process that labels them strictly according to their racial attributes, which may not be a positive experience for individual students. We can teach children about racism's negative effect on African Americans without labeling white children as "oppressors." This approach can instill in young minds feelings of tremendous guilt over something that has happened over generations before their births. As far as African American children, I think it is fair and right for them to know the horrendous treatment that their ancestors experienced in our nation and that racism continues today. I don't agree that they should be taught that they live in an oppressive regime currently in the United States and that they are "victims." That label can send a message that no matter what they do as individuals they cannot succeed. Yes, African American children should understand that there continues to be unfair treatment against African Americans, but that they are not "victims." We can teach diverse groups of students about discrimination without assigning labels that may contribute negatively to the self-identities of young children. Elementary school-aged children are not "oppressors" neither are they "victims." We must instill in our children the core beliefs that they are of great value due to their individuality and that they should seek out lives that will bring them happiness, while also contributing to the betterment of society.

## Diversity Training Beyond CRT (Closing)

I certainly don't want to come across as someone who is arguing that the factual history of racism or its vast negative effects on African Americans should not be discussed or taught in school in a comprehensive manner. The history of racism absolutely should be taught in our schools. However, this can be accomplished without what seems to be CRT's teaching philosophy that involves overly aggressive interference with each child's natural development in building a healthy, positive self-image. We should not personalize the crimes of the past by one race or the trauma of the past experienced by another race by placing these attributes onto the shoulders of children. This goes too far. Let's work together to teach what has happened and emphasize that so much more needs to be done to fight prejudice. This can be achieved without placing attributes, such as fault or victimhood, onto children for the multi-generational issue of racial inequality. This is where the approach of CRT training misses the mark.

Also, I wish to clarify that while I tend to side with the parents who oppose teaching Critical Race Theory in schools, it is only this approach that I see as not the best fit for our children when talking and teaching about race or racism. It is imperative that the history of racism is included in every school's curriculum. The goal should be to educate our students so they will grow up and take the lead in the effort of eradicating racism and discrimination on all fronts. In addition to my concerns expressed above about CRT, I am critical of the approach from the standpoint that CRT does not sufficiently communicate the progress that has been achieved for African Americans in our nation. Yes, progress has been too slow (this is an understatement, of course) as far as extending rights to African Americans, but our children need to learn that our governmental system laid the framework for this evolution of the extension of equal rights. I agree with CRT in that institutional racism still remains in our nation (and reforms are needed), but CRT does a grave injustice to the discussion by not acknowledging the role that our institutional, democratic system has played in establishing individual liberties. Our institutional, democratic system established by our U.S. Constitution protects these liberties which have been extended to all citizens, including those who have traditionally suffered the worst of racial discrimination. We need to teach our children this history as well.

Finally, I support teaching our young people that their generation has a responsibility to work towards continuing the effort that others have begun in achieving true inclusiveness, equal opportunity, and full acceptance of diversity for all Americans. I agree with the assertion that we cannot continue to move forward without our children fully understanding our nation's past. The future I believe is bright as far as achieving greater equality for all in America. I, for one, am in awe of the younger generations for their genuine desire to abolish hate and prejudice in our society. They integrate with one another without a thought of bigotry regarding others' race, ethnicity, or sexual identity. Those in their twenties today express themselves openly and unapologetically, displaying to others that differences are to be celebrated and not shunned. So, let's teach our children our history. Then, we should step back and watch in amazement and pride at the world that they will create. I am infinitely optimistic that our young people will succeed in ways that we cannot even imagine in the pursuit of ending racism and hate. I have no doubt that they will succeed where we have failed.

# 44. Dave Chappelle Is Wrong – Ye Should Be Called Out for Being Anti-Semitic

### Ye's Harmful Tweet

I disagree with Dave Chappelle's core opinion that he expressed during his *Saturday Night Live (SNL)* monologue (11/12/22) regarding Ye's anti-Semitic tweet ("Dave Chappelle Stand-up"). As an SNL fan and a Dave Chappelle fan, I watched the show televised live that evening. Mr. Chappelle said something to the effect that Jewish people have experienced terrible things all over the world, but you can't blame that on African Americans ("Dave Chappelle Stand-up"). Ye, the entertainer formerly known as Kanye West, specifically called out an entire people who follow the Jewish religion when tweeting he would "...go 'death con 3 on Jewish People,'" (Li and Sheeley). Now, Ye could have stated a specific company mistreated him, but in what the troubled entertainer stated, it was anti-Semitic.

Let me begin my argument by sharing some of my personal views on accusations of biased speech today. I do think some statements are too quickly interpreted as racist or anti-Semitic. Yes, I contend that the extreme political left has gone too far at times with calling statements, actions, or outcomes as biased, and proceed to unfairly "cancel" individuals. This "cancel culture" can unfairly ruin people's personal and professional reputations, even affecting their ability to earn an income. I'd like to share an example of how sometimes people become overly sensitive and ridiculous in an altruistic attempt at curbing hate speech. I am Jewish, but I live in the United States where a majority of the citizenry (although even this demographic is changing) are Christians. If someone wishes me a "Merry Christmas," I take it for what it more than likely is – just a statement of goodwill sent my way, not any type of anti-Semitic remark since I am Jewish. I think those who demand that we change our greeting to strictly "Happy Holidays" around Christmas are being overly sensitive. So, yes, it depends on the situation, context, and specific statement as to whether something said is racist, anti-gay, sexist, ageist, etc.

When Mr. Ye sends out an angry tweet like he did, it is pretty evident that his statement is anti-Semitic. He is in essence making a claim of being mistreated by the Jewish community. The statement gives a negative message about an entire group that in and of itself can incite others to initiate verbal, written or even physical attacks against Jews. Individuals or groups who are already anti-Semitic can take a statement like Mr. Ye's and become emboldened to continue or increase their prejudicial behavior. Clearly, Ye in calling out the religion of the people in the entertainment industry who he feels have mistreated him, is hateful behavior and is not acceptable in a civil society. It is no different than a racist Caucasian making a statement about African Americans as a group that promulgates a harmful, hateful stereotype.

Furthermore, Ye's statement lends itself to claims of Hollywood and the entertainment industry as being controlled by Jews. The false narrative here is that Jews have a lot of power and use it for nefarious goals – in this case to mistreat or cheat entertainers out of their rightful incomes. The statement by Mr. Ye also goes along with dangerous stereotypes and conspiracy theories that Jews run not only the entertainment industry, but also the financial world. In my opinion, Mr. Ye must make amends for spouting such hate against the Jewish people. So, I do disagree with Mr. Chappelle from the standpoint that Mr. Ye's statement in this specific situation is simply a case of a black American pushing hate against Jews. In this case, the fact that Mr. Ye is African American and belongs to a race of people who have suffered horribly, beginning with the days of slavery in this nation, does not and should not give him a pass on his statement of hate regarding Jews.

## Hate Speech

Yes, we should blame Mr. Ye for his totally inappropriate behavior and hold him accountable for his role if dangerous outcomes occur stemming from his tweet. Ye's tweet was very clearly hate speech. This type of speech is so dangerous in that it can trigger events, such as violence, discrimination and God forbid, another Holocaust. Am I exaggerating with mentioning the Holocaust as an outcome here? Perhaps, but my point is that hate speech if given an opportunity to disseminate to wide audiences can lead to horrific results for members of the targeted group. It can create an environment in which people start to be seen as not human, as we saw in Nazi Germany with Jews and, by the way, in the Southern United States during the times of slavery with African Americans. As *The 1619 Project* points out at length, the dissemination of false information on the physical attributes of African Americans, such as their ability to tolerate pain more than others or having deficiencies in their brain capacity (Villarosa), have led to mistreatment and lack of opportunities for African Americans up to the current day. The false narratives perpetuated against enslaved people in the early Americas essentially resulted in society viewing African Americas as subhuman for centuries.

Mr. Chappelle appears to be asserting that in these days of cancel culture that Jews are being overly sensitive to statements made by Ye and other African American celebrities. I don't agree completely with the cancel culture mentality. There are plenty of situations in which someone may have made a statement that was taken incorrectly, and the intention was not hostile at all. Yes, it is important that we do not rush to judgement and destroy someone's career and reputation over a misunderstanding. These statements, however, by Ye, do have a clear angry, antagonistic tone in calling out Jews specifically. I don't think there is a misunderstanding here. Dave Chappelle needs to simply call out Ye as making totally inappropriate and hateful statements against Jews. That's it. Now, when Ye issues a formal and sincere apology, then the healing can begin.

The other aspect here is that Dave Chappelle seems to be implying that African Americans are not a threat to Jews as blacks in this country have been a truly persecuted group. I totally agree that African Americans are members of a minority group who have been discriminated against and brutally treated throughout the history of this nation. However, that doesn't mean that members of a discriminated group are simply off the hook if they engage in acts of prejudice against other minority groups (or anyone else). Ye is African American, but like Dave Chappelle he has a powerful voice through media and social media avenues as a celebrity. As an aside here, I guess what I simply cannot fathom is when people from one minority group discriminate against people from another minority group. As minorities, we know what that feeling is of being targeted and experiencing that fear or vulnerability. Minorities can relate to one another in this regard. This is why I've always felt it is almost more of an ethical crime for a member of one minority group to express hate against a member of a different minority group, as opposed to when a member of a majority group expresses his or her prejudice. Of course, I am not saying that a member of a majority group who discriminates against a minority should be excused. My point here is that hate is wrong regardless of who initiates it. The fact that Ye is African American doesn't give him free unchallenged permission to express his hate. He should know better.

### Healing and Moving Forward

What is needed here is a sincere apology from Mr. Ye to the Jewish entertainment professionals he tweeted about, as well as to the entire Jewish community. Then, the Jewish community has a role. This friction that seems to be rising between African Americans and Jews in America needs to be addressed. There should be more dialogue between these communities. The entertainment industry is a great place to start since both African Americans and Jews have contributed significantly to the world of entertainment. These two minority groups should seek ways to interact, however, both in business and in their personal lives. Jews and African Americans should have a very close relationship since both have experienced worldwide discrimination. Jews like blacks have been banned from opportunities and having certain jobs. Both of these groups found success in areas like entertainment.

One stereotype is that Jews are shrewd businesspeople. What I say is that Jews do have a proud culture that has stressed education and they have done well in their careers as a group. The advantage of course that Jews have had, that African Americans have not enjoyed, is the same advantage that all whites have had – more time to accumulate wealth through multiple generations. The culture of discrimination has meant African Americans have had many more obstacles to overcome to achieve financial wealth compared to other groups. What Jews and others who have been successful in the business world should do is provide support to African Americans – lots of support. There should be initiatives to have black-owned recording companies, motion picture companies, as well as other entertainment-oriented businesses that can be supported by traditional companies with assistance also from government or non-profit entities. More African American business ownership in all sectors of our economy is necessary to correct past inequities.

## Free Speech Comedy with Compassion

I want to ensure that I do not leave out objections from the LGTBQ (Lesbian, Gay, Bisexual, Transgender and Questioning or Queer) community concerning some of Dave Chappelle's jokes. I do stand with those in the LGTBQ community and support their right to live a life free of discrimination and hate. As an individual, I know I need to do more to support this community. Of course, we certainly don't want comedians to have their free expression stifled by some type of "joke police" staffed by politically correct zealots. This can lead to an unreasonable limit on free speech. This is where collaboration and communication should occur.

One option is for comedians to take it upon themselves to review any potentially offensive material with some representatives of the groups who will be discussed during their shows. I had no problem with Dave Chappelle in his SNL monologue discussing his honest questions he had about the Jewish faith, such as to why some Jews "...dress like RUN DMC?" ("Dave Chappelle Stand-up"). Referring to the Jewish Friday night Shabbat dinner as "...Sha Na Na..." ("Dave Chappelle Stand-up") during his SNL monologue was just another humorous reaction, that a non-Jew might have if one did not have a full exposure to practicing, religious Jews. I found these comments to be simply funny and observational, even showing Mr. Chappelle's nonjudgmental attitude and openness to Jewish culture. These jokes had absolutely no ill-will whatsoever directed toward Jews.

I have been a huge Dave Chappelle fan since his *Chappelle's Show* in the early 2000's on the Comedy Central network. I always thought he shared a genius sense of humor that at times targeted race and the ridiculous nature of how humans try to separate themselves from other humans. He so often addresses race in his humor by making it inclusive. He pokes fun at different groups, but in a way that celebrates diversity. *Chappelle's Show* did such an impressive feat of finding the humor in diverse groups without it ever having a sense of intolerance or hate.

I think back and quickly recall just a few of the many examples of Dave Chappelle's comedic genius on his show that were truly celebrations of diversity. One skit on his show was about husbands who went to live with other families per a "wife swap" theme ("Trading Spouses"). It was hilarious seeing the interactions between how the African American dad handled his responsibilities as a husband and father with a Caucasian wife and child. This was compared to the interactions between the white husband and dad played perfectly by Dave Chappelle, who temporary lived with an African American wife and child. It did allude to some stereotypical differences, but it was done in a fun-loving, non-offensive way. I think the audience comes away from such a skit understanding that not all white men are sexually repressed or have a fetish involving women's underwear. That is part of the humor, but it in no way could be interpreted as a hateful or unfair depiction.

Another skit on *Chappelle's Show* that demonstrated Mr. Chappelle's talent at fully engaging his audience with humor to get a social message across, involved a Ku Klux Klan, white supremacist theme ("Clayton Bigsby"). The skit had a *60 Minutes* news show type of format in which a reporter was interviewing a member of a white supremacist group who dressed in a standard Ku Klux Klan outfit (hood and white sheet coverings) ("Clayton Bigsby"). The comedic aspect of this fake news show became apparent when it was revealed that this devoted follower of hate was a visually impaired African American who did not know he was black. Hilarity of course ensued in this individual's interactions with others as he went throughout the community spouting racial slurs, all the while confusing the white citizens he was confronting along the way. This skit in its creativeness showed how ridiculous racism really is, in that we are treating others differently solely on physical characteristics. The lesson became apparent when the African American hate group leader, Clayton Bigsby, played by Chappelle, learned that he was a person of color.

## Conclusion

In closing this essay, I felt Dave Chappelle overall missed the mark with his opening monologue on *SNL* on November 12, 2022. As much as I disagreed with the message and tone of his act, one great benefit of his statements is that people are having more open discussions about diversity and how we can all learn to live in a world where everyone is respected and valued. Mr. Chappelle seems to be in a mode recently of challenging politically correct speech as a threat to free speech. There is a valid concern about limiting free speech, but I do think it is a righteous endeavor to demand that speech that can incite hate or violence should be called out and addressed. We have reached a point in which making incorrect statements, blaming entire groups for society's problems, and calling for physical violence against groups should not be included in constitutionally, protected free speech.

I don't call for a "cancelling" of Mr. Chappelle. If the reader cannot tell, I am a big fan and I don't think this one monologue is a reason to cancel all the comedic joy he has brought to the world. I do not think in his heart that he is a man of hate based on his many years of comedy and frank speech. My hope is that he and others, who reach so many people because of their celebrity status, will speak their minds freely, but do so in a manner that is appropriately sensitive to how that speech can negatively affect others.

I look forward to Mr. Chappelle's next special or entertainment endeavor. Perhaps he will resurrect some of his famous characters from his former show and we can witness how they have turned their lives around for the better. One can envision Chappelle's Clayton Bigsby becoming a great civil rights leader fighting for the fair treatment of African Americans in the South. I would enjoy a storyline in which Tyrone Biggums, Chappelle's comical drug addict ("The Best of Tyrone Biggums"), finally kicks his drug habit to become a famous addiction recovery expert, now with a self-help book on *The New York Times Best Sellers* list. Yes, I am a fan. I could not finish this essay without noting the sad passing of one of my favorite contributors to *Chappelle's Show*, Charlie Murphy. He had a very different comedic style when compared to that of his famous brother Eddie, but to me Charlie was just as hilarious (if not more so) when it came to his story-telling style.

Finally, I have a message about comedy's current role in our society. Comedy has very effectively been used as political speech to highlight issues of significant social concern. This is nothing new and has always been the case for generations. George Carlin's political rants come to mind during the second half of the twentieth century. However, I'm concerned that in today's very combative world, we witness even comedy now becoming consistently a source of social contention. There is a time and place for political comedy, but I'd like to see during this period of such political disagreement, that comedy be used more as an instrument of healing by bringing joy to people. Maybe right now what we need from comedy is entertainment that uplifts everyone and brings people together, instead of adding to the climate of divisiveness.

# 45. "Jews Will Not Replace Us"

## My Reaction as a Jew to a March of Hate

"Jews will not replace us," was the chant. I felt almost numb watching CNN in the summer of 2017 as participants in the Unite the Right rally in Charlottesville, Virginia, marched in the night with eerily lit torches chanting these hateful, vicious words. It looked like something out of 1930s Nazi Germany, not the United States of the twenty-first century.

I had experienced mild, but never direct anti-Semitism when my family moved from New York City to North Carolina in the early 1980s as a child. As an American Jew, I knew there were individuals and hate groups that were always on the fringes of American society. These groups don't like Jews, African Americans, members of the LGBTQ (lesbian, gay, bisexual, transgender, queer or questioning) community and many others. This march was different in the openness of the participants and in their aggressive demeanor. They looked almost possessed and I tried not to look upon them as purely evil, but at the time I did not see any thread of humanity in them.

I experienced different emotions all at once and had questions. I felt fear, shock, and anger. How can people who don't even know me personally hate me, I thought? I'm sure this is the question many minorities have asked themselves when confronting hate. Of course, trying to answer this question rationally can't be done because it is irrational to hate members of a group one has never met. Some can and probably have said that American Jews always overreact to these instances of isolated hate intended for them. This may be true, but given the reality of the Holocaust, being on notice I suppose is part of being a Jew in this world. I admit I did feel fear as I looked upon this spectacle of indecency, wondering whether this was the beginning of a movement encouraging major acts of violence against Jews in the United States. Anger was another emotion I experienced. It seems incomprehensible that after the brutality and repugnancy of Nazi Germany that modern society has rejected, that such manic hate against Jews could manifest again, even by a small number of individuals and groups.

There is a dark history surrounding the usage of the term, "Jews will not replace us," but I want to express how those words struck me as an individual at that moment. We have this angry, frenzied mob with a maniacal demeanor, who looks as if the group belongs in 1930s Nazi Germany (not the United States in the 21$^{st}$ century), marching in the night with torches lit chanting hate-filled words. The immediate thought that came to mind when I was watching CNN is that this must have been what it looked like in Salem, Massachusetts in the 1600s when "witches" were rounded up to be burned at the stake. It seems people very quickly devolve into sub-human creatures when they fully embrace hating others, as this mob was doing on this dreadful night. This vision on my television didn't seem real, just a very scary horror film that ends in unimaginable suffering for the victims.

The mob in Charlottesville was calling out people like me as a threat to their existence. Watching this scene, I quickly concluded that either the mob had erupted into pure madness, or this was the execution of a plan by those with purely evil intentions. It is madness to conclude that such a small group of people who only make up 2% of the American population (Americans of Jewish descent or those who identify as Jewish) ("Jewish Americans in 2020") could pose an actual threat to any group or the public at large. I also wondered if this phrase was specifically and cleverly used to misguide the public. The wordplay is terrifying and is very reminiscent of George Orwell's book, *1984*. The reality is that the Jewish population has been under threat for centuries of being "replaced," not the other way around. Hitler's intention to kill every Jew in the world was an actual plan that to a significant degree had great success with the annihilation of six million Jews during World War II. This group chanting "Jews will not replace us," so incorrectly sends a message that American society is under threat from a very small group of people. The statement is absurd and ridiculous. No, the Jews are not a threat to others. We, like so many others, only wish to live in peace and worship as we choose. The guarantee of individual liberties, which includes our freedom of religion, is an essential component of our American national, ethical foundation based in the establishment and protection of human rights. This horrific event is a reminder to all patriotic Americans that we must always be ready to stand up and defend our Constitution, as well as the rights of all citizens as guaranteed per this sacred document.

## Removing Confederate Statues from Public Areas

This group of white supremacists came to Charlottesville to protest the proposed removal of a Robert E. Lee Confederate statue. The movement to remove Confederate statues across the South and elsewhere has gained steam as the appropriate action to eliminate what was a post-Civil War era movement to glorify or romanticize the Confederacy through the erecting of such statues ("Confederate Monument"). Clearly and correctly, in my opinion, these reminders of the Confederacy, whose intention in the Civil War was to maintain the unethical institution of slavery, do need to be taken down. These statues are a brutal reminder to African Americans of the Confederacy's great crime in fighting to keep this group of Americans as slaves – property, not citizens living freely in our nation. Romanticizing the Old South with these monuments is a farce and no doubt stirs up great pain and anguish for African Americans. Any fair-minded individual should be able to comprehend why it is wrong to keep these statues in place, given what they represent to African Americans and to mainstream Americans who patriotically reject a notion of a separate Southern nation apart from the United States.

I often wonder how Jewish people would feel living in modern Germany if there were numerous statues glorifying Hitler and the Nazi movement. The statue of Robert E. Lee was housed in Lee Park (now Market Street Park) (Montilla). One can only imagine the mortification and outrage if in Germany there was a statue of Hitler located in a "Hitler Park" after World War II. Now, I am providing this example to convey the message that individuals, movements, or messages that modern society finds discriminatory or inhumane (e.g. a government intent on eliminating Jews or one that is intent on keeping African Americans as slaves) should be rejected. I do want to note that I am in no way comparing Robert E. Lee to Hitler. As I point out elsewhere in this work, I do think that we have to be careful of completely rejecting individuals, such as some of our Founding Fathers, regarding the institution of slavery which was a worldwide practice in pre-modern times and in Colonial America. I do afford General Lee a bit of leeway (if you will) in that he was a citizen of the antebellum South and slavery was part of everyday life - the status quo. General Lee was a great military leader who did work to foster peace after the Civil War. One possibly fair criticism of General Lee is that he cannot be considered as a true American hero since he could have refused to resign his U.S. Army Commission at the beginning of the Civil War (Hall). He did have the opportunity to fight for the United States in the Civil War, but instead became the leader of the Confederate army (Blount). I leave it to historians to argue if this decision by Lee showed a lack of moral courage to do the right thing, or if he can be forgiven as a citizen of the then South who felt obligated to pledge his allegiance to the state of Virginia in which he was born and resided. I want to point out that Hitler displayed an evilness that has been matched by very few humans who have ever walked the Earth. This madman's attempt to take over the world and kill all Jews and others he judged not up to par with his image of the "master Aryan race" led to the killing of millions of innocent people. The overall point I am attempting to make in my comparison is that as a Jew I can relate to what African Americans must feel when seeing Confederate monuments whether they are of Robert E. Lee or other Confederate leaders. The Confederacy represented an initiative by some states to secede from the Union in order to ensure the continuance of the cruel institution of slavery in what is now the Southern United States. These monuments should not be destroyed but kept in museums as teaching tools. They are in fact part of history and should be allowed to remain as reminders of how humanity and America have progressed.

### Standing Up To Hate

I have gone into some discussion about the Robert E. Lee statue in order to provide a bit of background information as to the impetus for these white supremacists descending upon

Charlottesville, Virginia in the summer of 2017. I also wanted to express my opinion on what should be the fate of these Confederate monuments that have been allowed to remain standing until very recently. The other aspect that I hope to adequately communicate in this essay is how I plan to use this upsetting experience of watching this march of hate by those who chose to chant the phrase, "Jews will not replace us" as a personal call to action. I realize that as a secular Jew, I can walk down the street and I am viewed upon as any other white male in society. Now, I do want to comment that I think some factions of the liberal left have gone too far in blaming white males for all of society's ills, but I do realize the advantages that we hold in our society. White males have traditionally been able to access unlimited opportunities or resources to which minorities and women have been denied. I can exist without facing fear of being discriminated against or worse because of my appearance. Also, it is true that Jews in America have succeeded overall, and I make no secret of the fact that I am proud of my heritage which has focused on education and achievement. I do concede that success in America has been much more accessible for those of white, European ancestry. We have not had an "equal playing field" when it comes to socio-economic opportunities in the past and this must be corrected. Viewing this mob showing such hate to people of my background, does bring up some feeling of shame that I have not done enough to support other minorities (such as African Americans) and women as a white male. My hope is that I can use this expression of hate, that was displayed for all to see on national television, as a positive incentive to do whatever I can to not only fight hate and prejudice, but to work to change the minds of those who so wrongly have chosen the side of hate.

One of my goals in writing this work is to communicate a message that we must all come together and treat one another in a civil and respectful way with kindness, regardless of others' race, religion, ethnicity, sexual orientation, or gender self-identification. I am pledging to do more personally and ask others to do the same in supporting African American causes, such as shopping more at locally owned black businesses. It is important that we also support women-owned businesses so that women, who too-often have the majority of child-raising duties, can have flexible careers that pay them well enough to support themselves and their families. Hate and violence against Asian Americans that have arisen coming out of the COVID pandemic must be opposed and I vow to do my part to support this community. I may not fully understand all the pronouns used and issues facing the LGTBQ community, but I can do my part to support their right to live their lives as they choose, in adult, loving relationships with others (and seek to become better educated on their pronoun usage). Hate seems to spring up from time to time in society and when it does, we all have a moral obligation not only as Americans, but as righteous human beings to join together and loudly oppose it.

Finally, I feel compelled to mention in closing that southern Americans as a population group are too often bashed as being "racist, dumb and backward." The majority of people in the South should not be characterized by these stereotypes. Too often in the media, southerners are unfairly cast in unkind ways. This is hurtful to this group of Americans, and it must stop. Southerners, in my opinion, overall are kind, innovative, resilient, highly intelligent, generous and freedom-loving. We can come together as Americans for a brighter future in which kindness and compassion blunt out the disease of hate and violence against those who are different from ourselves.

# 46. Overcoming Negative Stereotyping of Southerners

## Introduction

A lot of effort is now properly spent on ending unfair treatment of others based on race, religion, ethnicity, and sexual identity in the United States. I did want to take some time to discuss another group of Americans who have been completely overlooked as far as being unfairly characterized through negative stereotyping. American southerners have been consistently stereotyped in a very negative light by the mass media and by citizens from other areas of the United States. They are classified as "backward, uneducated and racist." To be honest, I don't know of any other group that in today's environment of political correctness, who would not be calling for individuals to be fired from their jobs or, at the least, have to undergo intensive sensitivity training for so openly promoting such negative stereotypes to this degree.

I've lived most of my life in the rural or suburban (as the local metropolitan area has grown) South and consider myself to be a proud North Carolinian. Yes, my family was one of many who migrated to the sunny South beginning in the 1980s from states like New York, Ohio, and Pennsylvania. I want to point out that in this essay I am mainly discussing rural or suburban southerners versus individuals living in southern cities. The uniqueness of a geographical area's people becomes diluted in cities due to the very nature of metropolitan areas. Basically, all cities in the United States attract a very diverse melting pot of many ethnic, religious, and racial groups. Therefore, most cities house very diverse populations from all over the nation and world. This is in stark contrast to rural and suburban areas which have a higher percentage of residents who are native to the area and region.

## An Educated and Sophisticated South

My discussion is intended to represent my thoughts on the South as a whole, but I do use my home state of North Carolina as a prime example of a New South state. As far as education, North Carolina has an impressive community college system that is top notch at preparing North Carolinians for many front-line jobs, such as trade technicians (HVAC for example), police officers and nurses. I would argue that our system of higher education holds its own compared to the higher learning institutions of any other state in the nation. We have ACC (Atlantic Coast Conference) powerhouses like Duke, University of North Carolina at Chapel Hill, N.C. State and Wake Forest. In addition, we have other outstanding academic institutions such as Davidson College. North Carolina also can boast that we have an array of very well-respected Historically Black Colleges and Universities (HBCUs) which include North Carolina A&T State University, known for its Engineering program, and North Carolina Central University with one of the state's handful of Law Schools. I point to this higher educational system of the state to substantiate that a lot of North Carolinians have acquired higher levels of education past high school. Yes, there are many who come to North Carolina from outside of the state to study at our universities, but no doubt, these in-state schools support the education of a significant number of North Carolinians. The misguided stereotype of southerners as uneducated buffoons with limited IQs is simply not reality. North Carolina is one of the top states for businesses and industries to relocate their headquarters or branches to on a consistent basis. Actually, CNBC named North Carolina as the top state in the nation for business in 2023 (CNBC.com staff). Our educated and skilled workforce is one of the reasons why businesses can succeed in our state.

When comments are made that southerners are backward and unsophisticated, these adjectives paint an incorrect representation of people living in the South. No, in the rural South there are not huge museums like in the big cities, but there are many artistic endeavors occurring. The South is home to many diverse art forms, such as pottery-making – that is thriving in my area of western North Carolina. There are many small-town theatre guilds that offer impressive shows to the public. While my focus in this essay is the rural south, I do want to point out that in North Carolina, larger cities, such as Charlotte and Raleigh, offer Broadway and sophisticated local, acting productions. Of course, the South is famous for its culinary arts. The movement of eating local and "farm to table" is a somewhat progressive initiative that has been adopted by farm/restaurant businesses in the South. Great culinary art traditions, such as Low Country cuisine of the Charleston, South Carolina area and Louisiana fine dining are known not only throughout the nation, but throughout the world as very innovative and unique dining cultures. The South is indeed more than just barbecue, fried chicken, and grits.

### Southerners and Science

Another accusation is that southerners do poorly at following science, instead opting for religion or superstition to be their guide. Now, I do want to say that I totally disagree with those who opposed taking the COVID-19 vaccination shots, based on conservative talking points that had no basis (and still don't) in science. Yes, there was an issue in the South during the pandemic where some refused to get vaccinated in order to prevent serious illness and save lives. This is in contrast to many northern states that had significantly higher rates of vaccination participation. I feel very strongly on this issue and this lack of relying on science, somewhat may support the contention that southerners are "backward." On this issue, "backward," may be an accurate description, but those who rejected the science behind the COVID-19 vaccines were absolutely not isolated just in the South but included citizens in the Midwest and Northwest as well. I would say many conservative-leaning citizens in our nation and, yes, those in the rural South who are more likely to vote Republican, were misguided when it came to the vaccine and other recommendations by the CDC (Centers for Disease Control and Prevention) and medical experts when it came to the COVID-19 pandemic. I don't make excuses for these individuals, but I do think a medical crisis was politicized which led to this rejection of science. What I witnessed in rural North Carolina is that a lot of people have rejected the COVID safety guidelines of masking, social distancing and getting vaccinated ("How to Protect"), but interestingly enough, a high majority of those aged 65 years and over have been very diligent about getting their vaccines and boosters, along with wearing masks. My conclusion is correct according to statista.com which found per a study dated April 26, 2023, that the vast majority of Americans aged 65 and older in the southern states were fully vaccinated against COVID-19 (Vankar). This ranged from close to 85% in states like Arkansas, Alabama, and Mississippi to 95% in states like North Carolina and Virginia (Vankar). It seems clear that at the end of the day, regardless of geographic area or political affiliation, a large number of those who are most vulnerable to becoming very sick or dying from COVID-19, did in fact trust the science and did get vaccinated.

This brings me to the assertion of many that because there is a strong religious culture in the South that southerners often disregard science. The claim that southerners are backward or ignorant because they follow religion over science needs to be examined somewhat. There are many scientists and technology experts who are religious. No, being religious does not exclude one from following science. When science and religion seem opposed to one another, like in the case of Evolution versus Creationism, this has to be worked out and, yes, I would say the religious interpretation of biblical text may need to be reexamined in cases in which science clearly provides factual evidence in opposition to religious texts or beliefs. Religion, however, can provide mankind guidance on how to use the tremendous power of God's science. I want to point out that in my belief pattern I never see a conflict between religion and science because I see science as simply adhering to the rational laws of the universe that are created by God. Religion provides a strong ethical foundation for us to review when we need to determine the morality of how advanced science should be used. Morality based in religion compels us to ask ourselves if the use of new inventions, applications or tools created by science will contribute to the greater good of humanity. Just because we can clone a human does not mean it should be done. What were the implications of creating the atomic bomb that now has been mass-produced and can destroy the Earth many times over? My overall point is that those who have strong faiths should not be discounted. Some of the most thoughtful individuals are religious scholars who use their intellect intensely to determine how humanity can best follow God to help their fellow human. I contend that I put science fact above religious doctrine that seems to be in conflict with reality, but those who follow a particularly altruistic religious faith, such as Christianity, cannot be stereotyped as being "backward." I personally have a concern with Ultra-Orthodox sects of any religions (Jewish, Christian, Muslim, etc.) who claim their way is the only way which too often leads them to mistreat others who think differently. In general, however, I would argue that those who follow a religious faith are instilled by that faith to show caring and compassion for others. The good deeds that so many churches carry out in the South (and around the world) reflect in a sense a very progressive approach to improving society. Indeed, caring for the wellbeing of others is anything but "backward."

## The South and Racism

I would not be honest if I refuse to admit up front that I do find there to be an element of racism in the South. There is a history stemming from the Civil War that cannot be denied when one sees pick-up trucks with Confederate flag stickers on their bumpers, or simply Confederate flags literally attached to the backs of vehicles flapping in the wind. Perhaps the "heritage not hate" rationale that some supporters of the flag provide, is based on their authentic opinion that while they celebrate the Confederacy, it is not from a place of racial hatred. It is clear that the South does have a vocal element of racial hate, although small, stemming from its past with slavery that does need to be addressed. However, my overall conclusion based on personal experience is that most southerners are not racists. It should also be pointed out that the majority of African Americans in the United States reside in the southern states (Moslimani, Tamir, Budiman, Noe-Bustamante and Mora). This means there is greater interaction between whites and African Americans throughout the South than possibly in other areas of the country. Overall, there is peaceful co-existence between races in the South. The South has even been seen as a welcoming place for African Americans to relocate to from other regions in the United States in recent years.

I concede that there are vestiges of the old South that live on, but it's important to know that as the South has progressed and become more diverse, the current population is more accepting of diversity. It is also important to point out per recent incidents of police brutality against African Americans, that discrimination is not a monopoly in the American South. Racism is an issue throughout the United States, but clearly due to the geographical history of slavery in the South, the South is viewed as the home of racism. My claim is I wouldn't necessarily say that racism is worse here than in other parts of the country. In fact, what is interesting, as I've pointed out above, is that now there's a migration of African Americans flocking to the Southern United States. Some African American families whose grandparents and great grandparents fled the South in the post-slavery and segregationist eras, are finding that the urbanized North is not the land where their dreams of a good life have come to fruition. They are finding new success by moving to the South where there is a low cost of living and more economic opportunities in the Sun Belt. Yes, cities like Charlotte and Atlanta have attracted newcomers from the North and across the nation. As part of this migration some African Americans are finding they can make their dreams come true in the suburbs and rural areas on the outskirts of these major metropolitan areas. It is a heartwarming reality that the Old South is no longer and has been replaced by a welcoming New South that provides economic opportunities with upward mobility to African Americans.

I want to point out that the South is increasingly diverse with not only well-established African American communities, but with the growth of Asian and Hispanic populations as well. All these diverse groups seem to do just fine on the whole in coexisting together in peace. I do admit that while there is more to be done to achieve greater equality among all racial groups, the South is now a considerably more diverse environment than ever before. This is a positive step in the right direction. When we think of the South and its racial composition and diversity, we generally think of this region as mainly including whites and African Americans due to the prominent history of slavery. The new South of the twenty-first century consists of a vastly more diverse population than at any other time in the region's history. These include citizens from a variety of racial, ethnic, and religious backgrounds, as well as those from the LGTBQ community.

In addition, young people are leading the way in supporting diversity in all its forms – racial, ethnic, religious (or non-religious) and sexual orientation/preference. My subjective viewpoint is that increasingly dating and coupling patterns are reflecting that individuals from diverse groups are creating new lives together. We are seeing traditional and non-traditional coupling of individuals with varied backgrounds whether it be Caucasians and African Americans, or between other racial groups. Again, there are vestiges of the Old South. There is no doubt about that, but overall people from different races who marry or have romantic relationships together are not even paid much attention to in the New South. Yes, this new climate of acceptance and openness is true progress from the days when intermarrying between races was illegal in some states in the South.

I also want to avoid the stale debate (in my opinion) of whether the South is more racist and intolerant than other parts of the country. I don't think that's something that is measurable. All I will say is that the South still has work to do to end racism, but for that matter, so does our entire nation. Even in ultra-liberal California and New York we see great pockets of poverty occurring in African American communities. Does this mean that these blue states and cities are racist? I would say it does not, but I would argue that even these liberal areas have work to do in ensuring equal opportunity for minorities.

## Closing

As I close this essay, I admit that I have at times caught myself stereotyping the rural South. I found myself in disbelief this past June in my suburban, rural hometown in North Carolina. There was a Juneteenth festival being held in our downtown area. As I drove by, I observed a very diverse group of people walking through the downtown checking out the vendor booths and eating hot dogs like all Americans do on warm weather holidays. I admit it is difficult for all of us to overcome ingrained stereotypes, but through interaction and education we can obtain a more open-minded and extensive view of others.

Finally, I have focused in this essay on negative stereotyping of southerners, but one positive stereotype that is catching on is that people in the South are very nice. I would concur with this finding without taking anything away from all the great and friendly people who reside in the rest of the United States. Southerners are overall kind, down to earth and honest. I recall a few years ago before the pandemic that I was shopping at our local Walmart one afternoon. Later that evening I realized I was missing my wallet. I contacted my bank to cancel my debit card and researched online how to get a replacement driver's license. The next day I went by Walmart and figured I was wasting my time visiting the customer service desk to see if anyone had turned in a lost wallet. I was sure that someone quickly picked up the wallet, took the cash and cards, and tossed the rest in the trash. When I walked up to the customer service desk and told the representative my plight, she asked what color the wallet was. I told her the wallet was blue and after providing my name, she walked in the back and then came back handing me my wallet with everything in it. Some kind soul had found my wallet and turned it in to the store.

These days there is a lot of anger, disagreement, and divisiveness everywhere along racial, political, and even geographical lines. I in no way have set out to "sugar-coat" the rural South. There are still small, but intense pockets of hate and intolerance. Overall, however, the New South consists of diverse peoples who live together in peace and treat one another with great kindness. Strangers still wave to each other and help each other out (like turning in a lost wallet). Yes, faith and family are important to people in the South. This may seem outdated, but perhaps we all can learn from southerners that there are more important things than what car you drive or whether you have the latest smart phone. Southerners can teach us that trying to live in a fast-paced life constantly may not be healthy for us physically, mentally, or emotionally. So, I close by suggesting that the reader overlook the negative stereotypes of the South and delve deeper into the reality. Migration patterns don't lie. Many people of diverse backgrounds are flocking to the South because of greater economic opportunities, a more laid-back lifestyle, and friendly, warm-hearted people.

# 47. Dangers While Driving: Too Fast, Too Close and Too Angry

### Too Fast – Especially on Wet Roads

We had had several days in a row of rainy, foggy weather – a bit unusual for North Carolina. I truly love living in the sunny South. I was driving to work into the city on a Thursday around 6:30 a.m. and the rain was coming down. We have all learned in our driver education classes in high school that safety and basic physics call for us to slow down when it is raining. I found on this morning that many of the other drivers on the road were not following safety protocol. I did slow down according to what I thought was safe, noting pockets of standing water from the rain that had accumulated throughout the overnight hours. I could feel myself getting anxious as the car behind me edged up to my bumper at an alarmingly fast speed given the road conditions. As the vehicle eventually passed me traveling at a very high speed, I actually slowed down out of concern that the passing vehicle might swerve out of control on the wet road and collide with my vehicle.

Another concern that I have when driving during inclement weather, is that often other cars traveling toward me on two-lane roads do not slow down given the environmental conditions. I witness more and more drivers simply not slowing down at all during wet weather, disregarding the fact that vehicle tire traction on the road is going to be less dependable than in dry weather conditions. I always feel that I am psychologically and almost physically bracing myself when these cars come toward me, questioning whether the vehicles will stay in their lane. Often, I face vehicles approaching my vehicle traveling at 45 or 50 miles per hour through curves, disregarding the signage indicating vehicles need to slow down to 35 miles per hour through the sharp road bends. I do my best to get over near the shoulder of the road as much as possible in my lane just in case an oncoming car veers into my lane. These roads, particularly in the early mornings, have school buses traveling on them. God forbid, one of these senseless drivers crosses that center line and hits a school bus which is a real possibility when you combine high speeds and wet roads. One could say that I'm overreacting in my judgement of other drivers, yet I would offer that it is like clockwork in my area that when it rains we have at least one fatality on our Charlotte-area roadways. We also have many minor accidents. All of this could be avoided if people drove more safely.

I contend that we have to get speeding under control in inclement weather, but speed is a threat to public safety even during dry weather conditions. I have consistently held the belief that if a vehicle is traveling five miles over the speed limit, pulling the driver over and issuing a ticket or some form of citation would be an excessive and unreasonable action for a law enforcement officer to take. However, my perspective is that once a vehicle is traveling ten miles or more over the speed limit for more than a mile, then the driver should automatically receive some type of citation. This is why I continue to contend that many roadways should have speed cameras. The use of this tool would reduce speeds very quickly. Unfortunately, police can't be everywhere, but the technology we have can really assist in discouraging excessive speeding.

I would also like to see all speed limit signs transition to digital displays. The driver is always in charge of monitoring and judging how safely she or he can navigate a roadway and at what speed, but I support digital speed limit signs that can be adjusted as road conditions change due to the weather. I envision local departments of transportation being able to remotely reduce speed limits during rainy or icy road conditions. Perhaps someday digital speed limit signs will be able to measure precipitation in the atmosphere so they can automatically adjust their posted speed limits to match environmental conditions on the roads. The ability to lower posted speed limits would help reduce accidents during periods of inclement weather. There have been some successful traffic calming solutions that have been implemented quite well in communities, such as speed humps in neighborhoods. There is a neighborhood in Charlotte that had a four-lane road running right through it with many vehicles regularly traveling 10 or 15 miles per hour over the 35 miles per hour speed limit. The street has recently been redesigned and is now a two-lane road with traffic running one lane in each direction. The former vehicular lanes closest to the sidewalks in this very walkable community are now closed off to cars. Large planter boxes have been placed in these closed lanes and now act as barriers, providing some insulation to bike riders accessing these lanes, as well as to the pedestrians on the sidewalks. We must continue to come up with new roadway designs and other innovative solutions to slow down cars in order to protect the lives of drivers, cyclists, and pedestrians.

## Too Close

Our current driving environment consists of cars too often unsafely following the vehicles in front of them without allocating proper following distance. Tailgating is a serious threat to the safety of everyone on our roadways, especially on high-speed highways and thoroughfares. The other evening, I was waiting in a very busy Wendy's drive-through lane. There was no real danger to my vehicle or the passengers in it, but the super-sized pickup truck that seemed to dwarf my sub-compact crossover did make me pause. All I could see in my rearview mirror was a truck grill, while the young man kept inching his vehicle toward my tailgate, as if that would make the line go any faster at 8 p.m. on a Friday evening. Now, if this vehicle were to tap my back bumper in a drive-through lane at a fast-food restaurant, the outcome wouldn't lead to bodily harm to the passengers in my vehicle. However, if we were traveling at 55 miles per hour on the open road, then this type of tailgating behavior would become a serious hazard to the wellbeing of those in my vehicle, as well as to the wellbeing of this aggressive young man in the pickup truck. We need a drastic change in behavior when it comes to how closely we follow one another in our vehicles.

I recall in the 1980s when I took driver education, that we were taught to leave one car length between our vehicle and the car in front of us for every ten miles per hour that we are traveling. Also, we were taught that in inclement weather like rain, snow, and ice our following distance needs to increase. Recent safe driver training that I have attended now emphasizes that a vehicle should not pass a fixed location sooner than three to five seconds after the vehicle in front of it has passed the same fixed location. I prefer the car length rule of thumb, but the point is that we must all do a better job of following the guidance and avoid dangerous tailgating. Of course, the problem with tailgating is intensified with Americans' current love affair with super-sized SUVs (sport utility vehicles) and trucks. I often think there should be additional training required for those driving such vehicles just because these large trucks and SUVS have the potential to cause great destruction to vehicles and people. When these very large vehicles get into accidents, they can cause tremendous damage to other vehicles on the road, leading to more injuries and death to the drivers and passengers traveling in smaller vehicles. I admit that I changed from driving a sedan to a subcompact, crossover SUV in the hopes of providing some additional protection for my family. Of course, the super-sized trucks seem to still be twice the size of my vehicle when they come up behind me, even in my larger vehicle. Many drivers have had the unnerving experience of being in a smaller vehicle and having the large pickup truck or even the commercial eighteen-wheeler impatiently tailgating extremely closely behind them. In this type of driving situation, the driver of the large vehicle obviously realizes that if his vehicle were to collide with the smaller vehicle, it could lead to serious bodily injury and even death to the passengers in the smaller vehicle. This type of tailgating is simply a form of bullying and intimidation that society must collectively reject and stop.

I do think various enforcement and technological tools need to be implemented to curb tailgating. We need cameras to pick up information not just on speeding but also on tailgating behavior. More widespread use of roadway monitoring cameras, the issuing of additional citations handed out by law enforcement officers, and the installation of additional safety features on vehicles which prevent tailgating are all needed enhancements to stop this dangerous driving practice. I would like to see the dissemination of more public safety messages emphasizing the damage that can occur to vehicles and people due to following other vehicles too closely. We must communicate that all drivers need to ensure that they are maintaining safe following distances from the vehicles in front of them so that accidents can be avoided. We all need to drive so that everyone can arrive at their destinations safely.

## Too Angry

This brings me to the concern that too many of us are driving in an aggressive and angry mindset. As we are getting back to a "new normal" after two (or three) years of the COVID-19 pandemic, we are finding that our society is extremely divided on numerous political and social issues. People express their discontent and disagreement too often in angry speech and even through acts of violence. This behavior has extended onto our roadways. The vast majority of these angry interactions between motorists end in a few honked horns and some rude gestures, but these incidents can also end in crashes and people being seriously hurt or killed. Not only do drivers have to worry about being the victim of an angry driver hitting them with a car, now it appears that we have more incidents of angry drivers senselessly shooting at other motorists. We all get into that mode of "I'll show you," but we must adopt new strategies to keep the roadways calm. Again, technology can come into play. Not only should we have more cameras on the roadways, but I believe that front and rear cameras (and perhaps side cameras as well) should be standard (and required) on all new vehicles sold in the U.S. I understand the concern about too much "Big Brother" oversight by the government, but driving a vehicle as we know is a "privilege and not a right." When drivers know that they are being recorded, this will stop more aggressive driving. Yes, pulling out a phone and recording (or acting as if you are recording) can be effective at getting aggressive drivers to stop their behavior, but it also can incite them to really lose their self-control and become more dangerous. Having constant recording by roadway cameras and vehicle cameras can effectively communicate the message that we all need to behave. Our law enforcement officers are already short staffed coming out of the pandemic in many areas, but I'd like to see state troopers and municipal police focus specifically on aggressive drivers traveling in larger vehicles. Of course, drivers of smaller vehicles can be just as guilty of aggressive, dangerous driving as drivers of very large pick-up trucks, SUVs, and commercial eighteen-wheelers. The difference, as I've discussed, is the intensified threat of bodily harm that these larger vehicles pose to passengers in smaller vehicles that they encounter, not to mention any pedestrians or cyclists on or near the roadways. Our nation's increase in population, of course, has resulted in more vehicles on our roadways, creating an even greater challenge for law enforcement than in the past of policing dangerous driving behavior. I cannot stress enough my opinion that including the widespread use of cameras to monitor and record driving behavior is an effective policy in preventing excessive speeding, tailgating and other public safety threats. Technology must be used to assist our law enforcement officers in their ethical effort of increasing safety on our roadways.

## More Messaging and Better Education on Safe Driving

We don't want to distract already distracted drivers with more roadway signage, but we do need more messaging encouraging drivers not only to drive safely (no excessive speeding and tailgating) but to remain calm and patient. I'm sure behavioral experts can help with adding signage to our roadways that will encourage more calm behavior. Maybe next to stop lights to keep drivers calm, public art depicting tranquil scenes of nature, along with positive messages encouraging kindness, such as "Share your smile," or "Drive like your newborn is in the car in front of you," would help. I like the idea of a public information campaign encouraging safe driving like a "Speed Limit Saturdays" initiative. The idea is that particularly on the weekends when the majority of people are off work, there really is not a justifiable reason to speed even a little. If we all consciously make the decision to drive at the speed limit, then we can save lives. The goal would be to extend this behavior into the rest of the week with the emphasis on safety for everyone at all times. It seems that convenience and speed have won over our shared societal desire to keep our families and children safe on our roadways. We must reverse this trend and emphasize safety over speed.

I also think transportation planners and engineers can play a role by creating roadway environments that are easier to navigate, as well as aesthetically pleasing. How many of us have come upon road conditions that are very difficult to navigate, leading to incidents in which drivers are competing with one another. Four-way stop signs come to mind. This traffic arrangement may work in areas with little traffic, but in high traffic areas when cars are arriving at the intersection all at the same time, navigating through the four-way stop sign can be confusing and dangerous. Also, in areas where there are many stores and business establishments, speed limits should be reduced. The need to carefully navigate more stop lights with more drivers turning in and out of numerous businesses or residential areas requires everyone to drive more slowly to avoid accidents. What we want to do is create an environment in which confusion is lessened and in which we can keep in check the stress levels of drivers.

Some may say this is a silly proposal, but I think as part of an effort to change driving culture, we should require that each driver state a pledge before one can receive his or her driver's license. The pledge would be something like the following:

*I pledge to follow and respect all driving laws to the best of my ability each and every time that I get behind the wheel. I commit to driving safely at all times, understanding that I have a responsibility for the safety of all passengers in my vehicle, as well as to my fellow motorists traveling in the vehicles around me. I vow to drive in a courteous, polite, and cooperative manner. I am committed to the goal of everyone on our roadways reaching their destinations safely.*

## Closing

Yes, I am one of those who believe the future of driving is a collaborative system of self-driving vehicles with human drivers having the ability to take over when necessary (if technical issues arise, etc.). Any new system needs to have checks on human drivers – for example, if humans begin to drive in unsafe ways, the vehicle's computer system would take over the vehicle. I leave the details to the Elon Musks of the world to figure out how best to implement a new era of safety on the roads. We do need a new transportation system that emphasizes the safety of the traveler over convenience. Americans love to drive and experience that feeling of controlling our powerful transportation machines, but in my vision of the future, vehicles will be locked into at least a virtual transportation grid with more checks on dangerous and high-risk behavior. Yes, in my driving, transportation utopia of the future, the driver in his sports car will not be able to drive 80 miles per hour in a 55 miles-per-hour zone. The integrated computer system per my vision will not allow the car to travel that fast, or once the driver hits such a speed on his own, the vehicle will automatically pull over and simply be locked during which time law enforcement will arrive to ticket the driver. I do believe in more of a technologically integrated system in which there are limits on individual driver behavior.

In closing, I hope that I have communicated to the reader how passionately I feel about protecting the safety of everyone traveling on our roadways. Again, I do support some type of self-driving, autonomous system in the future. Unfortunately, any type of autonomous or semi-autonomous system could be decades away from full implementation. Given this reality, there are a lot of great ideas and policies that brilliant minds are coming up with to make our roadways safer for everyone now and in the near future. As far as steps in the near future to improve safety on our roadways, we can have police give out more tickets, cities can construct more traffic calming devices and we can set up video recording system that capture those displaying dangerous driving behaviors. A massive public education campaign can also help to convince people to change their driving habits. Another significant step in improving vehicle safety is for all of us (including yours truly) to make that commitment to putting everyone's safety first whenever we get behind the wheels of our vehicles.

## Follow-up Note

I did want to share a very disturbing incident that I read about in December of 2022 on my local NBC news outlet web site (Leshner). A family in Charlotte was traveling to a Christmas celebration when an agitated driver who was driving erratically, opened his car window displaying a gun. The family included a husband and wife with two teenagers in the back seat. They were terrified. In too many cases, it seems drivers get away with illegal behavior, such as in hit and run situations, because in the heat of the moment no one records their license plate numbers. I found it very interesting that the angry driver in this case was caught and charged. This family, you see, was traveling in a Tesla that had cameras which recorded the incident on video. The video was shared with police who were able to then locate the suspect. My contention is that when our driving environment becomes one in which all vehicles are being recorded by roadside cameras and vehicle cameras, then driver behavior will improve.

# 48. Long Live a Free Ukraine (written in late December of 2022)

<hr>

### President Zelensky Visits Washington

President Volodymyr Zelensky of Ukraine visited Washington D.C. on Wednesday, December 21, 2022, to meet with President Biden and to speak directly to the United States Congress. His visit marked the first time the Ukrainian president had left his nation since the beginning of Russia's inhumane invasion in February of 2022. I was greatly impressed by President Zelensky's speech to Congress. He expressed the gratefulness on the part of the people of Ukraine for all the help that the United States has provided in the war against Russia. In addition, he did make a plea to the United States government and directly to the people of the United States for continued support militarily.

The timing of President Zelensky's speech was critical to the effort by Ukraine to win continued support from Washington. Beginning in January, the party holding power in the House of Representatives will be the Republicans, not the Democrats. The Republicans have been overall supportive of the war in Ukraine, but their collective opinion is that it cannot be an unending situation in which the U.S. provides an open checkbook from which Ukraine funds its war with Russia. Hopefully Zelensky's speech will encourage Congress who holds the purse strings of the U.S. government to continue to support the Ukrainian effort, at least for the immediate future.

### We Must Continue to Support Ukraine

First, all Americans who value our place as leader of the free world should want to support Ukraine for the benefit of the people in that nation who wish to live in freedom. Secondly, I do see the war in Ukraine per a World War II, global perspective from which we should have learned how to deal with a tyrant. I won't delve into a comprehensive comparison of Hitler to Putin but what the West has learned when dealing with zealots intent on taking over other nations, is that they must be dealt with directly and immediately. This is challenging given that Russia has an impressive nuclear arsenal, but it still must be done. Putin has made it clear that he wishes to return to a Soviet-era existence in which the Soviet empire held power over numerous eastern European nations. This expansion cannot be allowed. These nations wish to remain free, democratic nation-states and have no desire to return to living under the repressive boot of the Kremlin. Western powers, with the North Atlantic Treaty Organization (NATO) at its helm, agree that Russian expansion and a new Cold War need to be prevented. The way to accomplish these goals is to continue to isolate Russia financially through sanctions, while wearing down its conventional military capabilities by funding the Ukrainian military. Furthermore, the hope is that the Russian people (and there are faint glimmers of hope) will tire of this war and force Putin's hand to retreat or look for a way to negotiate peace.

Zelensky's speech was critical in solidifying U.S. support for Ukraine, and it does look like the U.S. military will be providing more advanced missile defense systems (Lawler). In my opinion, we need to be cautious as far as how many advanced weapons systems we should provide to Ukraine. I think the United States has to walk this tightrope very carefully of standing with Ukraine, while not instigating a new world war or worse, a nuclear war with Russia. So far, the United States and NATO have walked that fine line of providing defense weapons to Ukraine, while limiting offensive weapons that could result in deep strikes into Russian territory. Now, my preference is for another member of NATO to provide Ukraine with more advanced defense systems. Even if the systems were American made, it would dampen the optics of the United States directly providing advanced weaponry in opposition to Russia. Overall, I do find myself supporting the allocation of advanced defense systems because of the brutality and inhumanity of Russia's continued missile attacks on civilian populations. The United Nations (UN) has even stated that these attacks in December seem to have been coordinated to knock out energy facilities across Ukraine. These power generating facilities are vital to ensuring Ukrainians have heat during the harsh winter months. The UN has stated these attacks on energy facilities and residential areas could amount to war crimes.

The goal of providing advanced defense weapons systems to Ukraine should simply be to establish some humanitarian ground rules. What Putin is attempting to do is to punish the Ukrainian people directly for opposing him. A sinister way to accomplish this is to send missiles into civilian areas and destroy the power grid as the Ukrainian people prepare to face a cold, harsh winter. Advanced weapons systems should equal the playing field somewhat. Both Ukrainian and Russian civilian areas should be off limits to military strikes. The defense systems will be put to the test in Ukraine to prevent incoming Russian missiles. The United States government should communicate to Russia and the world that providing these advanced defense systems should not be seen as an escalation of tensions between the superpowers, but that the focus of this effort is based on an immediate humanitarian need to protect Ukrainians civilians. Had Putin not inhumanely attacked civilian areas, there would be no need for the United States to introduce advanced defensive weapons into the war.

## Republicans Seek More Oversight on Funds Allocated to Ukraine

As we look to the political realities in the United States, it is important to note that Republicans, while overall they are supportive of Zelensky and the Ukrainian effort, would like to see more comprehensive oversight of the funds distributed to Ukraine. Now, if we recall there is some history here that could have Republicans less enthusiastic about Zelensky and Ukraine, than they otherwise would be for a nation fighting an international bully like Putin. Zelensky was asked by former President Donald Trump to investigate now President Biden and his son Hunter in 2019 during the 2020 presidential campaign. The question was whether there was any corruption on the part of both Hunter Biden and the current president while Hunter Biden sat on the board of a Ukrainian company. President Trump at the time clearly appeared to tie the distribution of financial aid to Ukraine essentially in exchange for Zelensky's cooperation to open an investigation. One could say that whether there was any true corruption or not, just the opening of an investigation could have been information used to discredit Joe Biden during the 2020 presidential election. Asking a foreign government for assistance in a U.S. political campaign is illegal under federal law (Chlopak). Mr. Trump's phone call to Mr. Zelensky, asking him to investigate the Bidens to determine if they committed any crimes or acts of corruption, did lead to Mr. Trump's impeachment by Congress. In my opinion, there is now a tendency of some Republicans based on political motivation to claim that Ukraine should have found wrongdoing by the Bidens. They seem to be shifting blame from President Trump and his inappropriate request to President Zelinsky, and falsely present the situation as a failure of a corrupt Ukrainian government which did not find illegal activity by the Bidens.

At the end of the day, my viewpoint is that regardless of the true reason why Republicans want more stringent oversight on funding and military support provided to Ukraine, it is not an unreasonable request. There is also a valid concern that while Ukraine's war against Russia needs the support of the West, corruption has been a problem within the Ukrainian government for some time. The balance, therefore, is to continue to support Ukraine, but with the establishment of a clear oversight review process of all funds, weapons and any other materials or services being provided to Ukraine. A cooperative initiative between the Republican-led House of Representatives, the Senate still led by the Democrats and the White House should be able to implement procedures to ensure acceptable oversight.

### Supporting Ukraine is Vital to the National Security of the United States

Oversight of what financially is being spent by the United States to support Ukraine is important, but again, we do need to remember that there is a national security issue for the United States in the case of Ukraine. We must prevent Putin from capturing any of the former Soviet-era nations per his stated desire of re-creating the former Soviet bloc. As we found out in World War II Germany, appeasement does not work with bullies, only showing strength in negotiation. We have a national security imperative to contain Russia by preventing Putin from taking over all of Ukraine. We must send a strong, although diplomatic message to a nuclear-armed Mr. Putin. Also, a key and ethical reason that we need to support Ukraine with weapons and financial support is that Ukraine has not asked America or NATO to provide any troops. The Ukrainians have been extremely brave and impressively resourceful at turning back the Russian invasion. Putin intended to quickly invade and completely capture the nation in a few days. The Russian leader basically envisioned a lightning-fast annexation of Ukraine. The nation would simply be incorporated as a new state within Russia. When this did not happen, it was an embarrassing, dismal failure. At the end of 2022, Russia and Ukraine are basically in a stalemate with Russia having to draft additional troops from civilian populations who are unlikely to be sufficiently trained for military combat. While it is difficult to truly measure public support of the war in Russia where open criticism is not tolerated by the Putin regime, news is coming out that mothers and families of soldiers are pleading for the war to end. These public pleas may indicate that the Russian people's support for Mr. Putin's military invasion of Ukraine may be fading fast. Unlike other nations (I think of Iraq and Afghanistan to some degree), Ukrainians are doing not just the brunt of the fighting, but all of the fighting to preserve their freedom. The Ukrainian people are not asking American or NATO troops to come fight for them. This truly is admirable and the brave fighting by the Ukrainians is a major reason why we must continue to support them. As a people, Americans have an obligation to support nations who wish to fight against totalitarianism in the quest to be part of the free world. This truth has been adeptly cited by Mr. Zelensky in his appeals to the West. The Ukrainians are on the actual front line, protecting the free world against Putin's evil intentions. We must remember that the fall of a free Ukraine means that Mr. Putin will continue his march to re-establish the former Soviet regime and its threat to all freedom-loving nations in Europe and beyond.

## Finding a Peaceful Resolution to the War in Ukraine

Now, there are those calling for Putin to be put on trial for war crimes per his unjustified invasion of Ukraine and subsequent attacks on civilian areas. I agree that Putin should be held responsible for his actions, but I also acknowledge the reality on the ground that until Putin is ousted, which may never happen, he still is the leader of a nation that has an impressive nuclear arsenal. I am no foreign policy expert, but if we sense that Putin is open to a way out, the United States should act as a broker of peace between Russia and Ukraine. This could be done behind the scenes through back channels, both as a way for Putin to save face, as well as to provide more open room for diplomatic discussion and open negotiation. Ukraine does not want to give up any land and I agree that giving up territory could encourage Putin to come back again, but we need to look for ways for

Russia to permanently withdraw from Ukraine. In order to accomplish this, Putin will have to walk away with something. Maybe this means some concessions with parts of the Donbas and Crimea regions being retained by Russia, but I would say the vast majority of these lands except for some eastern sections, should be returned to Ukrainian rule. A peace agreement could allow some port access for Russia to the Black Sea, but would return the significant port of Sevastopol back to full Ukrainian control. The port of Sevastopol has been a key location significantly enhancing Russia's ability to wage its military campaign in Syria (Cragg and Volochine). Putin failed to live up to the lease agreement with Ukraine for access to the port of Sevastopol per his annexation of Crimea in 2014 (Hille, Buckley and Farchy), and, therefore, in my opinion, should have limited access to this specific port in the future. This is a balancing act and, of course, we don't want to allow Putin to gain any significant areas of land that were not under Russian control before the invasion of February 2022 (or per Putin's annexation of Crimea in 2014). However, if Putin can save face and claim some type of victory, that could end the war.

Finally, some type of formal declaration by Ukraine stating that the nation will not join NATO could also be a desirable outcome for Putin. This would be a victory for Putin and to some degree would be a defeat to Ukraine which has sought entry into NATO. Such a declaration by Ukraine, however, may be part of a workable solution in the effort of establishing peace. Although it gives Russia a significant concession, it still allows the West to continue to provide direct military assistance to the Ukrainian people, who have proven that they perform quite well in holding their own against the Russian military. I would like to see that Ukraine is supported with an advanced missile shield and other major defensive armaments along the Russian border areas going forward. A strong border defense is needed to hopefully deter Mr. Putin from planning any future incursions into Ukraine. One must concede given Mr. Putin's world view, that there are no true guarantees for Ukraine, thus, the nation must always be defensively prepared. If Russia does take such barbaric military actions again, the people of Ukraine will be better able to prevent Russian troops from entering into their nation, or at least keep the fighting localized to border towns and areas.

### Long Live a Free Ukraine and Hope for a Future Free Russia

I close by stating that I do believe in the end Putin will fail to take Ukraine and gain traction in his attempt to resurrect the old Soviet-bloc system. The hope of the world should be that in the future, Russia will become more aligned with the West. Russia after the collapse of the Soviet Union in the late 20th Century did have great challenges transitioning to democracy and a free market economic system. The United States did attempt to support the transition for Russia, but the next time around, the West needs to do less gloating and celebrating that the old Russian system was defeated and place more emphasis on helping the Russian people for the long-term. Building a new bond of peace is essential to preventing a nation, which has lost a hot or cold war, from rebuilding in an effort to seek revenge and reclaim its "glory." The West learned this lesson much too slowly after two World Wars with Germany. We must continually communicate the message that although the United States may oppose Russia's governmental structure and Putin's reign of tyranny, we firmly stand with the people of Russia. Our American foreign policy should include a comprehensive plan to successfully transition Russia into a democratic state in which free markets can support wealth accumulation for the vast majority of its citizens. When Russia is ready, the West must be there with open arms.

# 49. Quiet Quitting: The Self-Empowerment of the Employee

---

### Quiet Quitting – Employees Protesting More and More Work

"Quiet quitting" is the term that has arisen post-pandemic for employees who are making a conscious effort to only perform their job and job tasks, nothing more. The rationale from what I understand is that employees feel underappreciated and underpaid. Often, as many employees have experienced, they are asked to do more and more outside of their core job tasks until they are completely overwhelmed. These employees are provided with insufficient support and understanding from their organization's management or ownership. This practice then is not an actual quitting of one's job, but a way of self-empowerment, in my opinion, to set healthy boundaries within one's work life. The high demand for goods and services coupled with a very low unemployment rate coming out of the COVID-19 pandemic, have resulted in an environment that has given employees confidence to demand more from their employers. Employees, therefore, feel empowered to insist on greater fairness and equity in the workplace.

### The Plight of the Employee during The Great Recession

Some of us who were working during the Great Recession, beginning around 2008, remember the widespread fear and panic that many workers experienced as mass layoffs were the result of a great economic decline. This economic crisis was due in large part to the end of a housing bubble. I do credit the federal government with quickly implementing policies to save the banks and the automobile industry in the United States. During this time, those of us who were fortunate enough to be employed realized that to keep our jobs we would have to do more with less. Indeed, if we did not receive pay cuts, we felt very fortunate. Of course, too many employers used this crisis to get more and more work out of their employees who were not let go with the unstated (and sometimes continually stated) threat that employees were dispensable. Many had to take on additional work tasks with miniscule or non-existent raises for multiple years. Incomes were stagnant. Employees fell into almost a malaise of accepting this less-than-ideal working world just to provide the basic necessities of food and housing for their families.

### The Workplace during the COVID-19 Pandemic

We fast forward to the year 2020 with the beginning of the COVID-19 Pandemic in March. Many employees, particularly in blue collar jobs, such as in healthcare, food service and public service (fire, police, sanitation, etc.) were required to work on site and in the community to perform their job duties. This on-site environment existed in stark contrast to the majority of white-collar employees who were able to work remotely through technological tools (laptop, desktop, and smartphone). The stories of employees who had to work on site, particularly before vaccines were available, really highlighted a reality in which many employees were not being treated with respect, dignity, or basic human consideration for their well-being. It was clear that employers simply weren't adequately addressing the health concerns of their employees. COVID-related illnesses and deaths demonstrated that employees were simply being neglected by their employers during this global health crisis. I recall a bus driver, whose story I watched on the national news, who succumbed to COVID-19 in 2020. The driver was exposed to others consistently throughout the workday due to the nature of his work. Mr. Jason Hargrove, a bus driver in Detroit, publicly expressed his frustration, via social media, with a passenger openly coughing multiple times on his bus (Levenson, Michael). Soon after his post, he contracted the virus and in a matter of days lost his battle with COVID-19. Another shocking situation covered by the media, that many of us can remember, involved meat packing plants in which employees complained that they were not being provided with sufficient supplies of masks and protective equipment. In addition, the management over these plants did not properly adjust workstations so employees could limit close contact with others (six feet apart of course is the recommended distance that individuals need to remain from one another to prevent the spread of the COVID-19 virus – a standard that has been thoroughly ingrained in everyone since the beginning of the pandemic). The dangerous environments in these meat processing plants during the pandemic led to multiple employees contracting COVID-19 with some tragically losing their lives (Hassan). We began to hear the term "essential employees," which introduced a new employee-based movement. Employees did not necessarily create and enter into formal unions through this movement, but large groups of employees did address their concerns by grouping together informally and demanding better working conditions and enhanced compensation. Additional pay was allocated to employees in food preparation, healthcare, public service, etc. as a way to acknowledge the additional health risk of working in-person during the pandemic.

We also need to remember what happened in 2020 when the pandemic first hit. Many in the service and retail sectors had their employment terminated because of COVID-19 restrictions. People early on in the pandemic were socially distancing and not traveling, eating out in restaurants, or attending entertainment events. It is important to look back and recall the great struggle of so many families. The stimulus checks, unemployment payments and rent deferment clearly saved millions from becoming homeless and not having enough food to eat. We all remember the long lines of cars full of people waiting at food banks and other charity organizations to get anything available so they could provide some sustenance for their families. There has been a heated debate as to whether the extended period in which unemployment and stimulus payments continued to be disbursed coming out of the pandemic, contributed to the inflationary situation we are experiencing in 2022 and 2023. This debate is important to have, but I would think most reasonably minded individuals would agree that the additional money families received, during the first year of the pandemic, was truly a Godsend. Then, as businesses began opening back up, what we found was that some employees who previously worked front line jobs were now able to land higher-paying jobs in other industries. Also, some decided to go back to school during this time. There were some who because of the stimulus and unemployment payments did not have to rush back to work. These citizens were able to hold out for jobs with better pay and benefits than they received in their pre-pandemic positions. We thus had a workforce who all of a sudden could demand more from their employers. Employees in this new work environment were able to demand and receive starting pay at $15.00 per hour and beyond. The pay increases in the food service, service sector, and many retail industries were significant. In a sense, employees everywhere continued an informal, but very successful lobbying effort in which employees banded together as a collective entity to demand higher, more livable wages. It was somewhat of a payback for the treatment employees received beginning with the Great Recession. Also, to be fair to the taxpayers, we had employees working for fast food companies and for "Big Box" stores (who will remain in this work unnamed, but readers are free to research this history on their own) who were working full time, but because their pay was so low, they still qualified to receive public assistance. Yes, it was time for pay and other benefits to be enhanced significantly. These large successful businesses were basically operating in a way in which taxpayers were subsidizing the unacceptably low incomes of their employees. Understandably, the use of public funds to provide this type of corporate welfare has been called into question as unacceptable. The viewpoint that large successful businesses need to pay acceptable, livable wages from their profits, rather than force their employees to seek financial support from governmental assistance to survive, gained widespread support during the pandemic.

### Employee Empowerment Coming out of the Pandemic

The dangers of working during the pandemic led to employees standing up more for their interests, but another aspect of the COVID-19 pandemic also affected how employees felt about their work. All of us experienced the fear of a very dangerous pandemic that has killed (to date) over one million Americans. Particularly before vaccines and effective treatments were widely available, the majority of us realized that one moment you could be living your life and within a week you could be unconscious, hooked up to a ventilator with the real possibility of never awakening. This realization that one could pass away very quickly from COVID-19 was a "wake-up call" that life is precious, and we all need to prioritize what is most important in our lives. We realized that relationships with loved ones and friends should be at the top of our priority lists. Too often when employees spoke about work-life balance in the past, employers really did not take their concerns seriously or worse - treated those employees as not being dedicated to their jobs and limited their upward mobility in their careers. Due to our societal, collective experience of the COVID-19 pandemic, however, the idea of a true work-life balance has quickly become an essential component of our working lives. Employers have done much better as far as respecting that balance and I want to give them credit for doing more to ensure employees do have time off and that their mental health is also being considered. The idea is that employees are people. We want to simply acknowledge that all people should be treated fairly and should receive fair pay, benefits, and time to live their lives. Employers are realizing that this approach is a "win-win" situation as happy employees are more productive. Flexible work schedules, such as four-day work weeks for blue collar, on-site jobs and hybrid work schedules for office workers have been very popular with employees. I can attest that having a work schedule of three days in the office and two days at home really has led to more work-life balance, more job productivity, and less stress in my life. Thanks to technology, meetings can almost always occur virtually with the meeting platforms now available. This allows for the time that we are in the office to become periods of great collaboration in a more informal way. Prior to the COVID-19 pandemic, how many working parents dreaded having to let their bosses know that the school just called, and they had to leave to pick up their sick children? Now it is no big deal – just a quick note to the boss that you had to leave the site, but within an hour or so you will be working from home. Better yet, you won't miss that late afternoon meeting as you can join Webex, Zoom, etc. from wherever you are.

Employees have made significant strides coming out of the pandemic. Low wages that I contend took root during the Great Recession are finally being increased across the workforce. Employees are now empowered to demand higher pay in a new market-based economy that requires a high number of employees to invigorate the American economy for the next quarter-century. Society is now looking at the workplace in a different light overall which has led to great improvements in working conditions for many employees. We know that employees who are happy and healthy will be more productive in their jobs. Citizens are overwhelmingly expressing that they want to have fulfilling careers, but they also want to live personally fulfilling lives. Truly, you can't get time back that has passed to spend with your family or to enjoy life. Coming out of the pandemic, we as a society have become more receptive to the idea of supporting everyone in not only their professional, but personal pursuits. The philosophy that I hope employers continue to embrace is a societal shift that no longer views employees as just tools to get the work done at potentially great harm to their physical and mental health, but as fellow human beings who need to be seen and treated as such. We need to continue on this path, noting that much more needs to be done to establish acceptable working conditions for all employees everywhere.

### Quiet Quitting – A Tool of Employees to Demand Fairness in a New Era

I want to say a bit more about the Quiet Quitting initiative that some employees are practicing in their jobs. Yes, I believe a lot of progress has been made coming out of the pandemic as far as how well employees are treated, but there are issues that still need to be addressed. Some employees are Quiet Quitting to express their desire for a better work-life balance. The other motivating factor with this practice is the feeling from employees that pay and promotions need to be better matched with their performance. How many employees have felt that they perform their job tasks at exceptional levels only to receive more work with seldom more pay and resources? It is all too often a practice in the workplace and indicates that management is not doing a good enough job of rewarding or promoting qualified staff. This practice of loading up employees who are already extremely busy with more work also demonstrates unfairness in the treatment of employees. Discrimination does play a role in this, but simply favoritism is perhaps a more closely linked factor in this practice. We have all witnessed conscientious employees, who are always busy with heavy workloads, while others always seem to have plenty of time to take weeklong vacations, especially around the major holidays. Not all employees have the desire to be in upper management for a variety of reasons, like work-life balance and family obligations, but employees who consistently go above and beyond in the performance of their core duties, should be paid for their efforts. This too often does not occur. Then, for those who do want growth, the obvious answer is to train these employees to be supervisors. Instead of one person trying to do all the work that is laid upon him or her by upper management, who obviously recognizes her or his abilities, upper management needs to swiftly recruit the employee to become the manager of many job tasks. This new manager then needs to oversee other employees performing these tasks. Empowering exceptional employees with the appropriate level of staff resources, helps to ensure that job tasks are completed in a timely manner without the risk of mistakes that can occur with just one employee struggling to keep up with an unreasonable workload. I do want to point out that in jobs involving healthcare, public safety, or other positions in which taking immediate action is necessary to protect lives or save them, Quiet Quitting is not an acceptable mode of protest. Other methods of communicating employment concerns or protesting work conditions need to be used in those areas.

### Closing

Quiet Quitting, in my opinion, is an expression of frustration that workers have with unfair workloads, particularly when taking into account their pay levels. I always say that most people are fair-minded and simply desire to get paid adequately for the work that they perform. There are always a few "bad apples" who want to "work the system" to get out of performing job duties, but overall, I think if Quiet Quitting is being practiced in an organization, then leadership needs to take a look and see if changes can be implemented to address inconsistencies in workloads, pay or upward mobility opportunities. In closing, I think Quiet Quitting is just another method for employees to express their building frustration which has been simmering for many years concerning a number of workplace issues. It is reminiscent of worker slowdowns that employees have used in the past as a method to protest poor working conditions or low pay. My hope is that as we continue to come out of the pandemic era in the coming years, that employees and employers can work together to improve the working environment for everyone so that strikes, protests, and other forms of expressing discontent, such as Quiet Quitting, will not be needed. We can enter into a new era of ensuring that everyone has a quality job that pays a living wage and also provides adequate leave time for family bonding, rest, and leisure. I do think when it comes to improving the work-life balance for employees by providing sufficient vacation and sick time, that Americans should take a look at the European model. I would argue that the American economy can both maintain its productivity edge in the world and ensure employees achieve true work-life balance. Every dedicated employee deserves a workplace environment that provides good pay, a healthy benefits package, advancement opportunities, flexible schedules, and reasonable workloads. Workloads should be considered "reasonable" only if employees are provided with the resources to complete their job tasks without working excessively long hours which can lead to fatigue or burnout. If we follow this employee-centered approach, there will be no need for anyone to feel justified in engaging in Quiet Quitting. Finally, we need to establish a workplace culture in which all employees in all areas and levels of the American economy are treated with the respect and dignity that all human beings deserve.

# 50. Final Thoughts: Let's Meet in the Middle

---

**The 2022 Mid-Term Elections – Americans Calling for Government from the Middle**

C-SPAN on a typical Friday night might show Congressional debates or some other Washington event from earlier in the week. This was not the case on C-SPAN and other news networks like CNN on Friday, January 6th, 2023 ("U.S. House of Representatives"). Those of us following the vote to elect the new U.S. Speaker of the House of Representatives viewed some late-night drama. The drama consisted of fourteen rounds of voting in which Kevin McCarthy was not able to garner enough votes from hardliner Republicans to secure the position. McCarthy, who really seemed to take it in stride how fervent the "Never Kevins" were in their intention to stop his election throughout the voting week that started on Tuesday (1/3/23), began to show his frustration on this late Friday night. He needed one more vote his way to clinch the Speaker position during this 14th round when the roll call came to Representative Matt Gaetz of Florida. Matt Gaetz like Lauren Boebert whom he was sitting beside voted "present." This vote option taken by Mr. Gaetz was not enough to elect McCarthy. What followed was McCarthy walking up the aisle of the House floor to confront Gaetz. The viewers, including myself, watching on television couldn't hear any audio, but clearly there were some heated words exchanged. As now Speaker McCarthy began to walk back down the aisle away from Gaetz, another Congressional member had to restrain Representative Mike Rogers of Alabama from lunging at Gaetz. Representative Richard Hudson of North Carolina stepped in and grabbed Mike Rogers, who was clearly angered by Gaetz not giving McCarthy the nod, before Mr. Rogers physically attacked Representative Gaetz.

The next motion initiated by North Carolina Representative Patrick McHenry (actually the representative for my North Carolina Congressional district) was intended to adjourn the voting process until Monday. As the vote was being conducted, it appeared that the House was going to vote for adjournment, but with some last-minute negotiating, the House decided to conduct a fifteenth round of voting. This time around, Kevin McCarthy was elected as Speaker with all the hardliners voting "present" which under House rules in combination with the affirmative votes for Mr. McCarthy, gave him sufficient support to claim his new position. Yes, as someone with a degree in Political Science, I am embarrassed to admit that I am not well-versed in the House rules on how the "present" vote works, but apparently the "present" votes can somehow reduce the number of "yes" votes needed to claim victory. Thus, in the very early hours of Saturday, January 7th, 2023,

Kevin McCarthy finally won the U.S. House of Representatives Speaker position for the 118th Congress.

Now, I'm discussing this contentious vote in my final thoughts of this work to make the point that having strong (non-violent of course) debate in which all perspectives have a voice is a key ingredient to a free, democratic society and government. Another key ingredient, however, to achieve a highly functional and free society is that there does have to be a point at which reasonable minds must compromise. As far as this vote for Speaker, I will give Republicans credit for their argument that the several votes it took to elect McCarthy is just part of democracy working. Now, if this had run into several days, then I would give more credibility to what some Democrats were contending, that this showed Republicans have too much infighting and too much resistance to compromise within their own ranks to effectively lead the House. The serious concern that I do have with obstructionists like Gaetz and Boebert who continue to support the false claim that President Biden did not win the presidency, is this willingness by a significant number of Republicans to put their personal, political desires ahead of the institutions set up by our U.S. Constitution. This behavior to win at all costs is a serious threat to our free system of government that depends on our leaders to actually support our democratic systems.

We have heard of how after contentious debates in the late twentieth century between the parties, political leaders in Washington would be civil and even formed close friendships. Republican President Ronald Reagan and Democrat Speaker of the House Tip O'Neill could disagree vehemently on policy, but were known to regularly have a drink together as friends (Trowbridge). Also, I have enjoyed learning about the close personal friendship between Supreme Court Justices Ruth Bader Ginsberg and Antonin Scalia who on the bench were polar opposites in their legal outlooks (Elkind). Yet, the two families of these justices became close and Justice Ginsberg's husband, Martin Ginsberg, would often cook dinner for both families (Elkind). We need to get back to civility. That is so important to strengthen our citizen bonds with one another.

I do agree with Republicans that the vote on January 6th, 2023, did end up being a fair process with representatives like Mr. Gaetz finally coming to the table of compromise when over 200 other House representatives voted for Mr. McCarthy as Speaker. This was not January 6, 2021, when the certification of the 2020 presidential election was interrupted by a gang of Trump-supporting insurrectionists who entered the Capitol with intentions of violently attacking members of Congress, as well as the Republican sitting Vice President of the United States. Any claims that the two January 6th events were similar in their threats to democracy, as some overly dramatic political commentators attempted to present, I reject. Yet, I do agree that this new group of Republicans who will lead the House does need to demonstrate a commitment to upholding our nation's fundamental democratic institutions and work for the betterment of the American people.

In addition, I think the politically divided makeup of the House of Representatives in 2023 in which Republicans hold a slight majority, demonstrates that Americans overall are asking for our leaders to compromise and find middle ground on issues. No one party has been given an overwhelming mandate to govern over the other. Many well-versed and educated political experts incorrectly predicted that this mid-term election would see Republicans taking both the House and more than likely the Senate. Typically, Americans do vote in mid-term elections for a divided government, giving the party that lost the White House more power in Congress. Yes, we as Americans want decisions made through compromise which really means moderate, level-headed political decisions. The rational consensus for the 2022 mid-term elections was that Republicans would take over the House and possibly the Senate given the state of high inflation and to some lesser degree, the Biden Administration's failure to effectively address the crisis at the southern border. The Democrats during the election cycle continued to emphasize how the Republicans supported the insurrection and the attempted unconstitutional taking of the presidency when President Biden was clearly, fairly elected. The mid-term results showed that these elections were very close and that while the Republicans did win the House, it was by a much smaller majority than what was being predicted. In fact, while Republicans hold the House it isn't by much of a majority. In the final vote for Speaker, McCarthy received 216 votes for the win compared to 212 votes that now Democrat Minority Leader Hakeem Jeffries received (*The Hill* staff). The American people have spoken, in my opinion. Republicans have a chance to address concerns of the economy, the crisis at the border and crime. Conservatives also have the opportunity to rein in what they consider to be (and in some cases I agree) extreme "woke" philosophies that children are being exposed to in our schools. Of course, the Democrats to my surprise held on to the Senate.

The media focuses so much on how our society is divided and to some extent this is true, but when we examine the outcome of the 2022 Congressional election, the clear message appears to be that the American people want to find common ground so our nation can move forward in unison. The current federal governmental leaders will have to compromise. Perhaps out of this compromise we can formulate and enact policies that are reasonable, based on common sense and will work for most Americans. President Biden finally provided a practical new policy for the southern border. This happened the week of the vote for the Speaker of the House in early January 2023. Millions have crossed the southern border in the first two years of the Biden Administration. 2.2 million migrants crossed the border illegally just during the 2022 federal fiscal year (Santana). Many critics argue that President Biden has not effectively addressed the issue of immigration, and, as a result of the election it appears, he finally felt the political pressure to act. The question is whether Biden would have moved so decisively if Democrats had won the House. After reviewing the main points of the policy ("Fact Sheet: Biden-Harris"), I find President Biden's policy to be a moderate response that appears to address criticism from the political right that he is soft on the southern border. Mr. Biden also frames his immigration plan with a humanitarian stance by allowing those seeking asylum to do so, an approach vital to retaining support from those on the political left for his overall immigration policy. The policy stresses that anyone entering the U.S. illegally will not qualify for future citizenship and will be returned to their home nation. I do want to be fair to the Biden Administration in that the president in his announcement on the new policy, really took time to stress that a good part of effectively addressing the immigration problem entails the need to provide substantial support to our neighboring nations to our south. A significant part of the solution is to improve the economic, social, and environmental conditions in these nations so that we won't have millions of people attempting to flee from their Latin American homes. As President Biden astutely pointed out, rational people aren't going to want to embark on an extremely dangerous journey over a thousand miles, possibly mostly on foot, to reach the United States if they have a high quality of life in their nations of birth.

The new Biden immigration policy is one example of how political pressure to move to the middle can result in more reasonable and sustainable solutions to very difficult challenges. We are a nation of immigrants, and we do and will accept some of those who wish to come, but allowing so many people to enter who have not been properly screened is a national security threat. The new policy is also not calling for the complete closing of the border as some on the political right would like. We need a reasonable, moderate immigration policy that acknowledges our moral responsibility to assist those seeking to come here based on humanitarian need, but with the understanding that we are not equipped with the resources to absorb millions into our nation on an annual basis. The new policy from the Biden Administration is a response not only to criticism from Republicans, but from Democrat leaders across the nation who have found themselves struggling to accommodate the large numbers of migrants arriving in their cities and towns. This was a correction back to a more middle of the road approach on immigration between the political extremes.

Let's look again just briefly at the U.S. Speaker of the House vote on a late Friday evening at the Capitol. The final election of Mr. McCarthy demonstrates how moving forces from the political extremes toward the middle can enable our nation to overcome divisiveness and gridlock to achieve effective outcomes. We had a small minority of Congressional representatives who were obstructing a vote with the clear realization that no other Republican would be able to obtain enough support to defeat Kevin McCarthy. These politically motivated outliers were preventing the U.S. House of

Representatives from beginning its business in the new session. What finally got the vote passed was the fact that those representatives who were acting fairly and rationally, put tremendous pressure on those holdouts to fall in line with the party. The pressure was finally successful when votes for other nominees beside McCarthy changed to "present" votes. This example can be viewed as a microcosm of our national electorate in general and provides some guidance for our society as we seek to become less divisive. We must continue to put pressure on the extremes to come to the middle, as well as meeting the vocal extremes with our own voices and actions to oppose them. One of my issues with those on the political extremes is the tendency for these individuals and groups to become inflexible and uncompromising. This can transition from extreme idealism to unacceptable behavior that extremists feel is justified (i.e. the ends justify the violent means). I put the insurrection on January 6, 2021, as behavior falling into this category, as well as some violent acts committed by groups on the extreme left, such as Antifa.

I have focused in this closing essay on the 2022 mid-term elections because my interpretation of the outcome is that the American people want a balanced government that works for the middle ground. Some have said that when we have a divided government, it is a sign that the American people want to curb governmental action – to limit it. I have the opinion that when we have divided government, Americans are saying that they want the president and the Congress to work together to formulate and implement fair, reasonable policies. My continued moderate approach to policymaking comes from a basic tenet that by meeting in the middle or near the middle, we can collectively find solutions that address the concerns of all stakeholders. This is the best method to achieve solutions that are win-win. Through compromise, all concerned parties get something that they want, even if they don't get everything that they want. In this decision-making environment, all parties feel like they have a say. This process can be the way out of severe division in which opposing sides of an issue get to a point at which it seems almost impossible to find common ground. We must make more of an effort at the local, state, and national levels to re-establish civil relationships with those who disagree with us.

Next, I briefly want to touch upon a few policy stances by the political extremes of both the Republican and Democrat Parties which demonstrate that such inflexible and fervent mindsets can lead to harmful outcomes for our American political and economic systems. As a Democrat, I do want to be fair and provide equal if not more examples of how Democrats on the far left have championed policies that are unreasonable and sometimes even intolerant, a description that I have rarely used to describe my party of overall inclusion.

**Right Wing Republicans Need to Support Our Free Electoral System**

Our Founding Fathers created a free electoral process in which all citizens have the power to vote for the candidates of their choice, as well as align with the political party per their free will. This right to vote for the candidate(s) of one's choice is a critical, primary component of our free, constitutional republic. The January 6th insurrection, however, is a clear example of zealot far right Republicans who chose not to adhere to the second critical component of our electoral system which is just as important as the first: After elections are completed, our system requires us to peacefully accept the outcomes, even if some of our candidates lose. Then, we come back together as one people under one system, under one United States government. We must reestablish our shared American ideals of fairness and equal opportunity, not to mention fair play. What children are taught from an early age is that when we win, we are to be gracious winners and acknowledge the efforts of the other competitors. Then, when we lose, we congratulate the winners and commit to working harder for the next competition (or election). I want to fully acknowledge that both political parties have work to do in the effort of putting the American people ahead of their political desires, but I do call out the Republicans for obstructing the 2020 presidential election because President Trump and his supporters were simply sore losers. The Trump way seems to be that candidates will only acknowledge that an election is fair if they win. If they lose, the claim is immediately that they were cheated. I submit Kari Lake, the defeated Republican candidate for governor in Arizona, as another example. Kari Lake claims that she was cheated out of victory for the governor's seat in the state of Arizona (Sievers). Of course, there has never been any credible evidence provided to support Ms. Lake's claim. Now, I am not denying any candidate from taking any legal action available to challenge election results, but it should be initiated based on a sound, legitimate reason, not just a political stunt intended to plant doubt in the electorate. Accepting an electoral loss is a key responsibility of any candidate running for public office. When candidates like Trump and Lake refuse to accept that they have lost fair and square, this poses a serious threat to our system of free elections. Republicans need to immediately cease such un-American behavior.

## Ultra-Liberal Policies of Democrats Can Be Unsustainable and Intolerant

I did support some enhanced unemployment payments and, overall, the stimulus payments from the federal government that many Americans desperately needed in order to survive financially during the pandemic. Furthermore, I did support the Biden Administration's short-lived tax credit for families with children. I do question, however, if the Biden Administration went too far in the distribution of payments, particularly that last round or two of stimulus checks to Americans, which along with extended unemployment benefits seem to have contributed to our current state of very high inflation. I am no economist, but it appeared to me that we had a situation as we moved out of the height of the pandemic, in which there were lots of Americans flush with cash ready to spend it, but employers did not have enough people working to produce the services and goods to meet the demand. Thus, I contend that our current high inflationary period, that we haven't seen since the early 1980s, is at least partially due to these additional payments which delayed Americans having to re-enter the workforce. As an overall policy approach, I contend that we have to reach that fine balance in which we have a financial safety net for Americans (again, I did overall support enhanced payments to Americans, particularly for those who lost their jobs during the pandemic), but not so much of a socialistic safety net that we don't have enough people actually working and producing core products and services to meet consumer demand. This is where I feel the ultra-liberal wing of the Democrat Party moves too far away from a capitalistic system with a reasonable safety net, and moves into endorsing an economic approach based too heavily on socialism. The middle-ground makes the most sense from a macro-economic standpoint. We know that capitalism with its free markets generates the most wealth, but we do need some safety-net features to ensure basic economic needs are met for those in the economy who fall on the lower end of the earnings spectrum. One final note on payments to citizens that I want to mention, is that I do support the idea of a universal basic income as endorsed by former 2020 Democrat presidential candidate Andrew Yang ("The Freedom Dividend"). I think the amount paid out per month is the key. The $1,000 per person amount seems reasonable in that it provides some assistance with living expenses, but it is critical that we cannot have any such payment system that pays so much that it disincentivizes people from actually working. Another preference that I have for a basic income system is that only low- and middle-income Americans should qualify. I would not be in favor of millionaires and very wealthy people receiving this monthly allotment. There are multiple economic policies on which I do stand with Democrats, which include the requirement for all Americans to be paid a living wage, the continuation of Social Security, the establishment of free tuition for public universities and even the implementation of an additional public option for health insurance. However, when the Democrats implement economic policies that move too far to the left, this can take away the free market incentive of attaining wealth through hard work and innovation that has made the U.S. the most successful economy in the world.

I agree with some Democrat ideas on crime, such as requiring illegal drug users to seek treatment over incarceration, and I am in favor to some degree of legalizing sex work. However, those on the far left, in my opinion, have gone too far in their bail reform policies. Defendants who have been accused of violent crimes with past violent criminal convictions belong in jail until their trials, not on the streets where they can commit more violence. We need a compassionate justice system that focuses on fairness to the accused, but with a clear emphasis on protecting public safety.

Also, too many on the left have moved from political correctness to cancel culture when it comes to free speech. Our current environment is one in which lives are quickly ruined without providing individuals with appropriate opportunities to explain the intentions of their spoken or written statements that have offended individuals or groups. Not everyone is up to date on the latest pronoun terminology or politically correct speech phrases that seem to be updated almost daily these days. I am very concerned about situations in which simply misunderstood speech is triggering the self-appointed speech police to "cancel" alleged offenders. The outcome of this cancelling behavior can result in ruining the honorable reputations of possibly well-intentioned individuals. Some even lose their livelihoods as a result of being "cancelled."

Those on the left must become more tolerant of those who disagree with them. Yes, we need to create a society that protects the rights of the LGTBQ community, but we also have to respect the rights of religious groups to follow their faith. Not an easy task and at some point, the idea of a free society requires us to say that legally all lifestyles between consenting adults should be respected. I am in total support of gay marriage as a legal institution that should be allowed under the equal protection of the law. However, I do completely understand parents up in arms about schools discussing sexual identity and preference with their young children. Being attacked for claiming that only biological women can have children or a menstrual cycle, is why Democrats at times seem on the fringe of reality. I do see the concern of parents of young girls who may have to potentially face a situation in which they could enter a public restroom or locker room with an adult biological male undressed in plain view. This delicate issue of restrooms and how to accommodate transgender individuals, must be approached in a sensitive manner to ensure everyone's rights are protected. I want to make it completely clear that I am in no way saying that members of the LGBTQ community are any more likely than anyone else to be child molesters, just that this type of situation is understandably a valid parental concern. How we discuss sex and gender differences with our children and at what age these topics should be discussed with them are complex decisions that should be determined through collaboration between parents, psychologists, and educators. My vote is that parents should have ultimate authority for younger children and that it would be best practice for schools not to discuss sex and gender with students at very young ages. Common sense would say this isn't age appropriate. Then, I'd say high school teenagers should be exposed to such discussions at school per a health class atmosphere. This would be age appropriate. Along with this theme, as a former competitive high school athlete, I can attest that there are some very talented, strong women who can compete with many men on the field or court. Having said this, we must concede that overall, there are differences in the male and female bodies as far as basic muscular strength and endurance. When we see transgender women or girls who are biologically male compete and overwhelmingly defeat their competition, it is clearly unfair. This does not promote the support of women's sports which have come so far in the past few decades. I want to emphasize that I agree with the intention of instilling in the next generation a sense of openness and tolerance of others. The LGBTQ community has faced tremendous discrimination, ridicule, and violence in our society through the generations. We do need to work to promote acceptance of all members of this community with the understanding that one's personal gender identification and sexual orientation must be respected and supported in any society that protects individual rights. I would say how one chooses to live his or her (or their) gender and sex life is a core right in a free society that cherishes individual liberty.

My point with these examples is to demonstrate that actions and policies initiated from both far ends of the political spectrum, can lead to the rejection of core principles of our political and economic systems that have resulted in the extension of rights and economic wealth to millions of Americans. Also, extreme political viewpoints are by their very nature intolerant of others' differing opinions. There is very little room allowed for compromise by those on the ends of the political spectrum. This exclusionary mindset leads to the rejection of different viewpoints. Aside from this approach not being very democratic by denying all interested parties a say, the narrow viewpoints on the extremes can also lead to the implementation of policies that don't work because a wide array of opinions and expertise are not allowed to be expressed.

## Final Discussion of Goals for this Work

I have set out in this collection of essays to achieve a few goals. First, I want to share some of my viewpoints with others. This is not primarily out of a belief that I have all the answers, although I do think I have some good ideas on addressing a variety of policy issues, but that I wish to be part of a political movement that brings America back to the political middle. I hope to effectively communicate the message that we can solve our differences through compromise and by toning down the divisive rhetoric on both sides of the political aisle. We need calm, rational approaches to address the many serious issues facing the world, not angry extremism that will delay effective action and leave groups out of the discussion and outcomes. Secondly, I hope to encourage others to get into the debate, but in a kinder more civil way. Social media has become so angry and divisive. It can be a great tool to enhance discussion and social interaction, but it rewards those who behave in shocking or offensive ways. We all must communicate in a more civil tone when debating areas of disagreement, in order to minimize the influence of the loud, angry voices. Effective communication requires us to listen to one another, not just shout at each other. There are so many out there who are great at organizing social and community events. We need these community organizers to bring people together both in person and through our amazing technology. I fear that social media sometimes becomes a virtual fence between people, instead of a virtual bridge between us. We need to use our technology to connect us, not divide us.

I want to discuss a third goal of this work in a bit of detail. A third goal I have in producing this work is that I hope I can contribute to a movement that creates a less partisan nation, at least one which is less politically divisive. I think debate between political parties is healthy for our democratic system, but when we think of ourselves primarily and foremost as red (Republican) or blue (Democrat) people instead of simply Americans (red, white and blue), then we are causing harm to the constitutional system that our Founding Fathers created for us. One of my favorite shows as a political junkie back in the early 2000s was *The West Wing*. The show ran on NBC for seven seasons beginning in 1999 and ending in 2006. Recently, I saw some reruns on television and I found myself thoroughly enjoying (or re-enjoying) watching this exceptionally written drama of life in the American White House. The theme of the show for those who have never seen it, is that the viewer gets an idea of what life is like in the White House from the perspective of the president and his staff. The show has been described as a dramatized version of the real thing, but when decisions are being made that affect millions of Americans, whether it is related to domestic or foreign policy, I would say working in the White House is a high tense, high demand, rewarding experience that involves more emotion and drama than any television show.

The audience in Season 2 of *The West Wing* was introduced to one of my favorite characters who was not on for all of the seven seasons. The episode, "In This White House," featured Ainsley Hayes, a young Republican, woman attorney from North Carolina. The audience was introduced to Ainsley when she participated in a debate on a political talk show with Sam Seaborn (played by famous actor Rob Lowe), a representative of the Democrat White House. Sam, a brilliant legal and political mind was quickly taken to task by the sharp intellect of Ainsley Hayes. President Josiah Bartlet (played by Martin Sheen) was so impressed with Ainsley that he had his chief of staff offer Ainsley a job. One of the many engaging scenes in this episode involves Ainsley's emotional, but comical debate with Leo McGarry (played by the late actor John Spencer), the White House Chief of Staff, on her dilemma as a Republican from North Carolina on whether to take a job "in this White House," thus connecting the audience to the episode's title. She was told by Leo to come back and let him know her decision. At the end of the episode while she was meeting some Republican friends at a restaurant who were mocking the Democrats in the White House, she very eloquently chided them saying to the effect, that they can question the Democrats' policy stances, but they should not question their loyalty to the nation. Ainsley then announced that she was their attorney and got up from the table in the restaurant to leave ("In This White House"), apparently in that instance making her decision to serve her country, regardless of political affiliation.

I wanted to describe this episode in some detail because I think the story of Ainsley Hayes highlights how love of our country should (and yes I know it is just a television show) be the highest priority for every citizen, not allegiance to any political party. Indeed, a White House controlled by one political party is very unlikely to hire someone from an opposing party. Every White House administration, while obviously seeking to advance particular policy approaches, should be more open to hiring not only those who agree with them, but those who are exceptionally qualified. As this episode progressed, it was evident that Ainsley Hayes was moved by the experience, witnessing firsthand the hard decisions being made at that level by the president and his staff in the White House. Her scene in the restaurant was absolutely inspiring with her obvious realization that to live up to her core ethical calling to serve her nation, this staunch, devout North Carolinian Republican decided that she must serve her nation, even if that meant working for a Democrat White House. Emily Procter, the actress who played Ainsley (of CSI Miami fame) did just an exceptional job in this role. I later learned that Emily Procter is in fact from North Carolina, so her accent wasn't being invented by a New York or Hollywood actress, yet this fact somehow doesn't diminish in the least her acting in this scene. The viewer can genuinely feel the character's strength and determination to be an honorable American, rather than focusing on petty partisanship.

The title of my work here referring to being a red, white and blue American is my perhaps not so clever attempt to allude to my platform which is a response to what is now a wide gulf between the left and right, along the political spectrum. Our nation has simply become too divided. Our flag represents a united nation, of course, but I want to use the colors of our flag to represent an ideal that our diverse allegiances ultimately must fall under one system founded in freedom. My wish is that red Republicans and blue Democrats put country over party. The white in our flag, I suppose, can represent a bridge for both colors/parties, as well as represent third parties like Independents who can fall in the middle of the political spectrum, or even the Green Party whose members currently are a very small minority, but could gain numbers with the climate change threat that is increasingly impacting the survival of our worldwide ecosystems. Yes, all political parties must fall in line under one flag.

## Closing

Some have said that we have not seen such divisiveness in our nation since the U.S. Civil War. Others claim that a new civil war is right around the corner. While I agree that there are pockets of great division and disagreement, I believe the real glue of our nation lies in the large numbers of citizens who voted in this past mid-term election for reasonable, rational middle-ground government. We are the silent majority that is not seen on CNN or Fox News or on social media posts. Moderates must remember that we have the numbers. We must continue to demand civil (and civilized) language and behavior promoting reasonable solutions to address challenging issues like climate change, national security, local crime, economic insecurity, discrimination, and the protection of our free system of elections.

As a parent and a concerned citizen, I often contemplate what kind of world we want our children to grow up in, so they can achieve their dreams and, in turn, support a civil and just society. It really comes down to ensuring that all children and their families have the core essentials for a stable life. We want all of our children to be able to reside in safe communities. Every child deserves a stable living arrangement in which he or she always has a home with a roof over their head, with plenty of healthy food necessary to grow the body and develop the mind. Schools in all districts need to have innovative and premiere educational programs. Excellent teachers need to be in all schools, not just in top private schools or in public schools in the wealthy areas of a city. All children need to be able to play in their communities in parks that are free from crime and have equipment that is safe and promotes their physical health. Access to medical care is a must as well for our children to succeed. Also, we want our children to have clean air to breathe and water to drink that is free from toxins and pollutants.

These core requirements for our children can only be achieved if we as adults do our part. When we drive on our public roads, we need to act as if the car in front of us is transporting our children or loved ones. We as adults must take personal responsibility for our actions. All citizens have a responsibility as rational beings to trust the expertise of the scientists, whether we are talking about climate change or vaccinations to protect us from contracting the COVID-19 virus. Teaching our children about our individual liberties as Americans is vital to the survival of our free society. We can instill in them the ideal that protesting against injustice is a basic right of all Americans, but we must set the example and engage in political debate in a civil way. It is important to teach our children that in a free society, while we have the right to protest and debate, we must also respect the rights of others to disagree. Of course, we must set the example that violating the law or committing acts of violence against property and especially people is never acceptable. In essence, we must set an example and teach our children "The Golden Rule" - to treat all others as we would want to be treated.

We have no small task in toning down the harsh language on the ends of the political spectrum and increasing civility. After the pandemic, many of us feel stressed out or burned out and are in no mood to be bright and cheerful, especially with others whom we completely disagree with on multiple issues. Yet, we must do our best, if not for ourselves, then for the children who look to us for guidance. There are two great tasks that we as Americans must undertake. The task of increasing civility and kindness among our citizens is the first order of business. The second great task is that we have to retake our seat as the leader of the free world in confronting the many challenges that humanity and the planet faces. As I've discussed in this work, as a red, white and blue, flag-waving American, I truly believe that the world is a much safer, kinder, and equitable place with the United States leading. We must teach the world by our example that free societies which honor the ideals of individual liberty, democracy, fairness, and civility, provide the foundation for a brighter future for all citizens of the world. I call upon my fellow Americans for us to unite under one flag, re-committing to these ideals.

Now forgive me for my over the top, somewhat annoying level of in-your-face patriotism, but I see the United States as the foundational stone needed to achieve a future of abundance, peace, and morality for the world. Issues like climate change, extensive world poverty, aggressive behavior by anti-democratic nation-states and mass-migration must all be effectively addressed. The current state of the world requires the United States to appropriately reclaim itself not as an egotistical and arrogant nation-state out in front, but as a humble leader of freedom, individual liberty and all that is righteous and good in the world. I was going to end this work comparing the United States to some type of fictional heroic character from the movies, but my understanding of copyright law is limited, so I've decided against it to avoid any copyright infringement issues. The reality is, however, that the United States is not a fictional character. It is a heroic, overwhelmingly benevolent force in the world and the world is waiting for Americans not to save them, but to work with them to save us all. My humble appeal to my fellow Americans is let us begin the greatest comeback story of all time by meeting in the middle.

# Works Cited

---

"Agreement for Bringing Peace to Afghanistan between the Islamic Emirate of Afghanistan which

is not recognized by the United States as a state and is known as the Taliban and the United

States of America." U.S. Department of State, 29 Feb. 2020,

www.state.gov/wp-content/uploads/2020/02/Agreement-For-Bringing-Peace-to-[1]

Afghanistan-02.29.20.pdf.

Ainsley, Julia. "Migrant border crossings in fiscal year 2022 topped 2.76 million, breaking

previous record." NBC News, 22 Oct. 2022,

www.nbcnews.com/politics/immigration/migrant-border-crossings-fiscal-year-2022-[2]

topped-276-million-breaking-rcna53517.

"Appointment of a Special Counsel." Office of Public Affairs, U.S. Department of Justice,

18 Nov. 2022, www.justice.gov/opa/pr/appointment-special-counsel-0[3].

"As Asylum-Seekers Report Ongoing Issues with CBP One App, Congressman Castro And House

Democrats Demand Action for DHS." Joaquin Castro, Congressman For The 20th District

Of Texas, 14 Mar. 2023, https://castro.house.gov/media-center/press-releases/
as-asylum-

seekers-report-ongoing-issues-with-cbp-one-app-congressman-castro-and-house-

democrats-demand-action-from-dhs.

---

1. http://www.state.gov/wp-content/uploads/2020/02/Agreement-For-Bringing-Peace-to-

2. http://www.nbcnews.com/politics/immigration/migrant-border-crossings-fiscal-year-2022-

3. http://www.justice.gov/opa/pr/appointment-special-counsel-0

Ballasy, Nicholas. "Biden-Buttigieg DOT to tap infrastructure spending to promote speed cameras nationwide." Just the News, 29 Jan. 2022, www.justthenews.com/government/congress/dots-national-roadway-safety-strategy-[4] includes-additional-speed-cameras-cities.

Bates, Josiah. "U.S. Crime Is Still Dramatically Higher Than Before the Pandemic." *Time*, 29 July 2022 (updated), www.time.com/6201797/crime-murder-rate-us-high-2022/.

———

BECKMAN, SARAH & RUFFES, Vanessa. "CMPD Chief Jennings wants state bond laws to change."

WCNC Charlotte, 22 July 2022, www.wcnc.com/article/news/crime/cmpd-chief-jennings-[5] wants-state-bond-laws-change/275-eddd8e1f-375b-4117-a8d6-

    4e58f65ca40d#:~:text=CHARLOTTE%2C%20N.C.%20—%20Charlotte-

    Mecklenburg,going%20back%20on%20the%20streets.

Benson, Samuel. "Trump says Secret Service blocked him from joining Jan. 6 march to the Capitol." *Politico*, 7 April 2022, www.politico.com/news/2022/04/07/trump-secret-[6] service-capitol-riot-00023737.

Bhutta, Neil; Chang, Andrew C.; Dettling, Lisa J.; Hsu, Joanne W. and Hewitt, Julia. "Disparities in Wealth by Race and Ethnicity in the 2019 Survey of Consumer Finances." FEDS Notes. Washington: Board of Governors of the Federal Reserve System, 28 Sept. 2020, www.federalreserve.gov/econres/notes/feds-notes/disparities-in-wealth-by-race-and-[7]

---

4. http://www.justthenews.com/government/congress/dots-national-roadway-safety-strategy-

5. http://www.wcnc.com/article/news/crime/cmpd-chief-jennings-

6. http://www.politico.com/news/2022/04/07/trump-secret-

7. http://www.federalreserve.gov/econres/notes/feds-notes/disparities-in-wealth-by-race-and-

ethnicity-in-the-2019-survey-of-consumer-finances-20200928.html.

Biden, Joseph R., President of the United States (inaugurated on 20 Jan.2021). "Remarks by President Biden on Afghanistan." The White House, 16 Aug. 2021,

www.whitehouse.gov/briefing-room/speeches-remarks/2021/08/16/ remarks-by-president-[8]

biden-on-

afghanistan/#:~:text=Our%20mission%20to%20degrade%20the,believed%20it%20never %20could%20be.

Biden, Joseph R., President of the United States (inaugurated on 20 Jan. 2021). "Remarks by President Biden on Bidenomics." The White House, 14 Sept. 2023, www.whitehouse.gov/briefing-room/speeches-remarks/2023/09/14/remarks-by-president-[9] biden-on-bidenomics-largo-md/.

"Bipartisan Senators Dare to Dream." National Immigration Forum, 10 Feb. 2023, www.immigrationforum.org/article/bipartisan-senators-dare-to-dream/.

"Black/African American Health." U.S. Department of Health and Human Services Office of Minority Health, accessed on 11 Oct. 2023, www.minorityhealth.hhs.gov/blackafrican-american-health.

Blackburn, Marsha. "Why Is Critical Race Theory Dangerous For Our Kids?" Marsha Blackburn, U.S. Senator For Tennessee, 12 July 2021, www.blackburn.senate.gov/2021/7/why-is-critical-race-theory-dangerous-for-our-kids.

Blakemore, Erin. "What really happened at Wounded Knee, the site of a historic massacre."

---

8. http://www.whitehouse.gov/briefing-room/speeches-remarks/2021/08/16/remarks-by-president-

9. http://www.whitehouse.gov/briefing-room/speeches-remarks/2023/09/14/remarks-by-president-

National Geographic, 19 Nov. 2021, www.nationalgeographic.com/history/article/what-[10]

really-happened-at-wounded-knee-the-site-of-a-historic-massacre.

Blount, Roy. "Making Sense of Robert E. Lee." *Smithsonian Magazine*, July 2003,

www.smithsonianmag.com/history/making-sense-of-robert-e-lee-[11]

85017563/#:~:text=Few%20figures%20in%20American%20history,end%20of%20the%

20Civil%20War.

Brown, Pamela; Perez, Evan and Lemon, Don. "FBI says Dylann Roof should not have been

cleared to purchase a weapon." CNN, 10 July 2015,

www.cnn.com/2015/07/10/politics/dylann-roof-fbi-gun-south-carolina/index.html[12].

Brown, Preezy. "Rihanna And Beyonce Make Forbes' Most Powerful Women List." Yahoo!

Finance, 7 Dec. 2022, www.finance.yahoo.com/news/rihanna-beyonc-forbes-most-[13]

powerful-210213526.html.

"Brown v. Board of Education (1954)." United States National Archives, Website page last

reviewed on 22 Nov. 2021, www.archives.gov/milestone-documents/brown-v-board-of-[14]

education#:~:text=In%20this%20milestone%20decision%2C%20the,1896%20Plessy%2

0v.%20Ferguson%20case.

Brownlee, Marques. "Tesla Self Driving vs. Everyday Roads!" *YouTube*, uploaded by Marques

Brownlee, 14 Dec. 2022, www.youtube.com/watch?v=9nF0K2nJ7N8[15].

---

10. http://www.nationalgeographic.com/history/article/what-

11. http://www.smithsonianmag.com/history/making-sense-of-robert-e-lee-

12. http://www.cnn.com/2015/07/10/politics/dylann-roof-fbi-gun-south-carolina/index.html

13. http://www.finance.yahoo.com/news/rihanna-beyonc-forbes-most-

14. http://www.archives.gov/milestone-documents/brown-v-board-of-

15. http://www.youtube.com/watch?v=9nF0K2nJ7N8

Brownstein, Scott; Devine, Curt and Griffin, Drew. "Here's why the US is behind in coronavirus

testing." CNN, Updated 21 Mar. 2020,

www.cnn.com/2020/03/21/politics/us-coronavirus-tests-invs/index.html[16].

Brueck, Hilary. "Switzerland has a stunningly high rate of gun ownership – here's why it doesn't

have mass shootings." Business Insider, 26 Oct. 2023,

www.businessinsider.com/switzerland-gun-laws-rates-of-gun-deaths-2018-2[17].

Bubalo, Mattea. "Three women among dozen publicly flogged in Afghanistan – Taliban official."

BBC News, 23 Nov. 2022, www.bbc.com/news/world-asia-63736271[18].

Bunn, Curtis. "Report: Black people are still killed by police at a higher rate than other groups."

NBC News, 3 Mar. 2022, www.nbcnews.com/news/nbcblk/report-black-people-are-still-[19]

killed-police-higher-rate-groups-rcna17169.

Byng, Rhonesha. "A Peek Inside Her Agenda: Janice Bryant Howroyd." Her Agenda,

16 Jan. 2023, www.heragenda.com/p/janice-bryant-howroyd/.

CNN Editorial Research. "Trayvon Martin Shooting Fast Facts." CNN, Updated 15 Feb. 2023,

www.cnn.com/2013/06/05/us/trayvon-martin-shooting-fast-facts/index.html.

Caldwell, Travis. "A timeline of the investigations into Tyre Nichols' death after a traffic stop

and arrest by Memphis police." CNN, Updated on 27 Jan. 2023,

www.cnn.com/2023/01/26/us/tyre-nichols-timeline-investigation/index.html.

"Carbon Capture Technology 'can never be an excuse' for business as usual, advocates say." CBS

News, *60 Minutes Overtime*, 30 April 2023, www.cbsnews.com/news/carbon-capture-[20]

---

16. http://www.cnn.com/2020/03/21/politics/us-coronavirus-tests-invs/index.html

17. http://www.businessinsider.com/switzerland-gun-laws-rates-of-gun-deaths-2018-2

18. http://www.bbc.com/news/world-asia-63736271

19. http://www.nbcnews.com/news/nbcblk/report-black-people-are-still-

technology-can-never-be-an-excuse-for-business-as-usual-advocates-say-60-minutes-2023-04-30/.

Chan, Louis. Dr. Oz faces backlash after China COVID tweet." AsAmNews, 4 Mar. 2022, www.asamnews.com/2022/03/04/false-claim-quackery-bad-medicine-dr-oz-politics/[21].

Chandler, Mark. "How Does Climate Change Affect Agriculture." Heifer International, 31 Mar. 2023, www.heifer.org/blog/how-climate-change-affects-agriculture.html[22].

Chenoweth, Erica and Pressman, Jeremy. "Black Lives Matter protesters were overwhelmingly peaceful, our research finds." Harvard Kennedy School for Human Rights Policy Carr Center, 20 Oct. 2020, www.carrcenter.hks.harvard.edu/publications/black-lives-matter-[23] protesters-were-overwhelmingly-peaceful-our-research-finds.

Cheney, Kyle. "Eastman plan to keep Trump in power faces a reckoning, as authorities seek his disbarment." *Politico*, 20 June 2023, www.politico.com/news/2023/06/20/eastman-disbarment-trial-trump-election-plan-[24] 00102784.

"Chien-Shiung Wu: Physicist, Columbia University." Atomic Heritage Foundation, Accessed on 20 June 2023, https://ahf.nuclearmuseum.org/ahf/profile/chien-shiung-wu/.

Chlopak, Erin. "Yes, President Trump Violated Campaign Finance Law by Asking Ukraine for a 'Favor.'" Campaign Legal Center (CLC), 3 Oct. 2019, www.campaignlegal.org/update/yes-president-trump-violated-campaign-finance-law-[25]

---

20. http://www.cbsnews.com/news/carbon-capture-

21. http://www.asamnews.com/2022/03/04/false-claim-quackery-bad-medicine-dr-oz-politics/

22. http://www.heifer.org/blog/how-climate-change-affects-agriculture.html

23. http://www.carrcenter.hks.harvard.edu/publications/black-lives-matter-

24. http://www.politico.com/news/2023/06/20/eastman-disbarment-trial-trump-election-plan-

asking-ukraine-favor.

Christian, Nnamdi. "Rich Dudes Floyd Mayweather's $450M Winning Streak Beyond the Ring." MoneyMade, 2 Aug. 2023 (updated), www.moneymade.io/learn/article/floyd-[26] mayweather-net-worth.

Cillizza, Chris. "Nancy Pelosi did what Donald Trump failed to do on January 6." CNN, 14 Oct. 2022, www.cnn.com/2022/10/14/politics/nancy-pelosi-mike-pence-donald-trump-[27] january-6/index.html.

Cillizza, Chris. "The long, dark history of Donald Trump's pledge to be a 'law and order' president." CNN, 2 June 2020, www.cnn.com/2020/06/02/politics/law-and-order-donald-[28] trump-protest-riots/index.html.

"Clayton Bigsby, the World's Only Black White Supremacist – Chappell's Show." Comedy Central, 11 Nov. 2019, www.youtube.com/watch?v=BLNDqxrUUwQ[29].

CNBC.com Staff. "America's Top States for Business." CNBC, 11 July 2023, www.cnbc.com/2023/07/11/top-states-for-business-north-carolina.html.

Cohen, Zachary; Perez, Evan; Murray, Sara and Grayer, Annie. "House January 6 committee handing over Investigative materials to DOJ." CNN, 20 Dec. 2022, www.cnn.com/2022/12/20/politics/january-6-committee-justice-department-[30] handoff/index.html.

---

25. http://www.campaignlegal.org/update/yes-president-trump-violated-campaign-finance-law-

26. http://www.moneymade.io/learn/article/floyd-

27. http://www.cnn.com/2022/10/14/politics/nancy-pelosi-mike-pence-donald-trump-

28. http://www.cnn.com/2020/06/02/politics/law-and-order-donald-

29. http://www.youtube.com/watch?v=BLNDqxrUUwQ

30. http://www.cnn.com/2022/12/20/politics/january-6-committee-justice-department-

"Confederate Monument Interpretation Guide." Atlanta History Center, Accessed on 19 March

2024,

    www.atlantahistorycenter.com/learning-and-research/projects-initiatives/
confederate-[31]monument-interpretation-
guide/#:~:text=While%20many%20Confederate%20memorials%20of,era%20beginning%20in%20t

Connley, Courtney. "Why Black workers still face a promotion and wage gap that's costing the

    economy    trillions."    CNBC,    16    Apr.    2021,    www.cnbc.com/2021/04/16/
black-workers-[32]

    face-promotion-and-wage-gaps-that-cost-the-economy-trillions.html.

Copp, Tara. "The U.S. Spent $83 Billion Training Afghan Forces. Why Did They Collapse So

Quickly?" Defense One, 14 Aug. 2021, www.defenseone.com/threats/2021/08/us-spent-[33]

83-billion-training-afghan-forces-why-did-they-collapse-so-quickly/184529/.

Coski, John. "Myths & Misunderstandings | The Confederate Flag." The American Civil War

Museum, 9 Jan. 2018, www.acwm.org/blog/myths-misunderstandings-confederate-[34]

flag/#:~:text="Heritage%2C%20not%20Hate"%20is,war%20is%20a%20false%20dichot

omy.

————————

CRAGG, GULLIVER AND Volochine, Elena. "The Crimean port of Sevastopol, a strategic link
between

Russia and Syria." France 24, 20 March 2019,

www.france24.com/en/20190320-focus-crimea-sevastopol-port-naval-base-russia-navy-[35]

31. http://www.atlantahistorycenter.com/learning-and-research/projects-initiatives/confederate-

32. http://www.cnbc.com/2021/04/16/black-workers-

33. http://www.defenseone.com/threats/2021/08/us-spent-

34. http://www.acwm.org/blog/myths-misunderstandings-confederate-

syria-war-operations-trade-tartus.

Creitz, Charles. "Sen. Johnson warns of 'unequal application of justice' as Capitol riot suspects sit in jail, vs Antifa, BLM." Fox News, 13 June 2021, www.foxnews.com/media/sen-johnson-capitol-riot-suspects-unequal-application-of-[36] justice-antifa-blm.

Cummings, William. "Trump tells congresswomen to 'go back' to the 'crime infested places from which they came.'" USA Today, 14 July 2019, www.usatoday.com/story/news/politics/2019/07/14/trump-tells-congresswomen-go-back-[37] counties-they-came/1728253001/.

Dahl, Julia. "Cops found AR-15 part, ammo in Dylann Roof's car months ago." CBS News, 26 June 2015, www.cbsnews.com/news/cops-found-ar-15-part-ammo-in-dylann-roofs-[38] car-months-before-charleston-massacre/.

Davis, Charles R. "While Trump incites his supporters with claims of fraud, Republicans privately insist he lost the election and will leave power, CNN's Jake Tapper says." Business Insider, 10 Nov. 2020, www.businessinsider.com/republicans-privately-insist-trump-lost-election-[39] and-will-leave-power-2020-11.

"Dave Chappelle Stand-up Monologue – SNL (2022) Transcript." Scraps From The Loft, 22 Jan. 2023, www.scrapsfromtheloft.com/comedy/dave-chappelle-monologue-snl-2022-[40] transcript/.

35. http://www.france24.com/en/20190320-focus-crimea-sevastopol-port-naval-base-russia-navy-

36. http://www.foxnews.com/media/sen-johnson-capitol-riot-suspects-unequal-application-of-

37. http://www.usatoday.com/story/news/politics/2019/07/14/trump-tells-congresswomen-go-back-

38. http://www.cbsnews.com/news/cops-found-ar-15-part-ammo-in-dylann-roofs-

39. http://www.businessinsider.com/republicans-privately-insist-trump-lost-election-

40. http://www.scrapsfromtheloft.com/comedy/dave-chappelle-monologue-snl-2022-

"DEMOGRAPHICS OF AFGHANISTAN." Statistics Times, 18 Nov. 2021,

www.statisticstimes.com/demographics/country/afghanistan-[41]

demographics.php#:~:text=The%20Sex%20Ratio%20in%20Afghanistan,million%20mor

e%20males%20than%20females.

DeBonis, Mike. "GOP Rep. Kinzinger wages a lonely fight against Trump's falsehoods and right-

wing disinformation." *The Washington Post*, 5 Dec. 2020,

www.washingtonpost.com/powerpost/trump-republicans-kinzinger-[42]

house/2020/12/05/753808a6-365d-11eb-b59c-adb7153d10c2_story.html.

"Dobbs v. Jackson Women's Health Organization (2022)." National Constitution Center,

Accessed on 9 June 2023,

www.constitutioncenter.org/the-constitution/supreme-court-case-library/dobbs-v-[43]

jackson-womens-health-

organization#:~:text=In%20Dobbs%2C%20the%20Supreme%20Court,law%20and%20o

verturned%20Roe%20v.

Dow, Cat. "What are the Six SAE levels of Self-Driving Cars?" Top Gear, 6 Mar. 2023,

www.topgear.com/car%20news/what-are-sae-levels-autonomous-driving-uk[44].

"Dr. Chien-Shiung Wu, The First Lady of Physics." U.S. National Park Service, Accessed on 20

June 2023, www.nps.gov/people/dr-chien-shiung-wu-the-first-lady-of-physics.htm.

Elkind, Elizabeth. "Antonin Scalia's son on his father's 'odd couple' friendship with Ruth Bader

---

41. http://www.statisticstimes.com/demographics/country/afghanistan-

42. http://www.washingtonpost.com/powerpost/trump-republicans-kinzinger-

43. http://www.constitutioncenter.org/the-constitution/supreme-court-case-library/dobbs-v-

44. http://www.topgear.com/car%20news/what-are-sae-levels-autonomous-driving-uk

Ginsburg." CBS News, Updated 19 Sept. 2020,

www.cbsnews.com/news/ruth-bader-ginsburg-supreme-court-antonin-scalia-friendship/[45].

---

45. http://www.cbsnews.com/news/ruth-bader-ginsburg-supreme-court-antonin-scalia-friendship/

"Early Estimates of Motor Vehicle Traffic Fatalities in 2021" (Crash Stats Brief Statistical Summary. Report No. DOT HS 813 283). U.S. Department of Transportation: National Highway Traffic Safety Administration (NHTSA), NHTSA National Center for Statistics and Analysis, April 2022, web site:

crashstats.nhtsa.dot.gov/Api/Public/ViewPublication/813283.

"Fact Sheet: Biden-Harris Administration Announces New Border Enforcement Actions." The White House, 5 Jan. 2023, www.whitehouse.gov/briefing-room/statements-releases/2023/01/05/fact-sheet-biden-[46] harris-administration-announces-new-border-enforcement-actions/.

"Fatality Facts 2021: Teenagers." The Insurance Institute for Highway Safety and Highway Loss Data Institute (IIHS-HLDI), May 2023, www.iihs.org/topics/fatality-statistics/detail/teenagers[47].

Felix, Mabel; Sobel, Laurie and Salganicoff, Alina. "A Review of Exceptions in State Abortion Bans: Implications for the Provision of Abortion Services." Kaiser Family Foundation, 18 May 2023, www.kff.org/womens-health-policy/issue-brief/a-review-of-exceptions-in-[48] state-abortions-bans-implications-for-the-provision-of-abortion-services/.

Fichera, Angelo. "Vice president doesn't have power to 'change the outcome' of elections." Associated Press (AP), 1 Feb. 2022, www.apnews.com/article/fact-checking-275776015398[49].

---

46. http://www.whitehouse.gov/briefing-room/statements-releases/2023/01/05/fact-sheet-biden-

47. http://www.iihs.org/topics/fatality-statistics/detail/teenagers

48. http://www.kff.org/womens-health-policy/issue-brief/a-review-of-exceptions-in-

49. http://www.apnews.com/article/fact-checking-275776015398

Fortin, Jacey. "Critical Race Theory: A Brief History." *The New York Times*, 8 Nov. 2021,

www.nytimes.com/article/what-is-critical-race-theory.html[50].

Fox News Staff. "LAURA INGRAHAM: We're witnessing an invasion by invitation." Fox

News, 25 Sept. 2023, www.foxnews.com/media/laura-ingraham-were-witnessing-[51]

invasion-by-invitation.

Frost, Robert. "Stopping by Woods on a Snowy Evening." Poetry Foundation,

www.poetryfoundation.org/poems/42891/stopping-by-woods-on-a-snowy-evening[52],

Accessed 11 Oct. 2023.

Fung, Katherine. "Read Liz Cheney's Concession Speech as Congresswoman Ousted in

Wyoming." *Newsweek*, 17 Aug. 2022, www.newsweek.com/read-liz-cheneys-concession-[53]

speech-congresswoman-ousted-wyoming-1734296.

Gaebler, Johann; Cai, William and Goel, Sharad. "Police stop Black drivers more often than

Whites. We found out why." *The Washington Post*, 15 Sept. 2022,

www.washingtonpost.com/politics/2022/09/15/driving-while-black-racial-discrimination-[54]

traffic-tickets/.

Garamone, Jim. "U.S. Central Command Releases Report on August Abbey Gate Attack." U.S.

Department of Defense, 4 Feb. 2022, www.defense.gov/News/News-[55]

Stories/Article/Article/2924398/us-central-command-releases-report-on-august-abbey-

gate-attack/.

---

50. http://www.nytimes.com/article/what-is-critical-race-theory.html

51. http://www.foxnews.com/media/laura-ingraham-were-witnessing-

52. http://www.poetryfoundation.org/poems/42891/stopping-by-woods-on-a-snowy-evening

53. http://www.newsweek.com/read-liz-cheneys-concession-

54. http://www.washingtonpost.com/politics/2022/09/15/driving-while-black-racial-discrimination-

55. http://www.defense.gov/News/News-

Gramlich, John. "What we know about the increase in U.S. murders in 2020." Pew Research

Center, 27 Oct. 2021, www.pewresearch.org/short-reads/2021/10/27/what-we-know-[56]

about-the-increase-in-u-s-murders-in-2020/.

Guzman, Chad De. "After Queen Elizabeth II's Death, Many Indians Are Demanding the Return

of the Kohinoor Diamond." Time, 9 Sept. 2022,

www.time.com/6212113/queen-elizabeth-india-kohinoor-diamond/[57].

Halbrook, Stephen. "Nazi Repression of Firearms Owners." Independent Institute, 1, Aug. 1999,

www.independent.org/publications/article.asp?id=2287#4[58].

———————————

HALL, NATHAN. "'IF Virginia Stands by the Old Union' – Robert E. Lee Resigns from the U.S.

Army." National Park Service, Last Updated 23 Aug. 2023,

www.nps.gov/rich/learn/historyculture/-if-virginia-stands-by-the-old-union-robert-e-lee-[59]

resigns-from-the-u-s-army.htm.

Hannah-Jones, Nikole. *The 1619 Project*: "Our democracy's founding ideals were false when they

were written. Black Americans have fought to make them true." *The New York Times

Magazine*, 14 Aug. 2019, www.nytimes.com/interactive/2019/08/14/magazine/black-[60]

history-american-democracy.html.

Hassan, Adeel. "Coronavirus cases and deaths were vastly underestimated in U.S. meatpacking

plants, a House report says." *The New York Times*, 28 Oct. 2021,

---

56. http://www.pewresearch.org/short-reads/2021/10/27/what-we-know-

57. http://www.time.com/6212113/queen-elizabeth-india-kohinoor-diamond/

58. http://www.independent.org/publications/article.asp?id=2287#a5c02393e59c943d6a75a9241140faca34

59. http://www.nps.gov/rich/learn/historyculture/-if-virginia-stands-by-the-old-union-robert-e-lee-

60. http://www.nytimes.com/interactive/2019/08/14/magazine/black-

www.nytimes.com/2021/10/28/world/meatpacking-workers-covid-cases-deaths.html.

Haywood, Shane. "Marvin Ellison Net Worth." North Carolina Employment Security

Commission (NCESC), 3 Oct. 2023 (last updated), www.ncesc.com/marvin-ellison-net-[61]

worth/.

"Health Care as a Human Right – Medicare for All." Friends of Bernie Sanders, Accessed on

5 July 2023, www.berniesanders.com/issues/medicare-for-all/.

"Healthy Soil: The foundation of organic farming." OCIA (Organic Crop Improvement

Association) International, 23 Aug. 2023, www.ocia.org/2023/08/23/healthy-soil-[62]

foundation-of-organic-farming/.

Hickel, Jason. "How Britain stole $45 trillion from India And lied about it." Committee for the

Abolition of Illegitimate Debt (CADTM), 31 Dec. 2018,

www.cadtm.org/spip.php?page=imprimer&id_article=16972[63].

Hille, Kathrin; Buckley, Neil and Farchy, Jack. "Putin tears up lease for Sevastopol naval base."

*Financial Times*, 2 April 2014, www.ft.com/content/5a610a56-ba85-11e3-8b15-[64]

00144feabdc0.

History.com Editors. "Sherman's March to the Sea." History.com, Updated 4 Oct. 2018,

www.history.com/topics/american-civil-war/shermans-march[65].

Hook, Jennifer Van; Gelatt, Julia and Soto, Ariel G. Ruiz. "A Turning Point for the Unauthorized

Immigrant Population in the United States." Migration Policy Institute (MPI), September

---

61. http://www.ncesc.com/marvin-ellison-net-

62. http://www.ocia.org/2023/08/23/healthy-soil-

63. http://www.cadtm.org/spip.php?page=imprimer&id_article=16972

64. http://www.ft.com/content/5a610a56-ba85-11e3-8b15-

65. http://www.history.com/topics/american-civil-war/shermans-march

2023, www.migrationpolicy.org/news/turning-point-us-unauthorized-immigrant-[66]

population.

"How to Protect Yourself and Others." Centers for Disease Control and Prevention (CDC),

Accessed 15 Nov. 2022, www.cdc.gov/coronavirus/2019-ncov/prevent-getting-[67]

sick/prevention.html#vaccines.

Hughes, Sam and Rapfogel, Nicole. "Following the Money: Untangling U.S. Prescription Drug

Financing." American Progress, 12 Oct. 2023,

www.americanprogress.org/article/following-the-money-untangling-u-s-prescription-[68]

drug-financing/.

*Human Rights Watch World Report 2023, Events of 2022.* Human Rights Watch, 2023,

www.hrw.org/sites/default/files/media_2023/01/World_Report_2023_WEBSPRE[69]

ADS_0.pdf.

Hussain, Grace. "Is Industrial Agriculture Really Making the World a Better Place." Sentient

Media, 2 July 2021, www.sentientmedia.org/industrial-agriculture/.

"In the Pashto language, the word 'sola' means 'peace.'" SOLA | School of Leadership

Afghanistan), Accessed on 12 Oct. 2023,

www.sola-afghanistan.org/the-need-for-[70]

sola#:~:text=In%20the%20Pashto%20language%2C%20the,sola"%20means%20"peace".

---

66. http://www.migrationpolicy.org/news/turning-point-us-unauthorized-immigrant-

67. http://www.cdc.gov/coronavirus/2019-ncov/prevent-getting-

68. http://www.americanprogress.org/article/following-the-money-untangling-u-s-prescription-

69. http://www.hrw.org/sites/default/files/media_2023/01/World_Report_2023_WEBSPRE

70. http://www.sola-afghanistan.org/the-need-for-

"IN THIS WHITE HOUSE." *The West Wing*, created by Aaron Sorkin, performances by Emily Procter,

Rob Lowe and John Spencer, Season 2, episode 4, Warner Bros. Television, 2000.

"Industrial Agricultural Pollution 101: From fertilizer runoff to methane emissions, large-scale

industrial agriculture pollution takes a toll on the environment." NRDC (Natural Resources

Defense Council), 21 July 2022, www.nrdc.org/stories/industrial-agricultural-pollution-[71]

101#whatis.

"Is St. Jude really free?" St. Jude Children's Research Hospital, Accessed 11 Oct. 2023,

www.stjude.org/about-st-jude/why-support-st-jude/no-bills.html.

Jackson, Samuel L. "'change is about to happen,' says Samuel L. Jackson." CNN, 8 June 2020,

www.facebook.com/CNNReplay/videos/change-is-about-to-happen-says-samuel-l-[72]

jackson/280707426412259/.

"Japanese American Incarceration: Records of the War Relocation Authority, 1942 – 1946." San

Francisco State University | J. Paul Leonard Library. Accessed on 10 June 2023,

www.library.sfsu.edu/japanese-american-incarceration-records-war-relocation-authority-[73]

1942-1946.

"Jewish Americans in 2020." Pew Research Center, 11 May 2021,

www.pewresearch.org/religion/2021/05/11/jewish-americans-in-2020/[74].

Kamps, Alice. *The Charters of Freedom at the National Archives: The Declaration of

Independence, The Constitution of the United States and The Bill of Rights.* Washington,

---

71. http://www.nrdc.org/stories/industrial-agricultural-pollution-

72. http://www.facebook.com/CNNReplay/videos/change-is-about-to-happen-says-samuel-l-

73. http://www.library.sfsu.edu/japanese-american-incarceration-records-war-relocation-authority-

74. http://www.pewresearch.org/religion/2021/05/11/jewish-americans-in-2020/

D.C., The National Archives Foundation, 2016.

Kates, Graham. "Timeline: The Trump investigation in Fulton County, Georgia." CBS News, Updated on 15 August 2023, www.cbsnews.com/news/trump-investigation-timeline-[75] fulton-county-georgia/.

Kelly, Tim. "11 richest NBA Players – ranked by 2023 net worth." Audacy Sports, 22 Feb. 2023, www.audacy.com/national/sports/gallery/11-richest-nba-players-ranked-by-net-worth[76].

Kelly, William. "U.S. Trade Deals From the 90s Set Up China as a Pollution Haven." *Inside Climate News*, 6 Mar. 2014, www.insideclimatenews.org/news/06032014/us-trade-deals-[77] 90s-set-china-pollution-haven/.

Key, Francis Scott, 1779-1843. The Star Spangled Banner. Garden City, N.Y.:Doubleday, Doran & company, 1942.

Kheel, Rebecca. "After messy Afghanistan withdrawal, questions remain." *The Hill*, 6 Sept. 2021, www.thehill.com/policy/defense/570810-five-questions-congress-wants-answered-about-[78] afghanistan-withdrawal/.

Knickmeyer, Ellen. "Costs of the Afghanistan war, in lives and dollars." AP News, 17 Aug. 2021, www.apnews.com/article/middle-east-business-afghanistan-[79] 43d8f53b35e80ec18c130cd683e1a38f.

Kumari, Kopal. "What is Oprah Winfrey's net worth in 2023." We Got This Covered (WGTC), 1 Sept. 2023, www.wegotthiscovered.com/celebrities/what-is-oprah-winfreys-net-worth-[80]

---

75. http://www.cbsnews.com/news/trump-investigation-timeline-

76. http://www.audacy.com/national/sports/gallery/11-richest-nba-players-ranked-by-net-worth

77. http://www.insideclimatenews.org/news/06032014/us-trade-deals-

78. http://www.thehill.com/policy/defense/570810-five-questions-congress-wants-answered-about-

79. http://www.apnews.com/article/middle-east-business-afghanistan-

in-2023/.

Kuznia, Rob and Abou-Ghazala, Yahya. "Bailed out, arrested again: These charities boomed after

The murder of George Floyd. They're under fire for bailing out violent offenders." CNN,

21 Mar. 2023, www.cnn.com/2023/03/21/us/bail-reform-bail-charities-invs/index.html[81].

Lawler, Dave. "Biden to announce U.S. sending Ukraine Patriot missiles during Zelensky visit."

Axios, 21 Dec. 2022,

www.axios.com/2022/12/21/biden-patriot-missile-system-ukraine-zelensky-visit.

Lazarus, Emma. "The New Colossus." Statue of Liberty. 1883. New York, New York.

LeBlanc, Paul. "New security video shows Officer Eugene Goodman potentially saving Mitt

Romney from mob during Capitol riot." CNN, Updated 10 Feb. 2021,

www.cnn.com/2021/02/10/politics/eugene-goodman-us-capitol-riot/index.html[82].

"LEGAL HIGHLIGHT: THE Civil Rights Act of 1964." U.S. Department of Labor, Office of the

Assistant Secretary for Administration & Management, Accessed 19 Aug. 2020,

www.dol.gov/agencies/oasam/civil-rights-center/statutes/civil-rights-act-of-[83]

1964#:~:text=In%201964%2C%20Congress%20passed%20Public,hiring%2C%20promo

ting%2C%20and%20firing.

Leshner, Chloe. "Video shows Charlotte driver brandishing gun in road rage incident." WCNC

Charlotte, 22 Dec. 2022, www.wcnc.com/article/news/crime/road-rage-charlotte-gun-[84]

---

80. http://www.wegotthiscovered.com/celebrities/what-is-oprah-winfreys-net-worth-

81. http://www.cnn.com/2023/03/21/us/bail-reform-bail-charities-invs/index.html

82. http://www.cnn.com/2021/02/10/politics/eugene-goodman-us-capitol-riot/index.html

83. http://www.dol.gov/agencies/oasam/civil-rights-center/statutes/civil-rights-act-of-

84. http://www.wcnc.com/article/news/crime/road-rage-charlotte-gun-

driver-tesla-video-camera-recording/275-aa9b1129-a7da-4d92-a049-dbcef0ef3f1f.

Levenson, Eric. "Former officer knelt on George Floyd for 9 minutes and 29 seconds – not the

Infamous 8:46." CNN, Updated 30 Mar. 2021, www.cnn.com/2021/03/29/us/george-[85]

floyd-timing-929-846/index.html.

Levenson, Michael. "11 Days After Fuming About a Coughing Passenger, a Bus Driver Died

From The Coronavirus." *The New York Times*, 4 Apr. 2020,

www.nytimes.com/2020/04/04/us/detroit-bus-driver-coronavirus.html.

Levey, Noam. "Investigation: Many U.S. hospitals sue patients for debts or threaten their credit."

NPR, 21, Dec. 2022,

www.npr.org/sections/health-shots/2022/12/21/1144491711/investigation-many-u-s-[86]

hospitals-sue-patients-for-debts-or-threaten-their-credit.

Levin, Bess. "Ex-White House Press Secretary: Trump 'Gleefully' Watched Insurrection on TV,

Hit 'Rewind' to Watch People Fighting Again." Vanity Fair, 6 Jan. 2022,

www.vanityfair.com/news/2022/01/donald-trump-stephanie-grisham-january-6[87].

—————————————

LEVITT, ZACH AND ENG, Jess. "Where America's developed areas are growing: 'Way off into the

horizon.'" *The Washington Post*, 11 Aug. 2021,

www.washingtonpost.com/nation/interactive/2021/land-development-urban-growth-[88]

maps/.

---

85. http://www.cnn.com/2021/03/29/us/george-

86. http://www.npr.org/sections/health-shots/2022/12/21/1144491711/investigation-many-u-s-

87. http://www.vanityfair.com/news/2022/01/donald-trump-stephanie-grisham-january-6

88. http://www.washingtonpost.com/nation/interactive/2021/land-development-urban-growth-

Li, David K. and Sheeley, Colin. "Ye locked out of Twitter after backlash for antisemitic posts."

NBC News, 10 Oct. 2022, www.nbcnews.com/news/us-news/ye-locked-twitter-violation-[89]

platform-policy-rcna51505.

Lincoln, Abraham, President of the United States (March 4, 1861 – April 15, 1865). "The

Emancipation Proclamation." The United States National Archives, Website page last

reviewed on 28 Jan. 2022, www.archives.gov/exhibits/featured-documents/emancipation-[90]

proclamation#:~:text=President%20Abraham%20Lincoln%20issued%20the,and%20henc

eforward%20shall%20be%20free."

Lindsey, Vickie. "She Had a Dream: Mae C. Jemison, First African American Woman in Space."

National Air and Space Museum, Smithsonian, 12 Sept. 2010,

www.airandspace.si.edu/stories/editorial/she-had-dream-mae-c-jemison-first-african-[91]

american-woman-space.

Logan, Justin. "Why Are American Troops Still in Iraq and Syria." Cato Institute, 10 Nov. 2023,

www.cato.org/commentary/why-are-american-troops-still-iraq-syria.

Lopez, Mark Hugo and Moslimani, Mohamad. "Key facts about the nations 47.2 million Black

Americans." Pew Research Center, 10 Feb. 2023,

www.pewresearch.org/short-reads/2023/02/10/key-facts-about-black-americans/[92].

Martin, Gary. "The meaning and origin of the expression: Necessity is the mother of invention."

The Phrase Finder, Accessed 12 Oct. 2023, www.phrases.org.uk/meanings/necessity-is-[93]

---

89. http://www.nbcnews.com/news/us-news/ye-locked-twitter-violation-

90. http://www.archives.gov/exhibits/featured-documents/emancipation-

91. http://www.airandspace.si.edu/stories/editorial/she-had-dream-mae-c-jemison-first-african-

92. http://www.pewresearch.org/short-reads/2023/02/10/key-facts-about-black-americans/

93. http://www.phrases.org.uk/meanings/necessity-is-

the-mother-of-invention.html.

Mastrangelo, Dominick. "Rupert Murdoch: Hannity, Ingraham 'went too far' in promoting Trump's false claims about 2020 election." *The Hill*, 7 March 2023, www.thehill.com/homenews/3888895-rupert-murdoch-hannity-ingraham-went-too-far-[94] in-promoting-trumps-false-claims-about-2020-election/.

Maurer, Roy. "Study Finds Productivity Not Deterred by Shift to Remote Work." The Society for Human Resources Management (SHRM), 16 Sept. 2020, www.shrm.org/topics-tools/news/study-finds-productivity-not-deterred-shift-to-remote-[95] work.

Mihalascu, Dan. "Join Kyle Connor For A Ride In The Boring Company's Las Vegas Loop." INSIDEEVs, 4 Jan. 2022, www.insideevs.com/news/558560/boring-company-tunnel-ride-[96] modely/.

Mir, Asfandyar. "The ISIS-K Resurgence." Wilson Center, 8 Oct. 2021, www.wilsoncenter.org/article/isis-k-resurgence[97].

Montanaro, Domenico. "Rising Violent Crime is Likely to Present A Political Challenge For Democrats in 2022." NPR, 22 July 2021, www.npr.org/2021/07/22/1018996709/rising-violent-crime-is-likely-to-present-a-[98] political-challenge-for-democrats-in.

Montilla, Desiree. "Charlottesville votes to rename parks yet again." WHSV News, 17 July 2018,

---

94. http://www.thehill.com/homenews/3888895-rupert-murdoch-hannity-ingraham-went-too-far-

95. http://www.shrm.org/topics-tools/news/study-finds-productivity-not-deterred-shift-to-remote-

96. http://www.insideevs.com/news/558560/boring-company-tunnel-ride-

97. http://www.wilsoncenter.org/article/isis-k-resurgence

98. http://www.npr.org/2021/07/22/1018996709/rising-violent-crime-is-likely-to-present-a-

www.whsv.com/content/news/Charlottesville-votes-to-rename-parks-yet-again-[99]

488407921.html.

Montoya-Galvez, Camilo. "CBP One app becomes main portal to U.S. asylum system under

Biden border strategy." CBS News, 11 April 2023,

www.cbsnews.com/news/cbp-one-app-us-border-asylum-biden/[100].

MORRISON, AARON. "BLACK Lives Matter movement marks 10 years of activism and renews its call

to defund the police." Associated Press (AP), 13 July 2023,

www.apnews.com/article/black-lives-matter-10th-anniversary-trayvon-martin-[101]

c2d79ae4639934ca1eb77d6b54c16f8b.

Moslimani, Mohamad; Tamir, Christine; Budiman, Abby; Noe-Bustamante, Luis and Mora,

Lauren. "Facts About the U.S. Black Population." Pew Research Center, 18 Jan. 2024,

www.pewresearch.org/social-trends/fact-sheet/facts-about-the-us-black-[102]

population/#:~:text=▶-,Multiracial%2C%20non-

Hispanic,and%20the%20Northeast%20(18%25).

"Neil deGrasse Tyson." Biography. Updated 26 Mar. 2021,

www.biography.com/scientists/neil-degrasse-tyson[103].

"Neil deGrasse Tyson." American Museum of Natural History, Seminars on Science, Accessed

on 26 Dec. 2023, www.amnh.org/learn-teach/seminars-on-science/about/faculty/neil-[104]

---

99. http://www.whsv.com/content/news/Charlottesville-votes-to-rename-parks-yet-again-

100. http://www.cbsnews.com/news/cbp-one-app-us-border-asylum-biden/

101. http://www.apnews.com/article/black-lives-matter-10th-anniversary-trayvon-martin-

102. http://www.pewresearch.org/social-trends/fact-sheet/facts-about-the-us-black-

103. http://www.biography.com/scientists/neil-degrasse-tyson

degrasse-tyson.

Niiya, Brian. "Ask a Historian: How Many Japanese Americans Were Incarcerated During WWII? Densho.org, www.densho.org/catalyst/how-many-japanese-americans-were-[105] incarcerated-during-wwii/.

"Operation Warp Speed: Accelerated COVID-19 Vaccine Development Status and Efforts to Address Manufacturing Challenges." U.S. Government Accountability Office, 11 Feb. 2021, www.gao.gov/products/gao-21-319.

"Our growing population." United Nations, Accessed on 12 Oct. 2023, www.un.org/en/global-issues/population[106].

"Our Founder Shabana Basij-Rasikh." SOLA | School of Leadership Afghanistan, Accessed on 12 Oct. 2023, www.sola-afghanistan.org/our-founder[107].

Patel, Dinyar. "Viewpoint: How British let one million Indians die in famine." BBC News, 11 June 2016, www.bbc.com/news/world-asia-india-36339524.

Pereira, Sheldon. "Tiger Woods And a $1 Billion Net Worth." Essentially Sports, 28 Feb. 2023, www.essentiallysports.com/golf-news-tiger-woods-and-a-billion-net-worth/[108].

Popli, Nik and Zorthian, Julia. "What Happened to the Jan. 6 Rioters Arrested Since the Capitol Attack." *Time,* 6 Jan. 2022, www.time.com/6133336/jan-6-capitol-riot-arrests-sentences/.

Powell, Alvin. "Wildfires are much worse than a sign of climate change." *The Harvard Gazette,* 23 Aug. 2023, www.news.harvard.edu/gazette/story/2023/08/wildfires-are-much-worse-

---

104. http://www.amnh.org/learn-teach/seminars-on-science/about/faculty/neil-%20%20%20%20%20%20%20
105. http://www.densho.org/catalyst/how-many-japanese-americans-were-
106. http://www.un.org/en/global-issues/population
107. http://www.sola-afghanistan.org/our-founder
108. http://www.essentiallysports.com/golf-news-tiger-woods-and-a-billion-net-worth/

than-a-sign-of-climate-change-says-expert/.

"QuickFacts." United States Census Bureau, Access 17 Aug. 2023,

www.census.gov/quickfacts/fact/table/US/RHI125222#RHI125222[109].

Ramirez, Rachel. "Billions of snow crabs have disappeared from the waters around Alaska.

Scientists say overfishing is not the cause." CNN, 16 Oct. 2022,

www.cnn.com/2022/10/16/us/alaska-snow-crab-harvest-canceled-climate/index.html[110].

Reuters. "More Than Half of World's Large Lakes Are Drying Up, Study Finds." Voice of

America & Reuters, 18 May 2023, www.voanews.com/a/more-than-half-of-world-s-large-[111]

lakes-are-drying-up-study-finds-/7099984.html.

Reagan, Ronald, President of the United States (20 Jan. 1981 – 20 Jan. 1989). "Farewell Address

to the Nation." Ronald Reagan Presidential Library & Museum, 11 Jan. 1989,

www.reaganlibrary.gov/archives/speech/farewell-address-nation[112].

"Retired NYPD Officer Sentenced to 10 Years in Prison For Actions Related to Capitol Breach."

United States Attorney's Office, District of Columbia, 1 Sept. 2022,

www.justice.gov/usao-dc/pr/retired-nypd-officer-sentenced-prison-actions-related-[113]

capitol-breach.

"Roe v. Wade, 410 U.S. 113 (1973)." Justia U.S. Supreme Court, accessed on 9 June 2023,

www.supreme.justia.com/cases/federal/us/410/113/#:~:text=A%20person%20may%20ch[114]

---

109. http://www.census.gov/quickfacts/fact/table/US/RHI125222#RHI125222

110. http://www.cnn.com/2022/10/16/us/alaska-snow-crab-harvest-canceled-climate/index.html

111. http://www.voanews.com/a/more-than-half-of-world-s-large-

112. http://www.reaganlibrary.gov/archives/speech/farewell-address-nation

113. http://www.justice.gov/usao-dc/pr/retired-nypd-officer-sentenced-prison-actions-related-

114. http://www.supreme.justia.com/cases/federal/us/410/

113/#_853ae90f0351324bd73ea615e6487517__4c761f170e016836ff84498202b99827__853ae90f0351324bd73ea615e6487517_tex

oose%20to,and%2028%20weeks%20after%20conception.

Rubin, Olivia. "Jury selection underway in Dominion's $1.6 billion defamation case against Fox News." ABC News, 13 Apr. 2023, www.abcnews.go.com/US/jury-selection-set-begin-dominions-16-billion-defamation/story?id=98547091.

Santana, Rebecca. "What's behind the influx of migrants crossing the U.S. southern border." PBS News Hour, 21 Sept. 2023, www.pbs.org/newshour/politics/whats-behind-the-influx-of-[115] migrants-crossing-the-u-s-southern-border.

"Sean Hannity: The mainstream media finally covers border crisis." Fox News, Accessed on 8 July 2023, www.foxnews.com/video/6317250218112[116].

Seligman, Lara. "'Speed equals safety': Inside the Pentagon's controversial decision to leave Bagram early." *Politico*, 28 Sept. 2021, www.politico.com/news/2021/09/28/pentagon-decision-leave-bagram-514456[117].

Shabad, Rebecca. "Biden blasts MAGA philosophy as 'semi-fascism.'" NBC News, 26 Aug. 2022, www.nbcnews.com/politics/2022-election/biden-blasts-maga-philosophy-semi-[118] fascism-rcna44953.

Shabad, Rebecca. "Contradicting Biden, top generals say they recommended a small force stay in Afghanistan." NBC News, 28 Sept. 2021, www.nbcnews.com/politics/congress/pentagon-[119] leaders-austin-milley-face-questions-chaotic-afghanistan-withdrawal-n1280230.

---

t_43ec3e5dee6e706af7766fffea512721_A_0bcef9c45bd8a48eda1b26eb0c61c869_20person_0bcef9c45bd8a48eda1b26eb0c61c869_20may_0bcef9c45bd8a48eda1b26eb0c61c869_20ch

115. http://www.pbs.org/newshour/politics/whats-behind-the-influx-of-

116. http://www.foxnews.com/video/6317250218112

117. http://www.politico.com/news/2021/09/28/pentagon-decision-leave-bagram-514456

118. http://www.nbcnews.com/politics/2022-election/biden-blasts-maga-philosophy-semi-

119. http://www.nbcnews.com/politics/congress/pentagon-

Sharp, Rachel. "New car data places Alex Murdaugh at the spot where wife's phone was

dumped – before he sped away." *The Independent*, 18 Feb. 2023,

www.the-independent.com/news/world/americas/crime/alex-murdaugh-car-phone-[120]

maggie-case-family-b2284612.html.

Shogan, Colleen. "Calvin *Coolidge* and Native Americans. A Complex History." The White

House Historical Association, 26 Oct. 2021,

www.whitehousehistory.org/calvin-coolidge-and-native-americans[121].

Sievers, Caitlin. "Kari Lake, who falsely claims she's the 'lawful governor' of AZ, files to run

for U.S. Senate." *Arizona Mirror*, 3 October 2023,

www.azmirror.com/briefs/kari-lake-who-falsely-claims-shes-the-lawful-governor-of-az-[122]

files-to-run-for-u-s-senate/.

Smith, Nick and Buchman, Cassie. "U.S. citizens most likely to be arrested for violent crime."

NewsNation, Updated 17 Feb. 2022,

www.newsnationnow.com/us-news/immigration/u-s-citizens-most-likely-to-commit-[123]

crimes-than-immigrants/.

"SC v. Murdaugh (2023)." Court Tv, Accessed on multiple dates during February and March

2023, www.courttv.com/trials/sc-v-murdaugh-2023/[124].

Srinivasan, Hiranmayi. "Patrick Mahomes Is Investing in F1-Here's His Net Worth."

Investopedia, 28 Oct. 2023, www.investopedia.com/patrick-mahomes-net-worth-[125]

---

120. http://www.the-independent.com/news/world/americas/crime/alex-murdaugh-car-phone-

121. http://www.whitehousehistory.org/calvin-coolidge-and-native-americans

122. http://www.azmirror.com/briefs/kari-lake-who-falsely-claims-shes-the-lawful-governor-of-az-

123. http://www.newsnationnow.com/us-news/immigration/u-s-citizens-most-likely-to-commit-

124. http://www.courttv.com/trials/sc-v-murdaugh-2023/

8383399.

Stahl, Lesley. "SOLA: Daring to educate Afghanistan's girls." CBS News, *60 Minutes*, 16 July

2023,           www.cbsnews.com/news/sola-afghanistan-education-60-minutes-transcript-
2023-[126]

07-16/.

Stobbe, Mike. "COVID helped make 2021 the deadliest year in U.S. history." Public Broadcasting

Service (PBS), 12 Apr. 2022, www.pbs.org/newshour/nation/covid-helped-make-2021-[127]

the-deadliest-year-in-u-s-history#:~:text=COVID-

19%20deaths%20rose%20in,is%20not%20solely%20to%20blame.

STRONG, SALLY. "AIR Pollution Dropped During Pandemic Lockdowns." University of
Houston,

9 May 2022,

www.uh.edu/news-events/stories/2022-news-articles/may-2022/05092242022-uh-

covid-air-pollutant-pollution-ghahremanloo-

choi.php#:~:text=As%20vehicle%20traffic%20lightened%20and,of%20potentially-

dangerous%20air%20pollutants.

"Subrahmanyan Chandrasekhar Facts." The Nobel Prize. Access on 20 June 2023,

www.nobelprize.org/prizes/physics/1983/chandrasekhar/facts/[128].

"Subrahmanyan Chandra: The Man Behind The Name." Chandra X-Ray Observatory. Accessed

125. http://www.investopedia.com/patrick-mahomes-net-worth-

126. http://www.cbsnews.com/news/sola-afghanistan-education-60-minutes-transcript-2023-

127. http://www.pbs.org/newshour/nation/covid-helped-make-2021-

128. http://www.nobelprize.org/prizes/physics/1983/chandrasekhar/facts/

on 10 June 2023, www.chandra.harvard.edu/about/chandra.html[129].

Takei, George. "Why I love a country that once betrayed me." *Ted: Ideas Worth Spreading,* June 2014, www.ted.com/talks/george_takei_why_i_love_a_country_that_once_ betrayed_me.

Tamir, Christine. "Key findings about Black immigrants in the U.S." Pew Research Center, 27 Jan. 2022, www.pewresearch.org/short-reads/2022/01/27/key-findings-about-black-[130] immigrants-in-the-u-s/.

Taylor, Kiara. "America's Top Black CEOs." Investopedia, Updated on 27 Feb. 2023, www.investopedia.com/top-black-ceos-5220330[131].

"10 Quick Facts on Global Hunger and the United Nations World Food Programme's Life-Changing Work." United Nations World Food Program USA, 20 Oct. 2021, www.wfpusa.org/10-quick-facts-hunger-wfps[132].

"The Best of Tyrone Biggums – Chappelle's Show." Comedy Central, 28 Apr. 2019, www.youtube.com/watch?v=oO3wTulizvg[133].

"The Freedom Dividend." Yang 2020, Accessed on 4 August 2023, https://2020.yang2020.com/policies/.

*The Hill* Staff. "House Speaker vote: McCarthy clinches Speakership." *The Hill,* 7 Jan. 2023, www.thehill.com/homenews/house/3802149-house-speaker-election-coverage-mccarthy-[134] allies-hope-to-hammer-out-deal-on-day-4-of-stalemate/.

---

129. http://www.chandra.harvard.edu/about/chandra.html

130. http://www.pewresearch.org/short-reads/2022/01/27/key-findings-about-black-

131. http://www.investopedia.com/top-black-ceos-5220330

132. http://www.wfpusa.org/10-quick-facts-hunger-wfps

133. http://www.youtube.com/watch?v=oO3wTulizvg

134. http://www.thehill.com/homenews/house/3802149-house-speaker-election-coverage-mccarthy-

*The King's Speech.* Directed by Tom Hooper, performances by Colin Firth and Geoffrey Rush,

The Weinstein Company, 2010.

"The Lord's Prayer." Crosswalk.com, accessed on 15 Oct. 2023,

www.crosswalk.com/faith/prayer/the-lords-prayer-be-encouraged-and-strengthened.html[135].

Tigue, Kristoffer. "Tucker Carlson Spread Lots of Climate Misinformation. His Replacement

Isn't Much Better." Inside Climate News, 21 July 2023,

www.insideclimatenews.org/news/21072023/tucker-carlson-jesse-watters-fox-news-[136]

climate-misinformation/.

"Tracking the Taliban's (Mis)Treatment of Women." United States Institute of Peace, Accessed

on 12 Oct. 2023, www.usip.org/tracking-talibans-mistreatment-women.

"Trading Spouses – Chappelle's Show." Comedy Central, 31 Dec. 2017,

www.youtube.com/watch?v=ZX5MHNvjw7o[137].

Trowbridge, Ronald L. "Reagan and O'Neill Were Friendly Opponents, so Why Must Today's

Partisans Spew Hatred?" Independent Institute, 2 October 2019,

https://blog.independent.org/2019/10/02/reagan-and-oneill-were-friendly-opponents-so-

why-must-todays-partisans-spew-hatred/.

"Tulsa Race Massacre: What You Didn't Learn in History Class." PBS, *Tulsa The Fire And*

*The Forgotten*, 10 June 2021, www.pbs.org/wnet/tulsa-the-fire-and-the-[138]

forgotten/2021/06/10/tulsa-race-massacre-what-you-didnt-learn-in-history-class/.

Turak, Natasha; Ng, Abigail and Macias, Amanda. "'Intelligence failure of the highest order' –

---

135. http://www.crosswalk.com/faith/prayer/the-lords-prayer-be-encouraged-and-strengthened.html

136. http://www.insideclimatenews.org/news/21072023/tucker-carlson-jesse-watters-fox-news-

137. http://www.youtube.com/watch?v=ZX5MHNvjw7o

138. http://www.pbs.org/wnet/tulsa-the-fire-and-the-

How Afghanistan fell to the Taliban so quickly." CNBC, 16 Aug. 2021,

www.cnbc.com/2021/08/16/how-afghanistan-fell-to-the-taliban-so-quickly.html.

University of Glasgow. "Marine fish are responding to ocean warming by relocating towards the

poles." Phys.org, 30 May 2023, www.phys.org/news/2023-05-marine-fish-ocean-

relocating-poles.html.

"Update: Three rounds of stimulus checks. See how many went out and for how much."

Pandemic Oversight, 9 Feb. 2023, www.pandemicoversight.gov/data-interactive-[139]

tools/data-stories/update-three-rounds-stimulus-checks-see-how-many-went-out-and.

U.S. Embassy Tbilisi. "Meet The U.S. Scientist Who Invented The N95 Mask Filter." U.S.

Embassy in Georgia, 12 August 2020, https://ge.usembassy.gov/meet-the-u-s-scientist-

who-invented-the-n95-mask-filter/.

"U.S. House of Representatives. House Session Part 1." C-Span, 6 Jan. 2023,

www.c-span.org/video/?525203-1/house-session-part-1[140].

"USA: Mandatory use of CBP One mobile application violates right to seek asylum."

Amnesty International, 8 May 2023,

www.amnesty.org/en/latest/news/2023/05/usa-mandatory-cbp-one-violates-right-

asylum/.

USAFacts Team. "Wealth inequity across race: what does the data show?" USAFacts,

Updated on 6 Apr. 2023,

www.usafacts.org/articles/wealth-inequality-across-races-what-does-the-[141]

---

139. http://www.pandemicoversight.gov/data-interactive-

140. http://www.c-span.org/video/?525203-1/house-session-part-1

141. http://www.usafacts.org/articles/wealth-inequality-across-races-what-does-the-

data-show/.

Vankar, Preeti. "Percentage of adults aged 65 and older in the United States who were fully vaccinated against COVID-19 as of April 26, 2023, by state or territory." Statistica, 29 Nov. 2023, www.statista.com/statistics/1254292/share-of-older-us-adults-fully-[142] vaccinated-against-covid-by-state/.

———

"VEGAN DIETS HAVE ONE-Fourth the Climate Impact of Meat-Heavy Diets, Study Finds." YaleEnvironment360, 21 July 2023, www.e360.yale.edu/digest/vegan-diet-climate-meat-vegetarian-pescatarian#:~:text=The%20analysis%20found%20that%20plant,of%20a%20deck%20of%20cards.

Verdon, Julian. "Unreliable Speed Cameras Line Government Pockets." 2023 Reason Foundation, 3 Feb. 2022, www.reason.com/2022/02/03/unreliable-speed-cameras-line-[143] government-pockets/#:~:text=Secretary%20of%20Transportation%20Pete%20Buttigieg's,means%2( o%20generate%20government%20revenue.

Villarosa, Linda. *The 1619 Project:* "Myths about physical racial differences were used to justify slavery – and are still believed by doctors today." *The New York Times Magazine,* 14 Aug. 2019, www.nytimes.com/interactive/2019/08/14/magazine/racial-differences-[144] doctors.html.

---

142. http://www.statista.com/statistics/1254292/share-of-older-us-adults-fully-

143. http://www.reason.com/2022/02/03/unreliable-speed-cameras-line-

144. http://www.nytimes.com/interactive/2019/08/14/magazine/racial-differences-

Waltower, Shayna. "Working From Home Increases Productivity." Business News Daily,

20 Oct. 2023,

www.businessnewsdaily.com/15259-working-from-home-more-productive.html[145].

"WATCH: Greg Jacob says Pence believed framers would not put election outcome in hands of

person.:" PBS News Hour, 16 June 2022, www.pbs.org/newshour/politics/watch-greg-[146]

jacob-says-pence-believed-framers-would-not-put-election-outcome-in-hands-of-one-

person.

"WATCH: 'Let's get back to work,' Pence urges Senate." PBS News Hour/YouTube,

6 Jan. 2021, www.pbs.org/newshour/politics/watch-lets-get-back-to-work-pence-urges-[147]

senate.

"Water and the global climate crisis: 10 things you should know." UNICEF, 02 March 2023,

www.unicef.org/stories/water-and-climate-change-10-things-you-should-know[148].

Weir, Kristen. "Nurtured by nature: Psychological research is advancing our understanding of

how time in nature can improve our mental health and sharpen our cognition." American

Psychological Association, 1 April 2020, www.apa.org/monitor/2020/04/nurtured-nature[149].

"What is President Biden's 'asylum ban' and what does it mean for people seeking safety?"

International Rescue Committee, 22 Mar. 2023, www.rescue.org/article/what-president-[150]

bidens-asylum-ban-and-what-does-it-mean-people-seeking-

---

145. http://www.businessnewsdaily.com/15259-working-from-home-more-productive.html

146. http://www.pbs.org/newshour/politics/watch-greg-

147. http://www.pbs.org/newshour/politics/watch-lets-get-back-to-work-pence-urges-

148. http://www.unicef.org/stories/water-and-climate-change-10-things-you-should-know

149. http://www.apa.org/monitor/2020/04/nurtured-nature

150. http://www.rescue.org/article/what-president-

safety#:~:text=The%20asylum%20ban%20bars%20asylum,U.S.%20government%20app

%20for%20smartphones.

"What is the sixth mass extinction and what can we do about it?" World Wildlife Fund, Accessed

13 Oct. 2023,

www.worldwildlife.org/stories/what-is-the-sixth-mass-extinction-and-what-can-we-do-[151]

about-it.

"What would reparations for Black Americans look like? An Expert does the math." PBS,

PBS News Hour, 1 June 2021, www.pbs.org/newshour/show/what-would-reparations-for-[152]

black-americans-look-like-an-expert-does-the-math.

"Why We Serve. Native Americans in the United States Armed Forces. World War I." 2020

Smithsonian Institute, National Museum of the American Indian,

www.americanindian.si.edu/static/why-we-serve/topics/world-war-1/. Accessed 11 Oct.

2023.

Wilkinson, Alissa. "Report: The Trump administration didn't order ventilators or masks until

mid-March." Vox.com, 5 Apr. 2020,

www.vox.com/2020/4/5/21208802/coronavirus-trump-ventilators-masks-march[153].

Wilkinson, Bard. "Churchill's policies to blame for millions of Indian famine deaths, study says."

CNN, 29 Mar. 2019, www.cnn.com/2019/03/29/asia/churchill-bengal-famine-intl-scli-[154]

gbr/index.html#:~:text="The%20Bengal%20famine%20of%201943,of%20the%20traged

y%2C%20he%20added.

---

151. http://www.worldwildlife.org/stories/what-is-the-sixth-mass-extinction-and-what-can-we-do-

152. http://www.pbs.org/newshour/show/what-would-reparations-for-

153. http://www.vox.com/2020/4/5/21208802/coronavirus-trump-ventilators-masks-march

154. http://www.cnn.com/2019/03/29/asia/churchill-bengal-famine-intl-scli-

Williams, Michelle. "Why Biden's premature COVID ending could help it surge." *The Hill,* 23 Sept. 22, www.thehill.com/opinion/healthcare/3658032-why-bidens-premature-covid-[155] ending-could-help-it-surge/.

Winton, Neil. "Computer Driven Autos Still Years Away Despite Massive Investment." Forbes, 27 Feb. 2022, www.forbes.com/sites/neilwinton/2022/02/27/computer-driven-autos-still-[156] years-away-despite-massive-investment/?sh=53225d9718cc.

Wolfe, Daniel and Dale, Daniel. "'It's going to disappear': A timeline of Trump's claims that COVID-19 will vanish." CNN, Updated 31 Oct. 2020, www.edition.cnn.com/interactive/2020/10/politics/covid-disappearing-trump-comment-[157] tracker/index.html.

Woodward, Aylin. "European colonizers killed so many indigenous Americans that the planet cooled down, a group of researchers concluded." Business Insider, 9 Feb. 2019, www.businessinsider.com/climate-changed-after-europeans-killed-indigenous-americans-2019-2.

Zdanowicz, Christina and Timm-Garcia, Jaide. "Tyre Nichols was a son and father who enjoyed Skateboarding, photography and sunsets, his family says." CNN, Updated 1 Feb. 2023, www.cnn.com/2023/01/25/us/tyre-nichols-memphis-profile/index.html.

---

155. http://www.thehill.com/opinion/healthcare/3658032-why-bidens-premature-covid-

156. http://www.forbes.com/sites/neilwinton/2022/02/27/computer-driven-autos-still-

157. http://www.edition.cnn.com/interactive/2020/10/politics/covid-disappearing-trump-comment-

# Don't miss out!

Visit the website below and you can sign up to receive emails whenever Eric Nachamie publishes a new book. There's no charge and no obligation.

https://books2read.com/r/B-A-ZTGEB-VELYC

**BOOKS 2 READ**

Connecting independent readers to independent writers.

# About the Author

Eric Nachamie was born in New York but moved with his family as a child to the Charlotte area of North Carolina in 1980 where he has lived for most of his life. He earned his undergraduate degree from North Carolina State University in Political Science and his Master of Public Administration from UNC-Charlotte. As someone who considers public service a special calling, Eric has worked in local government purchasing, administration and budgeting for over twenty years.

His personal interests include politics, health and fitness, and science fiction. "I am a Star Wars devotee from the beginning. I can remember as a child in New York City in the 1970s when the first movie came out - the lines to get into theatres were unbelievable".

During his leisure time, Eric enjoys having an active lifestyle which includes participating in running, strength training, Tai Chi and "driveway" basketball. Eric is also a YouTube fanatic and regularly accesses the platform for entertainment and educational pursuits.

Finally, his greatest joy is being a father to his now college-aged son who shares Eric's interest in politics. "A perfect Friday night is when my son and I get takeout, watch either CNN or Fox News (or both) and discuss and debate our support or opposition to the viewpoints being presented." Eric comically declares, "I have succeeded as a father, if I have taught my son to argue with the television like a deranged middle-aged man."

This work is the first published book by Eric who would like to see his collection of essays develop into an ongoing series.

Read more at https://www.redwhiteandblueamerican.com/.